SAMUEL JOHNSON

Painted by Opie – Engraved by C. Townley Engraver to his Majesty the King of Prussia & Member of the Royal Academys of Berlin & Florence
This Portrait of SAMUEL JOHNSON, L.L.D. is with the greatest Respect
dedicated to JAMES BOSWELL ESQ.
by his most obedient, humble Servant.
Charles Townley

SAMUEL JOHNSON

Literature, religion and English cultural politics from the Restoration to Romanticism

J. C. D. CLARK

CAMBRIDGE
UNIVERSITY PRESS

Published by the Press Syndicate of the University of Cambridge
The Pitt Building, Trumpington Street, Cambridge CB2 1RP
40 West 20th Street, New York, NY 10011-4211, USA
10 Stamford Road, Oakleigh, Melbourne 3166, Australia

First published 1994
Reprinted 1995

Printed in Great Britain at the University Press, Cambridge

A catalogue record for this book is available from the British Library

Library of Congress cataloguing in publication data

Clark, J. C. D.
Samuel Johnson – literature, religion and English cultural politics from the Restoration to Romanticism / J.C.D. Clark
p. cm.
Includes index.
ISBN 0 521 47304 7 (hc)
1. Johnson, Samuel, 1709–1784 – Political and social views.
2. Politics and literature – Great Britain – History – 18th century.
3. Culture – Political aspects – England – History – 18th century.
4. Great Britain – Politics and government – 18th century.
5. Johnson, Samuel, 1709–1784 – Contemporary England.
6. Authors, English – 18th century – Biography.
7. England – Church History – 18th century.
8. England – Civilization – 18th century.
I. Title
PR3537.P6C53 1994
828'.609–dc20 94-17934 CIP

ISBN 0 521 47304 7 hardback
ISBN 0 521 47885 5 paperback

CE

CONTENTS

ILLUSTRATIONS

PREFACE

This is a survey which takes Johnson as its starting point and remains bound by his preoccupations and commitments. A complete map of English cultural politics in his lifetime is beyond the scope of the present study: it would require a balanced treatment of many regions of that varied empire, especially the cultural and ideological nexus of the ministerial and of the opposition Whigs. This study attempts to fill in the details of only one province on the map; but its inhabitants, including John Dryden and Alexander Pope; William King, Thomas Ruddiman and Samuel Johnson, were not negligible, and they deserve to be seen for what they were.

The title deliberately limits this book to England's cultural politics. Although Scotland is briefly noticed when it impinged on Johnson's attention, I make no claim to carry the study of Scots cultural and intellectual history beyond the work of those authors whose research is extensively acknowledged in the footnotes. In particular, the poems of Ossian, a large subject in its own right, can only be briefly touched on here. But I hope that something has been gained by drawing new analogies between developments in England and Scotland, and that both the similarities and the differences will be illuminating. In particular, the pioneering arguments of Douglas Duncan on Scots Latinity as a cultural formation, as a political enterprise and as a matrix of national identity take on added meaning when compared with England's experience, and I have tried to do belated justice to Duncan's insufficiently-acknowledged work.

For the thesis in chapters 1 and 2 of the present work on the wider political significance of a late-humanist Latin culture I remain indebted both to David Duncan's *Thomas Ruddiman* (1965) and, importantly, to David Greenwood's *William King* (1969). I first used those books in the early 1980s while writing *English Society 1688–1832*, and although I have tried to make them better appreciated among historians and my pupils at Cambridge and Oxford, I believe that they may helpfully be drawn to the attention of students of English literature. Robert DeMaria's biography of Johnson came to hand after this work was largely completed; DeMaria rightly explores Johnson's interest in continental Renaissance Latinists, and his work, with that of Duncan and Greenwood, is my starting point for the extended argument which I seek to frame on the dynastic implications for English authors of the cultural politics of late humanism.

My chief debt is to Howard Erskine-Hill, who first identified the dynastic themes in early eighteenth-century English literature, and who has done more to illuminate that field than any other scholar; in this work I hope only to add to his achievement some observations from the perspective of an historian. Our academic exchanges on these questions began in the early 1980s, and encouraged me to include a brief discussion of Johnson in my book *English Society 1688–1832* (1985). I believed that this sufficiently placed Johnson against the ideological alignments of his age, but the publication in 1990 of a second edition of a monograph of 1960 which reasserted a Namierite interpretation made a fuller presentation of the evidence necessary.

I am grateful to those who have helped me in writing this book, although responsibility for its arguments rests with the author. For advice on specific points I am indebted to J. D. Fleeman, Eirwen Nicholson, Stuart Sherman, J. S. G. Simmons, Simon Swain, Kai Kin Yung and Charles Webster. David Brunton and Bruce Redford kindly offered many suggestions on a draft. I am grateful also to Richard Sharp, whose knowledge of eighteenth-century religion and iconography has brought this culture alive for me, and to Eveline Cruickshanks, who first among modern English historians made it possible to regard the dynastic nexus as a proper subject for scholarship.

For permission to print documents in their collections I am grateful to the University of Nottingham Manuscripts Department; the Bodleian Library, Oxford; the British Library; and the Public Record Office.

ABBREVIATIONS

BL Add MSS	British Library, Additional Manuscripts
Boswell, *Journal*	Frederick A. Pottle and Charles H. Bennett (eds.), *Boswell's Journal of A Tour to the Hebrides with Samuel Johnson, LL.D.* (New York, 1936)
Boswell, *Life*	George Birkbeck Hill and L. F. Powell (eds.), *Boswell's Life of Johnson* [1791] (6 vols., Oxford, 1934–50).
Brack and Kelley (eds.), *Early Biographies*	O M Brack, Jr., and Robert E. Kelley (eds.), *The Early Biographies of Samuel Johnson* (Iowa City, 1974).
Duncan, *Thomas Ruddiman*	Douglas Duncan, *Thomas Ruddiman: A Study in Scottish Scholarship of the Early Eighteenth Century* (Edinburgh, 1965)
Greene, *Politics*	Donald J. Greene, *The Politics of Samuel Johnson* (New Haven, 1960; 2nd edn, Athens, Georgia, 1990)
Greenwood, *William King*	David Greenwood, *William King: Tory and Jacobite* (Oxford, 1969)
Hawkins, *Life*	Sir John Hawkins, *The Life of Samuel Johnson, LL.D.* (2nd edn, London 1787)
HMC	Historical Manuscripts Commission
Johnson, *Letters*	Bruce Redford (ed.), *The Letters of Samuel Johnson* (5 vols., Princeton, 1992–4)
Johnson, *Lives of the Poets*	Samuel Johnson, *The Lives of the Most Eminent English Poets; with Critical Observations on their Works* (4 vols., London, 1781)
Johnson, *Works*	*The Yale Edition of the Works of Samuel Johnson*
William King, *Anecdotes*	William King, *Political and Literary Anecdotes of his Own Time* (2nd edn, London, 1819)

Orrery Papers	Countess of Cork and Orrery (ed.), *The Orrery Papers* (2 vols., London, 1903)
PRO SPD	Public Record Office, State Papers Domestic
Reade, *Johnsonian Gleanings*	Aleyn Lyell Reade, *Johnsonian Gleanings* (11 vols., privately printed, 1909–52)
Waingrow (ed.), *Correspondence*	Marshall Waingrow (ed.), *The Correspondence and other Papers of James Boswell relating to the Making of the Life of Johnson* (London, 1969)

INTRODUCTION

The life of Samuel Johnson, like much else about the eighteenth century, is further from us than it first appears. The literary idioms of that age, its ideological and political conflicts, and even the terminology in which they were expressed, call for the attention of the historian if their superficial similarities are not to betray us into a false confidence. This book is, in part, an historian's contribution to the study of Johnson's politics and religion,[1] but it has been drawn also to propose a new context for the cultural politics of his age. It is, of course, new only in relation to the research strategies of modern academic disciplines. Literary criticism achieved its autonomy in the English academic arena in the last decades of the nineteenth century and the first decades of the twentieth at a time when projects like the *Dictionary of National Biography* and the *Oxford History of England* engaged technical scholarship with a range of profoundly patriotic assumptions. Among the major premises which 'English' as a subject then acquired, and which has not been effectively revised since,[2] has been the self-sufficiency of the vernacular. As far back as we could look (it was assumed) England possessed an autonomous, free-standing, and vigorous vernacular literature: whether rough or polished, plebeian or middle class, provincial and plural or metropolitan and uniform, its autonomy was too seldom questioned. That assumption once secure, it was an easy next step to presume that that vernacular literature gave eloquent if changing expression to English national identities.

It is argued here that that assumption embodies only a part of the truth. The classics existed in close relation to the vernacular, and gave a privileged place to the translation and the imitation within English letters. The

[1] Many other themes in Johnson's ethical and philosophical thought deserve attention. For one important study, which does not, however, structure its material with respect to politics, see Nicholas Hudson, *Samuel Johnson and Eighteenth-century Thought* (Oxford, 1988).

[2] For an important example of a reviving attention to the interplay between the vernacular and the classical, see Howard D. Weinbrot, *Britannia's Issue: The Rise of British Literature from Dryden to Ossian* (Cambridge, 1993).

dominance of the classical tradition in this period is easily demonstrated from the landmarks of vernacular literature: England's national epic was Dryden's translation of Virgil's *Aeneid*; her leading military epic was Pope's translation of Homer's *Iliad*; her most popular play was Addison's *Cato*; her most distinguished satires were Pope's imitations of Horace. Johnson was sceptical of the viability and autonomy of different genres of vernacular literature in various ages before his own,[3] and the cultural politics of England between the Restoration and what is conventionally described as Romanticism, briefly outlined in this book, give grounds for endorsing his caution. Just as Englishmen of that period did not organise their collective identities by reference to a single matrix which can be labelled 'nationalism',[4] so the undoubted emergence of a self-sufficient vernacular was neither early nor inevitable. The episodes of cultural politics by which English literature and consciousness moved from the world of Milton and Cowley to that of the Victorian novelists is one context for the life and posthumous reputation of Johnson.

The processes included under the label 'the rise of the vernacular' were not only, and perhaps not chiefly, the positive affirmations of new ideals; they involved also the failure and the negation of old norms, especially ones to which the young Johnson had committed himself. The wider dimensions of the classics, and the implications of his cultural project in politics and religion, are a central theme of this study. Late humanist classicism, it is suggested, lasted for longer, and was more powerful, than historians or literary scholars have generally allowed; yet this unique historical formation lacks a name which would easily characterise it, and the decline in the twentieth century of knowledge of Latin and Greek has gradually closed off one half of a bilingual, or sometimes two thirds of a trilingual, culture from our appreciation. That culture is here called the Anglo-Latin tradition. It is not a wholly satisfactory term, since Greek, though secondary, was not insignificant; but it seems likely that the term 'neoclassical'[5] is already too replete with meanings from the history of art, in which it signifies a reaction against the Baroque, to identify a cultural formation which clearly included the Baroque and, in its later neo-Grecian phase,

3 See below, pp. 24–6.

4 J. C. D. Clark, *The Language of Liberty 1660–1832: Political Discourse and Social Dynamics in the Anglo-American World* (Cambridge, 1993), pp. 46–62.

5 For an argument against the prefix 'neo' in the term 'neoclassicism' on the grounds that classicism is always retrospective, see Bertrand Harris Bronson, 'When Was Neoclassicism', in Bronson, *Facets of the Enlightenment: Studies in English Literature and Its Contexts* (Berkeley, 1968), pp. 1–25.

even distinguished the Romanticism of the years before the 1830s from the Romanticism of the Victorians.[6]

In so far as the cultural polemics discussed here were an aspect of the conflict between 'ancients' and 'moderns', it is important that that conflict was not decided during the 'battle of the books' fought in the last decade of the seventeenth and the first decades of the eighteenth century. That battle, though loud, was inconclusive.[7] The conflict between the cultural systems of which the Anglo-Latin tradition and the vernacular tradition were (not wholly mutually exclusive) facets survived because there were profound religious and political polarities on which they drew. This was Johnson's world, at least until the 1750s. One contemporary tribute to *The Rambler*, reprinted in the *Gentleman's Magazine*, hailed its author in exactly this classical idiom: 'May the publick favours crown his merits, and may not the English, under the auspicious reign of GEORGE the Second, neglect a man, who, had he lived in the first century, would have been one of the greatest favourites of AUGUSTUS.'[8] Boswell was forced to add: 'This flattery of the monarch had no effect. It is too well known, that the second George never was an Augustus to learning or genius.'[9]

The young Samuel Johnson's ambition was to become a skilled and acknowledged exponent of the tradition of classical humanism.[10] But this was not merely a personal choice or a lonely elective affinity: Johnson chose the broad high road trod by the most able men of letters in England between the Restoration and the 1740s or 1750s. Nor was it merely a literary choice: the Anglo-Latin tradition was part of a wider political, social and cultural project both in England and Scotland. Such traditions were not disembodied: they reveal their purposes, and interconnections, in individual lives. For Johnson's cultural project to be understood in more than the two dimensions of the printed page, his life is here set in the context created by men whom he recognised as embarked in the same cause. In particular, William King at Oxford and Thomas Ruddiman at Edinburgh, both Latinists, cultural catalysts and social activists, help to define a phase of classical learning and its purposes in Britain. An analogy is not an identity: these men were not copies of each other. Ruddiman was a grammarian, editor, publisher and author of polemical historical pamphlets; King a neo-Latin poet, critic and satirist. But only the near-extinction

6 For a defence of the term 'neoclassical', see James William Johnson, *The Formation of English Neo-Classical Thought* (Princeton, 1967), pp. 3–30.

7 Joseph M. Levine, *The Battle of the Books: History and Literature in the Augustan Age* (Ithaca, 1991), p. 7, places the final and irreparable alterations of political life and historical consciousness 'sometime in the nineteenth century'.

8 *Gentleman's Magazine* 20 (1750), 465.

9 Boswell, *Life*, vol. 1, p. 209.

10 For which, see especially Robert DeMaria, *The Life of Samuel Johnson: A Critical Biography* (Oxford, 1993), pp. xi-xvi and passim.

of the classics in subsequent generations has obscured their stature, and prevented the analogy from seeming a self-evident one.[11] It may even be that King achieved higher eminence in his province of the republic of letters than Johnson did in his.[12] But King found no Boswell, and the defeat of Ruddiman's political cause in the 1740s cleared the ground with ruthless thoroughness for that idiom of enquiry later termed the Scottish Enlightenment (the idiom of Ferguson, Hume, Kames, Millar, and Smith) in which Ruddiman's scholarship not only had no place, but was to be systematically rejected. Again, an analogous process in England diminished Johnson's achievement after his death.

Scholars of Johnson, both literary critics and historians, confront an intractable evidential problem. The sources for his life before the 1760s are notoriously meagre, so that, as one literary scholar has observed, 'conjecture becomes a necessary tool if we are to make anything of the scant information at our disposal'.[13] The historian, by the use of circumstantial evidence and the construction of contexts, can contribute some rigour of method to this process. After Johnson's pension in 1762 and his emergence as a public figure, the problem is reversed: the evidence becomes copious, but much of it, and that the part hitherto the most used, was filtered through the powerful, retentive but highly individual mind of James Boswell.

To what degree Boswell created rather than neutrally recorded the character and opinions of the man whom he idolised has preoccupied literary critics. Accounts of Johnson by almost all scholars of English literature since the 1950s have largely or wholly adopted the thesis[14] that the proto-Romantic Boswell foisted onto the pragmatic, sceptical, apolitical Johnson a parody of the Tory and Jacobite identities which owed their final nineteenth-century form to the imagination of Sir Walter Scott. The Johnson whom Macaulay denounced, the bigoted and reactionary Tory and Jacobite, was – it is argued – Boswell's and Macaulay's own creation.

[11] Duncan, *Thomas Ruddiman*, pp. 148–9, assumed that Scotland's Latin culture was 'very different' from England's, and that the latter functioned as 'an assured and independent modern culture': this is to overstate the contrast. Similarly, Greenwood's *William King* did not explore Scots analogies.

[12] For an appraisal of the high stature of King's Latin literature see Greenwood, *William King*, pp. 327–61. Greenwood writes of 'the purity of his classical diction ... artistic and technical expertise ... a formal grandeur'; his prose has 'a richness of vocabulary, an amplitude of expression, and a lambent beauty of phrasing which constantly recall the Ciceronian prototype'.

[13] Paul J. Korshin, in W. H. Bond (ed.), *Eighteenth-Century Studies in Honor of Donald F. Hyde* (New York, 1970), p. 42.

[14] Propounded by Donald J. Greene, in a Columbia University doctoral dissertation of 1954 and in Greene, *Politics* (1960), passim. For an important early dissent from this view, see Howard Erskine-Hill, 'The Political Character of Samuel Johnson', in Isobel Grundy (ed.), *Samuel Johnson: New Critical Essays* (London, 1984), pp. 107–36.

The real Johnson, according to this interpretation, belonged naturally in the historical setting powerfully depicted by one of the most influential twentieth-century historians of England, Sir Lewis Namier (1888–1960).

It is, of course, an entirely proper historical exercise to seek to discern and strip away the subsequent layers of interpretation which may have obscured a subject. In this case, however, the exercise has failed because its chosen end point was deeply inappropriate. Namier's picture of eighteenth-century English society as secular and unideological, and English politics as conducted by small factional groups dedicated to the pursuit of material self-interest, has been qualified in many ways by historians since the 1970s, and has now been abandoned as a faithful portrait of Johnson's age. In place of a timeless and functional picture of interest-group politics, we now see a dynamic pattern of ideologically-fraught conflict which drove English politics through successive identifiable stages: the emergence of Whig and Tory parties in the Exclusion Crisis of the 1670s;[15] an alternating two-party struggle in the reigns of William and Anne;[16] a Whig supremacy under George I and George II failing to destroy a proscribed Tory party which formed the backbone of a bitter and unreconciled opposition;[17] the lasting possibility of a second revolution to break the Whig monopoly;[18] the survival of an ideological matrix for resistance which was the reverse of secular and contractarian;[19] the destruction of the old Whig and Tory parties in the factional conflicts of the 1750s;[20] the emergence in the 1760s of a pattern to persist for many decades, of coalition governments, sustained on a non-party basis by monarchical support and confronting a weakly-organised and fragmented opposition; the revival of party in the early nineteenth century and the arrival of party government after 1832, followed by a paradigm shift which changed men's perspectives on much of what had gone before.[21]

[15] Eveline Cruickshanks, 'Religion and Royal Succession – The Rage of Party', in Clyve Jones (ed.), *Britain in the First Age of Party* (London, 1987), pp. 19–43.

[16] Henry Horwitz, *Parliament, policy and politics in the reign of William III* (Manchester, 1977); Geoffrey Holmes, *British Politics in the Age of Anne* (London, 1967).

[17] Romney Sedgwick (ed.), *The History of Parliament. The House of Commons 1715–1754* (2 vols., London, 1970).

[18] Eveline Cruickshanks, *Political Untouchables: the Tories and the '45* (London, 1979); Bruce Lenman, *The Jacobite Risings in Britain 1689–1746* (London, 1980).

[19] J. P. Kenyon, *Revolution Principles: the Politics of Party 1689–1720* (Cambridge, 1977); Bruce Lenman, 'The Scottish Episcopal Clergy and the ideology of Jacobitism' in Eveline Cruickshanks (ed.), *Ideology and Conspiracy: Aspects of Jacobitism 1689–1759* (Edinburgh, 1982); J. C. D. Clark, *English Society 1688–1832: Ideology, social structure and political practice during the ancien regime* (Cambridge, 1985).

[20] J. C. D. Clark, *The Dynamics of Change: The Crisis of the 1750s and English Party Systems* (Cambridge, 1982).

[21] J. C. D. Clark, 'A General Theory of Party, Opposition and Government, 1688–1832', *Historical Journal* 23 (1980), 295–325.

Johnson's life spans two of those crucial watersheds. Born in 1709, his earliest years were spent in the Indian summer of Toryism: the famous ministry of the four last years of the Queen, Swift's history of which was for long a dangerous and unpublishable book. In 1714 the rules of English public life were profoundly changed, and Johnson's adolescence, early manhood and middle age were passed under that Whig ascendancy which the first two sovereigns of the Hanoverian dynasty rightly regarded as essential to their survival on the throne. Johnson participated fully in the Tories' experience of exclusion and proscription, and did so for a reason which greatly heightened his emotional response to this predicament: for reasons of religious scruple, he was unable to take the oath of allegiance to the new monarch or the oath of abjuration to deny all title in the rival claimant.

The evidence strongly suggests that in this phase of his career Johnson found reasons to acknowledge the legitimacy of the claims of the Stuarts to the throne from which James II, disastrous though Johnson considered him, had been, in Johnson's view, illegally excluded. In the 1750s this political landscape began to change in the aftermath of the final and crushing defeat of Jacobitism in 1746. Johnson's pronouncements on the dynastic question in the 1750s are open to a degree of ambiguity. He evidently acknowledged some title residing in long possession, in widespread support, and in personal virtue. In 1760 the accession of the young George III, untainted by the vices of his Hanoverian forebears, allowed Johnson, as it allowed many former Tories, to make his peace with the regime. Henceforth the terms 'Whig' and 'Tory' lost much of their force in the politics of Westminster and Whitehall.

The terms did not, of course, disappear from the memories of men whose lives spanned the reigns of monarchs before George III, or, to some degree, from political and religious polemic. Controversy over the legal status of the Established Church and its doctrinal integrity in the late 1760s and early 1770s, controversy over the strident political populism of John Wilkes, and controversy over British policy towards America all allowed polemicists in opposition, especially the Dissenting intelligentsia, to seek to keep the old terms alive. Johnson could be, and often was, condemned in language taken from the world before 1760. These terms were, to different degrees, anachronistic in the new reign;[22] yet to record this anachronism is not enough. Johnson's political identity derived from his experience in obscurity in the early decades of the century, not from the years of his fame. The recovery of the ideological and political alignments of early eighteenth-

[22] James J. Sack, *From Jacobite to Conservative: Reaction and Orthodoxy in Britain, c. 1760–1832* (Cambridge, 1993).

century England in recent scholarship allows us to say with confidence that Johnson was a Tory, a Nonjuror and a Jacobite within the meanings conventionally given to those words in the reign of George II.

Men of letters, like ideologues and practical politicians, did not display a simple, unchanging political identity as the pieces on a chess board display their coloration: the senses in which men drew political inferences from their theological commitments, attempted to express these through political parties, and understood the tactical options presented to them all evolved, and were sometimes in flux. Nevertheless, there was enough stability in those matters over time for Johnson's commitments to be explained in terms of the survival of an early-Hanoverian political nexus until the 1750s and its transformation in the 1760s.[23]

Johnson was a Tory. In the *Dictionary*, he gave 'Tory' as 'One who adheres to the antient constitution of the state, and the apostolical hierarchy of the church of England, opposed to a Whig': this was presumably sufficient not to call for a definition of 'Toryism'. 'Whig', by contrast, was 'The name of a faction', illustrated with a long and unflattering paragraph from Gilbert Burnet, and 'Whiggism', 'The notions of a Whig', illustrated from Swift: 'I could quote passages from fifty pamphlets, wholly made up of *whiggism* and atheism.' Although Johnson's definitions were in line with lexicographical precedent,[24] this is not evidence for unthinking repetition: as will be argued below, Johnson's opinions, like his definitions, show both conscious partisanship and an accurate understanding of the issues of principle which had divided the two parties in the reigns of George I and George II.

Johnson was a Nonjuror. That term is conventionally now restricted to the small group of men who separated from the main body of the Church of England in 1689 or 1714 and thereafter worshipped in separate congregations. Johnson did not join them, and held some of them in low regard; but his own understanding of the term, as will be shown, included within the ranks of Nonjurors that much larger number who refused the oaths and yet continued to worship with the juring Church. The evidence suggests not only that this was Johnson's practice, but also that he paid a high price for this resolute commitment of principle in career opportunities foregone.

Johnson was a Jacobite. This is perhaps the hardest of his three public affirmations to document, and the evidence for it is presented in this book. There is, of course, no evidence that Johnson was in arms during the

[23] For a scholarly explanation of these and other literary themes against this evolving tactical background, see Howard Erskine-Hill, *Poetry and the Realm of Politics: Shakespeare to Dryden* and *Poetry of Opposition and Revolution: Dryden to Wordsworth* (Oxford, forthcoming).

[24] James Sledd and Gwin Kolb, 'Johnson's Definitions of Whig and Tory', *Publications of the Modern Language Association of America* 67 (1952), 882–5.

rebellion of 1745,[25] or at any other time; but this military inactivity in the face of appalling personal risks is easily explicable, and was shared by almost all Englishmen who entertained some sympathy for the exiled dynasty. If only this most extreme test of armed rebellion is admitted as a means of establishing political identity, then few men at any time would satisfy it: such a simple criterion would, of course, entirely fail to register the motivations for assent, the ideological content of allegiance, or the ways in which allegiance changed in the face of tactical opportunity. Evidence on these questions is rehearsed here.

Boswell's unreliability as a witness has suggested itself most strongly to those scholars who accepted as their major premise the essential validity of Sir Lewis Namier's historical vision: it seemed to follow that Boswell's accounts of Johnson's provocative remarks against Whigs and Hanoverians were rhetorically heightened, and his claims that Johnson affirmed an attachment to the exiled house were Romantic fictions. Yet the re-instatement in recent scholarship of an intellectual nexus which embraced Tories, Jacobites and ministerial Whigs, and which shows why minorities of more extreme Whigs stood outside that dynastic idiom, removes the problem: none of Boswell's evidence is, on the surface, incompatible with the new historiography. If some of the passages in his *Life of Johnson* cannot be traced in his intermediate notes, this merely suggests their source in Boswell's remarkable memory rather than in his imagination.

Although Boswell once confided to his journal that he had 'a kind of *liking* for Jacobitism', his views on the dynastic question were undoubtedly Whig: in the same passage he called the Stuarts' title 'very casual and artificial'.[26] On his Highland tour with Johnson,[27] Boswell sided with Lord Kames and, by implication, against Thomas Ruddiman in the technical dispute of those men over the fundamental historical question whether the succession to the throne of Scotland in the middle ages had been strictly hereditary, or defeasible; uninterrupted, or broken.[28] Boswell even cited in his support William Blackstone, the Oxford Tory whose major work outlined the terms of his accommodation with the regime in the reign of

[25] John Buchan encouraged this belief (without evidence) in his novel *Midwinter* (1925). This blurring of fact and fiction, encouraging either Romantic assent or sceptical dismissal, has been a major obstacle to the scholarly reconstruction of the ideological and tactical options as Johnson saw them.

[26] See below, p. 206.

[27] Boswell, *Journal*, p. 237 (30 September 1773); Boswell, *Life*, vol. 5 (*Tour*), p. 272.

[28] Lord Kames, 'Appendix touching the Hereditary and Indefeasible Right of Kings' in Kames, *Essays upon Several Subjects concerning British Antiquities* (Edinburgh, 1747), pp. 192–217, replied to by Thomas Ruddiman, *A Dissertation concerning The Competition for the Crown of Scotland* (Edinburgh, 1748).

George III, and William Paley, the archetypal Cambridge Whig.[29] It was Johnson, not Boswell, who was the real Tory; and it was the committed Anglican Johnson who was the Jacobite, not the lapsed Presbyterian Boswell.

Boswell's records of Johnson's considered opinions on the Jacobite question date from the 1760s. By that stage, all serious possibility of a restoration was long past, and Johnson could discuss the question to some degree as an abstract one. But we have no records of his conversation on this point before the 1760s, and our estimate of it can never be other than circumstantial. It would, however, be realistic to infer from the evidence presented here that Johnson's comments as expressed in private conversation with men like Archibald Campbell, William Guthrie, William King, James Edward Oglethorpe, John, Earl of Orrery and Richard Savage were not restrained by any fundamental difference of orientation.

Nevertheless, even if Boswell were wholly disqualified, there would be sufficient evidence to place Johnson's political and religious views against the spectrum of possibilities presented by his age. Some of this evidence is provided by Johnson's first major biographer, Sir John Hawkins, who may have known his subject from 1739 and whose account in all major respects confirms Boswell's. Yet Hawkins was even less open than his competitor to a charge of having a proto-Romantic proclivity to Toryism which led him to father such views on Johnson. On the contrary, he consistently deplored the views of Nonjurors, Jacobites, Tories and even opposition Whigs: the aim of *The Craftsman*, like that of the opposition which supported it, was

> to blow the flame of national discontent, to delude the honest and well-meaning people of this country into a belief that the minister was its greatest enemy, and that his opponents, only, meant its welfare ... That Johnson has adopted these vulgar complaints, his poem [*London*] must witness. I shall not take upon me to demonstrate the fallacy of most of the charges contained in it, nor animadvert on the wickedness of those, who, to effect their own ambitious designs, scruple not to oppose the best endeavours of the person in power ...[30]

Johnson's views, thought Hawkins, were to be either condemned or excused; but his account of them, presented in this book, coincided with Boswell's.[31]

Boswell's *Life of Johnson* was a work of literature, but not necessarily a

29 Boswell, loc. cit., cited William Blackstone, *Commentaries on the Laws of England* (4 vols., Oxford, 1765–9), vol. 1, p. 205, and William Paley, *Principles of Moral and Political Philosophy* (London, 1785), book vi, chapter 3.

30 Hawkins, *Life*, pp. 60–1.

31 A full discussion of the evidential problem must await the publication of the complex manuscript draft of Boswell's *Life of Johnson*, volume 1 edited by Marshall Waingrow and volumes 2–4 by Bruce Redford (Edinburgh University Press, forthcoming).

work of fiction. In one small respect, an epitome of the larger whole, the biographer stood by his veracity. Macaulay was later to condemn Johnson for his personal eccentricities, including his overbearing manner, and to use these as symptoms of his authoritarianism; yet it was not thoughtlessness or artistic contrivance which led Boswell to preface many of Johnson's remarks with 'Why, Sir'; this really was a Johnsonian characteristic, and Boswell's usage was deliberate: 'I have even learnt a more curious expression, which is to resume a subject with "No, sir," though there is no negation in the case.'[32] Boswell only partly understood his subject's politics and his religion, but what he did understand he faithfully reported.

[32] Boswell, *Journal*, p. 292 (11 October 1773).

1

POLITICS, LITERATURE AND THE CULTURE OF HUMANISM

I. THE VERNACULAR AND THE CLASSICAL

'The chief glory of every people', announced Johnson in the Preface to his *Dictionary of the English Language*, 'arises from its authours'. Samuel Johnson himself chose to be 'an author by profession'.[1] Both as writer and as critic, he came to overshadow and overawe his contemporaries as no other man of letters had done since Dryden, and none was to do again. Yet his later reputation as an author within an autonomous vernacular literature was partly the result of a shift of perspective in the middle decades of the eighteenth century which subtly modified many contemporaries' understanding of the literary culture in which Johnson had grown to maturity. That was indeed a vernacular culture, but it was a vernacular which had developed in an intimate relationship with the classics and, especially, with the Latin prose and poetry of republican and imperial Rome.[2]

The content of education at English schools and universities was overwhelmingly classical; so it had been since the Reformation and was to be until the nineteenth century. In 1751 William Pitt, ill-rewarded adherent of the former opposition to Sir Robert Walpole, advised his nephew at Cambridge:

> I see the foundation so well laid, that I do not make the least doubt but you will become a perfect good scholar; and have the pleasure and applause that will attend the several advantages hereafter, in the future course of your life, that you can only

[1] Hawkins, *Life*, p. 27.

[2] For the literary dimension see especially Gilbert Highet, *The Classical Tradition: Greek and Roman Influences on Western Literature* (Oxford, 1949); J. A. K. Thomson, *The Classical Background of English Literature* (London, 1948); James William Johnson, *The Formation of English Neo-Classical Thought* (Princeton, 1967); R. R. Bolgar (ed.), *Classical Influences on Western Thought A.D. 1650–1870* (Cambridge, 1979); Craig Kallendorf, *Latin Influences on English Literature from the Middle Ages to the Eighteenth Century: An Annotated Bibliography of Scholarship, 1945–1979* (New York, 1982); Hanne Carlsen, *A Bibliography to the Classical Tradition in English Literature* (Copenhagen, 1985).

(a) Charles II as Augustus

Plate 1 The classical tradition. Classicism provided self-images and a vocabulary for authors as well as monarchs

(b) Samuel Johnson as Roman patrician

acquire now by your emulation and noble labours in the pursuit of learning, and of every acquirement that is to make you superior to other gentlemen.

I rejoice to hear that you have begun Homer's Iliad; and have made so great a progress in Virgil. I hope you taste and love those authors particularly. You cannot read them too much: they are not only the two greatest poets, but they contain the finest lessons for your age to imbibe: lessons of honour, courage, disinterestedness, love of truth, command of temper, gentleness of behaviour, humanity, and in one word, virtue in its true signification.[3]

All parties sought to use the classical tradition,[4] but for one party in particular it had a special significance. Francis Atterbury, later Bishop of Rochester, was aligned with this school of classical learning. He pursued an identification with the ancients that sought to recapture their essential spirit and to confer on the Englishmen of his age an easy, elegant, patrician style; he defined himself against the unmannerly, dogmatic, crabbed philological pedantry, as he saw it, of the new textual critics, especially the Cambridge Whig Dr Richard Bentley. As the editor of one of Atterbury's criticisms of Virgil, published in 1741, explained, Atterbury had shown himself to be 'a man of great learning, a deep critick, and a polite gentleman' who, by repeated reading of Virgil (by implication, rather than philological criticism) had 'made himself master of his genius and spirit':

This is what, in reading ancient authors, we ought to aim at, and endeavour to obtain; and then we may pretend to understand them, and to be capable of imitating them occasionally: the crowding together various readings, and mustering up quotations, according to the mode of modern critics, shews indeed their great labour in collating MSS. and old editions, in collecting passages from various authors, and turning over voluminous dictionaries; but is very far from being a proof of their understanding and observing those delicate strokes of the most refined art, and of their shewing themselves masters of the skill and peculiar manner of the writer. They rather confound and puzzle the reader, and cast dark clouds over the brightest passages of an author, whilst they are making a parade of Greek and Latin learning, wild conjectures, and far-fetched interpretations, in order to lay claim to the title of learned men and critics. No wonder, therefore, that these gentlemen, as has been generally observed, after all their pains taken, and time spent, in reading the classics, can neither think nor write in the delicate taste, and after the easy and elegant manner, of the ancients.[5]

3 William Pitt to Thomas Pitt, 12 October 1751, in W. S. Taylor and J. H. Pringle (eds.), *Correspondence of William Pitt, Earl of Chatham* (4 vols., London, 1838–40), vol. 1, p. 62.

4 For the use by Court Whigs of a political idiom drawn from Marcus Tullius Cicero, see Reed Browning, *Political and Constitutional Ideas of the Court Whigs* (Baton Rouge, 1982), pp. 210–56.

5 Anonymous editorial notes to Atterbury, 'Antonius Musa's Character, represented by Virgil, in the person of Iapys', in *The Epistolary Correspondence, Visitation Charges, Speeches, and Miscellanies, of the Right Reverend Francis Atterbury, D.D.* (4 vols., London, 1783–87), vol. 1, pp. 330–1. For the degree to which this attitude reflected Roman norms, see Edwin S. Ramage,

By contrast, the Whig William Pitt recommended a course of reading to his nephew including 'Horace and Virgil: of Horace the Odes, but above all, the Epistles and Ars Poetica ... Tully de Officiis, de Amicitia, de Senectute; his Catilinarian Orations and Philippics. Sallust'; but he preceded his list with 'Locke's Conduct of the Understanding; his Treatise also on the Understanding; his Treatise on Government, and Letters on Toleration', and quoted Persius, Satire I

> Compositum Jus, fasque animi; sanctosque recessus
> Mentis, et incoctum generoso pectus honesto

to recommend a Deistic religion of moral uprightness.[6]

Pitt's first author had a profound influence on the consciousness of the English elite. Horace 'as poet and as critic became fashionable only after 1660', but thereafter was soon ubiquitous both in school and university curriculae, in popular reading, as a point of reference and as a contemporary; Sir George Trumbull wrote in 1708 of 'our friend Horace', and numberless Englishmen throughout the century treated him as familiar, contemporary and relevant.[7] Johnson conceded a precedence to Horace second only to Virgil, had much of his poetry by heart, and had a habit of quoting it in apt allusion. It influenced his own poetry; it provided the mottoes for many of the essays in *The Rambler* and *The Adventurer*.[8] Horace 'by his satiric raillery had tried to lead his contemporaries into the path of civic virtue'; eighteenth-century authors enlisted him in a similar cause. Whigs could use him, especially the first six Odes of the Third Book, to recommend loyalty to the new regime.[9] Tories could use his satires to call in question that regime's moral foundations: Horace's careful apologias for the regime of Augustus were given a double or contrary meaning in Pope's

Urbanitas: Ancient Sophistication and Refinement (Norman, Oklahoma, 1973). For Virgil, see Angus Ross, 'Virgil and the Augustans', in Charles Martindale (ed.), *Virgil and his Influence: Bimillennial Studies* (Bristol, 1984), pp. 141–67.

6 William Pitt to Thomas Pitt, 12, 14 January 1754: *Chatham Correspondence*, vol. 1, pp. 64, 70 at 67, 75. Dryden's translation ran: 'A soul, where laws both human and divine,/ In practice more than speculation shine;/ A genuine virtue, of a vigorous kind,/ Pure in the last recesses of the mind.'

7 R. M. Ogilvie, *Latin and Greek: A History of the Influence of the Classics on English Life from 1600 to 1918* (London, 1964), pp. 34–73, at 44.

8 For a detailed study of Johnson's indebtedness to Horace, see Caroline Goad, *Horace in the English Literature of the Eighteenth Century* (New Haven, 1918), pp. 233–70, 544–85.

9 Goad, *Horace*, pp. 8–9. For a study of the contribution of the Horatian idiom to a social ideal, see Maren-Sofie Røstvig, *The Happy Man: Studies in the Metamorphoses of a Classical Ideal* (2nd edn, 2 vols., Oslo, 1962–71): 'As a rule, the poets who wrote about the Happy Man were conservative in their political and religious affiliation ... the figure of the Happy Man was created, more or less consciously, as a Royalist or humanist counterpart to the grim figure of the Puritan pilgrim'; not until the early eighteenth century did this motif enter the writings of Whigs and Dissenters: ibid., vol. 1, p. 317. It was a genre which also 'declined markedly' after 1770: ibid., vol. 2, pp. 9–10.

imitations of the 1730s. Indeed Pope's versions have been held to be closer to Juvenal than to their ostensible original:[10] with their cultural allusiveness, their patrician social constituency and their seditious political message, Pope's imitations identify better than any other works the literary context into which Johnson's earliest publications intervened.

In this cultural cocktail, the two classical languages were not equal.

Mr. Johnson told me that from twenty-one to fifty-six [i.e. from 1730 to 1765] he had read no Greek; at least not above five chapters of the New Testament. He saw a Xenophon's *Cyropaedia* in Mr. Thrale's library, and took it down; and he was not sensible that he had lost anything of it. He read all the New Testament that year, and has since read a good deal of Greek.[11]

For Johnson, as for many of his contemporaries, Latin and the political lessons conveyed in it were far more important. In 1773 he complained that the memorial inscription to Sir James Macdonald at Sleat 'should have been in Latin, as everything intended to be universal and permanent should be'.[12] Johnson drew a distinction between 'learning', classical learning, and modern knowledge, as when he praised Dr John Campbell's *Britannia Elucidata or Political Survey of Great Britain*: 'he has very extensive reading; not, perhaps, what is properly called learning, but history, politics, and in short that popular knowledge which makes a man very useful'.[13]

The social function of the classics was not constant; the present study seeks to highlight a particular phase of their wider role in England, from the 1660s to the 1750s, by exploring the political and ideological engagement which defined that period and by focusing attention on the cultural politics of its decline. Johnson importantly illuminates this process, for he was not merely a learned classicist among other classicists; he was the last great English man of letters able to write Latin verse to a high standard of technical and literary excellence, the last whose cultural inheritance was more a classical than a vernacular literature. His stature as a writer and a scholar of the Latin language had profound implications for his writings in English and for their social purpose, as this study will explore. If Johnson was the last of his line, it was a tradition of immense distinction extending from Cowley and Milton through Dryden and on to Addison, Swift and

10 Howard Erskine-Hill, *The Augustan Idea in English Literature* (London, 1983), pp. 291–349, at 294–5, 325, 329–30, 333, 342, 348; idem (ed.), *Pope: Horatian Satires and Epistles* (Oxford, 1964).

11 Boswell, *Journal*, p. 237 (30 September 1773). For a survey, see M. N. Austin, 'The Classical Learning of Samuel Johnson', in R. F. Brissenden (ed.), *Studies in the Eighteenth Century* (Canberra, 1968), pp. 285–306. For Johnson's Homeric allusions, see Joannes Gennadius, *Dr Johnson and Homer* (London, privately printed, 1924).

12 Boswell, *Journal*, p. 118 (5 September 1773).

13 Boswell, *Journal*, p. 316 (17 October 1773).

Pope, embracing also an academic tradition of men who were primarily Latin grammarians, like the Whig Dr Richard Bentley, Master of Trinity College, Cambridge, or the Tory Dr William King, Principal of St Mary Hall, Oxford. This academic liaison was, of course, essential for an obvious reason.

The literature of Greece and Rome was accessible only by scholarship, and it was by their scholarly standing, especially as Latinists, that Englishmen laid claim to the highest ranks in the republic of letters.[14] Throughout his early life, Johnson regarded himself as a scholar rather than a vernacular author. When Edward Cave agreed to be the publisher of *London*, Johnson thanked him for 'your regard to learning'.[15] In *The Vanity of Human Wishes* (1749), Johnson wrote:

> There mark what ills the scholar's life assail,
> Toil, envy, want, the garret, and the jail.

Attention has focused on the second line, where in the 1755 edition of the poem he famously replaced 'garret' with 'patron' to denigrate his disloyal patron Chesterfield, but in the first line he retained 'scholar's' where he could have written 'author's' without affecting the scansion. By contrast, vernacular political writers enjoyed little esteem in Johnson's youth. In 1740 'the Writers of all Parties' could plausibly be dismissed as 'a Set of very contemptible Fellows, following Party only as Hunger, Conveniency, or Ambition directs them; their Writings are secretly despised by those very Persons who affect to recommend them, and embrac'd only by those who find they chime in with their favourite Views or Passions'.[16] It is not surprising that Johnson, eager for fame, composed no systematic work on politics.

Yet Johnson was a scholar who had been denied a scholar's station in life for reasons which he saw to be political. He was at his most relaxed and expansive at the meetings of the Ivy Lane club, founded in 1749; but one of its members, the Whig lawyer John Hawkins, recorded that 'the greatest of all our difficulties' at these meetings was to restrain Johnson's behaviour towards another member, 'Dr Samuel Salter ... a Cambridge divine ... well-bred, courteous, and affable', and over seventy years old.

[14] For discussions of this subject by students of English literature, see Paul J. Korshin, 'The Literature of Neoclassicism, 1920–1968: A Bibliography', in Korshin (ed.), *Proceedings of the Modern Language Association Neoclassicism Conferences 1967–1968* (New York, 1970), pp. 85–157; Howard Erskine-Hill, *The Social Milieu of Alexander Pope: Lives, Example and the Poetic Response* (New Haven, 1975); Howard D. Weinbrot, *Augustus Caesar in "Augustan" England: The Decline of a Classical Norm* (Princeton, 1978); Erskine-Hill, *The Augustan Idea.*

[15] Johnson to Cave, c. April 1738: Johnson, *Letters*, vol. 1, p. 15.

[16] *An Historical View of the Principles, Characters, Persons &c. of the Political Writers in Great Britain* (London, 1740), p. 18.

And here I must observe, that Johnson, though a high-churchman, and by consequence a friend to the clergy as a body of men, was, with respect to individuals, frequently, not to say wanting in civility, but to a very great degree splenetic and pertinacious. For this behaviour we could but one way account: He had been bred in an university, and must there have had in prospect those advantages, those stations in life, or perhaps those dignities, which an academic education leads to. Missing these by his adverse fortunes, he looked on every dignitary under a bishop, for to those of that order he was more than sufficiently respectful, and, to descend lower, on every one that possessed the emoluments of his profession, as occupying a station to which himself had a better title, and, if his inferior in learning or mental endowments, treated him as little better than an usurper.[17]

The word 'usurper' had a double significance in that context. Neutrally, it applied to the person occupying the preferment to which Johnson would have thought himself entitled; but Hawkins's readers would inevitably have caught the political echo of that act of usurpation in 1714, the Hanoverian accession, that blocked careers in public life to those like Johnson who would not swear a solemn oath to acknowledge that event's legitimacy.

In 1755, in his famous letter of reproach to Lord Chesterfield for failing in his role as a patron, Johnson characterised himself as 'a retired and uncourtly Scholar'.[18] His command of the classics, and his role in the republic of letters in the first half of the century, fully justified this self-image: Johnson's learning was overwhelmingly in the classics, and in neoclassical Latin literature since the Renaissance. Johnson's astonishing memory was particularly exercised on the classics, as Boswell discovered in 1773:

Hay's translation of Martial was lying in a window. I said I thought it was pretty well done, and showed him a particular epigram, I think of ten, but am certain of eight, lines. He read it, and tossed away the book, saying, 'No, it is *not* pretty well.' As I persisted in my opinion, he said, 'Why, sir, the original is thus' (and he repeated it): 'and this man's translation is thus'; and then he repeated that also, exactly, though he had never seen it before, and read it over only once, and that too without any intention of getting it by heart.[19]

Buchanan's Latin poetry he also had by heart, as Hugh Blair was delighted to discover in 1773.[20] Nor was this random knowledge; Johnson could set out his understanding of the classical tradition systematically. In c. 1735 his cousin Samuel Ford (1717–93) asked his advice about reading before going to Oxford, where he was to matriculate at Trinity College in 1736. Johnson

17 Hawkins, *Life*, pp. 220, 251.
18 Johnson to Chesterfield, 7 February 1755: Johnson, *Letters*, vol. 1, p. 94.
19 Boswell, *Journal*, p. 363 (28 October 1773).
20 Hugh Blair to Boswell, 3 March 1785, in Boswell, *Journal*, p. 388.

recommended previous mastery of Cebes, Claudius Aelianus, Lucian, Xenophon, Homer, Theocritus and Euripides among the Greek authors; Terence, Cicero, Caesar, Sallust, Cornelius Nepos, Gaius Velleius Paterculus, Virgil, Horace and Phaedrus among the Romans; and no single work in the vernacular.[21] The same relentless grounding in Latin was the basis of Johnson's painstaking advice in 1763 to the young George Strahan, similarly preparing himself for University College: commenting on an early composition of Strahan's, Johnson remarked bleakly: 'You are angry that a theme on which you took such pains was at last a kind of English Latin; what could you expect more? If at the end of seven years you write good Latin, you will excel most of your contemporaries.'[22] Among these, Johnson was soon to include the young James Boswell, who unwisely forwarded to his mentor the Latin thesis on a theme from the Pandects which he presented to the Faculty of Advocates in order to be admitted to the Scots bar. Although it satisfied the lower linguistic standards of that Whiggish body, and although Boswell was duly admitted in July 1766, Johnson reproved him: 'your Latin wants correction ... *Homines nullius originis* for *Nullis orti majoribus* or *Nullo loco nati* is I am affraid barbarous. – Ruddiman is dead',[23] and with that greatest of Scottish grammarians, Johnson recognised, had died Scots Latinity.

For Gibbon's generation it was to be French, but for Johnson Latin was still the language of European learning. When Johnson was introduced at the house of the Bishop of Salisbury to 'Boscovich, the Jesuit, who had lately introduced the Newtonian philosophy at Rome',

> The conversation at first was mostly in French. Johnson, though thoroughly versed in that language, and a professed admirer of Boileau and La Bruyere, did not understand its pronunciation, nor could he speak it himself with propriety. For the rest of the evening the talk was in Latin. Boscovich had a ready current flow of that flimsy phraseology with which a priest may travel through Italy, Spain, and Germany. Johnson scorned what he called colloquial barbarisms. It was his pride to speak his best. He went on, after a little practice, with as much facility as if it was his native tongue.[24]

Johnson affirmed his affinity with this tradition in August 1734, when he 'issued a proposal, soliciting a subscription to an edition of Politian's Poems, with this title, "Angeli Politiani Poemata Latina, quibus notas,

21 Johnson to Samuel Ford, [c. mid 1735]: Johnson, *Letters*, vol. 1, p. 11.

22 Johnson to George Strahan, 19 February, 26 March, 16 April, 14 July, 20 September 1763: Johnson, *Letters*, vol. 1, pp. 217, 219–20, 224, 234.

23 Johnson to Boswell, 21 August 1766: Johnson, *Letters*, vol. 1, p. 271. For Ruddiman see below, pp. 21, 34–6 and passim.

24 Arthur Murphy, *An Essay on the Life and Genius of Samuel Johnson, LL.D.* (London, 1793), pp. 91–2. Murphy was present. Boswell, *Life*, vol. 2, p. 125, places the meeting in 1770.

cum Historia Latinae Poeseos a Petrarchae aevo ad Politiani tempora deducta, et Vita Politiani fusius quam antehac enarrata, addidit Sam. Johnson."' It was clearly Johnson's view of the importance of the history of late Latin poetry from Petrarch (1304–74) to Politian (1454–94),[25] rather than an awareness of the market for such a project that inspired him, and, 'not meeting with sufficient encouragement, Johnson dropped the design'. It formed part of his intention to become 'an author by profession', but, as Hawkins described it, 'either in the way of original composition, or translation, or in editing the works of celebrated authors'.[26] For Johnson's generation, these three functions had a far more integral relation than they were to enjoy in the autonomously vernacular culture which in the next century was to take the place of Anglo-Latin culture. To edit or to translate a classical author was still to work within a living tradition; to write an 'imitation' of a classical work was to appropriate that tradition by technical mastery of it, to give it renewed articulation, and to enlist the force and authority of a classic behind one's own statements.

A small but still influential part of this tradition was represented by original compositions in Latin verse. The age of Swift and Pope has been called 'the golden age of neo-Latin poetry in England', the culmination of a process in the seventeenth century by which Anglo-Latin poetry became 'more and more characteristically English'.[27] It did not last: after the 1750s there was a 'great falling off' in such poetry with only a brief flurry in the 1790s.[28] But until that decade, neo-Latin verse continued to be one of three vehicles by which this tradition expressed political and social ideals. This genre included the verse of Anthony Alsop (1672–1726), student and tutor of Christ Church until he accepted a country living in 1712: much of his poetry remained unpublished in his lifetime, and from the collected volume edited by Sir Francis Bernard in 1752 some was omitted because of its 'open expression of Jacobite hopes'.[29] It included also Benjamin Loveling,

25 For the 'crucially important' work of Politian (Angelo Poliziano), see Anthony Grafton, *Joseph Scaliger: A Study in the History of Classical Scholarship* vol. 1 (Oxford, 1983), pp. 9–100; Anthony Grafton and Lisa Jardine, *From Humanism to the Humanities* (London, 1986), pp. 94–7; F. A. Wright and T. A. Sinclair, *A History of Later Latin Literature from the Middle of the Fourth to the End of the Seventeenth Century* (London, 1931).

26 Hawkins, *Life*, p. 27.

27 Leicester Bradner, *Musae Anglicanae: A History of Anglo-Latin Poetry 1500–1925* (New York, 1940), pp. 9, 226. Bradner's valuable study does not, however, consider the phenomena of translation and imitation; nor does it consider the political message of this wider cultural project.

28 Bradner believed that 'It is not possible to assign any one major reason for this interval': ibid., p. 253. It may be suggested that the failure of the political cause of which the Anglo-Latin tradition was a part contributed. For the process by which 'Latin gradually ceased to be a living language' in schools and universities during the eighteenth century, see M. L. Clarke, *Classical Education in Britain 1500–1900* (Cambridge, 1959), pp. 46–73.

29 Bradner, *Musae Anglicanae*, pp. 229–36.

Johnson's Oxford contemporary and satirist of the 1730s, whose 'Festum Iustrale' has been described as 'the best descriptive poem of the century'.[30]

Following the work of Douglas Duncan, it is conventionally assumed that original composition in Latin was the salient defining characteristic of Scots culture. In a British context this needs qualification, however, since an original Scots neo-Latin tradition declined significantly before its English counterpart. The golden age of Scots Latin poetry evidently came in and after the accession of James VI to the throne of England in 1603, in the works of authors like Sir John Scot of Scotstarvet, Andrew Ramsay, Arthur Johnston and John Leech. It was a cultural movement which defined itself against Covenanting religion from the 1630s; this theme became intertwined with the dynastic one by the end of the century, especially in the work of Johnston and Archibald Pitcairne (1652–1713). He was a relatively isolated phenomenon: the stream of Scots Latin poetry, 'which had proceeded with unabated vigor for a hundred years, was practically at an end' at the Restoration.[31] But if it ceased to be written, it did not cease to be read, and read for its political content; kept alive in Scotland as a language by efficient schools and accessible universities, it was kept alive as a political culture not least by the activities of a brilliant cultural entrepreneur, Thomas Ruddiman. Yet England still had more of everything: England's culture in Johnson's lifetime supported not only a viable Anglo-Latin tradition but an emergent and extensive vernacular also.

Johnson used the medium of Latin for more than formal addresses: it was the vehicle for some of his most deeply personal statements in a classical idiom as well as for devotional sentiments in the idiom of the early Church.[32] Yet original composition in Latin was generally the third in importance of the three strands of England's Anglo-Latin tradition. More salient, especially from the political point of view, were the genres of translation and imitation. Imitation had a special significance; but imitation demonstrated the technical mastery and power of English men of letters, not their weakness of invention.[33] John Oldham explained his imitation of Horace's *Ars Poetica* as an improvement for the modern reader

30 Bradner, *Musae Anglicanae*, pp. 228, 237–8. He was the son of Benjamin Loveling, vicar of Banbury, Oxfordshire (born 1711); little is known of his life. Although he matriculated at Trinity College, Oxford, in 1728 he did not take a degree. It was probably this author whom Johnson described as 'a wit about town, who wrote bawdy Latin verses': Boswell, *Life*, vol. 2, pp. 91, 488. [Benjamin Loveling], *Latin and English Poems. By a Gentleman of Trinity College, Oxford* (London, no publisher, 1738) included verses on London whores.

31 Bradner, *Musae Anglicanae*, pp. 158–200, at 158, 182, 193–4, 198.

32 See Susie I. Tucker and Henry Gifford, 'Johnson's Latin Poetry', *Neophilologus* 41 (1957), 215–21.

33 Cf. Howard D. Weinbrot, 'Augustan Imitation: the Role of the Original', in Korshin (ed.), *Proceedings of the Modern Language Association Neoclassicism Conferences*, pp. 53–70, and Weinbrot, *The Formal Strain: Studies in Augustan Imitation and Satire* (Chicago, 1969).

by putting *Horace* into a more modern Dress than hitherto he has appeared in; that is, by making him speak as if he were living and writing now. I therefore resolved to alter the Scene from *Rome* to *London*, and to make use of *English* Names of Men, Places, and Customs, where the Parallel would decently permit, which I conceived would give a kind of new Air to the Poem and render it more agreeable to the relish of the present Age.[34]

This tradition reached its high point with Swift's imitations of Horace in 1713–14; in Pope's of the same author, written in 1733–8; and in Johnson's own *London* (1738) and *The Vanity of Human Wishes* (1749). Of Pope's imitations of Horace, Johnson wrote:

This mode of imitation, in which the ancients are familiarised, by adapting their sentiments to modern topicks, by making Horace say of Shakespeare what he originally said of Ennius, and accommodating his satires of Pantolabus and Nomentanus to the flatterers and prodigals of our own time, was first practised in the reign of Charles the Second by Oldham and Rochester, at least I remember no instances more ancient. It is a kind of middle composition between translation and original design, which pleases when the thoughts are unexpectedly applicable, and the parallels lucky. It seems to have been Pope's favourite amusement; for he has carried it further than any former poet.[35]

This was historically inaccurate: the imitation long preceded Oldham and Rochester.[36] Translation also was nothing new: a wide swathe of both Greek and Latin literature was already available in English by 1600.[37] What Johnson correctly sensed was the beginning in the 1660s of a special significance given to the classics, especially via the modes of translation and imitation,[38] within the scholarly and political tradition of which he was part. Between 1660 and 1700, at least fifty English poets produced translations or adaptations of Horace, let alone others of the ancients,[39] and

34 *The Works of Mr. John Oldham, Together with his Remains* (London, 1684), after p. 184 as *Some New Pieces* (London, 1684), sig. av (italics and Roman transposed): Weinbrot, 'Augustan Imitation', pp. 53–70, at 53.

35 Johnson, *Lives of the Poets*, vol. 4, pp. 117–8.

36 Harold F. Brooks, 'The "Imitation" in English Poetry, Especially in Formal Satire, before the Age of Pope', *Review of English Studies* 25 (1949), 124–40.

37 R.R. Bolgar, *The Classical Heritage and its Beneficiaries* (Cambridge, 1954), p. 328.

38 For debates on the genre since the Renaissance, and for imitation as 'the process of a poet's *relation to* rather than *approximation of* a standard or norm', see Anthony La Branche, 'Imitation: Getting in Touch', *Modern Language Quarterly* 31 (1970), 308–29. For one interpretation of the role of imitation in the eighteenth century, as an aesthetic liberation which depended on preserving the authority of classical models, see W. K. Wimsatt, 'Imitation As Freedom – 1717–1798', *New Literary History* 1 (1969–70), 215–36. Howard D. Weinbrot distinguishes four different modes of imitation in 'Augustan Imitation', pp. 53–70, and idem, *The Formal Strain*.

39 Robert M. Ogilvie, 'Translations of Horace in the 17th and 18th Centuries', *Wolfenbütteler Forschungen* 12 (1981), 71–80; Stuart Gillespie, 'A Checklist of Restoration English Translations and Adaptations of Greek and Latin Poetry, 1660–1700', *Translation and Literature* 1 (1992), 52–67.

after 1700 this stream became a flood.[40] Johnson's political allies clearly shared this literary tradition. Lord Orrery, proposing to pass the long winter evenings of 1740 in translating Pliny's *Epistles*, wrote:

to each Epistle I propose Notes, such as shall take in all Kinds of Learning, History, Humour, or agreeable Observations, so that the whole may be worth the Acceptance of the Publick. I have ever despised literal Translations: at best They are only fitt for School Boys, and they are what no Man of Taste can bring himself down to. I would make Pliny an Englishman: I would keep up his Sense and Spirit, but I would endeavour to use such Expressions as He himself would have chose had He written in English.[41]

William King agreed:

A Translation of *Pliny's Epistles* should not be attempted but by a polite Scholar and can never be well executed but by one, who very nearly resembles his author, and participates of the spirit and manners of that great Roman . . . In a word Pliny is not to be translated but by one, who speaks, and writes, and thinks, and lives like Pliny.[42]

In this context, Johnson's project for an edition of Politian and history of Latin poetry can be seen as a youthful affirmation of his place in a cultural tradition. Arthur Murphy commented:

It is to be regretted that this project failed for want of encouragement. Johnson, it seems, differed from Boileau, Voltaire, and D'Alembert, who had taken upon them to proscribe all modern efforts to write with elegance in a dead language. For a decision, pronounced in so high a tone, no good reason can be assigned. The interests of learning require, that the diction of Greece and Rome should be cultivated with care; and he, who can write a language with correctness, will be most likely to understand its idiom, its grammar, and its peculiar graces of style. What man of taste would willingly forego the pleasure of reading *Vida*, *Fracastorius*, *Sannazaro*, *Strada*, and others, down to the late elegant productions of Bishop Lowth? The history which Johnson proposed to himself would, beyond all question, have been a valuable addition to the history of letters; but his project failed.[43]

II. THE *LIVES OF THE POETS*: THE TRAJECTORY OF ENGLISH LETTERS

Johnson's understanding of the historical trajectory of the Anglo-Latin tradition was disclosed in his *Lives of the Poets* (1779–81), and although that

[40] Joseph William Moss, *A Manual of Classical Bibliography* (2 vols., London, 1825).

[41] Lord Orrery to Dr William King, 27 August 1739: *Orrery Papers*, vol. 1, p. 264. He later presented the two volumes of his translation to Bolingbroke: Orrery to Bolingbroke, 15 July 1751: ibid., vol. 2, p. 94.

[42] King to Orrery, 23 September 1739: Bodleian MS Eng hist d. 103, f. 7.

[43] Murphy, *Johnson*, pp. 26–7.

tradition itself was then receding into history, some contemporaries caught an echo of it in Johnson's special affinity for one precursor in particular: 'in his whole list of poets, there is no individual to whom the biographer bore so great a resemblance, in the general cast of his mind, in his political, and, I believe, in his religious notions' as Dryden.[44] The *Lives of the Poets* was an attempt to legislate for, as much as to record, a canon of English letters; Johnson did not acknowledge, and probably could not see, that his work was already the memorial of a tradition that had been profoundly modified. That modification was a result partly of the tradition's political failure, partly of the rise of hitherto-unsuspected alternatives. Thomas Warton's *History of English Poetry* was published in three volumes in 1774, 1778 and 1781. It was both a major landmark of scholarship and a decisive intervention in the cultural politics of its age: for the first time, the achievement of English poetry from Chaucer to the Elizabethans was retrieved and made accessible, and the ground was prepared for a shift in hegemonic style which the Romantics exploited.[45]

The *Lives of the Poets* was not Johnson's independent conception: it was driven by his publishers' commercial strategy, and by considerations of literary copyright. The established London booksellers who commissioned Johnson were prompted by what promised to be a definitive edition from the monopoly-threatening publisher John Bell, whose *The Poets of Great Britain Complete from Chaucer to Churchill*, printed in Edinburgh, appeared in 109 volumes between 1776 and 1782.[46] Nevertheless, Johnson's own cultural project largely coincided with the scope of the work chosen by his booksellers for commercial reasons. In Johnson's scenario, English poetry did not begin with Chaucer and a medieval vernacular, although he was well versed in such authors, nor even with Shakespeare. The early seventeenth century was similarly barren. By the standards of the Anglo-Latin tradition, the 'metaphysical' poets were sadly inadequate: where they should have sought to work within the conventions, 'Their wish was only to say what they hoped had been never said before ... Those writers who lay on the watch for novelty could have little hope of greatness; for great things cannot have escaped former observation.'[47] Especially, they could not have escaped the notice of the authors of antiquity. In Johnson's view, it was English poetry's links with Greece and Rome which affirmed its commitment to themes of general application to the human condition, to the

[44] [William Hayley], *Two Dialogues; containing a Comparative View of the Lives, Characters and Writings of Philip, the late Earl of Chesterfield, and Dr Samuel Johnson* (London, 1787), p. 120.

[45] See below, pp. 250–1.

[46] Thomas F. Bonnell, 'John Bell's *Poets of Great Britain*: The "Little Trifling Edition" Revisited', *Modern Philology* 85 (1987), 128–52. I owe this reference to Bruce Redford.

[47] Johnson, *Lives of the Poets*, vol. 1, pp. 30–1.

noble, and to the sublime. It was in these terms that Johnson praised the ancients: 'The peculiarity of Juvenal is a mixture of gaiety and stateliness, of pointed sentences and declamatory grandeur ... In the comparison of Homer and Virgil, the discriminative excellence of Homer is elevation and comprehension of thought, and that of Virgil is grace and splendor of diction.'[48] In all these respects, they were exemplary.

To Congreve was ascribed 'the cure of our Pindarick madness', that phase of English sensibility in the seventeenth century in which irregular rhetoric was excused as an imitation of Pindar. Cowley

first taught the English writers that Pindar's odes were regular; and though certainly he had not the fire requisite for the higher species of lyrick poetry, he has shewn us that enthusiasm has its rules, and that in mere confusion there is neither grace nor greatness.[49]

In Johnson's overview, modern English poetry began not with developments in the vernacular but with Cowley and Milton, 'of opposite [political] principles; but concurring in the cultivation of Latin poetry, in which the English, till their works and May's poem[50] appeared, seemed unable to contest the palm with any other of the lettered nations'. Cowley ranked above Milton in this respect, for Milton 'is generally content to express the thoughts of the ancients in their language; Cowley, without much loss of purity or elegance, accommodates the diction of Rome to his own conceptions'. Cowley was 'among those who freed translation from servility, and, instead of following his author at a distance, walked by his side'.[51] Johnson's admiration for Cowley extended to presenting 'the best edition' of his Latin poetry to Edmund Burke.[52]

Equally in the case of English prose, Johnson did not believe in the long existence of a vigorous vernacular. The *Tatler* and *Spectator* were new in this respect, he realised; before them, 'England had no masters of the common life'.

No writers had yet undertaken to reform either the savageness of neglect, or the impertinence of civility; to teach when to speak, or to be silent; how to refuse, or how to comply. We wanted not books to teach us our more important duties, and to settle opinions in philosophy or politicks; but an *Arbiter elegantiarum*, a judge of propriety, was yet wanting, who should survey the track of daily conversation, and

48 Ibid., vol. 2, pp. 163–5. 49 Ibid., vol. 3, p. 69.

50 Thomas May, *Supplementum Lucani* (London, 1640).

51 Ibid., vol. 1, pp. 18–19, 102. For Cowley see Brooks, 'The "Imitation"', pp. 127–31: Cowley's 'theory was in the main a plea for great latitude of paraphrase'. Denham 'appears to have been one of the first that understood the necessity of emancipating translation from the drudgery of counting lines and interpreting single words': Johnson, ibid., vol. 1, p. 117.

52 Johnson to Burke, 21 June 1770: Johnson, *Letters*, vol. 1, p. 340. This was Thomas Sprat (ed.), *Abrahami Couleii Angli, Poemata Latina* (London, 1668).

free it from thorns and prickles, which teaze the passer, though they do not wound him.

There were earlier periodicals, L'Estrange's *Observator* and Leslie's *Rehearsal*; 'but hitherto nothing had been conveyed to the people, in this commodious manner, but controversy relating to Church or State; of which they taught many to talk, whom they could not teach to judge'.[53]

Johnson gave priority to poetry over prose, and, within the genres of poetry, affirmed his esteem for one from which he derived his sense of the inception of modern English verse:

The affluence and comprehension of our language is very illustriously displayed in our poetical translations of the Ancient Writers; a work which the French seem to relinquish in despair, and which we were long unable to perform with dexterity. Ben Jonson thought it necessary to copy Horace almost word by word; Feltham, his contemporary and adversary, considers it indispensably requisite in a translation to give line for line ... Cowley saw that such *copyers* were a *servile race*; he asserted his liberty, and spread his wings so boldly that he left his authors. It was reserved for Dryden to fix the limits of poetical liberty, and give us just rules and examples of translation.[54]

The ancient Greeks had almost no translations; the Romans only a few. The Italians had been 'diligent translators', but had only a literal, pedantic version of the *Iliad.*

The French, in the meridian hour of their learning, were very laudably industrious to enrich their own language with the learning of the ancients; but found themselves reduced, by whatever necessity, to turn the Greek and Roman poetry into prose. Whoever could read an author, could translate him. From such rivals little can be feared.

In this literary form the English had excelled. This then had its effect on the vernacular: Pope's

version may be said to have tuned the English tongue; for since its appearance no writer, however deficient in other powers, has wanted melody. Such a series of lines so elaborately corrected, and so sweetly modulated, took possession of the publick ear; the vulgar was enamoured of the poem, and the learned wondered at the translation.[55]

[53] Johnson, *Lives of the Poets*, vol. 2, pp. 362–4.

[54] Ibid., vol. 2, pp. 123–4. For Dryden's theory of translation, see his 'Preface to the Translation of Ovid's Epistles' (1680) in W.P. Ker (ed.), *Essays of John Dryden* (2 vols., Oxford, 1926), vol. 1, p. 230–43.

[55] Johnson, *Lives of the Poets*, vol. 4, pp. 192–4.

Lesser figures commanded their place in Johnson's canon mainly as classicists: Richard Duke for his translations of Ovid and Juvenal; Thomas Sprat for his edition of Cowley's Latin poetry. Samuel Garth's last work was his edition of Ovid's *Metamorphoses*; Nicholas Rowe's was an edition of Lucan's *Pharsalia*, which Johnson praised as

> one of the greatest productions of English poetry; for there is perhaps none that so completely exhibits the genius and spirit of the original. *Lucan* is distinguished by a kind of dictatorial or philosophick dignity, rather, as Quintillian observes, declamatory than poetical; full of ambitious morality and pointed sentences, comprised in vigorous and animated lines. This character Rowe has very diligently and successfully preserved.[56]

Lesser figures paved the way for greater ones. Sir John Denham's 'versions of Virgil are not pleasing; but they taught Dryden to please better'.[57] Rochester, too, reaped the reward of a pioneer: 'His imitation of Horace on Lucilius is not inelegant or unhappy. In the reign of Charles the Second began that adaptation, which has since been very frequent, of ancient poetry to present times; and perhaps few will be found where the parallelism is better preserved than in this.'[58]

Ambrose Philips earned his place in the canon by his pastorals and his translations of Pindar. For the former he was praised by Addison and his friends, who were 'very willing to push him into reputation':

> The *Guardian* gave an account of Pastoral, partly critical, and partly historical; in which, when the merit of the moderns is compared, Tasso and Guarini are censured for remote thoughts and unnatural refinements; and, upon the whole, the Italians and French are all excluded from rural poetry, and the pipe of the Pastoral Muse is transmitted by lawful inheritance from Theocritus to Virgil, from Virgil to Spenser, and from Spenser to Philips.[59]

The translation of Pindar was similarly the claim to fame of Gilbert West. William Collins attracted Johnson's friendship about 1744, soon after publishing 'proposals for a History of the Revival of Learning'; Johnson or another friend rescued Collins from a bailiff by selling to the booksellers that author's proposal for 'a translation of Aristotle's Poeticks'.[60] Christopher Pitt was, as a schoolboy at Winchester, 'distinguished by exercises of uncommon elegance'; although he spent his life as rector of Pimpern in Dorset, he 'gave us a complete English Eneid' which ranked with Dryden's translation: 'It would have been pleasing to have an oppor-

56 Ibid., vol. 2, pp. 265, 284, 318, 333, 341.
57 Ibid., vol. 1, p. 117.
58 Ibid., vol. 1, p. 305; cf. p. 329.
59 Ibid., vol. 4, pp. 299–302, 309–10.
60 Ibid., vol. 4, pp. 316, 324–5.

tunity of comparing the two best translations that perhaps were ever produced by one nation of the same author.'[61]

Dryden, however, was the central figure in Johnson's scenario. Dryden's translation of Virgil, 'perhaps the most arduous work of its kind', was a triumph: 'He produced, says Pope, *the most noble and spirited translation that I know in any language* ... What was said of Rome, adorned by Augustus, may be applied by an easy metaphor to English poetry embellished by Dryden, *lateritiam invenit, marmoream reliquit*, he found it brick, and he left it marble.'[62] He did so, however, not by an unsupported achievement in the vernacular, but by drawing on the resources of the ancients.[63] In this project, Dryden was in profound sympathy with other figures of his age. One was the exiled royalist Wentworth Dillon (c. 1637–85), 4th Earl of Roscommon, who returned to England at the Restoration.

> He now busied his mind with literary projects, and formed the plan of a society for refining our language, and fixing its standard; *in imitation*, says Fenton, *of those learned and polite societies with which he had been acquainted abroad*. In this design his friend Dryden is said to have assisted him.
>
> The same design, it is well known, was revived by Dr Swift in the ministry of Oxford; but it has never since been publickly mentioned, though at that time great expectations were formed by some at least of its establishment and its effects.

Johnson could not restrain his own scepticism: 'Such a society might, perhaps, without much difficulty, be collected; but that it would produce what is expected from it, may be doubted.' In England such an academy would be corrupt, and its edicts 'would probably be read by many, only that they might be sure to disobey them': 'That our language is in perpetual danger of corruption cannot be denied; but what prevention can be found? The present manners of the nation would deride authority, and therefore nothing is left but that every writer should criticise himself.'[64] By the time Johnson wrote that passage, he had witnessed the process by which the ancients had largely lost that authority over the moderns which they had enjoyed in his youth.

Johnson's loyalty to that tradition even overrode political differences, just as the Scots episcopalian Thomas Ruddiman excused the politics of the Scots republican George Buchanan out of admiration for his Latinity. Despite Johnson's disapproval of Milton's politics, he recorded: 'I once heard Mr. Hampton, the translator of Polybius, remark what I think is

61 Ibid., vol. 4, pp. 243, 246. 62 Ibid., vol. 2, pp. 164, 166, 193.

63 For such themes explored in modern criticism, see Edward Pechter, *Dryden's Classical Theory of Literature* (Cambridge, 1975); Steven N. Zwicker, *Politics and Language in Dryden's Poetry* (Princeton, 1984); Taylor Corse, *Dryden's Aeneid: The English Virgil* (Newark, N.J., 1991).

64 Johnson, *Lives of the Poets*, vol. 1, pp. 320–2.

true, that Milton was the first Englishman who, after the revival of letters, wrote Latin verses with classick elegance.' But classical themes themselves were not enough to establish poetic stature: a work like *Lycidas* felt the full force of Johnson's criticism for a

> long train of mythological imagery, such as a College easily supplies. Nothing can less display knowledge, or less exercise invention, than to tell how a shepherd has lost his companion, and must now feed his flocks alone, without any judge of his skill in piping; and how one god asks another god what is become of Lycidas, and how neither god can tell. He who thus grieves will excite no sympathy; he who thus praises will confer no honour.[65]

Edmund Waller fell into a similar error:

> He borrows too many of his sentiments and illustrations from the old Mythology, for which it is vain to plead the example of ancient poets: the deities which they introduced so frequently, were considered as realities, so far as to be received by the imagination, whatever sober reason might even then determine. But of these images time has tarnished the splendour.[66]

Johnson was not merely a moralist: he was a Christian, an Anglican and a High Churchman, not afraid to term pantheism, paganism or atheists, infidels.

The partisanship of Whig and Tory could be suspended in Johnson's criticism in favour of those whose Latinity raised them to a higher level. If Milton was Johnson's main exception, a second was Joseph Addison, who according to Johnson, 'grew first eminent by his Latin compositions, which are indeed entitled to particular praise'.

> His next paper of verses contained a character of the principal English poets, inscribed to Henry Sacheverell, who was then, if not a poet, a writer of verses; as is shewn by his version of a small part of Virgil's Georgicks, published in the Miscellanies, and a Latin encomium on queen Mary, in the Musae Anglicanae. These verses exhibit all the fondness of friendship; but on one side or the other, friendship was too weak for the malignity of faction.

Addison's Latin poem on the Peace of Ryswick in 1697 was called by Smith '*the best Latin poem since the Aeneid*'; even Johnson conceded that 'the performance cannot be denied to be vigorous and elegant'.[67] He quoted Sir Richard Steele's praise of Addison: 'I have often reflected, after a night spent with him apart from all the world, that I had had the pleasure of conversing with an intimate acquaintance of Terence and Catullus'. Addison, however, fell short of the highest honours: 'His translations, so far as I have compared them, want the exactness of a scholar. That he

65 Ibid., vol. 1, p. 129, 225–6. 66 Ibid., vol. 1, p. 420.
67 Ibid., vol. 2, pp. 349, 351, 353, 395.

understood his authors cannot be doubted; but his versions will not teach others to understand them, being too licentiously paraphrastical.'[68] The highest honours were reserved for another.

Pope was 'first regularly initiated in poetry by the perusal of Ogylby's *Homer*, and Sandys's *Ovid* ... of Sandys he declared, in his notes to the *Iliad*, that English poetry owed much of its present beauty to his translations'. Pope demonstrated his early talent by translating, before the age of twelve, 'more than a fourth part of the *Metamorphoses*' of Ovid. At fourteen he 'made a version of the first book of the *Thebais*, which, with some revision, he afterwards published', and as well as a modern version of Chaucer, 'translated likewise the Epistle of *Sappho to Phaon* from Ovid'. Only after such achievements did the young author turn to French and Italian.[69]

Johnson praised Pope's translation of the *Iliad*: 'It is certainly the noblest version of poetry which the world has ever seen; and its publication must therefore be considered as one of the great events in the annals of Learning'. It was 'a performance which no age or nation can pretend to equal'.[70] Johnson praised in Pope an expertise which was specialised in the early eighteenth century, and obscure by the 1780s:

> Pope had sought for images and sentiments in a region not known to have been explored by many other of the English writers; he had consulted the modern writers of Latin poetry, a class of authors whom Boileau endeavoured to bring into contempt, and who are too generally neglected. Pope, however, was not ashamed of their acquaintance, nor ungrateful for the advantages which he might have derived from it. A small selection from the Italians who wrote in Latin had been published at London, about the latter end of the last century, by a man who concealed his name, but whom his Preface shews to have been well qualified for his undertaking. This collection Pope amplified by more than half, and (1740) published it in two volumes, but injuriously omitted his predecessor's preface. To these books, which had nothing but the mere text, no regard was paid, the authors were still neglected, and the editor was neither praised nor censured.[71]

68 Ibid., vol. 2, pp. 437–8.

69 Ibid., vol. 4, pp. 5–6, 9–10. For Pope's classical indebtedness see Howard Erskine-Hill (ed.), *Pope: Horatian Satires and Epistles* (Oxford, 1964); Thomas E. Maresca, *Pope's Horatian Poems* (Columbus, Ohio, 1966); Niall Rudd, *The Satires of Horace: A Study* (Cambridge, 1966); Howard Erskine-Hill, 'Satire and Self-Portrayal: The First Satire of the Second Book of Horace, Imitated and Pope's Reception of Horace', *Wolfenbütteler Forschungen* (München, 1981), 153–71; Frank Stack, *Pope and Horace: Studies in Imitation* (Cambridge, 1985); for Pope's and Dryden's, Charles Martindale and David Hopkins (eds.), *Horace Made New: Horatian influences on British writing from the Renaissance to the twentieth century* (Cambridge, 1993), pp. 127–98. Stack, *Pope and Horace*, pp. 281–3, provides a list of 38 imitations of Horace published 1730–40, in addition to Pope's.

70 Johnson, *Lives of the Poets*, vol. 4, pp. 47, 192.

71 Ibid., vol. 4, pp. 124–5.

Evidently unknown to Johnson, Pope's collection[72] was a re-edited version of that published by Francis Atterbury, Latinist, Christ Church don and Stuart conspirator.[73]

Johnson was too good a scholar to be an indulgent critic. Even Pope himself, whose *Iliad* received such praise, was reproved when he fell below his best. By the 1770s, Johnson's new emphasis on the vernacular, or need to establish his superiority as a classicist, led him to censure Pope's brilliant exercises in that genre:

> The Imitations of Horace seem to have been written as relaxations of his genius. This employment became his favourite by its facility; the plan was ready to his hand, and nothing was required but to accommodate as he could the sentiments of an old author to recent facts or familiar images; but what is easy is seldom excellent; such imitations cannot give pleasure to common readers; the man of learning may be sometimes surprised and delighted by an unexpected parallel; but the comparison requires knowledge of the original, which will likewise often detect strained applications. Between Roman images and English manners there will be an irreconcilable dissimilitude, and the work will be generally uncouth and party-coloured; neither original nor translated, neither ancient nor modern.[74]

Whatever Johnson thought by the 1770s of Pope's imitations of Horace, in 1738 Johnson himself, seeking a publisher for his poem *London*, had commended the genre: 'part of the beauty of the performance (if any beauty be allow'd it) consisting in adapting Juvenals Sentiments to modern facts and Persons'; it was for that reason that 'the Quotations [from Juvenal's Latin original] ... must be subjoined at the bottom of the Page'.[75]

In the *Lives of the Poets*, Johnson showed his need to claim mastery over the Anglo-Latin tradition by quietly disparaging its most famous practitioner. Pope's *Essay on Man* showed that he was 'not sufficiently master of his subject', that is, 'metaphysical morality': 'Never were penury of knowledge and vulgarity of sentiment so happily disguised.'

> In the conclusion it is sufficiently acknowledged, that the doctrine of the *Essay on Man* was received from Bolingbroke, who is said to have ridiculed Pope, among those who enjoyed his confidence, as having adopted and advanced principles of which he did not perceive the consequence, and as blindly propagating opinions contrary to his own.[76]

72 *Selecta Poemata Italorum Qui Latine Scripserunt. Cura cujusdam Anonymi Anno 1684 congesta, iterum in lucem data, una cum aliorum Italorum operibus, Accurante A. Pope* (2 vols., London, 1740).

73 ΑΝΘΟΛΟΓΓΑ *Seu Selecta Quaedam Poemata Italorum Qui Latine scripserunt* (London, 1684).

74 Johnson, *Lives of the Poets*, vol. 4, pp. 205–6. For Pope's imitations of Horace in the 1730s, see Erskine-Hill, *The Augustan Idea*, pp. 291–349.

75 Johnson to Edward Cave, April 1738: Johnson, *Letters*, vol. 1, p. 16.

76 Johnson, *Lives of the Poets*, vol. 4, pp. 100–9, 200–2.

Johnson the classicist and Johnson the theologian created Johnson the formidable critic.

The Lives of the Poets won lasting recognition as literary criticism, but within Johnson's cultural strategy the work was, in large part, a failure. It attempted to defend one conception of the canon, enshrining within it a host of relatively minor poets, like Samuel Garth, John Hughes, John Philips, John Pomfret, Edmund Smith, George Stepney, Gilbert West or Thomas Yalden; within a decade, Wordsworth and Coleridge had begun the process which eventually sank a whole culture, leaving only its peaks, Dryden and Pope, still projecting above the waters, seeming now like individual and isolated achievements of technically skillful versification alone. The *Lives of the Poets* reflected the criteria of the Anglo-Latin tradition, appraising English poets to a substantial degree in respect of their relation to the classics: these criteria were soon overlooked. More limiting still, Johnson's critical masterpiece implied a theory of the trajectory of modern English poetry, from nascent sophistication in Cowley and Milton through technical mastery in Dryden to fulfilment in Pope; but it contained no account of the later continuation of that trajectory, and Johnson's silence on this point left his disintegrating tradition without a clear rationale and so ultimately without a memorial. *The Lives of the Poets* was lastingly read for its many critical and biographical insights; its attempt to outline a tradition was forgotten.

III. THE POLITICAL SIGNIFICANCE OF THE ANGLO-LATIN TRADITION

Classical allusion came more easily to the English elite of c. 1660–1750 than to any other generation, and it came most easily of all in a political context. In 1715 Dudley Ryder (later, as Attorney General, to lead in the impeachment of Simon, Lord Lovat for his role in the Forty-five), noted his reading as a law student:

> Played upon my viol. Read some of Catiline Conspiracy.[77] It seems to be something like the case of England about the time of the rebellion when the Irish were sent for by King James [II]. Everybody were in a terrible consternation for fear of a massacre, the whole nation was in an uproar and news was spread about that the Irish were within a mile or two of them and were destroying everything they met with.[78]

Bolingbroke's writings for *The Craftsman* drew on many foreign countries for parallels, but, according to one pamphleteer,

[77] By Sallust.

[78] William Matthews (ed.), *The Diary of Dudley Ryder 1715–1716* (London, 1939), p. 70.

the most fruitful of all is the History of Old *Rome*. There you will meet with a *Cataline*, who had enter'd into a Plot to burn the City, and assassinate the Senate. You'll say, what Parallel can be drawn betwixt *Cataline* and a *British* Minister? Sir *R[ober]t W[alpol]e* sure has no Design to fire *London* and murder the Parliament? No; but an ingenious Character-monger will, when the literal Sense will not do, give it an Allegorical Term, and then they fit exactly: As for Example; The rest of the Ministry and Members of Parliament, who are on the Side of the Court, are the Conspirators with *Cataline*, *i.e.* Sir *R[ober]t*, to destroy the City of *London*, by ruining Trade, and to assassinate the Senate, *i.e.* to overthrow the Constitution. *Verres* is another top Character that has stood them in great Stead; and *Sejanus* has been a perfect Mine of smart Things that have been said against wicked Ministers.[79]

The young Lord Boyle described the scene in London at the news of George I's death and his son's accession: 'Nothing but Joy was seen; Nothing but Huzzas heard, and if you will allow a Classical Simile, it was like the Rejoicing of the Trojans described in Virgil, when they thought the Grecians were run away. Ruine and Destruction followed the Trojan Merriment; the Gods avert the Omen from the *English*!'[80] But this was more than a random choice of words, as Boyle's Jacobite politics were later to demonstrate. From the Restoration in 1660 to about the 1750s the classics served, among their other uses, one distinct and unique function which marked out that phase of English cultural politics. For the classics were one means by which a social order, dynastic, gentlemanly and episcopalian, came to conceive of itself and to resist what it defined as its enemies. It was in this spirit that Johnson repudiated with indignation the 'plebeian grossness' of the Wilkesites:

It is surely not unreasonable to hope, that the nation will consult its dignity, if not its safety, and disdain to be protected or enslaved by the declaimers or the plotters of a city-tavern. Had Rome fallen by the Catilinarian conspiracy, she might have consoled her fate by the greatness of her destroyers; but what would have alleviated the disgrace of England, had her government been changed by Tiler or by Ket.[81]

Johnson's early career was bound up with the conflicts generated by that project, and shared in the penalties more than the rewards which those conflicts showered on his contemporaries. The profession of letters in England was impoverished, as it was embittered, by political division. Arthur Murphy compared England unfavourably with the honours done by the French to 'their Poets, their Heroes, and their Philosophers'. The

79 *An Historical View of the Principles, Characters, Persons &c. of the Political Writers in Great Britain* (London, 1740), pp. 35–6.

80 Lord Boyle (later 5th Earl of Orrery) to William Byrd, September 1727, in *Orrery Papers*, vol. 1, p. 54.

81 I.e. Wat Tyler, leader of the Peasants' Revolt in 1381, and Robert Kett, leader of the rising of 1549. [Samuel Johnson], *The False Alarm* (London, 1770), pp. 49, 51.

French 'had, besides, an *Academy of Belles Lettres*, where Genius was cultivated, refined, and encouraged'. But in England the 'public mind, for centuries, has been engrossed by party and faction; by *the madness of many for the gain of a few*; by civil wars, religious dissentions, trade and commerce, and the arts of accumulating wealth. Amidst such attentions, who can wonder that cold praise has been often the only reward of merit?' Swift had the idea of an English Academy, 'and proposed it to Lord Oxford; but Whig and Tory were more important objects'.[82]

Both Whigs and Tories sought to master and appropriate the classical tradition, but Tories did so in larger numbers and normally with greater success than their opponents.[83] Johnson's alignment in this world was clear from the outset. It was no coincidence that Johnson, as his literary standing grew, came to be known through his work both to the Latinist Thomas Ruddiman (1674–1757), 'the foremost literary scholar in the Scotland of his day',[84] and to William King (1685–1763), England's 'last example of a Latin poet in the grand manner'.[85] Himself the protégé of the royalist poet Dr Archibald Pitcairne, Ruddiman excelled his patron not only as a Latinist but as a scholarly polemicist and publisher in the Stuart cause.[86] William King was one of the most committed and active of the English Jacobite intelligentsia.

Johnson's admiration for Ruddiman's scholarship was freely expressed, but he knew more of him than that: 'I hear,' wrote Johnson, 'that his learning is not his highest excellence.'[87] Boswell shrewdly recorded: 'His zeal for the Royal House of Stuart did not render him less estimable in Dr Johnson's eye.'[88] Although he was too old to take an active part in the Forty-five, one of Ruddiman's sons died in exile in 1747 after being transported for his participation in the rising.[89] In a manuscript note of 1755 to a pamphlet written against him, Ruddiman acknowledged that his principles were those of 'the nonjurant clergy of Scotland'.[90] His written contributions to that cause were made in self-defence, during the period of acrimonious polemic which followed the Forty-five,[91] but his position was already clear.

82 Murphy, *Johnson*, pp. 115–7.
83 Dr Bentley is, of course, the major exception to this rule.
84 Duncan, *Thomas Ruddiman*, p. 1 and passim.
85 Greenwood, *William King*, p. 352.
86 George Chalmers, *The Life of Thomas Ruddiman, A.M.* (London, 1794), pp. 24–5, 78, 286–93. For the seventeenth-century tradition of Scots Latinity, see Bradner, *Musae Anglicanae*, pp. 158–200.
87 Johnson to James Elphinstone, n.d. [1751–2] in Boswell, *Life*, vol. 1, pp. 210–11; vol. 2, p. 21.
88 Boswell, *Life*, vol. 1, p. 211.
89 Duncan, *Thomas Ruddiman*, p. 4.
90 Chalmers, *Ruddiman*, p. 287 n; Duncan, *Thomas Ruddiman*, p. 7.
91 Thomas Ruddiman, *An Answer to The Reverend Mr. George Logan's late Treatise on Government: in which (Contrary to the manifold Errors and Misrepresentations of that Author) The ancient*

In 1773 Johnson and Boswell paused on their tour of Scotland at Laurencekirk, 'where our great grammarian, Ruddiman, was once schoolmaster. We respectfully remembered that excellent man and eminent scholar, by whose labours a knowledge of the Latin language will be preserved in Scotland, if it shall be preserved at all.'[92] Johnson's perspective on Scots literary history was essentially Ruddiman's: Johnson 'owned that we were a very learned nation for about 100 years, from about 1550 to about 1650. But that we lost our learning during the Civil War and never recovered it.'[93] Johnson argued that

> the collection called *The Muses' Welcome to King James* (first of England and sixth of Scotland), on his return to his native kingdom, showed that there was then abundance of learning in Scotland ... He added, we could not now entertain a sovereign so; that Buchanan had spread the spirit of learning amongst us, but we had lost it during the civil wars. He did not allow the Latin poetry of Pitcairne so much merit as has been usually attributed to it, though he owned that one of his pieces ... was 'very well'. It is not improbable that it was the poem which Prior has so elegantly translated.[94]

This was no simple siding with the ancients over the moderns, for Johnson's sympathies were in many practical ways with the latter. When Lord Monboddo argued that 'our ancestors ... were better men than we are', Johnson contradicted him: '"We are as strong as they, and a great deal wiser." This was an assault upon one of Lord Monboddo's capital dogmas, and I was afraid there would have been a violent altercation', which Monboddo only avoided by his 'ancient *politesse*'. On one thing they did agree: 'We talked of the decrease of learning in Scotland, and of the *Muses' Welcome*. JOHNSON. "Learning is much decreased in England in my remembrance." MONBODDO. "You, sir, have lived to see its decrease in England, I its extinction in Scotland."' In England, according to Johnson, this went with the Whig stranglehold on the Church after 1714: 'Learning has decreased in England, because learning will not do so much for a man as formerly. There are other ways of getting preferment. Few bishops are now

Constitution of the Crown and Kingdom of Scotland, and the hereditary Succession of its Monarchs are asserted and vindicated (Edinburgh: W. and T. Ruddiman, 1747), 402 pp.; idem, *A Dissertation concerning The Competition for the Crown of Scotland, betwixt Lord Robert Bruce and Lord John Baliol, in the Year 1291. Wherein is proved, That ... the Right of Robert Bruce was preferable to that of John Baliol* ... (Edinburgh: W. and T. Ruddiman, 1748), 123 pp. For the controversy, see Chalmers, *Ruddiman*, pp. 190–224.

92 Boswell, *Journal*, p. 52 (21 August 1773).

93 Boswell, *Journal*, p. 210 (23 September 1773).

94 Boswell, *Journal*, pp. 37–8 (18 August 1773). On 21 August Johnson 'examined young Arthur, Lord Monboddo's son, in Latin. He answered very well, upon which he said with complacency, "Get you gone! When King James comes back, you shall be in the *Muses' Welcome*!"' (ibid., p. 56). It is not clear whether Johnson spoke figuratively of King James I (d. 1625) or King James III (d. 1766).

made for their learning.'[95] This was not an inflexible party point: English Whigs might be excepted, if good Latinists. Johnson 'thought very highly of Bentley; that no man now went so far in the kinds of learning that he cultivated'.[96]

In Scotland, similarly, Johnson like Ruddiman believed that the decline of learning went together with the advance of Presbyterianism. Johnson challenged one Scots audience:

> 'The clergy of England have produced the most valuable books in support of religion, both in theory and practice. What have your clergy done since you sunk into Presbyterianism? Can you name one book of any value in religion written by them?' We could not. Said he, 'I'll help you. Forbes wrote very well, but I believe he wrote before Episcopacy was quite extinguished'; and then pausing a little, he said, 'Yes, you have Wishart AGAINST repentance.'[97]

Johnson posed the same awkward question to Boswell's father Lord Auchinleck, who only escaped by boldly citing *Durham on the Galatians*, a title which he had, in fact, only 'read in catalogues': Johnson did not know it, and Auchinleck 'kept him at bay'.[98]

The attitude to the condition of their countries of such humanists, scholars and men of letters as the Scots Archibald Pitcairne and Thomas Ruddiman or the Englishmen William King and Samuel Johnson is well summed up by Douglas Duncan in the phrase 'patriotic despair'. In Pitcairne's poetry this took the form especially of a lament of 'the rise of Presbytery as an onslaught on the aristocratic culture of post-Restoration Scotland'. In Ruddiman's editing of historical texts it may have been, in addition, 'a face-saving consolation for loss of real political identity' following the Revolution of 1688 and the Union of 1707. Given these beliefs, by 1756 he naturally demonstrated a 'strange despair over the future of Scottish culture'.[99] Ruddiman's biographer has argued that he 'grew up to accept without question the assumption of the Scottish humanists that Latin should be the basis of the national culture and that Scotland's

95 Boswell, *Journal*, pp. 53, 55–6 (21 August 1773).

96 Boswell, *Journal*, p. 140 (10 September 1773).

97 Boswell, *Journal*, pp. 215–6 (23 September 1773), referring to Professor John Forbes (1593–1648), who was forced into exile for refusing to subscribe the Covenant, and to Dr William Wishart (d. 1753), author of a sermon against relying on a death-bed repentance: *An Essay on the Indispensible Necessity of a Holy and Good Life* (London: sold by A. Millar, 1753). Johnson was probably a customer of Andrew Millar.

98 It was not surprising that Johnson did not know it, for Auchinleck had made a mistake, probably thinking of James Durham (1622–58), *A Commentarie upon the Book of the Revelation* (1660): Boswell, *Journal*, p. 376 (6 November 1773).

99 Duncan, *Thomas Ruddiman*, pp. 18, 70–1, 145–55. Duncan terms this cultural pessimism 'an astonishing disregard of contemporary realities' (p. 152); relocated in its political setting on both sides of the border, it becomes explicable as the experience of many of Ruddiman's contemporaries.

achievements in that tongue entitled her to a proud place in the literary world'.[100] As Douglas Duncan has shown, Latinity, episcopalianism and dynastic legitimacy were united in the minds of such men as a necessary unity, and it was this vision with which Johnson sided when he deplored the ruin of Scottish religion, despoiled by 'presbyterian bigotry' and 'barbarian wantonness'.[101]

This was, in its essence, the idiom of William King. King's satire *Miltonis Epistola ad Pollionem* was published in London in 1738 with a dedication to Alexander Pope, and an English verse translation followed in 1740. Its first edition purported to be a Latin poem by John Milton, edited and annotated by 'F.S. Cantabrigiensis', addressed to Sir Patrick Hume, Baron Polwarth and first Earl of Marchmont (1641–1724), father of King's friend Alexander the second Earl (1675–1740), also styled Lord Polwarth and a prominent member of the opposition in the 1730s. King shielded himself behind the persona of a republican poet writing to a Presbyterian Whig in order to encourage the second Earl of Marchmont in his support for the Tory-inspired opposition to Sir Robert Walpole.

King's poem has been described as 'essentially a collection of escharotic laments on the corruption of the Whig government, and the venality of the times in general', showing a 'bitter disapproval of everything in the contemporary political scene which did not harmonize with his idealistic Tory and Jacobite principles'. In Latin of great technical sophistication and 'impeccable classical diction and vocabulary', King 'amply demonstrated that the contemporary policies of the high Tories and the nobility of the classical hexameter were capable of a very fine degree of synthesis'.[102] Making an inevitable use of coded language, King introduced the figure of a lion as a symbol of James III and of liberty itself. In the name of libertarian ideals, King exhorted Marchmont:

> Oh! were our Nations Rights as sacred held,
> As dear esteem'd by all our Popular Tribunes,
> And Princes of the Senate, as by thee!

If so, then

> A[NN]A's Golden Age should be restor'd:
> B[RITAI]N no more from her fond Mother torn,
> Should mourn th' unnat'ral Stepdame's rigid Yoke,
> Nor her Son's Sons th' insulting Tyrant dread.

100 Duncan, *Thomas Ruddiman*, pp. 12–13.
101 Johnson to Hester Thrale, 23 October 1773: Johnson, *Letters*, vol. 2, p. 105.
102 Greenwood, *William King*, pp. 89–96, at 92, 94–5.

Without that unspecified event (by implication, a restoration), virtue in public life was to no purpose:

> What can the steady Virtues now avail
> Of *CATO* or of *BRUTUS*? tho' the Voice
> And Energy of *CICERO* be thine,
> What Profit can thy dearest Country hope
> From thy Divine *PHILIPPICK*?[103]

The second Earl had previously resisted recruitment. 'I am persuaded my readiness and zeal will never be doubted of', he protested to his son, 'tho some are pleased to call me a Jacobite.'[104] How far King's verse now swayed him is not clear; but the literary idiom of King's politics was a powerful one.

It was the same set of preoccupations which informed his noble Latin oration at the opening of the Radcliffe Camera in 1749. William King praised the patrons of learning as 'the Ornament of Mankind' above 'those Heroes, foreign ones, I mean (for our own, as is becoming, I always except) who delight in the Slaughter of Men and Destruction of Cities, and cruelly contrive the Ruin of those they govern, as well as of others . . .' Such men (by implication, Hanoverians among them) were the enemies of everything for which Oxford stood:

> Shall these pretend to be adored by the People? These expect us, *Oxonians*, to adore them? Who are inveterate Enemies to this celebrated University, whose Glory they envy, and to Letters themselves, which they do not understand; who could wish to plunder the antientest Monuments of this Place, to rush into our Possessions, and to convert these beautiful Edifices into Stables for Horses.[105]

It was a clear echo of the fate of the university in the 1640s and 1650s. Oxford's enemies would naturally win favour among the ministers:

> it must always happen, that those, who from their Hearts detest both liberal Learning and Virtue itself, will avowedly detest these Seats of the Muses flourishing with all Learning and Virtue. It must happen, that those, who have determined to stigmatize the Nation with the Enormities of their Actions, will first of all Attempt to calumniate this illustrious University, the Ornament and Glory of the Nation.[106]

103 [William King], *Milton's Epistle to Pollio* (London, 1740), pp. 4–5. It is not known whether the translation was by King.

104 Alexander, Earl of Marchmont, to Lord Polwarth, 8 January 1736/7: HMC *Polwarth* vol. 5, p. 129.

105 *A Translation of a late Celebrated Oration. Occasioned by a Lible, entitled, Remarks on Doctor K—G's Speech* (London, 1750), pp. 35–6.

106 *A Translation*, p. 43.

King lamented the devastation caused by the European war just ended, deplored its instigators, and praised by implication the Tories who had ended another such war with the treaty of Utrecht in 1713.

But now how are all Things changed! The People grown utterly corrupt shew no Tokens of Shame or Remorse; no Sense of their original Majesty or Welfare! who set up their Votes to Sale, and often their Oaths in as public and open a Manner as they who sell Meat or Fish in a Market. If you enquire, what is the Cause, that has so entirely altered and inverted our whole People, 'til they have quite degenerated from the Behaviour and Glory of our Ancestors, I shall answer you in one Word, *Luxury*.[107]

Whatever had 'inverted all Things', argued King, 'God only can rescue us from so many Evils'. He therefore invoked the Deity in behalf of a cause which, as he proceeded, clearly united moral renovation with dynastic restoration:

RESTORE . . . to us our *Astrea*, or Justice herself . . .

RESTORE, at the same time, him the great Genius of *Britain*, (whether he is the Messenger or the very Spirit of God) the firmest Guard of Liberty and Religion; and let him banish into Exile, (into perpetual Exile) from among our Countrymen all barbarous Wars, Slaughters, Rapines, Years of Pestilence, haughty Usurpations, infamous Informers,[108] and every Evil.

RESTORE and prosper him, that the Common-wealth may revive, Faith be recall'd, Peace established, Laws ordained, just, honest, salutary, useful Laws, to deter the Abandoned, restrain Armies, favour the Learned, spare the Imprudent, relieve the Poor, delight all . . .

RESTORE and prosper him, that, while nothing can appear more illustrious than this Meeting, our other Countrymen, those especially who frequent the Court or the Senate, may resemble these glorious Patriots, may resemble you, Gentlemen of the University, though not in Brightness of Genius and Learning, yet in Probity and Diligence, yet in Magnanimity and Love of Liberty! . . .

RESTORE and prosper him, that this genial University may flourish through every Age . . . That whenever our noble and excellent Chancellor[109] shall depart (long hence, I hope) we may not see in his Place a Master, haughty, unmerciful, avaricious, illiterate, impious; but an easy and benign Ruler, devoted to Letters from his Childhood . . . surpassing the Glories of his Race in Virtue and Morals![110]

It was a high-water mark of Latin rhetoric and a central affirmation of the values of a whole culture; but the political cause it expressed was already lost.

King had forbidden the translation of his text, and the English prose

[107] *A Translation*, pp. 37–40. [108] For the significance of 'informers', see below, pp. 182–3.
[109] The Earl of Arran; for whom, see below, p. 102. [110] *A Translation*, pp. 47–54.

version was prepared by a zealous but anonymous supporter who wished to underline the political moral of King's work.[111] King himself had sheltered behind the grammatical ambiguity of Latin at the critical point: 'REDEAT simul magnus ille Genius Britanniae' and subsequent uses of 'REDEAT' could all refer back either to a person, 'magnus ille Genius Britanniae', or to an abstract 'Astrea nostra, aut quocunque nomine malit vocari ipsa Justitia'.[112] His audience would have been in no doubt. Nor were the Whigs. A witty parody in undistinguished English verse took every opportunity to ridicule the Latinist and trivialise his political ideals:

In me, ah! pity to behold!
A Wretch quite wither'd, weak and old;
Who now has pass'd, by heaven's decree,
The dangerous year of *Sixty-three*;
On asses milk, and caudle fed,
I doddle on my cane to bed,
Of every step I take, afraid;
My coat unbutton'd by my maid.
My memory oft mistaking names,
For G—RGE, I often think of J—MES;
Am grown so feeble frail a Thing,
I scarce remember *who is King!*
Th' imperial purple which does wear,
A lawful or a lawless Heir![113]

Unconsciously, it provided perfect evidence for King's thesis of the political significance of the degradation of culture and the decline of letters. But King's imagery was best appreciated in the circles to which it was most directly addressed. The medal struck to commemorate Charles Edward Stuart's second clandestine visit to London in 1752 carried a legend which quoted directly from King's Radclivian oration of 1749: REDEAT MAGNUS ILLE GENIUS BRITANNIAE.[114]

In Richard Savage's poem *Britannia's Miseries*, probably written in late 1716, the same dynastic cultural link had been made:

O Muse Britannia's Miseries rehearse,
Whilst inmost Sorrow flows in every Verse;
Mourn her Misfortunes in your pompous Lays

111 See the translator's footnote, *A Translation*, p. 54.
112 [William King], *Oratio in Theatro Sheldoniano Habita Idibus Aprilibus, MDCCXLIX. Die Dedicationis Bibliothecae Radclivianae* (London and Oxford, [1749]), pp. 29–30.
113 *A Satire upon Physicians, or an English Paraphrase, With Notes and References, of Dr King's most memorable Oration* ... (London, 1755), p. 2.
114 Edward Hawkins, *Medallic Illustrations of the History of Great Britain and Ireland to the Death of George II* (2 vols., London, 1885), vol. 2, p. 670; Noel Woolf, *The Medallic Record of the Jacobite Movement* (London, 1988), p. 121.

Correct her Foes, and give her Lovers Praise.
First grieve her King's a Royal Exile made,
Proscrib'd her Patriots and her Church betray'd,
Her laws corrupted, and her Land become
As sway'd by Tyrants was unhappy Rome![115]

Savage's idiom was the idiom also of Johnson's early poetry. Lord Orrery, an active Jacobite in the 1730s and '40s, deplored the times in which he lived in the same mode of 'patriotic despair':

can we wonder at the Errors of Youth when we see much greater Errors in the Age of Maturity? a Friend discarded, a Country betrayed, a Wife sold, Religion changed, Principles forsaken, these are Things we see every day; they are not the effect of youth, they flow from thought, design and experience, and these villainies are most elegantly encouraged and supported by the polite, the lively and the Great.[116]

Newly succeeded to his peerage, he added: 'as I am now become a Senator of Great Britain, it is time to enter into a more serious Train of Thinking, and to exert all the force and abilities of an individual towards the support and welfare of my Country, which seems, unhappy Island! to require the assistance of every Honest Heart to defend Her'.[117] Johnson and Orrery were appropriately drawn together by their common interest in the classics, and it seems that from 1751 Johnson joined with Orrery in an amicable scholarly controversy over the interpretation of Virgil.[118] Joseph Warton (1722–1800), whose edition of that author was published in 1753, was another close friend, and it was in his capacity as 'the Commentator on Virgil' that Johnson invited Warton to contribute essays to *The Adventurer*, Johnson's bi-weekly which ran from 7 November 1752 to 9 March 1754.[119]

Johnson's first two great poems addressed this classical tradition and derived much of their force from it: *London* (1738) was an imitation of Juvenal's third satire, *The Vanity of Human Wishes* (1749) an imitation of Juvenal's tenth.[120] In this, Johnson consciously associated himself with a poet writing under the early Roman emperors to deplore the loss of virtue and lament, by implication, the passing of a former regime. Decimus Iunius Iuvenalis, anglicized as Juvenal, born about AD 60, died after AD

115 Clarence Tracy (ed.), *The Poetical Works of Richard Savage* (Cambridge, 1962), p. 19.
116 Orrery to Major Cleeland, 2 November 1731: *Orrery Papers*, vol. 1, p. 100.
117 Orrery to Major Cleeland, 30 December 1731: ibid., p. 105.
118 Johnson to Orrery, [? late November 1751]: Johnson, *Letters*, vol. 1, p. 51; Paul J. Korshin, 'Johnson and the Earl of Orrery', in W. H. Bond (ed.), *Eighteenth-Century Studies in Honor of Donald F. Hyde* (New York, 1970), pp. 29–43.
119 Johnson to Joseph Warton, 8 March 1753: Johnson, *Letters*, vol. 1, p. 67.
120 See especially Niall Rudd, *Johnson's Juvenal* (Bristol, 1981, 1988). Rudd (p. ix) relies on Greene, *Politics* for his suggestion: 'We do not know exactly why Johnson was so hostile to Walpole.'

130, published a series of satires, beginning about 110 in the reign of Trajan and ending about 125 in that of Hadrian. The Stuart loyalist and Catholic John Dryden had begun the task of giving Juvenal a modern significance with his translation of five of Juvenal's satires, published in 1693 in the wake of the Revolution. Johnson owned Dryden's translation of Juvenal and took it with him to Oxford in 1728;[121] his knowledge of the social significance of this literary tradition dated from the 1720s, and did not wait for *The Lives of the Poets*.

London displays an intellectual engagement with this tradition, not an unthinking repetition of Country rhetoric or a naively rustic disapproval of the city.[122] Johnson was keenly aware of the drawbacks of life in the country and profoundly attached to the sort of sociability which he found, above all, in the metropolis;[123] in his poem *London* he made use of a hypothetically idyllic pastoral existence as an antithesis of urban corruption. It seems probable that *London* exploited classical allusion in this respect too, looking beyond Juvenal to Horace and the Arcadian vision that captivated authors from Milton to Tobias Smollett in his novel *The Expedition of Humphry Clinker* (1771). Another, and greater, poet than Johnson was about to make a similar point without reference to Arcadian visions.

Alexander Pope's poem *One Thousand Seven Hundred and Thirty Eight* was published three days after *London*; it too alluded to Horace, Pope inventing a Whig critic who compared him unfavourably to that poet:

> His sly, polite, insinuating stile
> Could please at Court, and made AUGUSTUS smile:
> An artful Manager, that crept between
> His Friends and Shame, and was a kind of *Screen*.

While Pope invoked the ancients to revive his flagging powers:

> O come, that easy *Ciceronian* stile,
> So *Latin*, yet so *English* all the while ...
> Then might I sing without the least Offence,
> And all I sung should be the *Nation's Sense*.

121 Reade, *Johnsonian Gleanings*, vol. 5, p. 225.

122 For the scholarly sophistication of Johnson's engagement with Juvenal, see Edward A. Bloom and Lillian D. Bloom, 'Johnson's *London* and its Juvenalian Texts' and 'Johnson's *London* and the Tools of Scholarship', *Huntington Library Quarterly* 34 (1970–1), 1–23, 115–39; idem, 'Johnson's "Mournful Narrative": The Rhetoric of "London"', in W. H. Bond (ed.), *Eighteenth-Century Studies in Honor of Donald F. Hyde* (New York, 1970), pp. 107–44; for a literary appraisal, Mary Lascelles, 'Johnson and Juvenal', in Frederick W. Hilles (ed.), *New Light on Dr Johnson* (New Haven, 1959), pp. 35–55.

123 For his candid expressions of these views at the time of his Scottish tour in 1773, see below, pp. 219–20.

– and recovered his voice sufficiently to lament how

All, all look up, with reverential Awe,
On Crimes that scape, or triumph o'er the Law:
While Truth, Worth, Wisdom, daily we decry -
'Nothing is Sacred now but Villany.'
Yet may this Verse (if such a Verse remain)
Show there was one who held it in disdain.[124]

In its sequel, Pope openly linked the classical idiom with politics:

How pleasing ATTERBURY's softer hour!
How shin'd the Soul, unconquer'd in the Tow'r!
How can I PULT'NEY, CHESTERFIELD forget,
While *Roman* Spirit charms, and *Attic* Wit . . .[125]

Johnson had a particular interest in Pope's 'two satires of *Thirty-eight*'. He recorded discussing them with their printer, Dodsley, and also with Savage, who showed that he had studied them with critical attention:

Of the two poems which derived their names from the year, and which are called the Epilogue to the Satires, it was very justly remarked by Savage, that the second was more strongly conceived, and more equally supported, but that it had no single passages equal to the contention in the first for the dignity of Vice, and the celebration of the triumph of Corruption.[126]

But Pope and Johnson were not alone: a group of men worked in the same idiom.

IV. THE JACOBITE CAUSE AS IDEOLOGY, SATIRE AND TRAGEDY

The social constituency of English Jacobitism was diverse: it embraced groups as far removed as Kingswood colliers and London aldermen, heirs to ancient titles and Newcastle keelmen. The reasons for which men subscribed to that cause were, similarly, not uniform. It possessed a high doctrine of divine, indefeasible, hereditary right to which only a few might adhere in its pure form; but this doctrine was not always on public display, and was not necessarily inconsistent with other critiques of the Hanoverian regime. Some, like Philip, first Duke of Wharton, could argue that they

124 Alexander Pope, *One Thousand Seven Hundred and Thirty Eight. A Dialogue Something like Horace* (London, 1738), pp. 2, 5–6, 10.
125 Alexander Pope, *One Thousand Seven Hundred and Thirty Eight. Dialogue II* (London, 1738), p. 7.
126 Johnson, *Lives of the Poets*, vol. 4, pp. 170, 205.

transferred their allegiance to James III on Whig principles.[127] Wharton announced his reverence for his father's memory:

He taught me those Notions of Government, that tend to the preserving of Liberty in its greatest Purity, when he extoll'd the Blessings of the unfortunate Revolution of 1688. He represented Triennial Parliaments as the greatest Bulwark against Tyranny and Arbitrary Power. The being freed from the Danger of a Standing Army in the Times of Peace, was by him esteem'd as a Blessing the Prince of *Orange* had introduced among us. The Security of the Church of *England*, the Liberty of the Press, and the Condemning the Right of the Dispensing Power in the Crown, were other Arguments that he us'd to employ, in order to justify the Dethroning his late Majesty.

With these Principles I entered upon the Stage of Life, when I soon beheld the Triennial Act repeal'd, standing Armies and Martial Law establish'd by Authority of Parliament; the Convocation of the Clergy prevented from meeting; the Orthodox Members of the Church discouraged, Schism, Ignorance and Atheism become the only Recommendation to Ecclesiastical Benefices; both Houses fill'd with the corrupt Tools of the Court; the Nation overwhelm'd with exorbitant Taxes; the Honour and Treasure of *England* sacrific'd to enlarge the Dominions of *Hanover*; *German* beggarly Favourites trampling on the ancient Nobility; the Act of Limitations disregarded; the Liberty of the Press abolish'd; and the Constitution of *England* thrown into the Mould of Corruption, to be modell'd according to the arbitrary Pleasure of Usurpation.

It was, on the surface, a purely Whig argument: 'those who follow the Maxims of the old *Whiggs* are obliged to resist such destructive Tyranny'.[128] But it combined easily with Wharton's account of meeting James III at Avignon after the Fifteen: 'I was struck with a becoming Awe, when I beheld Hereditary Right shining in every Feature of his Countenance, and the Politeness of Education illustrating the Majesty of his Person.' His was therefore a common cause: 'The *Tories*, according to their ancient Principles, are obliged to maintain and support Hereditary Right; and the *Whiggs*, unless they depart scandalously from the Maxims of their Predecessors, are bound by their Consciences to resist Arbitrary Power, in whatsoever Shape it appears, tho' colour'd with the specious Gloss of Parliamentary Authority.'[129]

Pragmatic motives also led men, whether or not paying respect to the full doctrine, to contemplate a Stuart restoration as a possible tactical option.

127 Philip, Duke of Wharton, *His Grace the Duke of Wharton's Reasons for Leaving his Native Country, and Espousing the Cause of his Royal Master King James III. In a Letter to His Friends in Great-Britain and Ireland* (1727), reprinted in *Select and Authentick Pieces Written by the Late Duke of Wharton* (Boulogne [i.e. London], 1731), pp. 86–97.

128 Wharton, *Reasons*, pp. 87–8.

129 Ibid., pp. 89–90, 96. The same claim that Whigs too must join the Jacobite cause on Whig principles was made in the pamphlet *Ex Ore Tuo Te Judico. Vox Populi, Vox Dei* ([London, 1719]), for which its printer, John Matthews, was hanged.

Dr William King, a man most likely to be fully acquainted with the movement's ideology, described (evidently in 1761) the motives of Charles Edward's supporters in the 1750s:

These were all men of fortune and distinction, and many of them persons of the first quality, who attached themselves to — as to a person who, they imagined, might be made the instrument of saving their country. They were sensible, that by WALPOLE's administration the English government was become a system of corruption, and that WALPOLE's successors, who pursued his plan without any of his abilities, had reduced us to such a deplorable situation, that our commercial interest was sinking, our colonies in danger of being lost, and Great Britain, which, if her powers were properly [footnote: 'As they were afterwards in Mr. PITT's administration'] exerted, was able to give laws to other nations, was become the contempt of all *Europe.*[130]

In Scotland the alignments were more simple, and more clearly along denominational lines. One pamphleteer defended the loyalty of his own sect:

do but inform yourself who composed the army of Rebels in *Scotland* in 1715 and in 1745, and you will find that there were not six *Presbyterians* amongst the many thousands that made up these Rebel Armies; and amongst some thousands of volunteers who ventured their lives against those Rebels, you won't find I believe six Scotch *Episcopals.*[131]

In England the alignments were more subtly expressed. It seems likely that the full-dress *jure divino* doctrine of the royalists of the 1670s and 80s, and the Nonjurors of the 1690s, was seldom heard by the 1730s, although the structure of its arguments was well known; rather, the anti-Hanoverian case was built around perceptions of moral, financial or electoral corruption, and expressed in terms of legal right and ancient precedent. Among the shifting options and tactical demands of public life, few politicians could afford the luxury of consistent public identification with an ideology, let alone that of divine, indefeasible, hereditary right. The existence of such ideologies shaped the options of practical men nonetheless. For those not swayed by denominational imperatives, political ideologies did not have to be subscribed to with such solemn earnestness; nor did the most active adherents of a cause necessarily make their motives plain. In 1732 Lord Orrery recorded a bantering exchange with his newly-appointed chaplain, the witty John Sandford (d. 1739):

130 William King, *Anecdotes*, pp. 208–9.

131 [Hugh Baillie], *An Appendix to a Letter to Dr Shebbeare. To which are added, Some Observations on a Pamphlet, entitled, Taxation no Tyranny* (London, 1775), p. 16.

I am afraid this Scarf[132] will effectually turn my Curate's Brain. He affirms it necessary for a Lord's Chaplain to be versed in politicks and history, and I found him last night deeply plunged into a book entituled *Hereditary Rights.*[133] He says He is of Fridays Night Club at Hornsey, where He heard this book much commended. He tells me it was written by Dr Harbin, a non-juring Clergyman, but was owned[134] by Mr. Bedford, another Non-juror, who was pilloried for it. You may be sure *Sic vos non vobis* did not escape him, and he was going on in a wild, or, as he calls it, his easy manner, when I said to him, with a serious countenance, Mr. Scarf, I am of opinion that, strictly speaking, there cannot be an Hereditary Gouvernment. You know, I dare say, that Mr. Lock, Mr. Sidney, and several other Authors have shewn all Government to be originally founded upon the Consent of the People, and therefore in Kingdoms called hereditary, when the son succeeds to the Father, it is by the tacit permission of the People, not by any natural Right or Interest that he possesses as Son to the preceeding King: and certainly the People have a just right to dethrone him after he is King if he violates their Laws: and likewise a right to exclude him before he comes to the Throne if they discover in him an incapacity to perform the duty of a good King.

Your Kings, I find, my Patron, (replied the Curate) are like the Deities of old; pieces of Wood either to be carved into Gods and Goddesses, or thrown into the Fire, but pray what think you of a Theocracy, such as the Jewish Institution?

When God himself, answered I, is pleased to interpose and give rules of government, there, my Curate, Man has nothing to do but obey all ordinances whatever without any reserve. I remember Josephus calls the Jewish Government a Theocracy, but where Government is left to the Wisdom of Men, as it always was since the Jewish œconomy, my doctrine, I think, must take place, or arbitrary power will get the better and overthrow all our rights and liberties.

Wherefore then, Earl Patron, has hereditary right been so constantly pursued in our Islands?

You mistake, my Curate, the lineal Succession has been so often disjointed in England that the People certainly imagine they may justly interrupt it whenever the good of the whole requires a link of the Chain to be broken. William Rufus and Henry the first were Kings while their brother Robert was alive. Stephen and John had neither of them hereditary Titles. Edward the third was crowned upon the deposition of his Father. The Henrys fourth, fifth and sixth were of the Lancastrian House, which was the youngest branch, and Henry the Seventh was of the same Family, nor could his marriage with the Heiress of the House of York mend his hereditary Title. Need I after this quote the Revolution?

Yet you see, Earl Patron, that ever since the Revolution we have followed Hereditary right as far as Religion would suffer us, for the present glorious and illustrious House are the most Protestant Relations to those whom we turned out: so that we have fished for the *jus hereditarium* even in a pool in Germany.

Away to thy Friday Nights Club, good Scarf, said I, and vent thy strange notions

132 An ecclesiastical vestment worn by a nobleman's chaplain.

133 [George Harbin], *The Hereditary Right of the Crown of England Asserted* (London, 1713).

134 I.e., the authorship was admitted to.

there. I shall be hanged because thou art my Chaplain, for heavens sake, quit politicks, and return to Love and Poetry.

A Pye for Poetry, and a Pudding for Love (replied He), I can talk out of the Pulpit, and I can talk in it; the first Sermon I preach before the Prince of Wales shall be in defence of hereditary right.

Do so, answered I, most political Curate, but trouble not his Royal Highness with any quotations out of Mr. Harbin's Book.[135]

However lighthearted Orrery could be about the political ideology of hereditary right, his cultural identity committed him wholeheartedly to the Stuart cause. Few men were more deeply implicated in active conspiracy, treasonable in Hanoverian eyes, from the late 1730s.[136] However improbable was the success of a restoration, and however loose and spasmodic was Jacobite organization, the emotional coherence of that dynasty's cause was considerable into the 1740s. One gauge of this was the bitterness and contempt which it reserved for those of its adherents who deserted it.

The chief of these was known to Johnson. Lord Gower's defection, recorded William King, was 'a great blow to the Tory party, and a singular disappointment to all his friends. For no one had entertained the least jealousy or suspicion of this part of his conduct ... The Tories considered him as their chief: they placed the greatest confidence in him, and did nothing without his advice and approbation.' Open and affable in manners, hospitable and frank, he sought to retain this image even in government, assuring his friends

that he went into employment with no other view than to serve his country, and that many articles tending to a thorough reformation were already stipulated. I had a letter from him (for I lived in some degree of intimacy with him for many years) to the purposes I have mentioned. Soon after I saw him, when he read the articles to me. If I rightly remember, they were thirteen in number: not one of which was performed, or ever intended to be performed. When this was at length discovered, he laid aside his disguise, adhering to the new system, and openly renouncing his old principles. He was then created an Earl: and this feather was the only reward of his apostacy.[137]

The culture of dynastic conflict involved many elements. Intellectually weighty controversies in political theory or ecclesiastical polity were the most durable but probably not the most widely encountered element. Far more common were its literary manifestations, and these can be assigned an identifiable trajectory. A small and distinct group of English poets, John Dryden the foremost in talent, had hailed the Restoration in 1660 with a

135 Lord Orrery to John Kempe, 18 March 1731/2: *Orrery Papers*, vol. 1, p. 107.
136 For which, see below, pp. 152, 169, 178–9.
137 William King, *Anecdotes*, pp. 46–7.

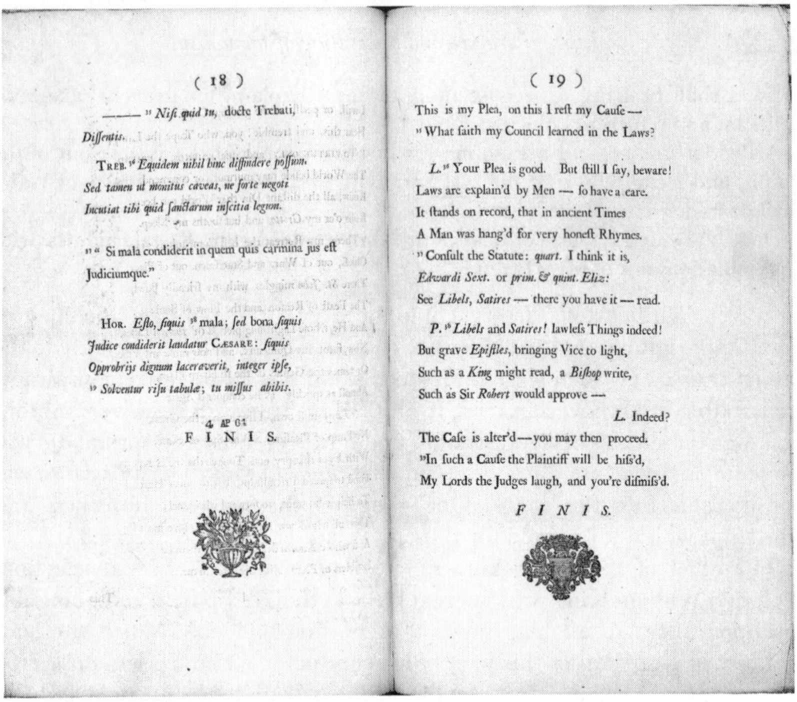

(18)

——— [37] *Nisi quid tu*, docte Trebati,
Dissentis.

TREB. [36] *Equidem nihil hinc diffindere possum.*
Sed tamen ut monitus caveas, ne forte negoti
Incutiat tibi quid sanctarum inscitia legum.

[37] " Si mala condiderit in quem quis carmina jus est
Judiciumque."

HOR. *Esto, siquis* [38] mala; *sed bona siquis*
Judice condiderit laudatur CÆSARE: *siquis*
Opprobriis dignum laceraverit, integer ipse,
[39] *Solventur risu tabulæ; tu missus abibis.*

F I N I S.

(19)

This is my Plea, on this I rest my Cause —
[37] What saith my Council learned in the Laws?

L. [36] Your Plea is good. But still I say, beware!
Laws are explain'd by Men — so have a care.
It stands on record, that in ancient Times
A Man was hang'd for very honest Rhymes.
[37] Consult the Statute: *quart.* I think it is,
Edwardi Sext. or *prim. & quint. Eliz:*
See *Libels, Satires* — there you have it — read.

P. [38] *Libels* and *Satires!* lawless Things indeed!
But grave *Epistles*, bringing Vice to light,
Such as a *King* might read, a *Bishop* write,
Such as Sir *Robert* would approve —
L. Indeed?
The Case is alter'd — you may then proceed.
[39] In such a Cause the Plaintiff will be hiss'd,
My Lords the Judges laugh, and you're dismiss'd.

F I N I S.

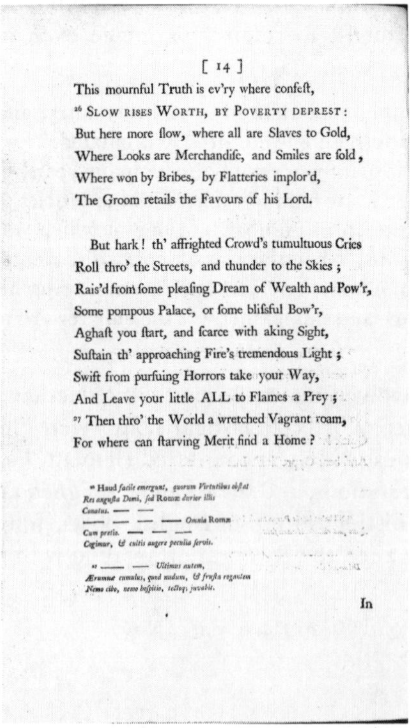

[14]

This mournful Truth is ev'ry where confest,
[26] SLOW RISES WORTH, BY POVERTY DEPREST:
But here more slow, where all are Slaves to Gold,
Where Looks are Merchandise, and Smiles are sold,
Where won by Bribes, by Flatteries implor'd,
The Groom retails the Favours of his Lord.

But hark! th' affrighted Crowd's tumultuous Cries
Roll thro' the Streets, and thunder to the Skies;
Rais'd from some pleasing Dream of Wealth and Pow'r,
Some pompous Palace, or some blissful Bow'r,
Aghast you start, and scarce with aking Sight,
Sustain th' approaching Fire's tremendous Light;
Swift from pursuing Horrors take your Way,
And Leave your little ALL to Flames a Prey;
[27] Then thro' the World a wretched Vagrant roam,
For where can starving Merit find a Home?

[26] Haud *facile emergunt, quorum Virtutibus obstat*
Res angusta Domi, sed Romæ *durior illis*
Conatus. —— ——
—— —— —— —— *Omnia* Romæ
Cum pretio. —— —— ——
Cogimur, & cultis augere peculia servis.

[27] —— —— *Ultimus autem,*
Ærumnæ cumulus, quod nudum, & frusta rogantem
Nemo cibo, nemo hospitio, tectoq; juvabit.

In

▲

(a) Alexander Pope's *The First Satire of the Second Book of Horace, Imitated* (1733) with a facing Latin text

◀

(b) Samuel Johnson's *London* (1738) with Latin footnotes

Plate 2
The classical tradition in letters. The genres of translation and imitation demonstrated modern authors' appropriation of the authority of the ancients

cultural project to trumpet the revival of arts and letters as a natural adjunct to the restoration of liberties through Charles II's triumph over his enemies.[138] Both could be, and often were, apostrophised in heavily classicised language and imagery. The monarch could, in Horatian vein, be hailed as Augustus, or, in Virgilian, as Aeneas. Those who were unhappy with the court naturally tested and challenged this myth, and after 1688 and 1714 the formal identifications with Augustus which were virtually forced on William III, George I and George II were the target for mounting satire by Dryden's heirs.[139]

Much of the Anglo-Latin poetry of the Restoration period in England, especially at Oxford, Cambridge, Eton and Westminster, was composed for official royal occasions and took the form of eulogy and panegyric; these occasional pieces were regularly issued in anthologies which, if not of a high order as Latin verse, did have the effect of associating a linguistic medium with a political message and a social constituency, the young noblemen and gentlemen generally entrusted with their recitation at Oxford's Encaenia celebrations (the verses were, in fact, often written by their tutors).[140] Thanks to the entrenchment of this genre in the English patrician (and especially Tory) elite, the linked collapse of letters, public morality and political virtue was as much a theme of the English opposition of the 1730s as it was of the Scots culture which Thomas Ruddiman laboured to preserve. Naturally, the ablest men of letters would find themselves in opposition to a court and a ministry that despised the arts, pensioned literary mediocrities and debauched the morals of the nation.

Pope's early poetry could be read as relatively unpolitical.[141] Swift congratulated him in 1723 that 'both partyes will approve your Poetry as long as you are known to be of neither', and reticence was certainly wise in the aftermath of the Atterbury Plot. In the 1730s Pope began to show his political hand more openly with his Horatian works, *The First Satire of the Second Book of Horace, Imitated* (London, 1733) and *The Second Satire of the*

[138] For the Augustan project in Restoration England, see especially Isabel Rivers, *The Poetry of Conservatism 1600–1745: A Study of Poets and Public Affairs from Jonson to Pope* (Cambridge, 1973), pp. 127–74; Howard Erskine-Hill, *The Augustan Idea in English Literature* (London, 1983), pp. 213–27. For the earlier origins of the motif, and its persistence since the late sixteenth century, ibid., pp. 134–212.

[139] James D. Garrison, *Dryden and the Tradition of Panegyric* (Berkeley, 1975); Howard D. Weinbrot, *Augustus Caesar in 'Augustan' England* (Princeton, 1978); Maximilian E. Novak, 'Shaping the Augustan Myth: John Dryden and the Politics of Restoration Augustanism', in Paul J. Korshin and Robert R. Allen (eds.), *Greene Centennial Studies* (Charlottesville, 1984), pp. 1–21; Howard Erskine-Hill, 'Dryden and the Augustan Idea', in J. P. Hardy and J. C. Eade (eds.), *Studies in the Eighteenth Century* 5 (1983), 3–15.

[140] Bradner, *Musae Anglicanae*, pp. 206–15.

[141] That this would have been a misreading is shown by Howard Erskine-Hill, 'Alexander Pope: The Political Poet in His Time', *Eighteenth Century Studies* 15 (1981–2), 123–48. For Pope, see also Rivers, *The Poetry of Conservatism*, pp. 175–219.

Second Book of Horace Paraphrased (London, 1734). *The Second Epistle of the Second Book of Horace, Imitated* (London, 1737) was Pope's open declaration of independence from the Court, and in the *Epistle to Augustus* (London, 1737) he extended this to an attack on George II. The political attacks mounted from *The Sixth Epistle of the First Book of Horace, Imitated* (London, 1738), through *The First Epistle of the First Book of Horace, Imitated* (London, 1738) to a peak in the *Epilogue to the Satires* (London, 1738), an open repudiation of Horace himself, associating him with servile courtiers; 'in a final note later appended to the *Second Dialogue*, [Pope] indicates that the government was threatening his freedom. The final *Dialogue* looks forward to the terrors of the last book of the *Dunciad* where, Pope makes clear, Walpole-Palinurus at the helm of the ship of state continues to lead the nation into dullness and spiritual death.'[142]

On the Stuart side the culture of dynastic legitimacy displayed a marked ability to reach out to include both the patrician and the plebeian. The intersection of the classical tradition and more earthy satire even produced a popular ballad entitled *The Turnip Song: A Georgick.*[143] One anthology of poems and songs, privately printed in 1750 and according to a manuscript note in the British Library's copy 'privately printed at Ragland Castle & a few Copies distributed as presents',[144] spanned just such a cultural range. It opened with 'An Ode, compos'd in the Year 1720, on the Birth of a great Prince', which proceeded from a Latin quotation from Virgil's fourth Eclogue. The author of another piece celebrating Cope's defeat at Preston Pans in 1745 closed his poem:

> But stop, my Muse; be conscious of thy Flight,
> Nor dare attempt beyond a mortal Height.
> Retire with Wonder and submissive Awe,
> A *Virgil* only can a *Caesar* draw.

But the collection extended easily to rousing vernacular drinking songs like *True Blue* and *The King Shall Enjoy His Own Again.*[145]

The genre of classical imitation could descend to doggerel satire, like the

142 Weinbrot, 'Augustan Imitation: the Role of the Original', pp. 65–6, quoting Swift to Pope, 20 September 1723.

143 Bodleian Douce Ballads 4, 246 (n.d.). The Elector of Hanover was popularly supposed to have been hoeing turnips when news arrived of his accession to the throne of England.

144 Raglan Castle was one of the seats of the Dukes of Beaufort.

145 *A Collection of Loyal Songs, Poems, &c. Printed in the Year 1750* (n.p.), pp. 3, 15, 36, 59. Another concluded: 'But stop, my Muse, be conscious of thy Flight,/ Nor dare attempt beyond a mortal Height;/ A HOMER only can a CHARLES draw,/ Retire with Wonder and submissive Awe': *To His Royal Highness Charles, Prince of Wales, &c. Regent of the Kingdoms of Scotland, England, France and Ireland* (n.p., 1745), p. 16.

verses of 1719 satirising George I in a drinking bout.[146] In general, however, it was used to make more elevated points. A Stuart supporter, evidently before the Fifteen, called on Horace to support his invocations to James:

> Return, be Guardian of a falling State,
> Dissolve the Senate, close their long Debate.

With that happy restoration,

> Fresh Grass shall on our Mountains Grow,
> Fat Oxen on our Meadows low,
> *Ceres* shall bless our Harvest with Increase,
> When *Albion* is possess'd of *J—s* and Peace.

It would bring moral transformation in its wake:

> Triumphant *Caesar* by divine Command,
> Shall purge the Errors of a guilty Land.[147]

The classical repertoire could furnish deliberately transparent disguises as well as generalised patrician allusions. Jacobite publicists seeking to place a favourable interpretation on the character of James III discussed him under the name of Aeneas; his sons figured as Ascanius (Charles Edward) and Benedictus (Henry Benedict),[148] the second son being an addition to the cast of Virgil's *Aeneid* dictated by the composition of the Stuart royal family.

Whigs too arranged, however implausibly, to be hailed in the same idiom: they were almost inevitably drawn to fight in the terms that Charles II's panegyric poets had dictated.[149]

> Vain are th'Attacks of Force or Art,
> Where *Caesar's* Arm defends a *Cato's* Heart

actually referred to James Stanhope.[150] Thomas Tickell called on Virgil to defend the accession of the House of Hanover and the defeat of the Fifteen.[151] The Whig opposition played on exactly these aspirations:

146 *The Ninth Ode of the Third Book of Horace, Imitated. Ben[so]n and G[eor]ge* (n.p., n.d. [?1719]).
147 *In Imitation of the 5th Ode of Horace. Lib. 4* (n.p., n.d.).
148 *Aeneas and His Two Sons. A True Portrait* (London, [1747]).
149 The Whig aesthetic seldom rose to the heights of their opponents, and has attracted less adequate literary criticism, e.g. Cecil A. Moore, 'Whig Panegyric Verse: A Phase of Sentimentalism', in idem, *Backgrounds of English Literature 1700–1760* (Minneapolis, 1953), pp. 104–44.
150 *An Imitation of the Ninth Ode of the Fourth Book of Horace. Inscribed to the Right Honourable James Stanhope, Esq.; One of His Majesty's Principal Secretaries of State* (London, 1715), p. 8.
151 [Thomas Tickell], *An Imitation of the Prophecy of Nereus. From Horace Book I. Ode XV.* (London, 1715).

> *Pultney* the coldest Breast with zeal can fire,
> And *Roman Thoughts* by *Attick Stile* inspire.[152]

None of it had the conviction carried by the Stuart apologists, but this concurrence on the opposition side contributed to the emergence of a distinct genre. Patriot poetry had its stock themes, as a ministerial writer was aware: until the favoured patriot replaced a courtier in office,

> Till that bless'd Time arrives, all Things go wrong;
> Our Counsels, *weak*, our Enemies are *strong*;
> The Publick's *pillag'd*, Liberty's *oppress'd*,
> And the whole Government, – a standing *Jest*.

Patriots were a 'motley Groupe'

> Where *Opposites*, unite their bickering Bands,
> And *Contradictions* join their jarring Hands;
> Where, Champions for *Hereditary Right*,
> Their Votes, with staunch *Republicans*, unite.[153]

Yet the very widespread currency of these themes in the classical heritage meant that opposition poets could develop a massive case for the profound corruption of English society, and, especially, of Whig society:

> Such are the evils, *Arcas*, such the crimes,
> Will make our age the scorn of future times.
> In letter'd story, shall this Aera stand
> The darkest, sure, that ever stain'd our land:
> No Glory now to awe, no wealth to aid,
> Abroad insulted, and at home betray'd:
> While Liberty hangs low her sickning head,
> And Honour, Virtue, Public Worth, are fled.
> Weep, Oh! my Friend, our Country sunk to shame,
> Whose glory long had rival'd *Roman* Fame.[154]

The most scholarly imitations of the ancients printed the Latin and English versions on facing pages. Some of these were restricted to moral reproof of the vices of London high society.[155] Another exhorted a young man to renounce domestic retreat –

[152] [James Bramston], *The Art of Politicks, In Imitation of Horace's Art of Poetry* (London, 1731), p. 13; the Latin text appears as footnotes to the imitation.
[153] *Modern Patriotism. A Poem* (London, n.d. [?1734]), pp. 23, 38–9.
[154] *One Thousand, Seven Hundred, and Forty-Five. A Satiric-Epistle; After the Manner of Mr Pope* (London: Printed for A. Dodd, opposite St *Clement's* Church in the *Strand*. 1746), pp. 11–12.
[155] E.g. *The Satirist: In Imitation of The Fourth Satire of the First Book of Horace* (London, 1733).

A good Estate, a Town-house, and a Seat,
The Grounds, the Garden, and the Park compleat,
With each domestic Blessing in a Wife,
These are the Joys! the Blandishments of Life!

– in favour of a life of public action.[156] Not every imitation was overtly seditious: Orrery, in 1741, drew from Horace a moral of rural retreat and literary endeavour.[157] Yet the majority made a political point, and often a dynastic point. In 1739 Walpole's corrupt administration, and his failure to declare war on Spain, came under Horace's adapted censure.[158] One author used facing Latin original and English imitation to satirise the greed of Sir Robert Walpole's brother;[159] one employed Horace in footnotes in an attempt to induce George II to return from his favourite Hanover.[160]

As the 1730s progressed, opposition writers made an increasingly ironical and critical use of Horace as a vehicle for satire, and turned more often to Juvenal[161] and Persius.[162] Persius was, even more than Juvenal, obliged to shelter behind obscurity and allusion to escape the vengeance of Nero: this was repeatedly pointed out by early-eighteenth-century commentators, as were the author's patrician status and personal virtue; of the Roman satirists his was the highest birth and fiercest indignation. Juvenal's satires too struck a particular echo: published in the reign of Hadrian, they reflect the bitterness the poet felt as an exile in the reign of his tyrannical predecessor, Domitian. Exile, usurpation, disinheritance and the corruption of public life were themes that could be made to seem strangely appropriate to England after 1688. English translations of Persius were also concentrated in this period: John Dryden (1693), Henry Eelbeck (1719), Thomas Sheridan (1728), John Senhouse (1730), John Stirling (1736), Thomas Brewster (collected edition, 1741–2), Edmund Burton (1752). Yet

156 *An Epistle in Verse to a Friend, in Imitation of the Second Epistle of the First Book of Horace* (London, 1739).

157 John, Earl of Orrery, *The First Ode of the First Book of Horace Imitated, And Inscribed to the Earl of Chesterfield* (London, 1741).

158 *Men and Measures characterised from Horace. Being An Imitation of the XVIth Ode of his Second Book* (London, 1739) included Horace's Latin text in footnotes.

159 *The Miser, a Poem: from the First Satire of the First Book of Horace. Inscrib'd to Horatio Walpole, Esquire* (London, 1735).

160 *An Ode to the Earl of Chesterfield, Imploring His Majesty's Return In Imitation of Horace. Ode II. Book IV* (London, 1737).

161 For Juvenal's influence on Pope's use of Horace see Howard Erskine-Hill (ed.), *Pope: Horatian Satires and Epistles* (Oxford, 1964), pp. 16–17.

162 For Persius, see William Frost, 'English Persius: The Golden Age', *Eighteenth-Century Studies* 2 (1968), 77–101; Cynthia Dessen, *Iunctura Callidus Acri: A Study of Persius' Satires* (Urbana, 1968); Howard D. Weinbrot, 'Persius, the Opposition to Walpole, and Pope', in Paul J. Korshin and Robert R. Allen (eds.), *Greene Centennial Studies* (Charlottesville, 1984), pp. 93–124, at 96–9, 104–5, 107–14. Weinbrot argues (pp. 114–24) for the earlier influence of Persius on Pope's use of Horace.

it was the imitation rather than the translation which gave him his main impact, with six different imitators in the 1730s.[163]

In 1739 Paul Whitehead's anonymous *The State of Rome, Under Nero and Domitian* linked the two tyrants who had poisoned the worlds of Persius and Juvenal for an emotional denunciation of modern vice in which 'Juvenal and Persius virtually become Pope' and echo the images of Pope's *One Thousand Seven Hundred and Thirty Eight* and *Epistle to Dr Arbuthnot* (1735). Whitehead pressed Juvenal and Persius into service together to condemn an age

> When black Corruption speads her Wings around,
> And Brib'ry, bare-fac'd, stalks the Senate Ground ...
> When was each Vice so dignify'd before?
> None, none can e'er out-do us – future Times
> Can't add one Scruple to our present Crimes.

It was an explicitly anti-Hanoverian vision:

> Here let *Arturius* live, and such as He,
> Such Manners will with such a Land agree;
> Chiefs who in Senates have the golden Knack
> Of turning Truth to Lies, and White to Black.
> Who build vast Halls to lodge their *wedded Whore*,
> And by Excise and Taxes starve the Poor.[164]

The poet applied the moral in denying it:

> Begin, *Calliope*, a Tale to sing,
> Of some past Booby, *Greek*, or *Roman* King.
> What Booby King? Why *Nero* let it be;
> Well, but his Times with ours can ne'er agree.
> Um – why that's true, – O no, not in the least,
> I only tell, and not apply the Jest.[165]

163 Weinbrot, 'Persius', pp. 94, 106–14, listing [John, Lord Hervey], *A Satire in the Manner of Persius: In a Dialogue between Atticus and Eugenio. By a Person of Quality* (London, 1730, 1739); *Advice to an Aspiring Young Gentleman of Fortune. In Imitation of the Fourth Satyr of Persius* (London, 1733); 'Griffith Morgan Danvers', *Persius Scaramouch: Or, a Critical and Moral Satire on the Orators, Scriblers and Vices of the present Times. In Imitation of the First Satire of Persius* (London, 1734); Dudley, *First Satire of Persius* (London, 1739); [? Paul Whitehead], *The State of Rome, Under Nero and Domitian: A Satire. Containing, A List of Nobles, Senators, High Priests, Great Ministers of State, &c. &c. &c.* (London, 1739); Benjamin Loveling, *The First Satire of Persius Imitated* (London, 1740).

164 *The State of Rome, under Nero and Domitian: A Satire. Containing, A List of Nobles, Senators, High Priests, Great Ministers of State, &c. &c. &c. By Messrs Juvenal and Persius* (London, 1739), pp. 4–5, 9.

165 Ibid., p. 13.

In 1740 this tide of satire produced Benjamin Loveling's *The First Satire of Persius Imitated*, printed by Samuel Johnson's publisher John Brett. It was another implicit parallel between the worlds of Nero and of George II, abandoning irony for a direct condemnation which, like Johnson's, included Walpole:

> Feign but a Senate where Corruption reigns,
> And leads her courtly Slaves in golden Chains,
> Where one directs three hundred venal Tongues,
> And owes his Grandeur to a People's Wrongs.[166]

Generally the point of these laboured, punning imitations was to reproach individuals,[167] but this critique could easily be extended in its application. One author confronted Horace's text with an open denunciation of the political corruption of St James's and Westminster.[168] Others besides Johnson enlisted Juvenal for an attack on Whig ministries. One poet echoed a theme of *London*: men of letters were undervalued and lacked patrons; they should prefer an Arcadian retreat:

> Ye Sons of Worth, whom Learning calls her own,
> Fly far from hence, and quit a senseless Town,
> To Fields, where *Thames* with smoother Current runs,
> Or where fair *Oose* delights her *Northern* Sons.

But this too was more than a pastoral lament. It had a political dimension:

> Fortune, who laughs at all we act below,
> The High depresses, and exalts the Low;
> From *Charles's* Brow the Wreath of Conquest tore,
> And made a short-liv'd King of *Theodore*;
> To *Norman* Bastards gave an *English* Crown,
> And plac'd a Rebel on a Martyr's Throne.[169]

The theme of a disillusioned poet turning his back on a corrupt metropolis and pronouncing a jeremiad on its vices was already known. Normally the setting was classical:

> O Glory! Empire! *Rome*! ye reverend Shades
> Of fam'd Antiquity! ye guardian Gods!
> What hideous Change approaches! what a Cloud

166 [Benjamin] Loveling, *The First Satire of Persius Imitated* (London: John Brett, 1740), p. 15. For this work see Cynthia Dessen, 'An Eighteenth-Century Imitation of Persius, Satire I', *Texas Studies in Literature and Language* 20 (1978), 433–56.

167 E.g. [James Miller], *Seasonable Reproof, A Satire, In the Manner of Horace* (London, 1735).

168 *The Fourth Satire of the First Book of Horace, Imitated. Address'd to Alexander Pope Esq* (London, 1733).

169 *The Seventh Satyre of Juvenal Imitated* (London, 1745), pp. 11–12, 14–15.

Of Woe broods sullen round her barb'rous Realms,
And frowns tremendous o'er degenerate *Rome*?[170]

Charles Akers dedicated this dire warning to the Duke of Argyll.

Johnson's *Marmor Norfolciense* of 1739 stood in a tradition of translation, like that published in 1737 to deride the fashionable plebeian poet Stephen Duck. Its title page adorned with Latin tags from Virgil's *Eclogues* and *Aeneid*, Duck was made to confess his ignorance of that language, and that he had 'with much Brain-labour ... *Thresh'd* into the following Poetical Form' the translation of 'an old *Popish-Priest*, and two eminent *Attorneys*'. Rehearsing a series of cryptic conjunctures, now fulfilled, the poem warned:

Then may the *White-cliff'd Isle* expect its Doom;
And dread the Projects of the Sons of Rome.[171]

The imagery of Jacobite verse had already anticipated the imagery of *Marmor Norfolciense*. One prophecy read:

When Savage Goths from Rhine return,
And Crowns aloft on Horns are worn.
When a dull Cuckold shall appear,
Usurper, Tyrant, Murderer;
With Fool, and Bastard to his Heir.[172]
A Strumpet's Breed, when Britons chuse,
And fetch their Princes from the Stews.
When a Red-Cow, of hideous Size,
The Throne with driv'ling Calves supplies;
(With monstrous Dugs that suit her Station,
As Nursing Mother to the Nation.)
When Turbants shall with Mitres vie,
And Loyal Peers on Scaffolds dye.
When Atheists shall the Church support,
And Harlots rule the State, and Court:
Then all Aegyptian Plagues succeed,
And the Sick Nation's doom'd to bleed.
Frogs, Serpents, Flies, on Thrones shall wait,
And Lice shall swarm in Beds of State.
Storms on the ripen'd Grain shall pour,
Or foreign Locusts all devour.

170 E.g. [Charles Akers], *The Loss of Liberty. A Poem* (London, 1733) [a reissue of the 1729 edition, entitled *The Loss of Liberty: or Fall of Rome*], p. 20.

171 *The Year of Wonders. Being a Literal and Poetical Translation Of an Old Latin Prophecy, found near Merlin's Cave. By S—N D—K* (London, 1737), pp. 3, 6.

172 George I was widely believed to have been cuckolded. Jacobites now replied to the implausible doubts about the birth of an heir to James II on 10 June 1688 with the devastating charge that George I was not the father of *his* heir.

When such dire Vengeance Heav'n has sent,
The guilty Land shall late repent.
An Exil'd King shall fight her Cause,
Protect the Church, restore the Laws.
The Bruns[wic]ke Stallion with disgrace,
Shall yield the British Lion place.
The Olive and the Laurel twin'd,
Plenty and Peace, with Conquest join'd.
This Isle, her ancient Glory gains,
For lo, her own AUGUSTUS Reigns.[173]

It was a captivating vision, but it was never to be realised. It was maintained even into the 1740s, and even in Latin verse: in May 1744 William King published *Antonietti Corsorum epistola ad Corsos de rege eligendo* 'attacking the politics of the Hanoverian dynasty and urging plainly, though under allegorical fiction, the return of the Stuarts'.[174] But from the failure of the rising of 1715, Tories and Jacobites could seldom escape the haunting fear that they were committed by conscience, by personal allegiance or by cultural affinity to a noble but a losing cause. These tragic themes of rejection and failure were explored, with enormous emotional force, in Johnson's biography of his Jacobite friend Richard Savage, published in 1744. Johnson's picture of Savage was of a man destroyed by self-deception, by a false sense of self-worth, and by an ambition and a view of his own abilities which made him lose touch with the realities of earning a living. Yet although Johnson condemned these faults, the clarity with which he did so disclosed his own affinity with them. Johnson, like Savage, was cheated by vain hope. Johnson's famous lines in *London*

This mournful truth is ev'ry where confess'd
SLOW RISES WORTH, BY POVERTY DEPRESS'D

are often interpreted as the protest of frustrated meritocracy. The *Life of Savage* placed them in a quite different context.[175] Johnson announced his black vision on the first page:

[173] *A Prophecy. By Merlyn, the famous British Prophet; found written upon an Old Wall in Saxon Characters; Dated the Year 482. about the Time of the Restoration of King Vortigern, to the British Throne; faithfully Transcrib'd from the Original* (n.p., n.d.). This overtly treasonable broadsheet poem naturally appeared with no indication of the name or place of publication, or the date; Queen Caroline's death on 20 November 1737 provides the latest date. *A Prophecy. By Merlyn* is not evidently recorded in the Eighteenth Century Short Title Catalogue; it is cited here from the copy in the Huntington Library, in a collected volume, shelfmark 299798.

[174] Bradner, *Musae Anglicanae*, p. 260.

[175] Johnson's footnote reference in *London* also shows that he here echoed a Juvenalian original: see plate 2.

It has been observed in all Ages, that the Advantages of Nature or of Fortune have contributed very little to the Promotion of Happiness; and that those whom the Splendor of their Rank, or the Extent of their Capacity, have placed upon the Summits of human Life, have not often given any just Occasion to Envy in those who look up to them from a lower Station. Whether it be that apparent Superiority incites great Designs, and great Designs are naturally liable to fatal Miscarriages, or that the general Lot of Mankind is Misery, and the Misfortunes of those whose Eminence drew upon them an universal Attention, have been more carefully recorded, because they were more generally observed, and have in reality been only more conspicuous than those of others, not more frequent, or more severe.[176]

Johnson's friend claimed that he was the son of Anne, Countess of Macclesfield, by an adulterous liaison with Richard Savage, 4th Earl Rivers (?1654–1712) and born in January 1697/8;[177] that his mother rejected him; that she would look

upon her Son from his Birth with a kind of Resentment and Abhorrence; and instead of supporting, assisting, and defending him, delight to see him struggling with Misery, that she would take every Opportunity of aggravating his Misfortunes, and obstructing his Resources, and with an implacable and restless Cruelty continue her Persecution from the first Hour of his Life to the last.[178]

Johnson's *Life of Savage* is a Senecan tragedy, the chronicle of a noble cause destroyed by blows of fate each more unnatural and more gross than the last. To a degree, Savage brought his ill fortune upon himself; but his failings were disproportionate to the sufferings with which fate overwhelmed him. His biography was more than the story of a noble spirit reduced to degradation. In the successive denials of his parentage, Savage's case paralleled that of James Francis Edward Stuart, whom Whigs consistently denied was the child born to James II's queen on 10 June 1688. Johnson did not write the *Life of Savage* as a deliberate piece of political propaganda, or even as a conscious allegory; but the strange emotional intensity which gives the work its peculiarly compelling quality was, it may be suggested, one consequence of the congruence of three overlapping cases. This moral drama of rejection and disinheritance was the tragedy of the House of Stuart, of Richard Savage, and ultimately of Johnson himself.

176 [Samuel Johnson], *An Account of the Life of Mr. Richard Savage, Son of the Earl Rivers* (London, 1744), pp. 1–2.

177 Earl Rivers had stood godfather to this illegitimate child, but under the assumed name of Captain John Smith; the child was therefore baptised as Richard Smith. Was this child Richard Savage, as he later claimed? Clarence Tracy, *The Artificial Bastard: A Biography of Richard Savage* (Cambridge, Mass., 1953), pp. vii–viii and 11–27, considered that 'his claim may be genuine', but the evidence is inconclusive.

178 [Johnson], *Life of Savage*, p. 5.

2

JOHNSON AND THE ANGLO-LATIN TRADITION

I. THE CULTURAL POLITICS OF REBELLION: WILLIAM LAUDER

After the Union, antiquarianism in Scotland lost little of its profoundly politicized orientation towards questions of modern Scottish national identity; it was a present-mindedness compelled by a 'post-Union national identity-crisis'.[1] That crisis was expressed in various ways in different literary genres, both classical and vernacular, and one episode in these cultural conflicts now spilled over into the English literary arena. Johnson's political and literary commitment to the humanistic Latin tradition both in its English and its Scots forms, and his charitable disposition towards other authors in that tradition, betrayed him into his most serious literary misjudgement. As Arthur Murphy explained, early in 1750 Johnson 'was induced, by the arts of a vile impostor, to lend his assistance, during a temporary illusion, to a fraud not to be paralleled in the annals of literature'.[2] The fraud was perpetrated by a Scot whom Johnson had befriended, William Lauder. A minor Latinist but ardent Jacobite, he had paid the price of a fragmented career that now went with that allegiance, but in 1742 finally obtained the humble post of Latin master at Dundee Grammar School.[3] Lauder's first cultural allegiance was precisely Johnson's, to the Anglo-Latin tradition of late humanism: Lauder's anthology *Poetarum Scotorum musae sacrae* (2 vols., Edinburgh, 1739) was 'the last serious publication of Scottish Latin poetry', prefaced by an Introduction

[1] Iain Gordon Brown, 'Modern Rome and Ancient Caledonia: the Union and the Politics of Scottish Culture', and Douglas Duncan, 'Scholarship and Politeness in the Early Eighteenth Century' in Andrew Hook (ed.), *The History of Scottish Literature Volume 2 1660–1800* (Aberdeen, 1987), pp. 33–64, at 33.

[2] Arthur Murphy, *An Essay on the Life and Genius of Samuel Johnson, LL.D.* (London, 1793), p. 59.

[3] For whom, see James L. Clifford, 'Johnson and Lauder', *Philological Quarterly* 54 (1975), 342–56, and Michael J. Marcuse, 'The Lauder Controversy and the Jacobite Cause', *Studies in Burke and His Time* 18 (1977), 27–47.

which one scholar has acknowledged to be 'full of genuine learning on the subject'.[4] His political allegiance aligned him with Johnson also. According to Andrew Henderson (fl. 1734–75), the Scots anti-Jacobite historian of the Forty-five,[5] Lauder had earlier associated with Thomas Ruddiman and a group of schoolmasters many of whom had participated in the Fifteen: under their influence Lauder became 'a most violent J-c-b-e, and zealous Admirer of Archbishop Laud'.[6]

Unknown to Johnson, Ruddiman had already come to doubt Lauder's personal qualities: 'I was so sensible of the weakness and folly of that man that I shunned his company, as far as decently I could'; Lauder's 'disappointments did not improve his temper; and his temper contributed to his disappointments'.[7] One chapter of Ruddiman's encounters with Lauder came during the period from September to November 1745 when, in the midst of the Stuart rebellion, Lauder laboured to persuade not only Ruddiman but John Murray of Broughton, Prince Charles's hard-pressed secretary, that Milton had been 'one of the most noted Plagiarists, I believe, that ever wrote'. Lauder conceded: 'I agree with you intirely in your sentiments, that a Poet is not to be thought guilty of Plagiarism who borrows thoughts, Lines, periods from others; for in that case almost everyone would be obnoxious. But that is far from being the case at present.'[8] Lauder sought the immediate publication of his 'discovery', and, presumably, the official approbation of the Prince: the denigration of Milton, republican and regicide, would presumably be a propaganda coup for the Stuart cause, and, by sinking Milton, Lauder would raise Charles I. The Jacobite enterprise did not build its ideology around a response to 1688 alone: before the Glorious Revolution came the Great Rebellion, and the issues of regicide (and restoration) had been at the centre of monarchical thinking long before the exile of James II raised issues of allegiance in the form still dominant in the 1740s.

Lauder's concern was not wholly unrealistic: the remarkable prominence of poetry as a medium of propaganda was recognised by the publication of an anthology of verse on Charles Edward Stuart in the midst of the rising.[9] Yet Ruddiman was incredulous that Lauder would trouble

4 Duncan, *Thomas Ruddiman*, p. 116; Leicester Bradner, *Musae Anglicanae: A History of Anglo-Latin Poetry 1500–1925* (New York, 1940), p. 291.
5 Arthur Henderson, *History of the Rebellion, 1745 and 1746* (Edinburgh, 1748).
6 [Arthur Henderson], *Furius; or, a Modest Attempt towards a History of the Life and Surprising Exploits of the Famous W.L., Critic and Thief-Catcher ... in a Letter from an Honest North Briton to His Friends in London* (London, [1748]), p. 19; Marcuse, 'Lauder Controversy', p. 33.
7 George Chalmers, *The Life of Thomas Ruddiman* (London, 1794), pp. 146–7, 150.
8 Lauder to Ruddiman, 4 September 1745: Duncan, *Thomas Ruddiman*, p. 159.
9 *A Full Collection of all Poems upon Charles, Prince of Wales, Regent of the Kingdoms of Scotland, England, France and Ireland, and Dominions thereunto belonging, Published since His Arrival in Edinburgh the 17th Day of September, till the 1st of November, 1745* ([Edinburgh], 1745).

John Murray with such a matter at such a moment. Whatever Murray's views about Buchanan or Milton, 'He very well knew that both of them, tho otherwise Men of singular Parts & Endowments, were arrant Villains & Traitors to their lawfull Sovereigns, & that Plagiarism, tho it could be fixt upon him, was in this last but a Peccadillo in Comparison of his other Crimes.' Nor did Lauder's evidence, which he had heaped on Ruddiman, persuade the greater scholar: 'notwithstanding the many foul Blots of his Character, there is none that will impartially read but two Pages of his Paradise Lost, but must be satisfy'd that he was such a masterly Poet, that he needed not to pilfer either Thoughts or Expressions from any other'. Although Ruddiman was 'a Lover of all learned & ingenious Productions', he refused his patronage to this one.[10]

This exchange lends credence to Henderson's statement that with the rising of 1745, Lauder 'espoused the Interest of the P-' and 'was obliged to decamp' from Dundee, not before a symbolic procession to the market cross, and taking leave of the town in a Latin oration to the effect, according to Henderson, 'I quit you all, in the Name of k. J[ames] VIII!'[11] It is known that Lauder resigned his position at the Dundee Grammar School on 31 October 1745 (the day Charles Edward Stuart left Edinburgh to invade England) though the school did not act to fill his post until 31 March 1746: it has been suggested that Lauder's departure for England occurred after that date.[12] In England he would be unknown, and safer from pursuit. In this he was only temporarily successful, for Arthur Henderson published his *Furius* in London in August 1748 as a warning against the personal and political character of the man who had now begun to make his career in the capital.[13] By that date, however, Lauder's scheme was already under way, and he had secured the credence and the patronage which Ruddiman had refused him.

Lauder's project remained the same, though he introduced it more cautiously. In the January 1747 issue of the *Gentleman's Magazine* appeared the first contribution to the controversy, 'An Essay on Milton's Imitation of the Moderns', signed 'W.L.' Although John Hawkesworth was by then undertaking the main business of the magazine, Johnson may have had a hand in late 1746 in the decision to publish Lauder's piece,[14] which indeed introduced the thesis of Milton's borrowing from recent Latin poets in mild terms. It was probably at this point that Johnson met Lauder and was moved to help a man of similar political commitments, denied recognition, without a career, in financial difficulty, and embittered by a physical

[10] Ruddiman to Lauder, 5 November 1745: Duncan, *Thomas Ruddiman*, p. 160.
[11] [Henderson], *Furius*, pp. 21–2.
[12] Marcuse, 'Lauder Controversy', p. 30.
[13] Marcuse, 'Lauder Controversy', p. 31.
[14] Clifford, 'Johnson and Lauder', p. 354 n. 4.

disability. In the April 1747 edition of the *Gentleman's Magazine* Lauder extended his account of Milton's borrowings, and after an exchange of letters in the magazine that summer Lauder's case seemed plausible enough to persuade Johnson to write for him the 'Proposals' for publishing by subscription Hugo Grotius's poem *Adamus Exsul*, with translation and notes, on which, it was claimed, Milton had drawn.[15] The issue now began to attract public attention, and was aired in issues of the *Gentleman's Magazine* through 1747, 1748 and 1749. In December 1749 Lauder published his most considered statement as a separate tract, *An Essay on Milton's use and imitation of the moderns, in his Paradise Lost.* It was shown in proof to the Ivy Lane club, recorded Hawkins:

> I could all along observe that Johnson seemed to approve, not only of the design but of the argument, and seemed to exult in a persuasion, that the reputation of Milton was likely to suffer by this discovery. That he was not privy to the imposture I am well persuaded, but that he wished well to the argument must be inferred from the preface, which indubitably was written by Johnson.[16]

Lauder's *Essay* indeed boasted as the Preface an extended version of Johnson's *Proposals* of 1747, and carried a new 'Postscript', also by Johnson, appealing for financial support for Milton's surviving granddaughter.[17]

Johnson had expressed a scarcely-qualified admiration for Milton, and understood the issue to be merely how Milton had worked within a neo-Latin tradition; that a study of his legitimate allusions and assimilations would be useful: it would be

> a retrospection of the progress of this mighty genius in the construction of his work, a view of the fabric gradually rising, perhaps from small beginnings, till its foundation rests in the centre, and its turrets sparkle in the skies; to trace back the structure through all its varieties to the simplicity of its first plan, to find what was first projected, whence the scheme was taken, how it was improved, by what assistance it was executed, and from what stores the materials were collected; whether its founder dug them from the quarries of nature, or demolished other buildings to embellish his own.[18]

But for Lauder the issue was no longer a scholarly one of Milton's intellectual affinities: it was a deliberately denigratory charge of outright plagiarism. Milton, claimed Lauder, had used without acknowledgement the work of lesser-known modern Latin authors like Masenius, Grotius,

15 William Lauder, *Proposals for printing by subscription Hugonis Grotii Adamus Exsul, tragoedia: with an English version, and the lines imitated from it by Milton subjoined to the pages* (London, 1747).
16 Hawkins, *Life*, p. 276.
17 In Allen T. Hazen (ed.), *Samuel Johnson's Prefaces & Dedications* (New Haven, 1937), pp. 77–84.
18 Hazen (ed.), *Prefaces*, p. 81.

Andrew Ramsay, Buchanan, Du Bartas, Molinaeus, Staphorstius, Taubmannus and Barlaeus.[19] Lauder stepped forward to claim credit for revealing Milton's sources and exposing his fraud. The result was a literary sensation, in which Johnson was innocently if carelessly implicated.

Hawkins obeyed as a lawyer the biographer's urge to set out the evidence:

The charges of plagiarism contained in this production, Lauder has attempted to make out by citations to a very great number, from a Latin poem of Jacobus Masenius a jesuit, intitled, 'Palaestra ligatae eloquentiae', from the 'Adamus exul' of Grotius, the 'Triumphus Pacis' of Caspar Staphorstius a Dutchman, from the Latin poems of Caspar Barlaeus, and the works of many other writers. For a time the world gave credit to them, and Milton's reputation was sinking under them, till a clergyman of great worth, learning and industry, Mr. now Dr John Douglas, prompted at first by mere curiosity, set himself to find out and compare the parallel passages, in the doing whereof he discovered, that in a quotation from Staphorstius, Lauder had interpolated eight lines taken from a Latin translation of the Paradise Lost, by a man named Hogaeus or Hog, and opposed them to the passage in the original, as evidence of Milton's plagiarism. Proofs of the like fraud in passages cited from Taubman and many others are produced by Dr Douglas; but a single instance of the kind would have been sufficient to blast the credit of his adversary.[20]

The fraud was detected by John Douglas, then rector of Eaton Constantine, Shropshire, who published in November 1750 *Milton Vindicated from the Charge of Plagiarism Brought Against Him by Mr. Lauder and Lauder Himself Convicted of Several Forgeries and Gross Impositions on the Public.* But Douglas recognised Johnson's innocence:

'Tis to be hoped, nay, 'tis *expected*, that the elegant and nervous Writer, whose judicious sentiments, and inimitable Stile, point out the Author of Lauder's Preface and Postscript, will no longer allow one to *plume himself with his Feathers* who appears so little to have deserved his Assistance; an Assistance which, I am persuaded, would never have been communicated, had there been the least suspicion of those Facts, which I have been the Instrument of conveying to the World ...[21]

Lauder's case collapsed; he admitted the charge to his publishers, who announced that they would henceforth sell his book only as 'a Masterpiece of Fraud',[22] and the *Gentleman's Magazine* of December 1750 carried a full apology, probably written by Johnson.[23] After John Douglas's discoveries,

19 Clifford, 'Johnson and Lauder', pp. 344–5.

20 Hawkins, *Life*, p. 276.

21 Douglas, *Milton Vindicated*, p. 77 [the title page is dated 1751, but the pamphlet was announced for publication earlier]; Murphy, *Johnson*, pp. 65–6; Clifford, 'Johnson and Lauder', p. 347.

22 Hazen (ed.), *Prefaces*, p. 79.

23 D. J. Greene, 'Some Notes on Johnson and the *Gentleman's Magazine*', *Publications of the Modern Language Association of America* 74 (1959), 75–84, at 83–4.

Johnson, whose ruling passion may be said to be the love of truth, convinced Lauder, that it would be more for his interest to make a full confession of his guilt than to stand forth the convicted champion of a lie; and for this purpose he drew up, in the strongest terms, a recantation in a Letter to the Rev. Mr. Douglas, which Lauder signed, and published in the year 1751.[24] That piece will remain a lasting memorial of the abhorrence with which Johnson beheld a violation of truth.[25]

Probably without Johnson's knowledge, Lauder had added a hasty Postscript to the *Letter to the Reverend Mr. Douglas* in which he tried to undo the apology by claiming that he had only been testing Milton's admirers with a ploy to expose their partisanship. Questioning the Scot's sanity, 'after the first week in January 1751 Johnson washed his hands completely of Lauder and never talked to him again'.[26]

Nor was Lauder silenced. In March 1751 he published *A Apology for Mr. Lauder, in a Letter Most Humbly Addressed to His Grace the Archbishop of Canterbury*, part of his campaign to retrieve his own reputation, and diminish Johnson's, by winning influential friends. In 1754 followed a tract entitled *King Charles I Vindicated from the Charge of Plagiarism Brought Against Him by Milton and Milton Himself Convicted of Forgery, and a Gross Imposition on the Public*. It began with Lauder's self-justification over his dealings with Johnson, who, he claimed, had tricked him in the apology he forced Lauder to sign: 'For, in place of acknowledging that such and such particular Passages only were interpolated, he gave up the whole Essay against *Milton* as Delusion and Misrepresentation, and thereby imposed more grievously on the Publick than I had done, and that too in Terms, much more submissive and abject than the Nature of the Offence required.'[27] The point of Lauder's new polemic was to reiterate his favourite charge of plagiarism. Milton, he claimed, had stolen a prayer from Sir Philip Sidney's *Arcadia* and forced the printer of *Eikon Basilike* to include it in that work as if the king were claiming authorship. It was, claimed Lauder, a 'Masterpiece of fraud & forgery committed by Milton against the memory of King Charles the First'. Still mouthing his favourite charge of plagiarism, Lauder left England in 1756 for Barbados, where he died in 1771.[28]

Murphy emphasised that 'if Johnson approved of the argument, it was no longer than while he believed it founded in truth'.[29] Yet despite Johnson's obvious rectitude and efforts to vindicate himself, the affair

24 William Lauder, *A Letter to the Reverend Mr. Douglas Occasioned by His Vindication of Milton* (London, 1751); the letter is dated 20 December 1750.

25 Murphy, *Johnson*, p. 66.

26 Clifford, 'Johnson and Lauder', p. 352.

27 Quoted in Clifford, 'Johnson and Lauder', p. 351.

28 Clifford, 'Johnson and Lauder', p. 353. For Lauder's attempts in the years after 1751 to ingratiate himself with English Jacobites, see Marcuse, 'Lauder Controversy', pp. 45–7.

29 Murphy, *Johnson*, p. 61.

continued to damage him. Hawkins claimed that Johnson's 'severe censure' of Milton's *Samson Agonistes* in *The Rambler* 'seems to have been prompted by no better a motive, than that hatred of the author for his political principles which he is known to have entertained, and was ever ready to avow'. As a Whig, Hawkins was indignant. Though not condoning Milton as a 'political enthusiast' or excusing his 'domestic manners', he insisted:

> But neither these nor those other qualities that rendered him both a bitter enemy and a railing disputant, could justify the severity of Johnson's criticism on the above-mentioned poem, nor apologize for that harsh and groundless censure which closes the first of his discourses on it, that it is 'a tragedy which ignorance has admired, and bigotry applauded'.

Hawkins linked Johnson's essay with the Lauder affair, which occurred 'about this time'.[30]

In his *Lives of the Poets*, Johnson again felt it proper to censure Milton's republican politics, and repeated Lauder's charge that Milton 'is suspected' of having 'interpolated' into Charles I's *Eikon Basilike* 'a prayer taken from *Sidney's Arcadia*, and imputing it to the King' to discredit him for using, as Milton put it, 'a prayer stolen word for word from the mouth of a heathen woman praying to a heathen god'.[31] Arthur Murphy wrote:

> Mr. Nichols, whose attachment to his illustrious friend was unwearied, shewed him in 1780 a book, called *Remarks on Johnson's Life of Milton*, in which the affair of Lauder was renewed with virulence, and a *poetical scale* in the Literary Magazine 1758 (when Johnson had ceased to write in that collection) was urged as an additional proof of deliberate malice. He read the libellous passage with attention, and instantly wrote on the margin: 'In the business of Lauder I was deceived, partly by thinking the man too frantic to be fraudulent. Of the *poetical scale*, quoted from the Magazine, I am not the author. I fancy it was put in after I had quitted that work: for, I not only did not write it, but I do not remember it.'[32]

Johnson's apologies either did not reach a wide enough public, or were disregarded by those who had an interest in doing so. The Dissenter and Socinian Joseph Towers, in his posthumous appraisal of the Anglican, claimed that 'It can hardly be doubted, but that his aversion to Milton's politics, was the cause of that alacrity, with which he joined with Lauder,

30 Hawkins, *Life*, pp. 274–5. Johnson, *The Rambler* no. 139, 16 July 1751, ended with that observation on *Samson Agonistes*; but Johnson's discussion mixed much praise with his criticism. Johnson continued his appraisal in no. 140, 20 July 1751, a questioning of 'Milton's learning'.

31 Johnson, *Lives of the Poets*, vol. 1, pp. 157–8.

32 Murphy, *Johnson*, pp. 66–7.

in his infamous attack on our great epic poet, and which induced him to assist in that transaction.'[33]

After this experience, Johnson's personal kindness to many individual Scots was more remarkable than his occasional generalisations about the Scottish character. One of the harshest of these was confided to Arthur Murphy, who first met Johnson in 1754 (and who met with an indulgent hearing when he called to apologise for translating into English and publishing as his own an essay in French which turned out to be a translation of one of Johnson's *Ramblers*).[34] Murphy recorded:

> The author of these memoirs well remembers, that Johnson one day asked him, 'Have you observed the difference between your own country impudence and Scotch impudence?' The answer being in the negative: 'Then I will tell you,' said Johnson. 'The impudence of an Irishman is the impudence of a fly, that buzzes about you, and you put it away; but it returns again, and flutters and teazes you. The impudence of a Scotsman is the impudence of a leech, that fixes and sucks your blood.'[35]

Johnson was not alone in his anti-Scottish dispositions, however, and his reaction was not out of line with contemporaries' harsh verdicts on national character. In 1716 John Bowes explained to his friend Dudley Ryder how he 'hated the name and sight of a Scotchman, for it was the genius and nature of that nation to be tricking cheating rogues that have always a design to deceive and defraud you'. Ryder thought Bowes 'too general in his invectives', but conceded 'I think that they have more generally a disposition to play the knave than the English. They have especially the art of dissembling and carry it with the greatest respect and outward deference.'[36] The cultural incompatibility of English and Scots was of long standing: it did not wait for the arrival in English politics of Lord Bute, and Johnson's pronouncements on the Scots could be paralleled from many other sources. In an age of dynastic politics, these cultural stereotypes had an added significance. Johnson had also been involved at a central point of his scholarly commitment, and it is difficult to miss the echo of personal experience in his laconic remark in *Lives of the Poets*: 'Men sometimes suffer by injudicious kindness.'[37] Lauder had evidently suffered by Johnson's patronage; so had the cause which they both supported.

33 [Joseph Towers], *An Essay on the Life, Character, and Writings of Dr Samuel Johnson* (London, 1786), p. 57.

34 W. Jackson Bate, *Samuel Johnson* (London, 1978), p. 322.

35 Murphy, *Johnson*, pp. 105–6.

36 William Matthews (ed.), *The Diary of Dudley Ryder 1715–1716* (London, 1939), p. 227 (26 April 1716).

37 Johnson, *Lives of the Poets*, vol. 4, p. 305.

II. THE FAILURE OF THE ANGLO-LATIN TRADITION AND THE RISE OF THE VERNACULAR

No amount of public acclaim or royal favour in the 1760s could conceal from Johnson the pointlessness of his endeavours. On the island of Skye, in 1773, he reflected:

> The return of my Birthday, if I remember it, fills me with thoughts which it seems to be the general care of humanity to escape. I can now look back upon threescore and four years, in which little has been done, and less has been enjoyed, a life diversified by misery, spent part in the sluggishness of penury, and part under the violence of pain, in gloomy discontent, or importunate distress.[38]

Behind this personal dejection lay the collapse of the tradition within which he had first worked. It meant, among other things, that his literary achievement appeared fragmentary or inexplicably small. *London* (1738) and *The Vanity of Human Wishes* (1749) would be fine prologues to major poetic achievements in mid- and late-career; but no such works were forthcoming, and those two poems stood at the end of an old tradition, not the beginning of a major new achievement. Johnson's poetry thereafter consisted of incidental pieces in English and Latin that display his talent without employing it to great ends. Likewise, the young Johnson regarded the verse drama as the noblest literary genre, and on coming to London in 1737 built his aspirations around his *Irene*; but when finally rescued and staged by his friend David Garrick in 1749 it seemed 'even more old-fashioned to a London audience', and Johnson never wrote another.[39]

Reactions to the failure of this political and social enterprise varied. Lord Orrery abandoned 'my native country' in disgust and settled on his estates in Ireland, describing their delights in Horatian terms.[40] In 1752 he addressed the historian Thomas Carte, who had sent the earl his formidable *History of England*:

> I retire, Sir, partly upon account of health, which of late has grown worse and worse. Another reason for my retirement is an absolute conviction that it is to no purpose to endeavour to save a Country which is resolved not to be saved. I have seen so many instances to confirm this melancholy opinion that the idle hopes of vain and visionary minds appear to me as airy bubbles not in the least to be regarded. My wishes for my Country will be the same to the last hour of my breath. My opinion of my Countrymen grows indeed less and less favourable every day. But, to say truth, we are a declining People: destined, I fear, to absolute destruction. We have had our Day. It ended with Queen Ann. Since her time all has been

[38] Johnson to Hester Thrale, 21 September 1773: Johnson, *Letters*, vol. 2, p. 75.

[39] This despite making the substantial sum of £295 from the performance and published edition: Bate, *Johnson*, pp. 264–5.

[40] E.g. Orrery to William King, 30 May 1747: *Orrery Papers*, vol. 2, p. 1.

Confusion and Discontent at Home; Folly and False Politics abroad; not to mention that Spirit of Slavery and Irreligion that is spreading itself throughout the several parts of the three Kingdoms. These are undeniable Truths. What then have we to hope? Or from whence? Not from Heaven, if we are to judge of the future by past events. Not from Heaven, if we are Judges of our own merits. Hopes may serve to fill Bumpers, but they will scarce at present be the entertainment of closet reflections or cool speculation. Retirement, therefore, is the best choice that the most healthy man can make, and to one with my wretched constitution it is not only eligible but necessary.[41]

In coded language, one Jacobite explained to another that no hope was left to them.

Another family shows the influence of these cultural cross-currents. Edward Gibbon (1675–1736), merchant, one of the Commissioners of the Customs in the great Tory ministry of the last four years of Queen Anne, lost his office at the accession of George I and as a South Sea Company director most of his fortune was confiscated by Parliament after the crash of 1720.[42] His politics were clear. His son Edward (1707–70) was educated by a private tutor, the Nonjuror William Law, then at Westminster and Cambridge; he left the University without taking a degree, but indulged the family resentment of Sir Robert Walpole as Tory MP for Petersfield (1734–41) and Southampton (1741–7). His elder son was the historian Edward Gibbon (1737–94) who, despite a career at Westminster school fragmented by ill-health, steeped himself in the classics. In retrospect, he looked back on his expulsion from Oxford after (like James Boswell) a brief conversion to Roman Catholicism as an emancipation from 'port and prejudice'. Just as the Earl of Eglinton 'cured' Boswell of Catholicism in 1760 'by turning him into a rake',[43] so Gibbon was emancipated, but into a fashionable Deism. Just as Boswell could write 'I am, I flatter myself, completely a citizen of the world',[44] so Gibbon abandoned the English and Anglo-Latin culture into which he had been born. Five years in Geneva as the pupil of a Calvinist minister, M. Pavillard, made him a modern, oriented to recent European learning.

Although Gibbon was awesomely well-read in classical literature, he added to it Locke, and his first publication was not only in the vernacular but in the language of European polite letters: *Essai sur l'étude de la littérature* (London, 1761). Alone of the survivors of the Anglo-Latin culture, Gibbon discovered a theme worthy of it: in 1764, on his single visit to Rome, he claimed he conceived the project of 'writing the decline and fall of the city'. It was to be Gibbon, not Johnson, who provided a monument to the

[41] Orrery to Thomas Carte, 5 August 1752: *Orrery Papers*, vol. 2, p. 116.
[42] Patricia B. Cradock, *Young Edward Gibbon* (Baltimore, 1982), pp. 7–8.
[43] Boswell, *Journal*, p. 48n. [44] Ibid., p. 10.

tradition into which he had been born. Returning from his continental tour in 1765, Gibbon began his labours on a work of which the first volume appeared in 1776. It contained repeated echoes of the Anglo-Latin critique of the Walpolian regime. The successors of Augustus had enjoyed 'absolute power':

> The military force was a blind and irresistible instrument of oppression; and the corruption of Roman manners would always supply flatterers eager to applaud, and ministers prepared to serve, the fear or the avarice, the lust or the cruelty, of their masters ... During fourscore years ... Rome groaned beneath an unremitting tyranny, which exterminated the ancient families of the republic, and was fatal to almost every virtue, and every talent, that arose in that unhappy period.[45]

By his victory at Actium, Octavianus Caesar held supreme power by right of conquest. The 'rich and polite Italians' practised passive obedience under his regime, preferring their 'ease and tranquillity'. Those among them 'of spirit and ability had perished in the field of battle, or in the proscription'. In their place, the new monarch brought with him a 'mixed multitude' who 'reflected disgrace upon their rank, instead of deriving honour from it'.[46] Gibbon echoed the military events of 1688 and the proscription of Stuart adherents which ensued.

Augustus, after his military victory, addressed the senate in an oration 'which displayed his patriotism, and disguised his ambition'. He spoke of 'filial piety'; he 'solemnly restored the senate and people to all their ancient rights'. The stratagem worked. The senate 'refused to accept the resignation of Augustus, they conjured him not to desert the republic, which he had saved', and pressed on him the title of emperor. It was as if Gibbon wrote of the Convention Parliament of 1689. Wisely, Augustus chose to conceal this military despotism and 'to reign under the venerable names of ancient magistracy'. Gibbon took a different view of his government: 'it may be defined [as] an absolute monarchy disguised by the forms of a commonwealth'.[47]

Gibbon subscribed to the Tory critique of standing armies. 'In the purer ages of the commonwealth, the use of arms was reserved for those ranks of citizens who had a country to love, a property to defend, and some share in enacting those laws, which it was their interest, as well as duty, to maintain.' Patriotism, however, 'which had rendered the legions of the republic almost invincible, could make but a very feeble impression on the mercenary servants of a despotic prince'. Augustus now combined in his person

45 Edward Gibbon, *The History of the Decline and Fall of the Roman Empire*, vol. 1 (London, 1776), pp. 79–81.
46 Ibid., pp. 60–1. 47 Ibid., pp. 62–3, 66, 69.

all the powers of republican offices; the republic's checks and balances were at an end; he acquired also 'the management of the religion ... of the Roman people'. One of the main safeguards of public liberty was henceforth turned against it: 'as soon as the senate had been humbled and disarmed, such an assembly, consisting of five or six hundred persons, was found a very tractable and useful instrument of dominion'.[48] So too was the Westminster Parliament, in the eyes of the new dynasty's opponents. So too did George I win control of the Church of England.

In some ways, Britain's case was worse. However great the power of the Roman emperors, most of them 'disdained that pomp and ceremony which might offend their countrymen'. Their household, 'however numerous or splendid, was composed entirely of their domestic slaves and freedmen. Augustus or Trajan would have blushed at employing the meanest of the Romans in those menial offices, which, in the household and bedchamber of a limited monarch, are so eagerly solicited by the proudest nobles of Britain.'[49] The argument cast some doubt on the adjective 'limited'. In another way, modern Britons were in a happier state because of the political division of Europe:

> A modern tyrant, who should find no resistance either in his own breast, or in his people, would soon experience a gentle restraint from the example of his equals, the dread of present censure, the advice of his allies, and the apprehension of his enemies. The object of his displeasure, after his exile or escape from the narrow limits of his dominions, would easily obtain, in a happier climate, a secure refuge, a new fortune adequate to his merit, the freedom of complaint, and perhaps the means of revenge.[50]

So the Stuarts, in a 'happier climate', exercised some restraint on their successors. Monarchy had an inherent problem: 'unless public liberty is protected by intrepid and vigilant guardians, the authority of so formidable a magistrate will soon degenerate into despotism'. The clergy would not prevent this: 'such is the connexion between the throne and the altar, that the banner of the church has very seldom been seen on the side of the people'. Gibbon looked for a remedy elsewhere: 'A martial nobility and stubborn commons, possessed of arms, tenacious of property, and collected into constitutional assemblies, form the only barrier which can perpetually resist the perpetual enterprises of an aspiring prince.'[51] Thus had the opposition to Walpole and to George II fought a stubborn and tenacious battle in defence of liberty and property.

Gibbon's readers would have found a still more exact parallel in his account of the state of the arts and of public virtue. The age of the

[48] Ibid., pp. 9–10, 67–8. [49] Ibid., pp. 69–70. [50] Ibid., pp. 83–4.
[51] Ibid., p. 60.

Antonines had been an age of polite learning: 'the most northern tribes of Britons had acquired a taste for rhetoric: Homer as well as Virgil were transcribed and studied on the banks of the Rhine and Danube; and the most liberal rewards sought out the faintest glimmerings of literary merit'. But the decline of political freedom went with the decline of letters. 'The name of Poet was almost forgotten; that of Orator was usurped by the sophists. A cloud of critics, of compilers, of commentators, darkened the face of learning, and the decline of genius was soon followed by the corruption of taste.'[52] Gibbon echoed the cultural critique of the Anglo-Latin tradition. The strongest echo of all was in the work's central theme. Gibbon declared that he had 'described the triumph of barbarism and religion'. It was the verdict of Samuel Johnson, William King and Thomas Ruddiman on their own societies; from the viewpoint of a religious sceptic, Gibbon now projected it onto the widest canvas as an account of the fall of Rome itself.

Jeremy Bentham's Tory-Jacobite family background in London was similar to Gibbon's. Bentham later recorded that he was, when very young, once in Goldsmith's presence 'in an eating-house in Clement's Churchyard', and once in Johnson's at the Mitre Tavern, but was 'too young and too insignificant to be talked to'.[53] In 1763 Bentham's father Jeremiah exploited a distant acquaintance to enlist Johnson's help in correcting the Latin verses[54] with which the young Bentham, then an Oxford undergraduate, hoped to be chosen to speak at the Encaenia to celebrate the Peace of Paris. But Bentham's verses were bad, Johnson merely pointed out the mistakes rather than returning a revised poem, his comments arrived a day too late, and Bentham was not successful: later in life, Jeremy Bentham showed little attachment to his father's and to Johnson's tradition.[55]

Few men enjoyed like Orrery the luxury of turning their Arcadian literary conceits into a pattern of life. Most continued in their old habitations. Even in Oxford, however, the new age found literary expression, and it did so in a way that illuminates the strategy which underpinned Johnson's own writing: the decline of the Anglo-Latin tradition seemed to demand, and was soon met with, an assertion of the antiquity and dignity

[52] Ibid., p. 58. Gibbon's work contained, of course, many other themes, some of them inconsistent, like his scorn for monarchy ('Of the various forms of government, which have prevailed in the world, an hereditary monarchy seems to present the fairest scope for ridicule', p. 171) and ironic challenges to orthodox religion. These should not obscure the survival in Gibbon's pages of much of the opposition rhetoric of the 1730s.

[53] John Bowring (ed.), *The Works of Jeremy Bentham* (London, 1838–43), vol. 10, p. 124.

[54] No longer extant; Johnson's suggestions are BL Add MSS 54225, f. 59.

[55] For this episode see Paul J. Korshin, 'Dr Johnson and Jeremy Bentham: An Unnoticed Relationship', *Modern Philology* 70 (1972–3), 38–45. I owe these references to Dr J. D. Fleeman and Dr Kai Kin Yung. For the possibility that Johnson helped Dr William King on this occasion, see below, p. 201.

of a native English vernacular tradition. The old world lasted unapologetically into the 1750s, but the idiom of satire drawn from classical imitation seemed now to tire. A militia bill called forth a satiric doggerel which hid behind a classical imitation,[56] but it was a weak performance. Thomas Neville, Fellow of Jesus College, Cambridge, still used Horace's Satires and Epistles in the same way as earlier metropolitan satirists.[57] His colleague Edward Burnaby Greene, Fellow of Corpus Christi College, similarly congratulated himself on his rural retreat:

> High in unpension'd honesty I sit,
> Free as the patriot-soul of steady P[it]t.[58]

But the Seven Years' War would soon seem to belong to the moderns, not the ancients.

Already a change of direction was evident in English cultural politics as one generation gave way to another. Johnson's university illustrated the realignment nicely. Oxford's Professor of Poetry until 1756 was the Rev. William Hawkins, Fellow of Pembroke (whom Johnson may have wished to succeed in his professorship);[59] his collected works, published in three octavo volumes at Oxford in 1758, consisted of *Tracts in Divinity* (volume 1); in English, *Dramatic and other Poems, Letters, Essays, &c.* (volume 2) dedicated to George Henry, Earl of Lichfield;[60] and, in Latin, *Praelectiones Poeticae in Schola Naturalis Philosophiae, Oxon. Habitae*, the latter dedicated to Oxford's Jacobite Chancellor, the Earl of Arran. The subscribers to Hawkins's collected works were a roll-call of Tory Oxford, beginning with the Earl of Arran himself and proceeding through Sir Walter Wagstaffe Bagot (MP 1724–54, 1762–8), the Duke of Beaufort, Norborne Berkeley (MP 1741–63), William Blackstone (MP 1761–70), Sir Francis Dashwood (MP 1741–63), Sir William Dolben (MP 1768–1806), Charles Gray (MP 1742–55, 1761–80), William King, the Earl of Lichfield, Sir John Philipps (MP 1741–64), Sir John St Aubyn (MP 1747–72), Sir Charles Kemys Tynte (MP 1745–74), Sir Richard Vyvyan and Arthur Vansittart (MP 1757–74) to Sir Watkin Williams Wynne. The names included two of Johnson's friends: Bennet Langton and Topham Beauclerk.

Vernacular verse, even Shakespeare's, only received Hawkins's professorial attention after he had translated it into Latin. In his own English

56 *An Imitation of The 22nd Ode in the First Book of Horace* (London, n.d. [?1756]).
57 Thomas Neville, *Imitations of Horace* (London, 1758).
58 [Edward Burnaby Greene], *The Tenth Epistle of the First Book of Horace. Imitated* (London, 1756), p. 5.
59 See below, p. 120.
60 It contained Hawkins's *Henry and Rosamond. A Tragedy*, with a dedication dated 13 March 1749 to Sir John Philipps.

verse, Hawkins echoed exactly the more lofty scorn of the classical poets for their own era:

> But in this wooden Age, these dastard Times,
> O'er run with Follies, and foul-stain'd with Crimes;
> When Vice gigantic takes her public Stand,
> And bids Corruption deluge all the Land,
> Sculks now no more in Holes from Place to Place,
> But stares astonish'd Virtue in the Face;
> When Chiefs blaspheme the God for whom they fight,
> And all religion is to be polite;
> In such a Day as this secure to steer,
> With spotless Honour from Contagion clear,
> To cherish still the dying patriot Fire,
> Unaw'd by Menace, and unbought by Hire,
> To own, and to defend the Christian Name,
> And fix on Infidels the Mark of Shame,
> Is the first Point of Praise; and let the Nine
> Sound with their Harps this Praise, fair *Oxford*, thine.[61]

Hawkins's successor was the Rev. Thomas Warton (1728–90), who held the chair of poetry from 1757 to 1767 and whose interests were very different: his *Observations on The Faerie Queene of Spenser* (1754) and *History of English Poetry* (1775–81) 'strengthened the idea of a native English poetic tradition'[62] in a way, it might be suggested, quite foreign to the intention of William Hawkins; but Warton was Johnson's friend. There were, of course, few men who yet saw their cultural options as mutually exclusive alternatives. As Professor of Poetry, Thomas Warton's lectures included the Greek poets, and in 1770 he published an edition of Theocritus.[63] Yet Warton's main orientation was, and was seen to be, towards the vernacular. Johnson indeed praised him for 'the advancement of the literature of our native Country', and, in 1754, enlisted himself in the same cause: 'The Reason why the authours which are yet read of the sixteenth Century are so little understood is that they are read alone, and no help is borrowed from those who lived with them or before them. Some part of this ignorance I hope to remove by my book which now draws towards its end'[64] – Johnson's *Dictionary*.

The passage of generations and of cultural priorities symbolised at Oxford by the succession of Thomas Warton to William Hawkins was

61 Hawkins, *An Essay on Genius* in *Works*, vol. 3, p. 246. The poem is undated.
62 Bruce Redford, in Johnson, *Letters*, vol. 1, p. 81n.
63 It did not rank high as classical scholarship, however: M. L. Clarke, *Greek Studies in England 1700–1830* (Cambridge, 1945), pp. 63–4. Warton's real interests lay elsewhere.
64 Johnson to Thomas Warton, 16 July 1754, in Johnson, *Letters*, vol. 1, p. 80.

equally symbolised in Edinburgh by the contested election of David Hume to succeed Thomas Ruddiman as Keeper of the Advocates' Library, then the centre of Scots historical research. Ruddiman, Keeper since 1730, had naturally filled the library with heavyweight works in the old tradition: civil and canon law, Greek and Roman classics, the history and antiquities of Britain.[65] In 1752 David Hume took over,[66] and by 1754 was engaged in a highly charged conflict with the Curators over his decision to include three new volumes which the curators considered 'indecent books, and unworthy of a place in a learned library' but which Hume regarded as integral to the culture of European *bienpensants*. Hume's view swiftly prevailed, and by the 1770s the Library was assiduously completing its collections in the vernacular literatures of Europe, the *belles lettres* which came to define a new age's idea of a vernacular culture, what in the nineteenth century was to be called the Enlightenment.[67]

The cultural and political enterprise on which the young Johnson had been embarked, and which he shared with authors like Dryden, Pope, Swift, King and (in a different setting) Ruddiman, had failed. It may be that Johnson's *Dictionary* was, in part, intended to be the foundation stone of a newly-strengthened vernacular culture, to replace the old: English was now to be raised to the dignity of Latin and Greek as a medium for cultural expression. William Warburton had lamented in 1747 that 'the English tongue, at this Juncture, deserves and demands our particular regard ... For we have neither Grammar nor Dictionary, neither chart nor Compass, to guide us through this wide sea of words':[68] just before the publication of the *Dictionary* Johnson quoted that phrase in looking forward to the accomplishment of his project.[69]

In the Preface to his *Dictionary*,[70] Johnson explained that he had taken his 'examples and authorities from the writers before the restoration [of 1660], whose works I regard as *the wells of English undefiled*'. Since that time,

65 Alexander Brown's Preface of 1772 to the catalogue of 1742: Douglas, *Thomas Ruddiman*, p. 37.

66 Hume claimed that 'The violent cry of deism, atheism, and scepticism, was raised against me ... nothing since the rebellion has ever so much engaged the attention of this town, except Provost Stewart's trial', that is, the trial of Archibald Stewart in 1747 for having, as Lord Provost of Edinburgh, surrendered the city to the Jacobites in 1745: William K. Dickson, 'David Hume and the Advocates' Library', *Juridical Review* 44 (1932), 1–14.

67 Ernest Campbell Mossner, *The Life of David Hume* (Oxford, 1970), pp. 252–4; Duncan, *Thomas Ruddiman*, p. 38. One of the three volumes was Bussy Rabutin's *Histoire amoureuse des Gaules*: the Curators had a point.

68 Quoted by Redford in Johnson, *Letters*, vol. 1, p. 92n.

69 Johnson to Thomas Warton, 1 February 1755: Johnson, *Letters*, vol. 1, p. 91.

70 For which, see James H. Sledd and Gwin J. Kolb (eds.), *Dr Johnson's Dictionary: Essays in the Biography of a Book* (Chicago, 1955); Robert DeMaria, Jr., *Johnson's Dictionary and the Language of Learning* (Chapel Hill, 1986); Allen Reddick, *The Making of Johnson's Dictionary 1746–1773* (Cambridge, 1990).

English had 'been gradually departing from its original *Teutonick* character, and deviating towards a *Gallick* structure and phraseology, from which it ought to be our endeavour to recal it'. He attempted to do so not only by a dictionary, but a dictionary prefaced by chapters on 'The History of the English Language' and 'A Grammar of the English Tongue'. It was to be a systematic response to the problem, and complete in itself. Johnson said that he had 'long thought of' the project of an English dictionary even before the publisher Robert Dodsley put the suggestion to him;[71] but his decision to accept the publisher's invitation and embark on this daunting enterprise was made in the spring of 1746, as the Stuart cause was going down to crushing and final defeat. His prospectus for a consortium of publishers, 'A Short Scheme for compiling a new Dictionary of the English Language', was dated 30 April 1746; the battle of Culloden had signalled the Jacobite nemesis on 16 April.

Yet Johnson did not simply abandon one cultural tradition in order to promote another, either in 1746 or at any later date. *The Vanity of Human Wishes* (1749), his second great 'imitation' of Juvenal, was still in the future. Nevertheless, new purposes can be discerned in his writings. Johnson's periodical *The Rambler* appeared twice weekly from 20 March 1750 to 14 March 1752, and was his most sustained achievement in English prose to that date. Although seemingly vernacular essays in the style of the *Tatler* (1709–11) and the *Spectator* (1711–12), the acknowledged models in the genre, they carry a very different cargo, part Anglican moralising, part neoclassical precept.[72] Many of the references in its pages are to Renaissance humanists like Bellarmine, Camerarius, Cardano, Castiglione, Cornaro, Cujacius, Descartes, Erasmus, Fabricius, Gassendi, Lipsius, Politian, Pontanus, Sannazaro, the Scaligers, and Thuanus, in a way that recalls his project for a history of neoclassical poetry centering on Politian.[73] The *Rambler* met some resistance on its first appearance because of its prose style, recorded Hawkins: 'The vulgar opinion is, that the style of this century is the perfection of our language, and that we owe its ultimate and final improvement to Mr. Addison.'[74] Johnson's prose was blamed for differing from that model.

71 Boswell, *Life*, vol. 1, p. 182; vol. 3, p. 405.

72 For a detailed study of Johnson's use of the classical motto, see Robert C. Olson, *Motto, Context, Essay: The Classical Background of Samuel Johnson's Rambler and Adventurer Essays* (New York, 1984). Johnson's 239 texts were taken from Horace (80), Juvenal (34), Ovid (27), Martial (22), Virgil (14), Homer (7), Lucan (6), Seneca (6).

73 Bate, *Johnson*, p. 294; Samuel Johnson, *The Rambler*, ed. W. J. Bate and A. B. Strauss (3 vols., New Haven, 1969), vol. 1, p. xxxii: 'Of the 669 quotations or literary allusions in the *Rambler* ... well above half – 406 (60 per cent) – are from Greek (104) or classical Latin (302) authors ... Of the 251 quotations and references to works since the beginning of the Renaissance, only 37 are to eighteenth-century writers.'

74 Hawkins, *Life*, pp. 270.

By contrast to *The Rambler*, Johnson's next periodical, *The Idler*, published weekly from 15 April 1758 to 5 April 1760, consciously sought an easy vernacular style. Its prose was markedly different from that of *The Rambler*, and *The Idler* has been seen as a deliberate attempt to match the relaxed and informal idiom of Addison and Steele. The enterprise may also have been Johnson's excuse to himself for his failure to make progress with a grander and definitive project in the vernacular, an eight-volume edition of Shakespeare.[75] The contract for this work, signed on 2 June 1756, provided for completion within eighteen months; but Johnson postponed and postponed. It is possible that he was inhibited by the importance of the task, and reluctant that this second monument to English letters should fall short of his far more laborious achievement in the *Dictionary*.[76] Nevertheless, when it eventually appeared, Johnson's Preface to his edition of Shakespeare (1765) systematically argued to elevate his subject. Antiquity had its 'votaries' who 'reverence it, not from reason, but from prejudice'; but there was a rational esteem for what had been long tested and long approved. Consequently, 'The poet, of whose works I have undertaken the revision, may now begin to assume the dignity of an ancient, and claim the privilege of established fame and prescriptive veneration.'[77]

Yet Johnson's project for the vernacular was, in its own terms, not a success. Arthur Murphy attempted an explanation:

> It is remarkable, that the pomp of diction, which has been objected to Johnson, was first assumed in the Rambler. His Dictionary was going on at the same time, and, in the course of that work, as he grew familiar with technical and scholastic words, he thought that the bulk of his readers were equally learned; or at least would admire the splendour and dignity of the style. And yet it is well known, that he praised in Cowley the easy and unaffected structure of the sentences. Cowley may be placed at the head of those who cultivated a clear and natural style. Dryden, Tillotson, and Sir William Temple, followed. Addison, Swift, and Pope, with more correctness, carried our language well nigh to perfection. Of Addison, Johnson was used to say, *He is the Raphael of Essay Writers*. How he differed so widely from such elegant models is a problem not to be solved ... Determined to discard colloquial barbarisms and licentious idioms, he forgot the elegant simplicity that distinguishes the writings of Addison.[78]

75 For the intellectual context of this work, see especially R. D. Stock, *Samuel Johnson and Neoclassical Dramatic Theory: The Intellectual Context of the Preface to Shakespeare* (Lincoln, Nebraska, 1973).

76 Bate, *Johnson*, pp. 330–6, 343. It was finally published in October 1765: ibid., pp. 390–8. If the Tory Richard Farmer, Fellow and later Master of Emmanuel College, Cambridge, was the anonymous instigator of Johnson's pension, it may be relevant that Farmer presented Johnson with a copy of his *An Essay on the Learning of Shakespeare* (Cambridge, 1767). J.D. Fleeman (ed.), *A Preliminary Handlist of Copies of Books associated with Dr Samuel Johnson* (Oxford, 1984), p. 18.

77 Johnson, *Works*, vol. 7, pp. 59–61.

78 Murphy, *Johnson*, pp. 156–8.

Boswell aptly noted of Johnson: 'It has been often remarked that in his poetical pieces (which it is to be regretted are so few, because so excellent) his style is easier than in his prose.'[79]

Perhaps the root of the problem was that Addison, 'not so profound a thinker', had a different relation to the classics:

His Latin Poetry shews, that he relished, with a just selection, all the refined and delicate beauties of the Roman classics; and when he cultivated his native language, no wonder that he formed that graceful style, which has been so justly admired; simple, yet elegant; adorned, yet never over-wrought; rich in allusion, yet pure and perspicuous; correct, without labour, and, though sometimes deficient in strength, yet always musical.

Addison is

the Jupiter of Virgil, with placid serenity talking to Venus:

Vultu, quo coelum tempestatesque serenat.

Johnson is JUPITER TONANS: he darts his lightning, and rolls his thunder, in the cause of virtue and piety. The language seems to fall short of his ideas . . .[80]

English prose after Johnson was seldom deeply indebted to his style. If he sought an easy, informal vernacular, his contemporaries could find better models in Defoe or Smollett, Addison or Steele. If Johnson sought to raise the vernacular to a higher level of dignity, his ultimate loyalty to a learned tradition only made him seem portentous. His style could be parodied, but was seldom imitated. Johnson ultimately sided with critical acuity and moral integrity against the rising fashions of the vernacular, the Gothic or the Celtic. This last preference involved him in the best-known of his conflicts over the politics of language.

III. 'CALEDONIAN BIGOTRY': THE POEMS OF OSSIAN

Two themes ran through Johnson's experiences during his tour of Scotland in 1773: the theme of failure, in the story of the rising of 1745; and the swelling theme of increasing Scots assertions of the antiquity and dignity of their culture through claims for the authenticity of the poems of Ossian.[81]

79 Boswell, *Journal*, p. 7.   80 Murphy, *Johnson*, pp. 158–9, 161.

81 James Macpherson first issued, anonymously, *Fragments of Ancient Poetry, Collected in the Highlands of Scotland, and Translated from the Galic or Erse Language* (Edinburgh, 1760), with a preface, again anonymous, by Hugh Blair. Perceiving a market niche, Macpherson then devised an epic poem about Fingal, a Celtic hero, written in the third century by Fingal's son, the poet Ossian: this appeared as *Fingal. An Ancient Epic Poem, in six books; together with several other Poems, composed by Ossian, the son of Fingal; translated from the Galic language by James Macpherson* (London, 1762); the second instalment was published as *Temora, an Ancient Epic Poem, in eight books; together with several other Poems, composed by Ossian, the son of Fingal;*

In England the most obvious inference about the purpose of Johnson's Highland tour was that it echoed Johnson's sympathy for the Stuart cause; but in Scotland the cultural conflicts and preoccupations were, by the 1770s, very different. From the 1760s, one prominent mode of asserting Scots identity had become the championing of a vernacular, indeed a Gaelic, literature as the authentic and ancient voice of a Scots nation. The poems of Ossian, recently edited (or forged) by James Macpherson,[82] at once aligned commentators for and against. Johnson was among their most persistent critics, resolutely doubting the authenticity of the published text.

Hawkins saw the exact analogy: the argument over the poems of Ossian 'was continued with a degree of asperity equal to that which was shewn in the controversy concerning the genuineness of Phalaris's epistles'.[83] This set-piece controversy[84] over the spurious epistles of the Greek tyrant Phalaris had a significance far beyond philological scholarship. It was an opening round in that battle between ancients and moderns which, in different forms, was to last beyond Johnson's own life. This small issue thus became a symbolic contest between the Whiggish moderns, especially those of Trinity College, Cambridge, and the Tory ancients, especially those based at Christ Church, Oxford, a contest expressing not merely two different styles of classical scholarship but two conflicting religious and political traditions. Unusually, it was fought on the territory of Greek, not Latin, and began with Sir William Temple's 'Essay upon Ancient and Modern Learning' of 1690, which openly espoused the cause of the ancients. This was replied to by Dr Richard Bentley's protégé William Wotton (1694), which in turn was the occasion for a riposte (1698) by Dean Henry Aldrich's unimpeachably patrician pupil Charles Boyle (1676–1731), later 4th Earl of Orrery, in a work substantially ghosted for him by a group of Christ Church dons including Francis Atterbury,[85] Anthony

translated from the Galic language by James Macpherson (London, 1763). By 1765 the two latter had been combined, with revisions, as *The Works of Ossian, the Son of Fingal, in two volumes. Translated from the Galic language by James Macpherson ... To which is subjoined a critical dissertation on the poems of Ossian. By Hugh Blair, D.D.* (London, 1765).

82 From the extensive literature on the Ossian controversy, see especially Edward D. Snyder, *The Celtic Revival in English Literature: 1760–1800* (Cambridge, Mass., 1923); Derick S. Thomson, *The Gaelic Sources of Macpherson's 'Ossian'* (Edinburgh, [1951]); Malcolm Chapman, *The Gaelic Vision in Scottish Culture* (London, 1978); Ian Haywood, *The Making of History: A Study of the Literary Forgeries of James Macpherson and Thomas Chatterton in Relation to Eighteenth-Century Ideas of History and Fiction* (London, 1986); Fiona J. Stafford, *The Sublime Savage: A Study of James Macpherson and The Poems of Ossian* (Edinburgh, 1988); Paul deGategno, *James Macpherson* (Boston, 1989); Howard Gaskill (ed.), *Ossian Revived* (Edinburgh, 1991).

83 Hawkins, *Life*, pp. 491–2.

84 See, in general, Joseph M. Levine, *The Battle of the Books: History and Literature in the Augustan Age* (Ithaca, 1991), pp. 47–120 and passim.

85 For whom, see above, p. 14.

Alsop[86] and George Smalridge. Bentley's crushing *Dissertation upon the Epistles of Phalaris* (1699) may have settled the philological issue for later and uncommitted scholars, but it did not change Charles Boyle's politics: he spent six months in the Tower in 1721 on suspicion of complicity in the Atterbury plot, and narrowly escaped prosecution. Ossian, like Phalaris, was from the outset a cultural icon, a point of inevitable conflict in the cultural politics of Johnson's Britain.[87]

Johnson's unhappy experience at the hands of his unbalanced protégé William Lauder carried over to his more careful scepticism over the alleged poems of Ossian. This disbelief dated from the early 1760s, but the issue was forced on his attention during his Scottish tour. Hardly had Johnson reached Edinburgh than he confronted at dinner 'Sir Adolphus Oughton, then our Deputy Commander-in-Chief, who was not only an excellent officer but one of the most universal scholars I ever knew', boasted Boswell: he 'had learned the Erse language, and expressed his belief in the authenticity of Ossian's poetry. Dr Johnson took the opposite side of that perplexed question', and hostilities were narrowly averted.[88] In Aberdeen, Boswell and Johnson

> spoke of *Fingal*. He [Johnson] said, 'If the poems were really translated, they were certainly first written down. Let Mr. Macpherson deposit the MS in one of the colleges at Aberdeen where there are people who can judge, and if the professors certify the authenticity, then there will be an end of the controversy. If he does not take this obvious and easy method, he gives the best reason to doubt, considering too how much is against it *a priori*.[89]

Johnson now began to encounter what he could only regard as deliberate misrepresentation. Martin Macpherson, Presbyterian minister of Sleat on the Isle of Skye, 'told Mr. Johnson that there was an Erse Bible; that he had compared the new Erse Testament by Mr. Stuart with the former one; that here were many Erse manuscripts – all of which circumstances we afterwards found not to be true'.[90] Something similar happened when Donald Macqueen, Presbyterian minister of Kilmuir, spent time with Johnson.

86 For whom, see above, p. 20.

87 Macpherson's was not an isolated achievement. For the crucial role played by his allies and promoters among the campaigners for a Scots militia and the Moderate party of the Presbyterian Church of Scotland, see Richard B. Sher, '"Those Scotch Imposters and their Cabal": Ossian and the Scottish Enlightenment', *Man and Nature* 1 (1982), 55–63. Hugh Blair, Alexander Carlyle and Adam Ferguson 'suspected all along that Macpherson had taken "liberties" in piecing together "separate or broken fragments" to create his Ossian epics', but their need to devise a Scots national epic led them to ignore Macpherson's fabrications: ibid., p. 60.

88 Boswell, *Journal*, p. 27 (16 August 1773).

89 Boswell, *Journal*, p. 67 (23 August 1773).

90 Boswell, *Journal*, pp. 122–3 (7 September 1773).

Mr. Johnson asked him as to *Fingal*. He said he could repeat some passages in the original. That he heard his grandfather had a copy of the poem; but that he did not believe that Ossian composed that poem as it is now published. This came pretty much to what Mr. Johnson has always held, though he goes farther and maintains that it is no better than such an epic poem as he could make from the song of Robin Hood; that is to say, that, except a few passages, there is nothing truly ancient but the names and some vague traditions. Mr. Macqueen alleged that Homer was made up of detached fragments. Mr. Johnson denied it; said that it had been one work originally, and that you could not put a book of the *Iliad* out of place; and he believed the same might be said of the *Odyssey*.[91]

At Ullinish, Johnson's

notion as to the poems given by Macpherson as the works of Ossian, was confirmed here. Mr. Macqueen had always evaded the point, saying that Mr. Macpherson's pieces fell far short of what he knew in Erse, and were said to be Ossian's. Said Mr. Johnson, 'I hope they do. I am not disputing that you may have poetry of great merit, but that Macpherson's is not a translation from ancient poetry. You do not believe it. I say before you, you do not believe it, though you are very willing that the world should believe it.' Mr. Macqueen could not answer to this. Said Mr. Johnson, 'I look upon Macpherson's *Fingal* to be as gross an imposition as ever the world was troubled with. Had it been really an ancient work, a true specimen how men thought at that time, it would have been a curiosity of the first rate. As a modern production, it is nothing.'

Boswell too was angry at this evasion. Macqueen 'always harped on this: "Macpherson's translations are far inferior to Ossian's originals." "Yes," said I, "because they are not the same. They are inferior as a shilling is to a guinea, because they are not the same." It was really disagreeable to see how Macqueen shuffled about the matter.'

Boswell then had Rorie MacLeod, son of his host Alexander MacLeod, who spoke Erse, compare James Macpherson's English text with what Donald Macqueen claimed were fragments of the original: one passage Rorie MacLeod declared to be 'pretty like'.

When Mr. Johnson came down, I told him that Mr. Macqueen had repeated a passage pretty like; and that he himself had required Macpherson's Ossian to be no liker than Pope's Homer. 'Well,' said he, 'this is just what I always said. He has found names, and stories, and phrases – nay passages in old songs – and with them has compounded his own compositions, and so made what he gives to the world as the translation of an ancient poem.' 'But,' said I, 'it was wrong in him to pretend that there was a poem in six books.' JOHNSON. 'Yes, sir. At a time too when the Highlanders knew nothing of *books* and nothing of *six* – or perhaps were got to the length of counting six ...'[92]

[91] Boswell, *Journal*, p. 129 (8 September 1775).
[92] Boswell, *Journal*, pp. 204–6 (22–23 September 1773).

Johnson had Macqueen in mind when he recalled in his *Journey* 'a very learned Minister in Sky' who urged on him the genuineness of the poems: 'He wished me to be deceived, for the honour of his country'; but he evidently did not believe in the genuineness of *Fingal* himself. The Scots in general were 'seduced by their fondness for their supposed ancestors. A Scotchman must be a very sturdy moralist, who does not love *Scotland* better than truth: he will always love it better than inquiry; and if falsehood flatters his vanity, will not be very diligent to detect it.'[93] Andrew Henderson, outraged by this passage, defended the originality of *Fingal* against the *Iliad* and the *Aeneid*;[94] but it was left to Boswell to puncture this pretence with a devastating metaphor. Though there were some grand images in Macpherson's poem,

> there was [a certain sameness] in *Fingal*, though not every one is sensible of it. That it was like the paper with which a room is finished, where you have a number of birds and a number of figures and a number of trees and a number of flowers; and as there is a variety of objects, one does not at once perceive that the finishing is composed of pieces all exactly the same. By the time your eye has made the round of the pattern, you forget what you first looked at. So it is with Ossian's poetry to a considerable degree.[95]

Boswell 'read some of Macpherson's *Dissertations on the Ancient Caledonians*, etc. I was disgusted at the unsatisfactory conjectures as to antiquity before the days of record.'[96] Johnson agreed about the book: 'you might read half an hour and ask yourself what you had been reading. There were so many words to so little matter, there was no getting through the book.'[97] Not only the sceptical Johnson but the partisan Boswell was unhappy with the state of the evidence. Even 'very warm advocates for its authenticity' admitted that *Fingal* contained *some* editorial linking passages, and was not wholly 'a translation from the Gaelic'; why were those not produced? Their absence cast doubt on the authenticity of the whole, Boswell conceded.[98] He added an important rider:

> For the satisfaction of those on the north of the Tweed, who may think Dr Johnson's account of Caledonian credulity and inaccuracy too strong, it is but fair to add that he admitted the same kind of ready belief might be found in his own country. He would undertake, he said, to write an epic poem on the story of Robin Hood, and

93 Samuel Johnson, *A Journey to the Western Islands of Scotland* [1775], ed. J. D. Fleeman (Oxford, 1985), pp. 98–9.

94 Andrew Henderson, *A Letter to Dr Samuel Johnson, on His Journey to the Western Isles* (London, [1775]), pp. 18–21.

95 Boswell, *Journal*, pp. 288–9 (10 October 1773).

96 Boswell, *Journal*, p. 122 (7 September 1773).

97 Boswell, *Journal*, p. 165 (13 September 1773).

98 Boswell, *Journal*, p. 381 (10 November 1773).

half England, to whom the names and places he should mention in it are familiar, would believe and declare they had heard it from their earliest years.[99]

Johnson's quarrel was not with Scotland but with the idea of a culture and a national identity built around a mythical vernacular literature.[100] He had, indeed, already made the same objection in England, in his devastating parody of ballad poetry:

I put my hat upon my head,
And walk'd into the Strand,
And there I met another man
With his hat in his hand.[101]

It was, specifically, a retort to Thomas Percy's *The Hermit of Warkworth: A Northumberland Ballad* (London, 1771). Johnson was not hostile to ancient verse as such. From June to August 1764, Johnson had been the guest of Bishop Percy at Easton Maudit in Northamptonshire, intending to push forward the edition of Shakespeare. Percy was finishing the work to be published in 1765 as *Reliques of Ancient English Poetry*, and enlisted Johnson's help in that enterprise. Despite Johnson's scepticism of the ballad form, he contributed the Glossary and Dedication to his friend's book.[102] What Johnson objected to was the polemical misuse of this tradition (as he saw it) for political ends.

In his *Journey to the Western Islands*, Johnson explained:

I suppose my opinion of the poems of Ossian is already discovered. I believe they never existed in any other form than that which we have seen. The editor, or author, never could shew the original; nor can it be shewn by any other; to revenge reasonable incredulity, by refusing evidence, is a degree of insolence, with which the world is not yet acquainted; and stubborn audacity is the last refuge of guilt. It would be easy to shew it if he had it; but whence could it be had? It is too long to be remembered, and the language formerly had nothing written. He has doubtless inserted names that circulate in popular stories, and may have translated some wandering balads, if any can be found; and the names, and some of the images

99 Boswell, *Journal*, p. 380 (10 November 1773).

100 Any such process of nation-building is highly problematic, and more research on this theme is still necessary. For the complex emergence of a nationalist vernacular literature, see John Lucas, *England and Englishness: Ideas of Nationhood in English Poetry 1688–1900* (London, 1990); for a study of the cultural dynamics of Scots national identity, see Murray G. H. Pittock, *The Invention of Scotland: The Stuart myth and the Scottish Identity, 1638 to the present* (London, 1991).

101 Joseph Cradock, *Literary and Miscellaneous Memoirs* (4 vols., London, 1828), vol. 1, p. 207; Boswell, *Life*, vol. 2, pp. 136, 212–3.

102 Boswell, *Life*, vol. 1, pp. 49, 486, 553–4. Again, Johnson's scepticism was well founded. For doubts about Thomas Percy's use of his sources similar to those more often raised about Macpherson, see Haywood, *The Making of History*, pp. 105–14.

being recollected, make an inaccurate auditor imagine, by the help of Caledonian bigotry, that he has formerly heard the whole.[103]

Macpherson discovered the nature of this passage within two days of Johnson's book being distributed to the booksellers. When his attempts to put pressure on the printer, William Strahan, to cancel the paragraph failed, Macpherson turned to the author. In one of the more remarkable passages of literary history, Macpherson composed a grovelling apology which he sent to Johnson with a demand that he sign it within three hours. When this failed, Macpherson threatened physical violence. These literary tactics only served to produce one of Johnson's most famous letters in reply, robustly defending his integrity and casting yet more scorn on Macpherson's translation of the *Iliad* into 'Ossianic' prose. More practically, Johnson acquired a cudgel, 'an oak-plant of a tremendous size' as Hawkins described it, and Macpherson's threat was heard of no more.[104] But after his experience of the literary ethics of Lauder and Macpherson, Johnson's sceptical attitude to Scottish claims becomes more intelligible.

A Scots vernacular did exist, but not in Ossian. Not only did a Scots vernacular literature in English assert itself to challenge an older Latin humanistic culture;[105] within Gaelic too, the formal, precedent-bound bardic traditions were giving way to something new. It did not check the repeated expressions of support for the exiled dynasty found in Gaelic verse.[106] Scotland's humiliation and defeat in 1745–6[107] indeed provoked a bitter Jacobite cultural backlash, especially in Gaelic poetry like that of Alexander Macdonald (c. 1700–70); but his was far removed from Ossian's Homeric uplift, being, as was noted even in 1744, 'stuffed with obscene language', and, as a modern critic has characterised them, 'scurrilously magnificent' in the poems' 'most vivid and explicit imagery'.[108] By contrast, James Macpherson's inventions were formulaic in just the right

[103] Johnson, *Journey* (ed. Fleeman), p. 98.

[104] Hawkins, *Life*, pp. 490–1; Boswell, *Life*, vol. 2, pp. 292–8, 511–13; Johnson to James Macpherson, 20 January 1775: Johnson, *Letters*, vol. 2, p. 168; Bate, *Johnson*, pp. 519–22.

[105] For the Scots vernacular in English, see especially Thomas Crawford, *Society and the Lyric: a study of the Song Culture of eighteenth-century Scotland* (Edinburgh, 1979); William Donaldson, *The Jacobite Song* (Aberdeen, 1988).

[106] Derick S. Thomson, 'Gaelic Poetry in the Eighteenth Century: the Breaking of the Mould' in Andrew Hook (ed.), *The History of Scottish Literature Volume 2 1660–1800* (Aberdeen, 1987), pp. 175–89.

[107] For one study which dates a 'crisis of identity' among Scots to c. 1740, see Kenneth Simpson, *The Protean Scot: The Crisis of Identity in Eighteenth Century Scottish Literature* (Aberdeen, 1988), p. 3.

[108] Duncan Glen, *The Poetry of the Scots: An Introduction and Bibliographical Guide to Poetry in Gaelic, Scots, Latin and English* (Edinburgh, 1991), p. 70.

way for an audience steeped in an older classical tradition[109] which was seeking to break out into a newly dignified but 'polite' vernacular. In that sense his fictions might be described as retro-Homeric more than proto-Romantic. 'The plushy green headlands, the blue bays, the wind groaning in the pines and oaks, the ships, halls, caves, tombs, and campfires, the running deer and boars, the thrusting and the bleeding warriors, the spears, swords, harps, armor and gems – the whole bardic idiom of Homeric and Miltonic imitation – constituted a distinct poetic invention on the part of Macpherson, if no very subtle one.'[110]

The Ossianic cult was not as much the spontaneous effusion of a native vernacular tradition as it claimed to be. Its roots were at least as much in Scottish classical scholarship,[111] for the image of Ossian as a Scots Homer derived in part from the work of the Aberdeen professor Thomas Blackwell, who helped to popularise an image of the Greek author as a *Naturmensch.*[112] This theme was reinforced, and the link was established by Hugh Blair in 1763, who compared Homer and Ossian at length, not always to the Greek's advantage.[113] Such explicit recognition helped prompt James Macpherson to produce his translation of the *Iliad* in the style of his Ossianic inventions (1773).[114]

James Macpherson was probably a pupil of Thomas Blackwell, an inspirational teacher as Professor of Greek at Marischal College, Aberdeen, from 1725 to 1757.[115] Blackwell's assumption that the functions of social historian and literary critic were essentially similar helped to spread the linked assumption that Homer and his age were as barbaric as the events described in the *Iliad* and, therefore, to elevate modern Scotland by

109 For Renaissance humanism remaining 'a central source of ideal and image to educated Scots', see Hugh Ouston, 'Cultural Life from the Restoration to the Union' in Andrew Hook (ed.), *The History of Scottish Literature Volume 2 1660–1800* (Aberdeen, 1987), pp. 11–30, at 21.

110 W. K. Wimsatt, 'Imitation As Freedom – 1717–1798', *New Literary History* 1 (1969–70), 215–36, at 228.

111 For the attention of Scots intellectuals to the relations between Homer and Ossian, see Donald M. Foerster, *Homer in English Criticism: The Historical Approach in the Eighteenth Century* (New Haven, 1947), pp. 41–62; Margaret Mary Rubel, *Savage and Barbarian: Historical Attitudes in the Criticism of Homer and Ossian in Britain, 1760–1800* (Amsterdam, 1978).

112 Thomas Blackwell, *An Enquiry into the Life and Writings of Homer* (London, 1735). See the index to this work, *sub* 'Nature'.

113 [Hugh Blair], *A Critical Dissertation on the Poems of Ossian, the Son of Fingal* (London, 1763), pp. 22–3, 28, 30, 74. Virgil came a poor third: 'His perfect hero, Aeneas, is an unanimated, insipid personage', pp. 32, 62.

114 M. L. Clarke, *Greek Studies in England 1700–1830* (Cambridge, 1945), pp. 129–30, 134–6.

115 For the origins of Macpherson's vision in the Jacobite, Episcopalian, Scoto-Latin culture of the north east of Scotland, see Pittock, *Invention of Scotland*, pp. 73–9; George Pratt Insh, *The Scottish Jacobite Movement* (Edinburgh, 1952), pp. 168–75.

comparison. James Beattie, Adam Ferguson and Lord Kames all subscribed to that comfortingly patriotic view.[116] For Hugh Blair, 'the ancient Scots were of Celtic original', and the Celts were 'a great and mighty people, altogether distinct from the Goths and Teutones'. Ossian was their bard:

> There we find the fire and enthusiasm of the most early times, combined with an amazing degree of regularity and art. We find tenderness, and even delicacy of sentiment, greatly predominant over fierceness and barbarity. Our hearts are melted with the softest feelings, and at the same time elevated with the highest ideas of magnanimity, generosity, and true heroism.

Ossian recorded 'the most illustrious scenes which that age could exhibit, both of heroism in war, and magnificence in peace'. The moral of *Fingal* was highly comforting to Scots: 'That Wisdom and Bravery always triumph over brutal force; or another nobler still; That the most compleat victory over an enemy is obtained by that moderation and generosity which convert him into a friend.'[117]

This magnanimity was not always evident in Fingal's descendants. Johnson's critics dwelt on his unfairness to Scotland, and were almost as preoccupied with refuting his emblematic charge that that country was denuded of trees[118] as they were to vindicate Scots letters, partly the classics, but chiefly, of course, Ossian. One Scots Presbyterian minister, in response to Johnson's cool account of that country, mounted an impassioned defence of the poems and claimed that 'it was the great object of the Doctor's *Journey*, to find out some pretence or other for denying the authenticity of the ancient compositions in the *Gaelic* language'.[119] M'Nichol clearly perceived Johnson's attitudes not only as English prejudice, but as bound up with a certain use of classical culture: 'as it was a custom with the Greek and Roman authors to call every thing rude and barbarous which did not belong to themselves, our traveller, perhaps, may think himself entitled to take an equal liberty with whatever is not *English.*' Johnson's disbelief of 'the dignified sentiments, the exalted manners' imputed to Highland society by the poems of Ossian reflected 'those confined notions concerning the character of ages and nations, which are

116 Foerster, *Homer in English Criticism*, pp. 42–7.

117 [Blair], *Critical Dissertation*, pp. 11, 16, 25.

118 *Remarks on a Voyage to the Hebrides, in a Letter to Dr Samuel Johnson, LL.D.* (London, 1775), pp. 4–6; Andrew Henderson, *A Letter to Dr Samuel Johnson, on His Journey to the Western Isles* (London, [1775]), p. 9.

119 Donald M'Nichol, *Remarks on Dr Samuel Johnson's Journey to the Hebrides; in which are contained, Observations on the Antiquities, Language, Genius, and Manners of the Highlanders of Scotland* (London, 1779), pp. 242, 344–71.

too often entertained in certain universities. With the literature of Greece and Rome, they imbibe such an exalted idea of classic character, as induces them to consign to ignorance and barbarism, all antiquity beyond the pales of the Greek and Roman empires.'[120]

This strategy was not confined to Scots. Even Gibbon described the legends of Fingal and the poems of Ossian as a 'pleasing supposition' and thought Fingal's Celts a useful foil to 'the degenerate Romans, polluted with the mean vices of wealth and slavery'.[121] Yet M'Nichol loyally sought a new way of apologising for his nation and claiming its place on Mount Olympus by elevating its vernacular:

> The powers of the soul are in every country the same. Why then should not the Celtic *Druid* be as capable of impressing useful instruction on the followers of his religion, as the bare-footed *Selli*, who sacrificed to *Jupiter* on the cold top of *Dodona*? Or, by what prescription has the neighbourhood of the *Hellespont* a right to sentiments more exalted than those of the chieftain who inhabits the coast of the Vergivian ocean? Have not many nations, who have been called barbarians, excelled the Romans in valour, and in that most exalted of all virtues, a sincere love for their country?[122]

M'Nichol was Johnson's inferior in scholarship, in letters, and in common courtesy;[123] but it was he, not Johnson, who could seize the cultural moment. John Hawkins felt obliged to apologise for Johnson's pronouncements on Scotland: many of his criticisms were contradicted by his own evidence; if Johnson 'stigmatized Scotland as a country, and the Scots as a people, his compliments to individuals, in some measure atone for it'. Hawkins commented: 'I will not repeat, for I do not wish to perpetuate, those passages that have given disgust. I have ever esteemed the Scots as a brave, hospitable, and virtuous people, and should be very sorry if they imagined Johnson's prejudices common to their southern neighbours.'[124] But Hawkins was a Whig. As another Whig observed, reacting against Johnson's charge that 'A Scotchman must be a very sturdy moralist who does not love Scotland better than truth': 'Strange that a man pensioned by the Government should write so unlike a gentleman, revive the national distinction abolished by the Union, the very first article of which ought to

[120] Ibid., pp. 297, 354–5.

[121] Edward Gibbon, *The History of the Decline and Fall of the Roman Empire* vol. I (London, 1776), p. 133. Gibbon confided to a footnote (p. xx, n.14) a scholarly doubt which in fact exposed Macpherson's fraud.

[122] Ibid., pp. 355–6. For an argument that James Macpherson was responsible for some scurrilous passages interpolated into M'Nichol's text, see Robert F. Metzdorf, 'M'Nichol, Macpherson, and Johnson', in W. H. Bond (ed.), *Eighteenth-Century Studies in Honor of Donald F. Hyde* (New York, 1970), pp. 45–61.

[123] See below, p. 238. [124] Hawkins, *Life*, pp. 483–4.

make you ashamed.'[125] By 1787 Scotland had been redefined in the current English perspective from a haven of Jacobite rebellion to be a model of Whig uprightness.

[125] Henderson, *Letter to Dr Samuel Johnson*, pp. 25, 46. Henderson, as an historian of the forty-five, insisted that very few Scots had been 'in actual rebellion', and that this was evidence for their loyalty to King George (p. 48).

3

THE POLITICAL CULTURE OF OXFORD UNIVERSITY, 1715–1768

I. OXFORD'S PUBLIC IMAGE

Classical learning naturally pointed the young Johnson in one direction, and as the horizon of his world expanded, the political significance of his cultural commitments became ever more prominent. From a school and family background in which (as will be shown) the issues of hereditary right, sacred monarchy and political allegiance were explicitly understood, Johnson passed to Oxford University. Before considering his career there, the political culture which Oxford and Cambridge then sustained must be established as the appropriate context for Johnson's own conduct. For these politico-theological issues were not merely the atavistic concerns of a rural backwater like Lichfield; they were debated and contested at national level also by the intellectual and social elite, above all at the universities. Dr Matthew Panting (c. 1683–1739), Master of Pembroke during Johnson's residence, Johnson called 'a fine Jacobite fellow'.[1] It is important to know how widely such perceptions were entertained.

Whigs were in little doubt on the issue. Dudley Ryder, a Dissenter and later Attorney General, predicted in July 1715 that the securely Protestant university of Leyden would henceforth be 'very much frequented by the English, ours having so little advantage for learning and besides extremely corrupt in principle, that the Whigs will be afraid to send their sons there'.[2] His opinion was not based on personal knowledge, for as a Dissenter he was excluded; this did not prevent Whigs from making more public what had been widely known since the Revolution. With the accession of William III

[1] Boswell, *Life*, vol. 1, p. 73.

[2] William Matthews (ed.), *The Diary of Dudley Ryder 1715–1716* (London, 1939), p. 65; cf. his entry for 11 August 1716 (p. 74): Samuel Powell (matriculated at Queen's College, Oxford, in 1714) called. 'I inquired about the University of Oxford. He says they are so busy about the church and politics that nothing else goes forward with them: learning or politeness has nothing to do there, and they are so infected with their Tory principles that a Whig is a kind of monster to them and carries in its [sic] ideas with them the worst of characters, everything that is ill' (cf. Powell's second report, ibid., p. 143).

in 1689, Tories had been confronted by a new and bleak prospect of discrimination and future exclusion from all forms of office and preferment, whether in central government, the armed forces, the church, the law or the universities; Jacobites faced in addition a campaign of persecution aimed at searching them out and expelling them from the posts which they currently held. In 1714, with the accession of George I, this persecution was renewed and intensified.[3] Members of the Old Interest had their doctrinal integrity to vindicate but also their livelihoods to defend: they responded by creating enclaves in many walks of life in which men of similar principles would be recognised, respected and protected. Chief among these enclaves was the University of Oxford.

In the aftermath of the Fifteen, Whigs responded to the fact of widespread subversion with a call for a purge of disloyal clergy, and traced both their political principles and their allegedly irregular private lives to the same source:

> What wonder will it be, that the inferior Clergy are debauch'd in Morals, disloyal in Politicks, heretical in Principles, prophane in Conversation, when we shall trace them back to their Erudition, and find that they were bred up in all these at the Colleges, where they were placed to be furnish'd with Learning and good Morals, and where they suck in Vice instead of Virtue, profligate Manners instead of Modesty and Sobriety, and Prophaneness instead of Piety; that there they learnt to trifle with Oaths, swallow them carelessly, observe them negligently, and construe them Jesuitically![4]

Dissenters, too, took seriously the religious obligations of oaths, and could argue that such practices at the universities promoted a lasting dishonesty which violated a sacred obligation:

> this Excuse for taking Oaths at random, is made use of by the same Persons after they come from the University; and when we now charge the Jacobite Clergy, with having taken the Oaths to the Government; the Abjuration, *&c.* and to challenge them for not observing them, their Answer is, that these Oaths are but Matters of Form, taken of Course, that are Customary upon every change of Government, and like the Customary Oaths at the University; no Body takes any Notice of them, or troubles themselves about them.[5]

What occurred at the universities was nevertheless of particular importance:

[3] Eveline Cruickshanks, *Political Untouchables: The Tories and the '45* (London, 1979), pp. 4–5.

[4] [?Daniel Defoe], *Reasons for a Royal Visitation; Occasion'd by the Present Great Defection of the Clergy from the Government. Shewing The Absolute Necessity of Purging the Universities, and Restoring Discipline to the Church* (London, 1717), p. 15.

[5] Ibid., p. 20.

We are a Nation miserably divided into Parties and Factions, and the Spirit of Division having spread over the whole Kingdom, it is no wonder that we find it over-running our Universities also. But there are, who say that this Spirit of Division is propagated, and spread, even by, and from the Universities, as it respects the Disaffection to the Person of the King, and to the Succession of his whole Race; and that the Spirit of Jacobitism has so effectually possess'd the Colleges and Students in both the Cities of *Oxford* and *Cambridge*; that they are at this Time the Centre of Disaffection and Disloyalty to the whole Body of the Kingdom.[6]

If Matthew Panting, Master of Pembroke College during Johnson's residence, held the views Johnson ascribed to him, it is less surprising that Panting was soon led to devote a sermon to the nature of 'Religious Obligations', especially those 'Voluntary Engagements', vows. If, argued Panting, 'a Vow, when lawfully and regularly made, carries always an Obligation of Duty along with it, the Breach of it must consequently be always attended with Guilt, or an Obligation to Punishment'. There was, of course, an escape: 'those Vows must of themselves be null and void, which would seem to oblige to any thing unlawful'.[7] One author even condemned the practice of drinking healths (by implication, to the Pretender) as 'an *abuse* of a sacred Ordinance; and a performance of that Action *privately* to *man*, which should be applied to none but CHRIST, and in our *solemn* worship'.[8] A rationale like Panting's could nevertheless defend the survival of a widespread political culture. Lady Binning, in Oxford in 1738, characterised the place for her uncle: 'All the news I can tell you is that we are all Jacobits'; she had heard a story that a Colonel Campbell had been at Court 'when a noble Lord, whom he wou[l]d not name, told the King St Marry Hall was a nest of all the Scots Jacobits who came there on purpose to support it ... We were also told we were obliged to some of our friends and countrymen of Christ Church for that character.'[9]

Such identifications are easily explicable in the aftermath of 1688, but they remained as vivid in the wake of the Fifteen and can be found, just as stridently expressed, in the years immediately following the Forty-five. The very extremism of Whig and anticlerical denunciations, especially in the decade following the accesssion of George I, can be used to suggest that

6 Ibid., p. 33. For a review of similar attacks see *The Danger of the Church-Establishment of England, From the Insolence of Protestant Dissenters ... In a Letter to Sir John Smith* (London, 1718), esp. pp. 45–52.

7 Matthew Panting, *Religious Vows. A Sermon Preach'd at the Consecration of a Chapel in Pembroke-College in Oxford, On Monday, July 10. 1732* (Oxford, 1732), pp. 9, 24–5.

8 [Peter Browne], *A Letter to a Reverend Gentleman in Oxford, On the Subject of Drinking Healths* (London, 1722), pp. 6–7.

9 Rachel Baillie, Lady Binning, to Alexander Earl of Marchmont, 22 March 1738: HMC *Polwarth*, vol. 5 (1961), p. 213.

most Oxonians were moderates, or politically disengaged. But however much successive Vice Chancellors and Heads of Houses sought to mitigate or disguise the evidence,[10] continued minor instances of disorder and seditious libel kept Oxford in the news as a place where dynastic disaffection was not far beneath the surface.[11] One famous instance was the Jacobite riot of 23 February 1747/8, during the course of which, as was testified at his trial, James Dawes accosted a proctor with the words, 'I am the man that dare say God bless King James the 3d and tell you my Name is Dawes of St Mary Hall. I am a man of an Independent Fortune and therefore am afraid of *no one or no man*.'[12] It was unlucky that Dawes chose to address the Whig informer and placehunter Richard Blacow, who exploited the incident to secure a canonry of Windsor for himself and a two year prison sentence for the undergraduate. In other circumstances such declarations went unpunished; indeed they were condoned.

More important than these minor disturbances, and giving significance to them, was the long persistence of a certain ideological framework which preserved the dynastic issue at its high level of political and theological sophistication and prevented its dismissal as sentimentality. Whigs indeed wished to dismiss the rebels of 1715 as 'the vicious, the wicked, the profligate, and profane', but one Whig conceded in 1749:

> Yet I must confess there was a great Number amongst them of a different Stamp, Persons who did really act upon Principle, who believ'd in their Consciences, that the *Pretender* was the only rightful Heir to the *Crown*, and in Consequence of such a Persuasion concluded that he had a legal Right to their Aid and Assistance. And here it shou'd be carefully observed, that the Seeds of Disloyalty and Disaffection had for a long Time been sewing, in our Universities, and other more private Seminaries of Learning; the Minds of great Numbers of our Nobility, Gentry, and Commonalty, had been greatly corrupted and depraved, by those who had the Charge of their Education. They had been educated in all the old, absurd, and ridiculous Notions of Government, as *passive Obedience, Non-resistance,* and that of an *absolute indefeasible hereditary Right,* and had been always accustomed to hear, a parliamentary Right to the Crown treated as a most wicked and infamous Usurpation.[13]

Even after the suppression of the Fifteen, 'the Spirit of Rebellion was far from being quelled; the old Principles still prevailed; and those who had corrupted and depraved the Minds of the People, were still left in Possession

[10] P. Langford, 'Tories and Jacobites' in L.S. Sutherland and L.G. Mitchell (eds.), *The History of the University of Oxford*, vol. 5 (Oxford, 1986), pp. 99–127.

[11] For which, see especially W.R. Ward, *Georgian Oxford: University Politics in the Eighteenth Century* (Oxford, 1958), pp. 52–213.

[12] M. Sharpe to Hardwicke, 4 November 1748: BL Add MSS 35887, f. 24.

[13] *A Blow at the Root: or, an Attempt to Prove, That no Time ever was, or very probably ever will be, so proper and convenient as the Present, for introducing a further Reformation into our National Church, Universities, and Schools* (London, 1749), pp. v–vi.

of that great and important Trust, the Education of our Youth'. This was still true, claimed the pamphleteer, after the Forty-five.[14]

It had been true enough in an earlier decade for William Murray (1705–93), at Christ Church from 1723 to 1727. He later pursued a brilliant but uneasy career within the Hanoverian establishment as Solicitor General (1742–54) and Attorney General (1754–56), before finally abandoning the House of Commons with relief, moving to the Lords as Lord Mansfield on taking the post of Lord Chief Justice (1756–88). His undergraduate loyalties were rather different. In Paris in the long vacation of his second year at Oxford, Murray had written to his brother-in-law John Hay, Earl of Inverness and Secretary of State to James III:

> I flatter myself you will excuse the ambition of a young man, if I make use of the freedom I at present have, to desire you to make a tender of my duty and loyalty to the King; a very small present, but all I have to offer. Twill in some measure excuse my presumption for offering my service, though in so private a station as not to be able to render any considerable, that I do it at a time when so many are wanting to their duty, that 'tis some merit to protest against it ... The chief end I would propose from my studies and education, and the greatest glory I can aim at is to be able to serve his Majesty in any way that he pleases to command me.[15]

But Murray's youthful commitment was a secret that could not be kept, caused a crisis in 1753 which he only narrowly survived,[16] and blocked his rise to the highest office under George II. Nor was Murray the only figure in public life with a skeleton in his cupboard.

Oxford's predominant loyalties were common knowledge: so was the contradiction which this created with the formal professions of Oxonians. One pamphleteer in 1750, outraged by William King's evocation of Oxford's loyalties at the opening of the Radcliffe Camera,[17] addressed the dons of the university with heavy irony:

> who is it that is ignorant that *you* take the *Oaths* to *King George*, and *abjure* the *Pretender*, not a *Man* of you *excepted*? It is likewise, I believe, pretty well known even at Paris, and at *Rome*, what *Sort* of *People* are *most caressed* at *all* your *publick Meetings*, your *Races*, your *High Borlace*,[18] &c. and how you dispose of your Places of *Honour*, *Trust*, and *Profit*. Your *Members* of *Parliament* too! How *warmly* they have *always* spoken of the *Revolution*? Their *Respect* how singular to the *present Government*? How *zealous* in *its Defence* in the *late Rebellion*?

14 Ibid., pp. vii, xv.

15 Murray to Hay, 6 August 1725: Stuart Papers, Windsor, 85/21, quoted in Romney Sedgwick (ed.), *The History of Parliament: The House of Commons 1715–1754* (2 vols., London, 1970), vol. 2, p. 285.

16 J. C. D. Clark (ed.), *The Memoirs and Speeches of James, 2nd Earl Waldegrave, 1742–1763* (Cambridge, 1988), pp. 48–64.

17 For which, see above, pp. 38–40.

18 The High Borlace was an Oxford festivity which occurred annually in August.

Central to this claim were the oath of allegiance and the oath of abjuration, 'which *Oaths* they *all* take, as above observed, and *most* of them again and again'.[19] The issue had refused to fade away, and had survived as a major problem for the intellectual integrity of a large section of the English intelligentsia. Even in 1755, the prospect of a French invasion led one Whig to speculate on the sources of support in England for such an adventure: 'If they have any encouragement to it, it must procede from that spirit of Jacobitism, which is so industriously nursed up in that University, of which Dr Huddesford their Vice Chancellor has the impudence to say, that there is not a body of Men in England who are more sincerely attached to King George than the generality of them are. Hardily asserted! But God forbid that the possession of the present Family should ever depend upon their voice!'[20] It was to George Huddesford that Samuel Johnson in the same year addressed his letter of thanks for Oxford's honorary degree.[21]

II. STATE OATHS AND THE INTELLIGENTSIA

The problems of allegiance which Oxford confronted were given a particular focus by the state oaths imposed (and sometimes evaded) in the aftermath of the Revolution of 1688.[22] Such oaths were aimed principally at office-holders in church and state, but the universities were carefully provided for also. For those not instinctively in sympathy with the new regime, new legislation might seem like a formidable code of legal persecution. The Act of I W & M, s. 1, c. 8 imposed the oaths of allegiance and supremacy on Heads of Houses, Fellows and Professors, as well as on civil and military officers.[23] After the Hanoverian accession, the Act of I Geo I, s. 2, c. 13 reasserted the duty of taking oaths for a list of persons including all 'Heads, or Governours, and all other Members of Colleges and Halls in either University, being of the Foundation, or who enjoy any Exhibition (being of the Age of 18.) And all Persons teaching or reading to Pupils in the Universities, or elsewhere'; and two or more JPs were authorised to tender the oaths 'to any Persons they shall suspect to be disaffected'. The

19 *Oxford Honesty: or, a Case of Conscience, Humbly put to the Worshipful and Reverend The Vice-Chancellor, The Heads of Houses, The Fellows, &c. of The University of Oxford. Whether One may take the Oaths to King George; and yet, consistently with Honour, and Conscience, and the Fear of God, may do all one can in Favour of the Pretender? Occasioned by the Oxford Speech, and Oxford Behaviour, at the Opening of Radcliff's Library, April 13, 1749* (2nd edn, London, 1750), pp. 5–6; first published as *A Case of Conscience* ... (London, [1749]).

20 Thomas Edwards to Samuel Richardson, 4 February 1755: Bodleian MS Bodl 1012, f. 188.

21 For which, see below, pp. 182–3.

22 For the working of this system at local level, see E. H. Carter, *The Norwich Subscription Books: A Study of the Subscription Books of the Diocese of Norwich 1637–1800* (London, 1937).

23 *A Summary of the Penal Laws relating to Nonjurors, Papists, Popish Recusants, and Nonconformists* (London, 1716), pp. 58–61.

oaths of allegiance and supremacy remained in the same form as those prescribed by I W & M, s. 1, c. 8; the oath of abjuration was brought up to date to focus on James III.[24]

The existence of national oaths imposed duties on members of the universities, junior and senior. Oxford's statutes gave effect to them and provided a procedure for tendering the oaths, adding to much older provisions to secure religious conformity. As they were summed up in the age of reform,

By the Statutes of the University of Oxford up to the year 1837, all students above sixteen years of age were required to sign the Thirty-nine Articles of the Church of England, to take the oath of supremacy, and the oath to observe the Statutes. Students above twelve and under sixteen were *only* required to sign the Thirty-nine articles.[25]

That this was a correct account of the requirements at matriculation as they stood in Johnson's Oxford is proved both by the full text of the Statutes, and by the handbook to them produced for undergraduate use. In the University Statutes, Title II, De Matricula Universitatis, read:

Quotquot autem in Matriculam Universitatis redigendi accedunt, si decimum sextum suæ ætatis annum attigerint, Articulis fidei & Religionis subscribant, & de agnoscendo primatu Regiæ Majestatis; nec non de fidelitate Universitati exhibenda; Statutis, Privilgeiis, & consuetudinibus eiusdem observandis, juxta formam hactenus usitatam, corporale juramentum præstent.

Quod si infra decimum sextum & supra duodecimum ætatis annum extiterint, Articulis fidei & Religionis duntaxat subscribent, & in Matriculam redigentur.[26]

As a record of matriculation, the undergraduate would receive a document like that given to Johnson's near-contemporary at Pembroke College, Joshua Ellis:

Oxoniae. Dec. 14. Anno Domini 1727.

Quo die comparuit coram me Joshua Ellis e Coll Pembr generosi fil et subscripsit Articulis Fidei, et Religionis; et juramentum suscepit de agnoscenda suprema Regiae Majestatis potestae; et de observandis Statutis, Privilegiis et Consuetudinibus huius Universitatis.

Jo. Mather, Vice-Can.[27]

[24] Ibid., pp. 94–104.

[25] H.A. Pottinger, *University Tests: A Short Account of the Contrivances by which the Acts of Parliament abolishing Tests and Declarations have been evaded at Oxford* (London, 1873), p. 3.

[26] *Parecbolae sive Excerpta è Corpore Statutorum Universitatis Oxoniensis. Accedunt Articuli Religionis XXXIX. In Ecclesia Anglicana recepti: nec non Juramenta Fidelitatis & Suprematus. In Usum Juventutis Academiae* (Oxford, 1729), p. 4.

[27] George Birkbeck Hill (ed.), *Johnsonian Miscellanies* (2 vols., Oxford, 1897), vol. 2, p. 85.

It is clear, then, that undergraduates were not required to take the oaths of allegiance and abjuration on matriculation.[28]

The requirement that those of twelve years of age or upwards subscribe the Thirty-nine Articles of the Church of England on their matriculation dated back to a university Statute of 1581; it was a requirement which became the central point of controversy only in the 1770s with the advance of heterodoxy. One advocate of the relaxation of subscription to the Articles was obliged to argue against any parallel with the case of 'young Men of sixteen or eighteen abjuring the Pope's Supremacy, which Abjuration is at that Age required': the latter was 'one simple Proposition' required from those who had attained the age of discretion; the former was a series of complex and profound points required from boys below that age.[29] In 1772, at the time of the Feathers Tavern petition to Parliament against the imposition of subscription to the Thirty-nine articles, Johnson defended requiring this subscription from undergraduates: 'the meaning of subscribing is, not that they fully understand all the articles, but that they will adhere to the Church of England'.[30] Johnson again defended subscription in 1773: 'As all who come into the country must obey the King, so all who come into an university must be of the Church.'[31] Clearly it was not oaths as such which troubled Johnson, nor the problems of youthful subscription, nor the renunciation of Popery, but certain oaths in particular. These would face the student at a later stage of his Oxford career.

Title IX, §3, 'De subscriptione ante Praesentationem exigenda', laid down the procedure on graduation:

Cum Præsentandus vel Præsentandi, ad Apodyterium Domui Congregationis vicinum devenerint, eorum quilibet Articulis Fidei & Religionis in Synodo Londini Anno Dom. 1562. editis & confirmatis (lectis prius, vel alio recitante, auditis in præsentia Præsentatoris sui) necnon tribus Articulis in 36. Canone comprehensis (lectis prius ibidem, & publice, coram Præsentatore, in præsentia Procuratorum) subscribet; qui quidem tres Articuli descripti sunt Canone 36. Libri Constitutionum & Canonum Ecclesiasticorum, in Synodo Londini coepta Anno Dom. 1603.[32]

28 Greene (*Politics*, pp. xxx–xxxi), arguing that Johnson was not a Nonjuror, asks 'what had graduation to do with taking oaths?' and suggests that these oaths would have been required of undergraduates, by implication at matriculation. This requirement in fact applied only to undergraduates 'of the foundation', i.e. to those holding scholarships, servitorships, etc. There was evidently no procedure which would have required their subscription of all undergraduates (foundationers excepted) before graduation.

29 *A Complete and Faithful Collection of the Several Papers which have been Published in Oxford, On the Subject of Subscription to the XXXIX Articles, Required from Young Persons at their Matriculation* (Oxford, 1772), pp. 56–7.

30 Boswell, *Life*, vol. 2, pp. 150–1.

31 Boswell, *Journal*, p. 43; Boswell, *Life*, vol. 5 (*Tour*), pp. 64–5.

32 *Parecbolae*, p. 108; cf. *Corpus Statutorum Universitatis Oxoniensis* (Oxford, 1768), p. 92.

The Undergraduate could then turn to an Appendix to find these oaths in full. The first was as set out in the Church of England's 36th Canon of 1562:

Three Articles in the 36th Canon.

I. That the Queen's Majesty under God, is the only Supream Governour of this Realm, and of all other her Highness Dominions and Countreys, as well in all Spiritual or Ecclesiastical things or causes, as Temporal; and that no Foreign Prince, Person, Prelate, State or Potentate, hath or ought to have any Jurisdiction, Power, Superiority, Preeminence or Authority, Ecclesiastical or Spiritual, within her Majesty's said Realms, Dominions and Countreys.

II. That the Book of Common Prayer, and of Ordering of Bishops, Priests and Deacons, containeth in it nothing contrary to the word of God, and that it may lawfully be used, and that I my self will use the Form in the said Book prescribed in publick Prayer, and Administration of the Sacraments, and none other.

III. That I allow the Book of Articles of Religion agreed upon by the Arch-Bishops and Bishops of both Provinces, and the whole Clergy in the Convocation holden at *London* in the year of our Lord God, One thousand five hundred sixty and two: and that I acknowledge all and every the Articles therein contained, being in number Nine and thirty, besides the Ratification, to be agreeable to the Word of God.

The Oath of Allegiance.

I A.B. do sincerely Promise and Swear, That I will be faithful, and bear true Allegiance to His Majesty King *George*.

So help me God, &c.

The Oath of Supremacy

I A.B. do Swear, That I do from my Heart Abhor, Detest, and Abjure, as Impious and Heretical, that damnable Doctrine and Position, *That Princes Excommunicated or Deprived by the Pope, or any Authority of the See of* Rome, *may be Deposed or Murthered by their Subjects, or any other whatsoever.*

And I do declare, That no Foreign Prince, Person, Prelate, State or Potentate, hath, or ought to have any Jurisdiction, Power, Superiority, Preeminence, or Authority Ecclesiastical or Spiritual within this Realm.

So help me God, &c.[33]

A literally-minded Jacobite and Nonjuror would be able, without violating his conscience, to matriculate: the oath of supremacy, disowning the authority of any 'Foreign Prince', would not, for him, apply to the elder member of the House of Stuart. He could not, however, graduate, for that would require the oath of allegiance; still less could he take a fellowship, for that would call for the oath of abjuration comprehensively disowning the

[33] *Parecbolae*, pp. 227–8.

exiled dynasty. The only degrees Nonjurors could obtain were honorary ones,[34] as, in 1728, the degree of Doctor of Medicine was conferred by diploma on the Nonjuror Dr William Fullerton, though in the face of politically-motivated opposition in Convocation.[35]

Partly in response to the Jacobite riot on 23 February 1747/8, the birthday of Prince Henry Stuart,[36] one officious Whig tutor (Edward Bentham, Fellow of Oriel) compiled an 'Antidote for the Use of his Pupils', necessary since 'the wretched Spirit of Party-Zeal seldom fails to enflame their Imaginations, and betray them into various Extravagancies'. The antidote was:

You would do well therefore to consider seriously, that, "*If any shall endeavour advisedly or directedly, to hinder any Person, who shall be next in succession to the Crown for the Time being*, (according to the Limitation by the 1 & 2 W. & M. Sess. 2 C. 2 and the 12 W. III C. 2) *He is guilty of High-Treason. And those that maliciously and directly affirm the same by Preaching, or advised Speaking shall incure a* Praemunire. 1 & 2 Anne, C. 17.

By the 13 W. III C. 3. *To have Correspondence or keep Intelligence with the pretended Prince of* Wales, *or knowingly with any Person employed by him, or to pay Money for his Use, is High-Treason.*

By the 4 Anne, C. 8. 6 Anne, C.7. *Whosoever shall advisedly and directly, by writing or printing, maintain that the pretended Prince of* Wales, *or any other, hath any Right to the Crown otherwise than by the* 1 and 2 W. and M. Sess. 2. C. 2. and the 12 W. III. C. 2. Or, *that the Kings of this Realm by the Authority of Parliament cannot make Laws to limit and bind the Crown as to the Descent and Government thereof, shall be guilty of High-Treason.*[37]

But Bentham addressed a hypothetical pupil of very different inclinations: 'Do you not ... consider yourself as the rightful Subject of one whose only Claim to your Subjection is his being a Lineal Descendant of a Person formerly invested with Royal Power?'[38] Bentham offered a defence of the

34 Oxford in the early eighteenth century conferred large numbers of honorary degrees: the political position of their recipients deserves study. See *A Catalogue of all Graduats in Divinity, Law, and Physick: and of all Masters of Arts and Doctors of Musick: Who have regularly Proceeded, or been Created, in the University of Oxford, Between October 10th. 1659, and October 10th. 1726* (Oxford, 1727); *The Catalogue of Graduats &c. in the University of Oxford, Continued from October 10. 1727. to October 10. 1735*, continued ... *October 10. 1735 to October 10. 1747* and ... *October 10. 1747 to October 10. 1760.*

35 A.D. Godley, *Oxford in the Eighteenth Century* (London, 1908), p. 183; Charles Webster, in *The History of the University of Oxford*, vol. 5 (Oxford, 1986), pp. 687–8.

36 For which, see Ward, *Georgian Oxford*, pp. 170–1, and Richard Blacow, *A Letter to William King LL.D., Principal of St Mary Hall in Oxford; containing a Particular Account of the Treasonable Riot at Oxford, in February 1747* (London, 1755); cf. *An Answer to Mr. Blacow's Apology* (London, 1755).

37 [Edward Bentham], *A Letter To a Young Gentleman. By a Tutor, and Fellow of a College in Oxford* ([Oxford], 1748), pp. 9–10. For the occasion of this pamphlet, see pp. 91, 182–3.

38 Ibid., p. 14.

Revolution, and urged his pupil to give serious thought to it, since 'Upon your promotion to any *Degree*, you will be called upon to take the Oath of *Allegiance*; and if advanced to any Preferment, in or out of the University, any Office Military, Civil, or Ecclestiastical, you must necessarily take the Oath of *Abjuration*.' This applied at Oxford too: 'All Heads, Fellows and Foundationers of Colleges or Halls, all Readers or Tutors in the University are required to take the Oath of *Abjuration*, under penalty of forfeiting their Places, and Five hundred Pounds, if exercising any Office.'[39]

For the benefit of the Oxford of 1750, Edward Bentham then printed the texts of the oaths in force. The first was difficult enough; but even a man torn in his conscience, who might acknowledge some right in the House of Hanover, might be repelled by the second.

The Oath of Allegiance

I A.B. *do sincerely promise and swear, that I will be faithful, and bear true Allegiance to his Majesty King* George:

So help me God.

The Oath of Abjuration

I A.B. *do truly and sincerely acknowledge, profess, testify, and declare in my Conscience, before God and all the World, That our Sovereign Lord King* George *is lawful and rightful King of this Realm, and all his Majesty's Dominions thereunto belonging. And I do solemnly and sincerely declare, That I do believe in my Conscience, that the Person pretended to be the Prince of* Wales, *during the Life of the late King* James, *and since his Decease, pretending to be, and taking upon himself the Stile and Title of King of* England, *by the Name of* James *the Third, or of* Scotland, *by the Name of* James *the Eighth, or the Stile and title of King of* Great-Britain, *hath not any Right or Title whatsoever to the Crown of this Realm, or any other the Dominions thereto belonging: And I do renounce, refuse, and abjure any Allegiance or Obedience to him. And I do swear, that I will bear true Faith and true Allegiance to his Majesty King* George, *and him will defend, to the utmost of my Power, against all Traiterous Conspiracies and Attempts whatsoever, which shall be made against his Person, Crown, or Dignity. And I will do my utmost Endeavour to disclose and make known to his Majesty, and his Successors, all Treasons and Traiterous Conspiracies which I shall know to be against him, or any of them. And I do faithfully promise, to the utmost of my Power, to support, maintain, and defend the Succession of the Crown against him the said* James, *and all other Persons whatsoever; which Succession, by an Act, intituled,* An Act for the further Limitation of the Crown, and better securing the Rights and Liberties of the Subject, *is and stands limited to the Princess* Sophia, *Electress and Dutchess Dowager of* Hanover, *and the Heirs of her Body, being* Protestants. *And all these Things, I do plainly and sincerely acknowledge and swear, according to these express Words by me spoken, and according to the plain and common Sense and Understanding of the same Words, without any Equivocation, mental Evasion, or secret Reservation whatsoever. And I do make this Recognition, Acknowledgement, Abjur-*

[39] Ibid., p. 27.

ation, Renunciation, and Promise, heartily, willingly, and truly, upon the true Faith of a Christian.

So help me God.[40]

Whigs were outraged that Tories might seem to escape the consequences of a solemn oath. Even in 1750, a Whig don protested:

He, who can, for his own Temporal Advantage, enter into Obligations *sacred* and *solemn*, as the Oaths of *Allegiance* and *Abjuration* are, and This done, dispute, clamour, drink, or riot for the Person whom He has abjured, then wipe his Mouth and say 'I have done no Wickedness,' must have a System of Morality peculiar to Himself, must be deaf to the Voice of *Persuasion*, must be left to the Lashes of a *Fiend* of his own creating, an *Evil Conscience*.

Oxford dons had all taken the oaths of allegiance and abjuration: were they not perjured? Why, except in two or three colleges, were all candidates for fellowships rejected 'as labour under a Suspicion of any Zeal for the Government'?[41] Defining and defending the regime in this way had its predictable effect. By mid-century, a lawyer deplored 'the general Disregard to the Obligation of Oaths'. The author offered, as one explanation:

The frequent Imposition of Oaths by late Acts of Parliament, and annexing them to such Things as concern the Interest, and, in some Instances, the very Being and Subsistence, of the Taker of the Oath, must have greatly contributed to the Increase of Perjury ... I believe the general Oath of Allegiance, imposed some Years since, occasioned more Perjury than Religion could prevent in Half a Century: Never was an Oath more profaned. It is remembered how Persons, of all Conditions and Denominations, flocked in Crowds to make this faithless Test of their Allegiance; and yet, after all this wise Precaution, could the King count one Friend more? Were there not as evident Marks of Disaffection after, as before; and even by those who had made this mock Testimonial of the Loyalty?[42]

Samuel Johnson never profaned such an oath; he never took it.

III. TEMPORA MUTANTUR, 1750–1768

By the 1750s, some sought a different way of formulating Tory identity. Henry Brooke attempted to reconcile the Tories by taking them at their word:

[40] [Bentham], *A Letter To a Young Gentleman*, pp. 29–31. Ironically, Bentham was to support Johnson for a honorary DCL in 1775, after Lord North had proposed it following Johnson's pro-ministerial pamphlets; Bentham had a speech ready in case there was opposition to the Grace in Convocation proposing the degree, though none materialised. Johnson to Edward Bentham, 8 April 1775: Johnson, *Letters*, vol. 2, p. 196.

[41] [Henry Brooke], *A Letter to the Oxford Tories. By an Englishman* (London, 1750), pp. 4–7.

[42] *A Treatise concerning Oaths and Perjury* (London, 1750), pp. 6–7.

I call you *Tories*, because such you call yourselves: But the real and essential Difference between a Church of England Academick *Tory* and a Church of England Academick *Whig* is, I confess, a Secret to my Understanding; both these having subscribed the same Articles of *Religious* Faith; both having given to the same Government the same Solemn Security for their *Civil* Obedience: Surely then there can be no Absurdity in an Assertion that a Distinction made between Members of the same Communion, *sworn* Subjects to the same *Prince*, is a Distinction without a *Difference*, an Opposition in *Name* only, destitute of any Foundation in *Fact*.

Tories were 'eager on all Occasions to disavow the Creed of *Jacobitism*': this proved that real Jacobites were 'inconsiderable' in number. But how reasonable was that supposition, if, 'on a fair Scrutiny into the Conduct of the Leaders of your Party, for more than thirty Years last past, it shall appear that no one *Minister*, no one *Measure* of Government has obtained your Approbation, or escaped your Displeasure'? Was it not reasonable to think 'that your Dislike to *every* Publick Measure proceeds from a determined Aversion to "*the Powers that Be*?"'[43] Brooke may have sought a reconciliation, but no sooner did he turn to review the actual conduct of the Oxford Tories than his bitter resentment showed how difficult that task was to be.[44] With a closing threat which perhaps echoed Johnson's *Marmor Norfolciense*, Brooke warned: 'the little Efforts of *Malice* and *Scurrility*, low *Libels* in Prose and Verse, in *Monkish* or in *Modern* Rhime, the petulant Ingenuity of *Grubstreet*, or the more sonorous Oratory of *Billingsgate* shall not deprive me of a Moment's Rest'.[45]

One pamphleteer hoped to win Tories to the idea that they were 'True-blues'; he had himself been 'educated in *True-blue* Principles ... My Father and Grandfather were both *True-blues*' who laboured 'in promoting every Measure, and bringing about every End, that could in the least contribute to the *Welfare* of the Kingdom, the *sole* object our Party ever had in View, and *have* to this Day'. These 'Principles of *True-bluism*', first upheld by Hampden, secondly by Lord Russell, were to be understood as libertarian and anti-Catholic, and quite different from the 'Old Interest', if this was to be defined as 'the Old Jacobite Interest'.[46] Nevertheless, although a shift in the wind began to be discerned in the 1750s, many of the figures of an earlier era were still the leading actors of that decade. When Johnson obtained his honorary MA from Oxford in 1755, the diploma was brought to him in London by Dr William King, Principal of St Mary Hall since

[43] [Brooke], *A Letter to the Oxford Tories*, pp. 3–6.
[44] Cf. the defence of Edward Bentham of Oriel (p. 7) or his attack on the 'Spleen and Malevolence' of William King's oration at the opening of the Radcliffe Camera (p. 23).
[45] Ibid., p. 24.
[46] *True-Blue: or, a Letter to the Gentlemen of the Old Interest in the County of Oxford* (London, 1754), pp. 4–7, 18.

Plate 3
The installation of the Earl of Westmoreland as Chancellor of the University of Oxford, 6 July 1759. Samuel Johnson attended this celebration of Tory triumph and may be represented in Worlidge's group portrait

1720.[47] Boswell added: 'We may conceive what a high gratification it must have been to Johnson to receive his diploma from the hands of the great DR. KING, whose principles were so congenial with his own.'[48] It seems that in this as in many other matters Johnson had been reticent on this sensitive subject, and Boswell had nothing explicit to quote.

King's Jacobite oration at the opening of the Radcliffe Library in 1749 was to be followed by an even more fervent public celebration. In 1759 Johnson was at Oxford '(which he visited almost every year)' during the instalment of the Earl of Westmoreland, the new Chancellor of the university: on which occasion he wore his academical gown in the theatre, where, he wrote, 'I have clapped my hands till they are sore, at Dr King's speech.'[49] The seventh Earl of Westmoreland was the Tory candidate for this life appointment, elected after some anxiety by the Tory interest following the demise aged 88 of the Tory-Jacobite Earl of Arran.[50] Westmoreland had an even more vivid background: he was one of those introduced to Charles Edward during the Prince's clandestine visit of 1750; in 1753, at a later stage of the Elibank plot, the Earl Marischal referred to Westmoreland and William King as 'Les deux principales personnes en Angleterre dans le secret'.[51] He was a natural successor to the brother of the attainted Duke of Ormonde, argued John Wilkes: 'To the earl of *Arran*, lord *Westmorland* succeeded, by the strongest of all recommendations to the university; for he was said to be the man in the kingdom most *personally* obnoxious to our late Sovereign.'[52] Westmoreland was expected by Tories, not unreasonably, to be the continuing patron and defender of the Tory cause, and the celebration of his installation reflected their triumph and relief.[53] It was no coincidence that Johnson's poems *London* and *The Vanity of Human Wishes* were reprinted in Oxford in 1759 as *Two Satires. By Samuel Johnson, A.M.*: their significance would be correctly appreciated in such an intellectual milieu.[54]

47 Hawkins, *Life*, p. 343. 48 Boswell, *Life*, vol. 1, p. 282n.

49 Thomas Tyers, 'A Biographical Sketch of Dr Samuel Johnson' in Brack and Kelley (eds.), *Early Biographies*, p. 89; Johnson to unknown, [July 1759]: Johnson, *Letters*, vol. 1, p. 186.

50 James Butler, 2nd Duke of Ormonde (1665–1745), was dismissed from his post of Captain-General soon after the arrival of George I in England in September 1714; in June 1715 he was impeached and in August left for exile in France. In September that year his brother Charles Butler, Earl of Arran (1671–1758) announced to the University of Oxford Ormonde's resignation as Chancellor and was elected in his place. Arran's secretary from his election in 1715 to December 1721 was William King, later Johnson's friend.

51 Earl Marischal to Frederick the Great, 7 May 1753: *Politische Correspondenz Friedrich's des Grossen* (39 vols., Berlin, 1879–1925), vol. 9, pp. 437ff; Greenwood, *William King*, p. 238.

52 *The North Briton*, no. 32 (8 January 1763).

53 Richard Sharp, 'The Oxford Installation of 1759', *Oxoniensia* 56 (1991), 145–53.

54 Two hundred and fifty copies of the work were printed 'At the Clarendon Printing House' as a private commission; Dr J. D. Fleeman suggests that Thomas Warton may have arranged it. I am grateful to Dr Fleeman for advice on this point.

By the 1760s, it was more evident that times were changing. In 1763 an anonymous pamphleteer assumed in print that role of licensed satirist which was once performed in person at Encaenia celebrations by the individual filling the occasional office of Terrae Filius. He reflected on how astonishingly politics had developed:

I can remember the Time, and indeed it is but a very little while ago, when a *Place* was esteemed at Oxford as a Badge of Corruption, and a *green* Coat the Livery of Servitude. I can remember too that a certain great Patriot informed the House of Commons, that *Oxford* was *paved* with Disaffection and Jacobitism.[55] But now the old *True Blue* is faced, according to the Court-fashion, with *Green*, and the red and white Roses were not more closely twined together by the Union of the Houses of York and Lancaster, than the OLD and NEW INTEREST in this County by the Coalition and Compromise at the late Election of Lord *Charles Spenser*, and Sir *James Dashwood*. We have lived to see the staunch Doctor *Blackstone* on the Point of being sent to *Ireland* as a Judge, and honoured with a Patent of Precedency and a Silk Gown. We have lived to see Sir *Francis Dashwood* created Lord *Le Despenser*, and appointed Chancellor of the Exchequer, and Master of the Wardrobe. Sir *John Philipps* it is well known is a Privy Counsellor, and our Right Honourable Chancellor is Captain of the Band of Pensioners.

Tempora mutantur, et nos mutamur in illis.

The Tories are all at Court, and Oxonians are made bishops. The *Cocoa-Tree*[56] is running a Race with *Arthur's*[57] towards the golden Goal of St James's;[58] and, it is said, that at the next Meeting of the Parliament a Bill will be brought in for *cleaning*, *lighting*, and NEW-PAVING the Streets of Oxford by the Right Honourable Mr. PITT.[59]

Hostile observers complained in similar terms:

If arbitrary Power is not the present favoured system, why is this notorious predilection for Toryism, so conspicuous? ... Has not the cocoa tree, for these many years *emptied* it's members into the chief *offices* of Trust and profit? Are not men of highflying tenets chosen to the highest departments of the state? ... Does it not seem

55 William Pitt, in the House of Commons on 27 November 1754: J. C. D. Clark, *The Dynamics of Change: The Crisis of the 1750s and English Party Systems* (Cambridge, 1982), p. 121.

56 The Cocoa Tree Chocolate House in Pall Mall was converted into a private club in c. 1745–6: its members were often 'suspected of Jacobite sympathies ... When Lord Bute came to power in 1761, the Cocoa Tree was known as the "Ministerial Club"': Bryant Lillywhite, *London Coffee Houses* (London, 1963), p. 164.

57 For the complex history of this institution see Lillywhite, *London Coffee Houses*, p. 92. Arthur's was the home of White's Club, which in the early eighteenth century was clearly identified with the Whigs.

58 I.e. St James's Palace and ministerial office.

59 *Terrae-Filius. Number IV. Friday, July 8, 1763* (London, [1763]), pp. 55–6. Greene (*Politics*, p. lii) argues that the idea that Tories were welcomed back into office in the early 1760s was merely Whig propaganda. Such evidence as this shows how Oxford Tories shared that perception.

as if having been friends to the Stuarts, was the strongest recommendation to favour?[60]

It was a critique now aimed at Johnson himself.

Yet not everything changed. Principles were more persistent than persons. In 1768 Johnson was in Oxford for the general election, and delighted that 'The Virtue of Oxford has once more prevailed' over 'the slaves of power, and the solicitors of favour'. The contest was a difficult one, prompted by the death of one of the sitting Members, Sir Walter Bagot, 5th Bt. (1702–68); Johnson witnessed the return of the survivor, Sir Roger Newdigate, 5th Bt. (1719–1806) with Francis Page, 'an Oxfordshire Gentleman of no name', against two government supporters, Charles Jenkinson and George Hay. Johnson commended the electors: 'it must be for ever pleasing to see men adhering to their principles against their interest, especially when you consider that these Voters are poor, and never can be much less poor but by the favour of those whom they are now opposing'.[61] If this was Johnson's disposition as late as 1768, how are the facts of his own family background and brief career as an undergraduate in 1728–9 to be interpreted?

60 *The Pamphlet entitled 'Taxation no Tyranny', candidly considered, and it's Arguments, and pernicious Doctrines, Exposed and Refuted* (London, [1775]), p. 117.

61 Johnson to Hester Thrale, 24 March 1768: Johnson, *Letters*, vol. 1, p. 299.

4

JOHNSON'S CAREER AND THE QUESTION OF THE OATHS, 1709–1758

I. JOHNSON'S FAMILY BACKGROUND

Johnson's family background was not distinguished. He called his cousin the Rev. Cornelius Harrison (1700–48) 'the only one of my relations who ever rose in fortune above penury or in character above neglect'.[1] Samuel Johnson began his career in urgent need of patronage and encouragement, and found these things, where he could, on either side of the party divide. Johnson's acquaintance in Lichfield included many Whigs. His grandfather on his mother's side was Cornelius Ford (1632–1709), a small landowner and evidently a Whig; his son, Johnson's mentor and cousin the Rev. Cornelius Ford (1694–1731) was clearly of that party. So was Gilbert Walmesley (1680–1751), whose father, William Walmesley (c. 1650–1713), had briefly been a Whig MP. Gilbert, Register of the Ecclesiastical Court of the Diocese of Lichfield from 1707 to his death, was an active patron of the young Johnson and his point of contact with the social circle of Lichfield Cathedral close; Johnson later recorded Gilbert Walmesley's zealous Whiggism.[2] Johnson's earliest biographers might easily have pointed to such social circles had they sought a context for their subject's Whig commitments, or for his wide and apolitical sympathies. They did not do so: on the contrary, they explored Samuel Johnson's Lichfield acquaintance to explain how he came to adopt the opposite opinions.

To Walmesley's memory, Johnson paid a magnanimous tribute: 'He was a Whig, with all the virulence and malevolence of his party; yet difference of opinion did not keep us apart. I honoured him, and he endured me.'[3] This was the Walmesley who had left Lichfield in disgust when the Tory peace of Utrecht was being celebrated in 1713; his Whig commitments

[1] Johnson to Hester Thrale, 12 August 1773: Johnson, *Letters*, vol. 2, pp. 48–9. Harrison had been a Fellow of Pembroke Hall, Cambridge, and was Perpetual Curate of Darlington, Co. Durham, 1727–48. Johnson might have mentioned his other cousin, the Rev. Cornelius Ford, but his early death presumably disqualified him.

[2] Greene, *Politics*, pp. 49–50, 62–5.

[3] Johnson, *Lives of the Poets*, vol. 2, p. 258.

were not in doubt. Much later, Boswell guessed that it was Walmesley whom Johnson meant in his observation on the subject of 'difference in political principles'. 'JOHNSON. It is much increased by opposition. There was a violent Whig, with whom I used to contend with much eagerness. After his death I felt my Toryism much abated.'[4] But Walmesley did not die until 1751, and Johnson's political commitments until that decade remained vivid. This was clear to contemporaries: when Johnson's *Life of Edmund Smith* was reprinted in the *St James's Chronicle* of 31 July 1779, the remarks on Gilbert Walmesley which it contained were seized on and quoted by a hostile critic as a self-condemnation out of Johnson's own mouth. Johnson had written that Walmesley was a Whig, and that Johnson was of 'different notions and opinions. But we are well informed, that Mr. Walmesley was no republican, but strongly attached in principle to the succession of the House of Hanover.' What then must Johnson's principles have been, asked his critic, if opposite to these?[5]

Although Staffordshire in general and Lichfield in particular had a royalist and Tory reputation, it was mixed in its historic allegiances, and had been profoundly divided in the 1640s: local families had been engaged on both sides as combatants during the Civil War. Yet this did not inspire in Johnson a desire to reconcile his contemporaries or do justice to Crown and Parliament, as the Whig James Boswell sought an eirenic perspective on the more recent 'civil war' (as he neutrally termed it) in Scotland. On the contrary, Johnson looked back on England's Civil War with horror. Even Milton shared in this censure: his republicanism was 'founded in an envious hatred of greatness, and a sullen desire of independence; in petulance impatient of controul, and pride disdainful of superiority. He hated monarchs in the state, and prelates in the church; for he hated all whom he was required to obey.' Milton was guilty of the faults of his age:

> It is scarcely possible, in the regularity and composure of the present time, to imagine the tumult of absurdity, and clamour of contradiction, that perplexed doctrine, and disturbed both publick and private quiet, in that age, when subordination was broken, and awe was hissed away; when any unsettled innovator who could hatch a half-formed notion produced it to the publick; when every man might become a preacher, and almost every preacher could collect a congregation.[6]

This historical perspective on the Civil War meant that Johnson was clearly marked out to his friends as 'a cordial well-wisher to the constitution in Church and State'. This led him to view English Dissenters with extreme caution:

[4] Boswell, *Journal*, p. 378 (10 November 1773).
[5] [Francis Blackburne], *Remarks on Johnson's Life of Milton* (London, 1780), pp. 113–4.
[6] Johnson, *Lives of the Poets*, vol. 1, pp. 217, 290.

Their religion, he frequently said, was too worldly, too political, too restless and ambitious. The doctrine of *cashiering* kings, and erecting on the ruins of the constitution a new form of government, which lately issued from their pulpits, he always thought was, under a calm disguise, the principle that lay lurking in their hearts. He knew that a wild democracy had overturned King, Lords, and Commons; and that a set of Republican Fanatics, who would not bow at the name of JESUS, had taken possession of all the livings and all the parishes in the kingdom. That those scenes of horror might never be renewed was the ardent wish of Dr Johnson; and though he apprehended no danger from Scotland, it is probable that his dislike of Calvinism mingled sometimes with his reflections on the natives of that country.[7]

Many of Johnson's early biographers sought to account for or excuse such political views as an inheritance from his family or his Lichfield acquaintance. This was not always easy to do if, as was commonplace in the three decades after the Glorious Revolution, men were often secretive about their true feelings for prudential reasons. This was evidently true of Samuel Johnson's father Michael, and may have given rise to the elder Johnson's reputation for Hanoverian probity in at least one local family. The poet Anna Seward noted in February 1763 that her grandfather John Hunter, master of the grammar school at Lichfield,

perceiving Johnson's abilities, had, to his own honour, taken as much pains with him as with the young gentlemen whose parents paid an high price for their pupilage; but my grandfather was a Jacobite, and Sam. Johnson had imbibed his master's absurd zeal for the forfeit rights of the house of Stuart; and this, though his father had very loyal principles; but the anxiety attendant on penurious circumstances, probably left old Johnson little leisure or inclination to talk on political subjects.[8]

Anna Seward implied that Samuel's father was publicly uncommunicative about his political views. John Hawkins, perhaps drawing on his subject's testimony, knew more about Michael: 'It may here be proper, as it will account for some particulars respecting the character of his son Samuel, to mention, that his political principles led him to favour the pretensions of the exiled family, and that though a very honest and sensible man, he, like many others inhabiting the county of Stafford, was a Jacobite.'[9] Hawkins's testimony was assured and unambiguous. It must however be weighed against the evidence of the father's public acceptance of the House of Hanover. At the time of the first major crisis of the new regime

[7] Arthur Murphy, *An Essay on the Life and Genius of Samuel Johnson, LL.D.* (London, 1793), pp. 107–8.

[8] Walter Scott (ed.), *The Poetical Works of Anna Seward* (3 vols., Edinburgh, 1810), vol. 1, p. lxx.

[9] Hawkins, *Life*, p. 3.

Michael Johnson signed the loyal address to the king by the Lichfield Corporation of 20 August 1715, and at other times subscribed the oaths of allegiance and abjuration required of those who took local office.[10] On 19 July 1712 he was elected a magistrate of Lichfield, and took the oaths on 25 July; he did so again on 7 October 1726,[11] subscribing the oaths of allegiance, supremacy and abjuration as required by I Geo. I, s. 2, c. 13. It may however be relevant that although Michael Johnson took the oaths, there is record of one of his former apprentices failing to do so.[12]

This second act of subscription in 1726 must have made an impression on the seventeen year old Samuel, who had just returned to Lichfield from Stourbridge School, and been in his mind when he went up to Oxford two years later. His father's conduct in this area evidently troubled Samuel; when Boswell 'pressed him upon it' he snapped '*That*, Sir, he was to settle with himself.'[13] The implication is clearly that Samuel Johnson believed that his father had Jacobite sympathies and had compromised his integrity by swearing such oaths. Presumably on stronger grounds than inference, Boswell wrote that Michael Johnson was 'a zealous high-churchman and royalist, and retained his attachment to the unfortunate house of Stuart, though he reconciled himself, by casuistical arguments of expediency and necessity, to take the oaths imposed by the prevailing power'.[14] Johnson would speak of his father, to Hawkins, 'as of a man in whose temper and character melancholy was predominant'.[15] Michael Johnson, like his son, had evidently enlisted in a losing cause, and paid an emotional price for his attempts to retain his integrity in a world now publicly precommitted against him.

The regime re-established in 1660 as an antidote to the religious wars of the first half of the seventeenth century had ascribed a special importance to oaths as definitions and defences of social order. What became the chief moral handbook of restored Anglicanism, *The Whole Duty of Man*, laid especial stress (chapter 4) on the binding nature of oaths and the sinfulness of taking unlawful oaths; it was a work which had a particular influence on the young Samuel Johnson. But this was not a matter of private morality alone. The monarchy of Charles II consciously sought to entrench itself in the consciences of Englishmen by a redefinition of the duties of the subject through newly-imposed oaths. This question attracted so much attention from the Anglican intelligentsia since it was obliged to argue both that oaths were sacred and inviolable, and also that oaths to the usurping

10 James L. Clifford, *Young Samuel Johnson* (London, 1955), pp. 38–9.
11 Reade, *Johnsonian Gleanings*, vol. 3, pp. 67, 165; vol. 4, pp. 201–3, which prints the oaths.
12 Simon Martin, at Leicester on 3 July 1727: Reade, *Johnsonian Gleanings*, vol. 1, p. 18.
13 Boswell, *Life*, vol. 2, p. 322.
14 Boswell, *Life*, vol. 1, pp. 36–7.
15 Hawkins, *Life*, p. 288.

powers taken during the rebellion were of no effect – including the Solemn League and Covenant, which Charles II had himself subscribed in 1651 as the price of Scots support. The Act of Uniformity of 1662 indeed imposed a counter-oath:

I A. B. Do Declare, *That it is not lawful upon any pretence whatsoever to take Arms against the King, and that I do abhor that Trayterous Position, of taking Arms by His Authority against His Person, or against those that are Commissionated by Him; And that I will conform to the Liturgy of the Church of* England, *as it is now established: And I do Declare, That I do hold there lies no Obligation upon me, or on any other person, from the Oath commonly called,* The Solemn League and Covenant, *to endeavour any change or alteration of Government either in Church or State; and that the same was in it self an unlawful Oath, and imposed upon the Subjects of this Realm, against the known Laws and Liberties of this Kingdom.*[16]

Once this problem had been resolved, the way was open for many Anglican writers to place a formidable stress on the 'awfull' and 'inviolable' character of oaths. One pamphleteer of 1660 had provided just such an account of the oaths of supremacy and allegiance: no more sacred obligation could an individual lay upon himself, he urged, but, more extensively, a state oath was of so much more importance that it bound not only those individuals who took it but the whole nation, including 'their succeeding Posterity, that are within the designe, and purpose of the said Oaths'. Such oaths were not revocable, so that 'no Engagement, Covenant, Protestation or Oath of Abjuration, contrary to the Oaths of Supremacy or Allegiance can be taken, without an horrid Sin against God'.[17] It was this solemn injunction that confronted Englishmen in 1688 and 1714. Nor did their awesome theological sanction cease to weigh with the orthodox. In the *Dictionary*, Johnson defined 'sacrament' in three ways, as '1. An oath; any ceremony producing an obligation. 2. An outward and visible sign of an inward and spiritual grace ... 3. The eucharist; the holy communion.'

It may be significant that it was his mother who in 1712 took Johnson to London to be touched by Queen Anne for scrofula, the 'King's evil' (his mother even concealing her pregnancy to make the journey), for a consistent Jacobite would have regarded this royal gift as residing in the elder male line alone, that is, with James III. Sir John Hawkins, as a Whig, felt obliged to take sides on the question, adding as a footnote 'that the vindication of this power, as inherent in the pretender, by Mr. Carte,

16 [John Stileman], *A Discourse of the Nature and Obligation of Oaths: wherein Satisfaction is tendered touching the Non-obligation and Unlawfulness of the Oath called, The Solemn League and Covenant* (London, 1662), pp. 1–2.

17 *The Resurrection of Loyalty and Obedience, out of the Grave of Rebellion: By the sacred Force of the Oathes of Supremacy and Allegiance, which have lain as dead, and out of minde, for diverse years; and here raised up out of the dust, and discovered in their great inviolable Force and Power unto the People* (London, 1660), pp. 4–5, 8.

destroyed the credit of his intended history of England, and put a stop to the completion of it'.[18] Thomas Carte, a close friend of Samuel Johnson's friends, committed himself to this position (though hiding behind ambiguous wording) when the first volume of his *A General History of England* was published in 1747 after the Whig Lord Egmont had accurately predicted that 'there is reason to believe that his history will be wrote to support the doctrine of indefeasible hereditary right, in order to serve the Pretender'.[19] This claim to a charismatic healing power was still an inescapable challenge, but had been a regular part of the public persona of Restoration monarchy. It is difficult to imagine that Michael Johnson was not present when James II performed the ceremony of healing in Lichfield Cathedral on 31 August 1687. Michael's sister had married the brother of James II's nurse and woman of the bedchamber; and he could hardly not have had views on the issue.[20]

Johnson claimed that he 'always retained some memory' of being taken to London to be touched for the evil by Queen Anne;[21] to Mrs. Thrale he confided: 'He had, he said, a confused, but somehow a sort of solemn recollection of a lady in diamonds, and a long black hood'.[22] This is evidence not for the communication of political views by that ceremony, but for Samuel's early and continued awareness of the wide issues which it raised.[23] He was indeed well aware of the dynastic significance of such ceremonies. For Johnson, the Wilkesite controversy of the late 1760s was an artificial contest compared with what had gone before: 'One part of the nation has never before contended with the other, but for some weighty and apparent interest. If the means were violent, the end was great. The civil war was fought for what each army called and believed the best religion, and the best government. The struggle in the reign of Anne, was to exclude or restore an exiled king.'[24] In the *Dictionary*, Johnson gave as one sense of 'evil' 'Malady; disease; as, the *king's evil*', and supported it from Shakespeare's *Macbeth*:

> At his touch
> Such sanctity hath heaven given his hand,

18 Hawkins, *Life*, p. 5.

19 J. C. D. Clark, *English Society 1688–1832: Ideology, social structure and political practice during the ancien regime* (Cambridge, 1985), pp. 160–1.

20 Reade, *Johnsonian Gleanings*, vol. 3, pp. 22–4, 65–6. Greene (*Politics*, p. xxxiii) implies that Boswell is the only source for Michael Johnson's political opinions. This is not the case.

21 [Richard Wright, ed.], *An Account of the Life of Dr Samuel Johnson, from his birth to his eleventh year, written by himself* (London, 1805), p. 16.

22 Hesther Lynch Piozzi, *Anecdotes of the late Samuel Johnson, LL. D. during the last twenty years of his life* (London, 1786), p. 10.

23 Cf. Greene, *Politics*, p. xxxiii: 'Presumably the royal touch helped to convert the two-and-a-half-year-old toddler to Jacobitism'.

24 [Samuel Johnson], *The False Alarm* (London, 1770), p. 51.

They presently amend.
— What's the disease he means?
— 'Tis called the *evil*.

Shakespeare had clearly given credence to the royal power, and Johnson did not correct him. On his death in 1788, Johnson's friend Dr John Taylor bequeathed to the 5th Duke of Devonshire 'the same piece of gold which was given to my late friend Dr Samuel Johnson deceased by her late Majesty Queen Anne, and which he wore suspended by a ribbon and on which piece of gold is the following inscription Soli Deo Gloria and on the reverse Anna D.G. Br. F.D. Reg'.[25] It was Johnson's 'touch piece', which he not only retained throughout life but had continued to wear, as the recipients of such tokens[26] normally did. Such attachment to an object argues for more, on Johnson's part, than mere recollection; but for Taylor, as a firm Whig, the object had to be factually described rather than called by a name which might acknowledge the claim which it symbolised. Whatever Taylor's view, it is unlikely that he was unaware of the opinion on that momentous question of his schoolfriend and undergraduate contemporary. Boswell would have relished such an anecdote: it seems a reasonable inference that Johnson did not confide in him on this point.

Divine-right monarchy was represented to its subjects in a literary as well as a ceremonial and thaumaturgic tradition, and these literary sources were fully accessible to the son of a provincial bookseller. In his *Lives of the Poets*, Johnson much later recalled:

In 1681, Dryden became yet more conspicuous by uniting politicks with poetry, in the memorable satire called *Absalom and Achitophel*,[27] written against the faction which, by lord Shaftesbury's incitement, set the duke of Monmouth at its head.

Of this poem, in which personal satire was applied to the support of publick principles, and in which therefore every mind was interested, the reception was eager, and the sale so large, that my father, an old bookseller, told me, he had not known it equalled but by *Sacheverell's* trial.[28]

25 Thomas Taylor, *A Life of John Taylor LL.D., of Ashburne* (London, [1876]), p. 76; Reade, *Johnsonian Gleanings*, vol. 3, p. 62. Edward Hawkins acquired it in 1844 from the Devonshire collection; from him it passed to the British Museum.

26 Noel Woolf, *The Sovereign Remedy: Touch-Pieces and the King's Evil* (Manchester, 1990).

27 For the 'theme of national redemption' and 'the satanic nature of the enemy' in this poem, see Steven N. Zwicker, *Dryden's Political Poetry: The Typology of King and Nation* (Providence, 1972), pp. 83–101: 'the plot of the poem and the various characters argue (with or without their own knowledge) that throughout the poem Charles reflects the godhead; the relationship that exists between the paternal role of the earthly and heavenly monarchs also exists between God as sovereign and the king in his official capacity' (pp. 88–9).

28 Johnson, *Lives of the Poets*, vol. 2, pp. 59–60.

(a) Charles II performing the ceremony of touching for the king's evil

(b) Samuel Johnson's touch piece (1712)

Plate 4 Charismatic monarchy. The thaumaturgic claims of the Stuarts continued to provide a litmus test of their adherents and to be repudiated by Whigs

The Tryal of Dr Henry Sacheverell, before the House of Peers, for High Crimes and Misdemeanours; upon an Impeachment (London, 1710) was indeed a best-seller, reprinted in folio and octavo editions, and circulated widely as a compendium of political theory; but it was especially valued by Tories as recording the collapse, under scrutiny, of the Whig interpretation of the revolution of 1688.[29] It was of more than anecdotal significance that a Lichfield tradition recorded the three-year-old Samuel 'perched upon his father's shoulders' to hear Sacheverell preach or conduct a service in Lichfield Cathedral, possibly in early 1713:

> Mr. Hammond ask'd Mr. [Michael] Johnson how he cou'd possibly think of bringing Such an Infant to Church and in the Midst of so Great a Croud. He answer'd because it was impossible to keep him at home for young as he was he believ'd he had caught the Public Spirit and zeal for Sachaverel and woud have staid forever in the Church Satisfied with beholding him.[30]

Lichfield was a narrow place, embittered by long memories and stubborn resentments. Not until 1737 did Johnson discover, like James Thomson (1700–48) that 'the only stage on which a poet could appear, with any hope of advantage, was London; a place too wide for the operation of petty competition and private malignity, where merit might soon become conspicuous, and would find friends as soon as it became reputable to befriend it'.[31] Meanwhile, if Johnson did not enjoy a wide arena for his talents, he had the immense advantage of being born the son of a bookseller. His access to English and European culture was broad. One component of his early knowledge was an exposure to Nonjuror theology: Thomas Brett's collection of liturgies, published in 1720,[32] was known to Johnson before his father's death in 1731. It demonstrated a profound interest in such matters in provincial Lichfield. Hawkins recorded:

> Johnson once told me, he had heard his father say, that when he was young in trade, king Edward the Sixth's first liturgy was much enquired for, and fetched a great price; but that the publication of this book, which contained the whole communion-office as it stands in the former, reduced the price of it to that of a common book.[33]

Evidence like this does not conclusively establish that Samuel Johnson adopted such views from his family background; but it does establish that the issues and ideologies which convulsed English society in the three

29 Geoffrey Holmes, *The Trial of Doctor Sacheverell* (London, 1973); J. P. Kenyon, *Revolution Principles: The Politics of Party 1689–1720* (Cambridge, 1977), pp. 128–45.

30 Boswell, *Life*, vol. 1, pp. 35n, 39, based on Mary Adey to Boswell, 26 February 1785, in Waingrow (ed.), *Correspondence*, pp. 63–6, at 64. For a different interpretation, see Greene, *Politics*, p. xxxiv.

31 Johnson, *Lives of the Poets*, vol. 4, p. 253.

32 For which, see below, p. 132.

33 Hawkins, *Life*, p. 448.

decades from the accession of James II to the rising of 1715 were vividly present in Johnson's milieu, and that he was lastingly aware of that fact.

II. A NONJUROR AT OXFORD, 1728–1729

Boswell's compulsive candour, his need to confess, tends to obscure the fact that Johnson's own nature was quite otherwise. There were areas of his early life on which he was reticent or ambiguous to the point of being misleading. Johnson was, for unexplained reasons, nervous about his private papers, ordering masses of them to be burned a few days before his death. These included 'two quarto volumes, containing a full, fair, and most particular account of his own life, from his earliest recollection'. Boswell, Hawkins and, it seems, George Steevens, among Johnson's would-be biographers, were eager to see these volumes, and Johnson equally anxious that they should not do so. Hawkins pocketed one of the volumes during Johnson's last days, which was with difficulty retrieved, and, suggested Boswell, 'The agitation into which Johnson was thrown by this incident, probably made him hastily burn those precious records which must ever be regretted.'[34] Even from a fragmentary account of his early life which did survive, rescued by his servant Francis Barber, Johnson had torn thirty-two pages.[35]

Uncertainty to the point almost of mystery has surrounded some aspects of Johnson's Oxford career, especially the issue of whether his failure to graduate was a consequence of his inability to take the oath of allegiance which graduation would have required. This thesis would be more persuasive had Johnson (as was once believed) completed three of the four years' residence normally required for a degree, but is not wholly dependent on the length of his time at Oxford: as will be shown, other evidence tends to support it. The evidence for Johnson's period in residence actually supports neither of his major biographers. He matriculated at Pembroke College in October 1728 and left in December 1729, yet seemingly allowed Hawkins and Boswell to believe that he completed nearly three years, leaving in the autumn of 1731.[36] There is, however, some uncertainty. Johnson claimed in 1773 to have known George Whitefield early in the latter's life, by implication at Pembroke; Whitefield matriculated on 7

[34] Boswell, *Life*, vol. 1, p. 25; vol. 4, pp. 405–6.

[35] [Richard Wright, ed.], *An Account of the Life of Dr Samuel Johnson*, p. v. The destruction of papers was common in early-eighteenth-century Tory-Jacobite circles.

[36] Boswell (*Life*, vol. 1, p. 78) recorded that Johnson left Oxford in the autumn of 1731. This statement was based on misleading information from Dr William Adams (1706–89), Master of Pembroke 1775–89, in response to Boswell's enquiry after Johnson's death (Waingrow, *Correspondence*, p. 58); but Boswell had evidently never questioned Johnson about it.

November 1732. Visiting Oxford in 1782, Johnson showed off his college to Hannah More, explaining (as she recorded) 'This was my room; this Shenstone's.' The poet William Shenstone matriculated on 25 May 1732.[37] Against this must be set Johnson's remark in 1778 of his undergraduate contemporary Oliver Edwards that he 'had not seen me since 1729': Edwards was at Pembroke from June 1729 to April 1730.[38] On the matter of the financing of his Oxford education, Boswell merely recorded: 'The subject was too delicate to question Johnson upon.'[39] Clearly the source of the difficulty was not in any sense of ill-treatment by his university, for Johnson always spoke in warm terms both of Oxford and of Pembroke College. Nevertheless, uncertainty has surrounded both the dates of his residence, and his reasons for leaving without a degree.

According to Hawkins, Johnson's time at Oxford was divisible into two parts: the first from matriculation on 31 October 1728 until he left in December 1729, 'the reason whereof, was a failure of pecuniary supplies from his father'; the second when, 'meeting with another source, the bounty, as it is supposed, of some one or more of the members of the cathedral [at Lichfield], he returned, and made up the whole of his residence in the university, about three years, during all which time his academical studies, though not orderly, were to an astonishing degree intense'.[40] Finally, however, 'It is little less than certain, that his own indigence, and the inability of his father to help him, called Johnson from the university sooner than he meant to quit it ... The non-attainment of a degree, which after a certain standing is conferred almost of course, he regretted not ...'[41] – an implausible disregard, given the zeal of Johnson's studies and his efforts in 1739 to obtain an honorary MA from Trinity College, Dublin, to enable him to pursue a career as a schoolmaster. Why Johnson's supposed Lichfield patrons, having allegedly financed him through three years of Oxford, should withdraw their support only a year short of graduation is unexplained. So is the absence of any resentment by Johnson at this treatment, all the more remarkable in view of his later eloquent reproach of Chesterfield for failing to perform the duties of a patron.

Yet the documents clearly establish that Johnson did not reside for three years. The Master's Account Book of Pembroke College contains the Rev. Matthew Panting's entry of 10 October 1728 which recorded the receipt of

37 Boswell, *Life*, vol. 4, p. 151 n; vol. 5, p. 35 (*Tour*); Boswell, *Journal*, p. 20; Reade, *Johnsonian Gleanings*, vol. 5, pp. 37–8, 43.

38 Boswell, *Life*, vol. 3, p. 302; Reade, *Johnsonian Gleanings*, vol. 5, p. 36.

39 Boswell, *Life*, vol. 1, p. 58. Boswell recorded only a few anecdotes of Johnson's Oxford career; that most of those were from Dr Adams and Dr Taylor is revealed in Waingrow (ed.), *Correspondence*, passim.

40 Hawkins, *Life*, pp. 15–16.

41 Ibid., p. 17.

the entrance fee from Johnson. On 31 October Johnson paid his caution money of £7, a security against possible debts: this he never reclaimed, 'perhaps because he continued to hope that he might return to college'. Johnson signed the University Matriculation Register on 16 December 1728, and his charges appear in the Battel books of his college until his last term, Michaelmas 1729.[42] The length of Johnson's residence at Oxford has been investigated in the light of Pembroke College's records, and these sometimes-ambiguous documents have been the subject of controversy.[43] The most detailed study of the question establishes that Johnson was continuously in residence until the week of 5–12 December 1729, and that thereafter he was out of residence, paying only nominal charges but with his name remaining on the books, until 8 October 1731.[44]

Might he nevertheless have continued his studies at Oxford had he wished to do so? Others in similar financial circumstances found ways of completing the course for a degree. Samuel Johnson's Oxford education was made possible by a legacy of £40. This would have covered a year's expenses as a commoner, but George Whitefield, at Pembroke in the more humble status of servitor from November 1732, cost his family only some £8 a year.[45] The possibility remains that Johnson could have completed his course and obtained a degree by accepting this menial but traditional office. In 1773, Johnson commended the institution of servitor at Oxford, and undertook to arrange such a post for the son of some Scottish hosts:[46] perhaps his youthful pride has been overstated.

> He could not, at this early period of his life, divest himself of an opinion, that poverty was disgraceful; and was very severe in his censures of that oeconomy in both our universities, which exacted at meals the attendance of poor scholars, under the several denominations of servitors in the one, and sizers in the other: he thought that the scholar's, like the christian life, levelled all distinctions of rank and worldly pre-eminence; but in this he was mistaken: civil policy had, long before his coming into the world, reduced the several classes of men to a regular subordination, and given servitude its sanction.[47]

The possibility also exists that, as Hawkins recorded as fact, Johnson might have obtained financial backing from Lichfield patrons. He

42 *An Exhibition for the Johnson Club at Pembroke College, Oxford, Saturday, 6 July, 1975* [Oxford, 1975], p. 1.

43 Reviewed in Reade, *Johnsonian Gleanings*, vol. 5, pp. 45–51.

44 Ibid., pp. 51–63, 153–75.

45 Johnson's battels from October 1728 to December 1729 were £23–5–4d. To these would have been added room rents and college fees. Reade, *Johnsonian Gleanings*, vol. 3, pp. 180–1, vol. 5, pp. 37, 160; George Birkbeck Hill, *Dr Johnson His Friends and His Critics* (London, 1878), p. 9.

46 Boswell, *Journal*, p. 89; Boswell, *Life*, vol. 5 (*Tour*), p. 122.

47 Hawkins, *Life*, p. 18.

evidently did neither. Nor did he obtain a scholarship from his college;[48] but, as a 'foundationer', a scholar like a servitor would be required to take the oaths. This was made clear in 1753 by William Murray, MP, trying vainly to vindicate himself before the Privy Council from allegations of Jacobitism:

> When I went to the university, as I was upon a foundation, I took all the oaths to the Government. When I took them I well knew the force of those engagements. I was not ignorant of the nature of the question, if it can be called a question, for I never could see the doubt. That a Protestant should reason himself into a Jacobite is as incomprehensible in politics as it is in religion that a man should reason himself into an atheist.[49]

But Murray lied: his written promise of allegiance to James III in 1725 was at that moment in the Stuart papers at Rome.

Johnson's name was kept on the college books; he continued to pay certain fees; he left his library of over 100 volumes at Oxford in the care of a friend, John Taylor, until 1735:[50] evidently he intended to return but was unable to do so. But his whereabouts after leaving Oxford in December 1729 are unknown until, in the summer of 1731, he unsuccessfully applied for the post of usher at Stourbridge School.[51] Uncertainty continues to surround this period, added to rather than explained by Johnson's acute mental disturbance, verging in some sense on insanity.[52] The fact that Johnson did not complete three years' residence, as Hawkins had some reason to believe, does not dispose of the problem of the oaths.[53] Johnson, like other men of high religious or political principle, was confronted by a major dilemma.

III. A CAREER FRUSTRATED, 1729–1758

Johnson's lack of a university degree must have been foreseen as a handicap at an early date: in 1731 he applied for the post of usher at Stourbridge School; from March to July 1732 he held such a post at Market Bosworth

48 There is evidence that Johnson was eligible for a small scholarship, and might have been elected to one in 1730: Reade, *Johnsonian Gleanings*, vol. 5, p. 36.

49 BL Add MSS 33050 f. 331, quoted in Romney Sedgwick (ed.), *The History of Parliament: The House of Commons 1715–1754* (2 vols., London, 1970), vol. 2, p. 287.

50 Johnson wrote to Gilbert Repington on 18 May 1735 (Johnson, *Letters*, vol. 1, p. 7) to ask for the books, which Taylor had entrusted to John Spicer in 1730. Reade, *Johnsonian Gleanings*, vol. 5, p. 27.

51 Joseph Wood Krutch, *Samuel Johnson* (London, 1948), pp. 30–1; Johnson to Gregory Hickman, 30 October 1731 (the first letter by Johnson now extant) in Johnson, *Letters*, vol. 1, p. 3.

52 W. Jackson Bate, *Samuel Johnson* (London, 1978), pp. 115–29. At Stourbridge, Johnson was beaten by a rival candidate from Trinity College, Oxford, who had a BA.

53 Greene, *Politics*, p. xxx argues that it does so dispose of the question.

School;[54] in the latter month he applied for a similar post in the school at Ashbourne.[55] Given the prospect of a need to make his living in this way, quite apart from his high regard for scholarship and its dignities, Johnson is unlikely to have neglected to take his degree, had it been possible for him to do so. Nor did he lose touch with Oxford: his abortive plan to print an edition of the poetry of Politian was made in the spring of 1734; on 15 June 1734 the works of that author were borrowed for him from the library of his college.[56] Johnson still considered himself a grammarian, and a career as a schoolmaster was (as it had been for Thomas Ruddiman) a natural if unglamorous course. A similar obstacle threatened to prevent this, as it had seemed to close off a university career: schoolmasters were liable by statute to take the oaths.[57] But (unlike university graduates or fellows of colleges on election) there was no automatic ceremony on appointment to a school which would have required this: the tyrannical Sir Wolstan Dixie is unlikely to have been scrupulous about these formal observances, and it is likely that the oaths were only formally tendered on any systematic basis at times of political emergency. The records of the diocese of Norwich suggest that far fewer schoolteachers than clergy ever took the oaths; that the number of teachers subscribing fell off markedly after the Atterbury plot and before the Forty-five; but that clergy continued to subscribe in large numbers throughout the early part of the century.[58] Certain undoubted English Nonjurors, like Ambrose Bonwicke (1652–1722) and Elijah Fenton (1683–1730) did become schoolmasters;[59] it was not unreasonable that Johnson sought so hard to do the same.

Only after these possibilities had failed did Johnson's career take a different direction. Others beside him trod that familiar but rocky path, like Nicholas Amhurst (1697–1742), who wrote *Terrae Filius* after being expelled from Oxford, tried his fortune in 'the common Resort of Want, Wickedness and Wit', London, and offered his services to Sir Robert Walpole; the minister was not impressed, and Amherst was soon running *The Craftsman* for the opposition. One reason for his conversion was financial, according to a journalist colleague; another was 'the Treatment he

[54] Its chief trustee, Sir Wolstan Dixie, in appointing Johnson, flouted the requirement of the school's statutes that the undermaster have the BA degree: Bate, *Johnson*, p. 130.

[55] Ashbourne school did not require a degree; two men without degrees were preferred to Johnson: Bate, *Johnson*, p. 132.

[56] Pembroke College library borrowing register, reported in *An Exhibition for the Johnson Club at Pembroke College, Oxford, Sunday, 6 July, 1975* [Oxford, 1975], and Reade, *Johnsonian Gleanings*, vol. 5, p. 100.

[57] Greene, *Politics*, p. xxxi.

[58] E. H. Carter, *The Norwich Subscription Books: A Study of the Subscription Books of the Diocese of Norwich 1637–1800* (London, 1937), pp. 5–6, 90–100.

[59] J. H. Overton, *The Nonjurors* (London, 1902), pp. 259, 264–6; Paul Kléber Monod, *Jacobitism and the English People 1688–1788* (Cambridge, 1989), pp. 274–5.

imagin'd he had received from Sir *R[ober]t*, which was very provoking to a Man just come from the University of *Oxford* full of *Greek* and *Latin*, and fuller of himself than either'.[60]

Johnson, however, fought longer to resist the pressures that threatened to drag him down to the level of a Grub Street hack. In 1738, according to Boswell, Dr William Adams of Pembroke was approached 'by a common friend' to secure for Johnson a honorary Oxford MA, to qualify him to be a schoolmaster; but 'it was then thought too great a favour to be asked'.[61] Johnson's poem *London*, published in May 1738, attracted the praise of the sympathetic Alexander Pope.[62] Discovering Johnson's difficult circumstances, Pope, unknown to Johnson, intervened with the still-Jacobite Earl Gower to persuade him to act on Johnson's behalf.[63] How Pope was induced to intervene is unknown, but his doing so is evidence for a shared political milieu embracing Johnson, Pope, King, Gower and Swift. On 1 August 1739 Gower wrote to a friend of Jonathan Swift in an attempt to persuade the Dean to procure Johnson the degree of MA from the University of Dublin to qualify him under the statutes of a school to be its master; but the application failed.[64] Boswell was forced to record that Johnson always displayed 'a certain degree of prejudice' against Swift, and tried to rescue his subject from an obvious charge: 'Mr. Thomas Sheridan imputed it to a supposed apprehension in Johnson, that Swift had not been sufficiently active in obtaining for him an Irish degree when it was solicited'.[65]

Probably in late 1745 or early 1746, Johnson again approached Dr Adams to ask that he intercede on his behalf with Richard Smalbroke, son of the Bishop of Lichfield,[66] who had just taken the Oxford degree of DCL and begun to practice as an advocate in Doctors' Commons, the court of civil and canon law. Johnson wished to discover whether the court would

60 *An Historical View of the Principles, Characters, Persons &c. of the Political Writers in Great Britain* (London, 1740), pp. 27, 29.

61 Boswell, *Life*, vol. 1, p. 133; Dr Adams to Boswell, 17 February 1785: Waingrow (ed.), *Correspondence*, p. 58.

62 For Pope's politics, see Howard Erskine-Hill, 'Alexander Pope: The Political Poet in His Time', *Eighteenth-Century Studies* 15 (1981–82), 123–48.

63 Waingrow (ed.), *Correspondence*, p. 10.

64 Boswell, *Life*, vol. 1, pp. 133–4; Reade, *Johnsonian Gleanings*, vol. 6, pp. 76, 96–114, identifies the school as Appleby.

65 Boswell, *Life*, vol. 4, p. 61; vol. 5, p. 44.

66 The Smalbroke family may have been sympathetic to one of Johnson's politics: Richard Smalbroke, bishop of Lichfield 1730–50, preached at St Clement Danes, later Johnson's church, on 27 April 1735: Richard Parkinson (ed.), *The Private Journal and Literary Remains of John Byrom* (2 vols in 4 parts, Manchester, 1854–7), vol. 1, p. 595. For St Clement Danes and its churchmanship, see below, pp. 139–40, 154–7. Smalbroke was unusual among the bishops for his open Toryism: he voted for the dismissal of Walpole in 1741, and in 1747 featured for his politics in a satirical print, 'A Sight of the Banging Bout at Lichfield', illustrated in Eveline Cruickshanks, *Political Untouchables: The Tories and the '45* (London, 1979), plate 8.

waive the qualification of a DCL and allow him to begin a career as an advocate there without that degree; but the application failed, the court being unwilling to dispense with that requirement.[67] The law would have been a new field for Johnson, but scholarship, and poetry, were not. Thomas Tyers recorded that Johnson, after the completion of his *Dictionary*, 'wished, for a moment, to fill the chair of a professor, at Oxford, then become vacant, but he never applied for it'.[68] He probably referred to the Professorship of Poetry, vacated by William Hawkins in 1756; but, again, there was an obstacle. A chair, and its attendant fellowship, would have required the oaths; Johnson's honorary Oxford MA, awarded to him by the university in 1755, did not.

The problem of public oaths was not only an abstract problem of political and theological speculation; it recurred during the Seven Years' War in an unexpected practical context. The iniquity of standing armies and the superior virtue of citizen militias was a familiar theme of the opposition to the Hanoverian regime. A Bill for just such a scheme was introduced into the Commons in March 1756 by George Townshend as part of the campaign of William Pitt to subvert the ministry of the Duke of Newcastle, of which he was a nominal but disruptive member. Newcastle and his allies secured the defeat of the Bill in the Lords on 24 May, but not before Johnson had given it powerful but ineffectual endorsement in the *Literary Magazine*. His detailed account of the provisions of the Bill had to confront an awkward problem. The militia was a favourite Tory device, but recruits to it would presumably have to take the oath of allegiance. Johnson rehearsed the obvious objection: 'Shall then the defence of the king be intrusted to those who will not swear allegiance? That is undoubtedly absurd.' Uneasily, Johnson explored the alternatives:

> Yet surely nothing has more tendency to make bad subjects than irreligion, and nothing will sooner make men irreligious, than the frequency of oaths ... Every man who takes these oaths is or is not already faithful to his king. If he be faithful, how is his fidelity increased? If he be not, how is his loyalty improved, by diminishing his honesty? It is undoubtedly intended, that men of disloyal principles should be forced to discover their tenets by refusing their test. But this those who intend it do not expect. They know, what every one knows, that mean men called before those whom they have always regarded with veneration, will be more afraid of man than God, and will take the oath taken and offered by their betters, without understanding, without examining, perhaps without hearing it ... The frequent

67 Reade, *Johnsonian Gleanings*, vol. 6, p. 116 and Bate, *Johnson*, pp. 232–3, date the episode to late 1745, after Smalbroke had begun his practice in Doctors Commons and before April 1746, when Johnson began the *Dictionary*. Boswell, *Life*, vol. 1, p 134, places it in 1738. Dr Adams to Boswell, 17 February 1785 and 12 July 1786: Waingrow (ed.), *Correspondence*, pp. 59, 161.

68 Tyers, 'Biographical Sketch', in Brack and Kelley (eds.), *Early Biographies*, p. 77.

imposition of oaths has almost ruined the morals of this unhappy nation, and of a nation without morals it is of small importance who shall be king.

What then is to be done? Let the officers who must be supposed to know the state of their own counties choose those whom the government may trust without an oath.

It was a weak conclusion, but Johnson recoiled from imposing on men's consciences a 'hateful oath'.[69] Johnson himself may have shied away from taking the oath in similar circumstances: Boswell recorded that Johnson was once picked to serve in the Trained Bands, or militia, of the City of London, and went so far as to provide himself with a musket, sword and belt; but he chose at additional expense to hire a deputy to serve in his place.[70] Edward Gibbon, with a far less robust physique, had renounced such scruples, and when Pitt's Militia Bill passed the following year he served in person, later boasting in print of how valuable his military experience had been to the historian of the Roman Empire.

Johnson had been shut out of a university and a church career; but, in a sense, this was self-exclusion. Sir John Hawkins dated to about 1758 Johnson's refusal of preferment in the church, an explicit offer made by Mr. Langton of Langton, Lincolnshire, father of his friend Bennet Langton:

About this time he had, from a friend who highly esteemed him, the offer of a living, of which he might have rendered himself capable by entering into holy orders: it was a rectory, in a pleasant country, and of such a yearly value as might have tempted one in better circumstances than himself to accept it; but he had scruples about the duties of the ministerial function, that he could not, after deliberation, overcome. 'I have not,' said he, 'the requisites for the office, and I cannot, in my conscience, shear that flock which I am unable to feed.' – Upon conversing with him on that inability which was his reason for declining the offer, it was found to be a suspicion of his patience to undergo the fatigue of catechising and instructing a great number of poor ignorant persons, who, in religious matters, had, perhaps, every thing to learn.[71]

Hawkins's puzzlement is evident. Nor is Johnson's own account fully convincing. He was a fluent author of sermons commissioned from him by Anglican clergy, certainly as early as that which he composed for Henry Hervey Aston in 1745, and the twenty eight which survive are, it has been suggested, only a fraction of his total output.[72] Few Anglican laymen in the

69 [Samuel Johnson], 'Extract of the Bill for the Better Ordering the Militia Forces in the Several Counties of That Part of Great-Britain Called England, As Altered and Amended by the Committee, with Remarks', *Literary Magazine* no. 2 (15 May – 15 June 1756), pp. [57]–63, in Johnson, *Works*, vol. 10, pp. 151–66, at 158–60.

70 Boswell, *Life*, vol. 4, p. 319.

71 Hawkins, *Life*, pp. 365.

72 Johnson admitted to authorship of 'about forty' sermons. Johnson, *Works*, vol. 14, pp. xix, xxi–xxiii. This suggests that the identity of many of the clergy for whom they were composed has been lost: Johnson's Anglican milieu in London was evidently wider than

eighteenth century, and still fewer lay authors, had such a commitment to their religion. Johnson's wide theological knowledge, and active charity towards the poor, make his excuses to Hawkins seem, at most, false modesty. But an ecclesiastical post would probably still have required the oaths, and would certainly have required Johnson to recite those prayers for the Hanoverian royal family, by name, which were inseparable parts of the morning and evening services of the Church of England. In this context it may be relevant that one of Johnson's own prayers, undated but conjecturally ascribed to 1759, includes the petition that he might be helped 'to overcome and suppress vain scruples; and to use such diligence in lawful employment as may enable me to support myself and do good to others'.[73] Johnson's desperate need for a stable career was agonizingly prolonged.

Johnson's early life-experience was one of exclusion and rejection; it is not surprising that this found echoes in his writing. Elijah Fenton, a Nonjuror, was unable to take a degree at Cambridge. Johnson defended him:

> By this perverseness of integrity he was driven out a commoner of Nature, excluded from the regular modes of profit and prosperity, and reduced to pick up a livelihood uncertain and fortuitous; but it must be remembered that he kept his name unsullied, and never suffered himself to be reduced, like too many of the same sect, to mean arts and dishonourable shifts. Whoever mentioned Fenton, mentioned him with honour.[74]

As in Johnson's *Life of Savage*, the autobiographical parallel is inescapable.

Yet this was a moral predicament which, however disastrous for a career, could not be revealed without peril to men who did not themselves share it. It seems that Johnson was uncommunicative to the point of secrecy about his time at Oxford. Some of this may have to do with poverty; more, it seems, with the acute melancholia, perhaps verging on insanity, which gripped him from that time. How much of his distress was caused by the prospect that his labours were futile because he would in any event be unable to qualify himself to take a degree is unknown. What is certain is that no evidence has been presented that he ever did take the oath of allegiance or the oath of abjuration at Oxford, or anywhere else. His agonisingly scrupulous honesty was, however, very obvious. 'The late Mr. Tyers, who knew Dr Johnson intimately, observed, "that he always talked as if he was talking upon oath."' Arthur Murphy agreed.[75] It was an attitude which set limits to Johnson's political conduct, as he made clear by

can now be established. One of its members may have been the Rev. John Rogers, lecturer at St Clement Danes: ibid., p. 30n.

[73] Johnson, *Works*, vol. 1, p. 70.

[74] Johnson, *Lives of the Poets*, vol. 3, p. 110.

[75] Murphy, *Johnson*, p. 146.

implication in his *Lives of the Poets*. Abraham Cowley was in the service of Charles II at Paris in the 1650s, was sent to England in 1656, captured, and released by 'the usurping powers' only on a security of £1000; yearning for 'retirement', he seemed to make a submission to the Commonwealth. Johnson commented: 'let neither our reverence for a genius, nor our pity for a sufferer, dispose us to forget that, if his activity was virtue, his retreat was cowardice'. Yet he acknowledged extenuating circumstances:

> The man whose miscarriage in a just cause has put him in the power of his enemy may, without any violation of his integrity, regain his liberty, or preserve his life, by a promise of neutrality ... He that is at the disposal of another, may not promise to aid him in any injurious act, because no power can compel active disobedience. He may engage to do nothing, but not to do ill.[76]

Johnson accidentally disclosed his own refusal to subscribe in April 1773, in conceding some de facto title to the House of Hanover:

> Talking of the family of Stuart, he said, 'It should seem that the family at present on the throne has now established as good a right as the former family, by the long consent of the people; and that to disturb this right might be considered as culpable. At the same time I own, that it is a very difficult question, when considered with respect to the House of Stuart. To oblige people to take oaths as to the disputed right, is wrong. I know not whether I could take them: but I do not blame those who do.' So conscientious and so delicate was he upon this subject, which has occasioned so much clamour against him.[77]

Plainly, and by his own confession, Johnson had not taken the oaths: neither his pension nor his honorary Oxford MA had required them.

These oaths, but especially the formidable oath of abjuration, he deeply resented. In 1775, Johnson looked forward to a hypothetical future in which England would have been defeated in the revolutionary war, and the American colonies would have established their independence. Surely, then, suggested Johnson, commercial relations would go on as before? The treaty of peace, he hoped, would then provide that

> if an Englishman be inclined to hold a plantation, he shall only take an oath of allegiance to the reigning powers, and be suffered, while he lives inoffensively, to retain his own opinion of English rights, unmolested in his conscience by an oath of abjuration.[78]

[76] Johnson, *Lives of the Poets*, vol. 1, pp. 14–16. [77] Boswell, *Life*, vol. 2, p. 220.
[78] [Samuel Johnson], *Taxation no Tyranny; an Answer to the Resolutions and Address of the American Congress* (London, 1775), pp. 90–1.

This was, in essence, Johnson's own position in the reign of George III: realistic acknowledgement of a *de facto* regime without renouncing a superior *de jure* obligation elsewhere. But he was unwise to raise again the sensitive subject of oaths. One critic seized on the closing passage in *Taxation no Tyranny* about a future independent America which knew no oath of abjuration, 'the which, (unless my memory hath failed me,) you gratefully refused to take, in the moment when you did his present Majesty the honor to accept of an inconsiderable pension'.[79]

[79] *Taxation, Tyranny. Addressed to Samuel Johnson, LL.D.* (London, 1775), p. 80.

5

JOHNSON AND THE NONJURORS

I. THE NONJURORS: SURVIVAL AND DECLINE

Johnson's view of the territory of English literature differed in two fundamental ways from that which came to prevail after his lifetime. He gave, as we have seen, a role to the classics which profoundly modified the nature of the vernacular. Second, he regarded religion as having an integral relation with literature. The *Dictionary* was a profoundly theologically-conscious work.[1] In 1781, when Topham Beauclerk's library was sold in London,

> Mr. Wilkes said, he wondered to find in it such a numerous collection of sermons; seeming to think it strange that a gentleman of Mr. Beauclerk's character in the gay world, should have chosen to have many compositions of that kind. JOHNSON. 'Why, Sir, you are to consider, that sermons make a considerable branch of English literature; so that a library must be very imperfect if it has not a numerous collection of sermons ...'[2]

Boswell placed first in his character sketch of Johnson that he was 'a sincere and zealous Christian, of high-Church-of-England and monarchical principles, which he would not tamely suffer to be questioned'.[3]

To Boswell's astonishment, Johnson produced cogent reasons for preferring Roman Catholicism to Presbyterianism, including 'apostolical ordination'; he even admitted that he saw 'nothing unreasonable' in the Roman doctrine of Purgatory.[4] But this was evidently provoked by the comparison with Scots religion, for Johnson was equally capable of speaking against Roman Catholicism, observing, 'In every thing in which they differed from us they are wrong.'[5] In the presence of non-Anglicans, Johnson manifestly closed ranks with the Church of England. John Dun,

[1] See below, pp. 211–12. [2] Boswell, *Life*, vol. 4, p. 105.

[3] Boswell, *Journal*, p. 6. For one study of the ecclesiastical basis of Johnson's politics see Chester Chapin, 'Religion and the Nature of Samuel Johnson's Toryism', *Cithara* 29 (1990), 38–54.

[4] Boswell, *Life*, vol. 2, pp. 103–6; cf. p. 163. [5] Ibid., vol. 3, p. 407.

Presbyterian minister of Auchinleck, was unwise enough to air his prejudices concerning Johnson's church: he

> discovered a narrowness of information concerning the dignitaries of the Church of England, among whom may be found men of the greatest learning, virtue, and piety, and of a truly apostolic character. He talked before Dr Johnson of fat bishops and drowsy deans; and, in short, seemed to believe the illiberal and profane scoffings of professed satirists or vulgar railers. Dr Johnson was so highly offended that he said to him, 'Sir, you know no more of our church than a Hottentot.'[6]

Elsewhere, however, Johnson's internal differences with other Anglicans surfaced, especially in his critical view of Whig clergy.[7] How far did these problems divide Johnson from his own denomination?

The negative evidence that Johnson never took the oaths of allegiance and abjuration and sought ways of securing a degree while evading the obligation to do so does not in itself establish his professed position on the Nonjurors.[8] Yet the High Church and Nonjuring positions had been and remained points of active controversy in the circles in which Johnson moved during his early years. As an undergraduate, he might have heard a round assertion of the divine right of the clergy in a university sermon, and read an indignant low-church reply.[9] Oxford sustained a learned and sophisticated debate on these issues into the 1750s, and saw contributions by Whigs as well as Tories. One pamphleteer in 1748 outlined the Nonjuror's charge to a Low Church opponent:

> Your notions of government are so tinctured with *Hoadlianism*, which has been exploded, and so solidly answered, in the best answer ever was made, and to which no answer ever will be made, (which I will lend you if you will read it)[10] that there need be little said upon that head: for the laws of God, and man forbid resistance, upon any pretence whatever, and no government of what nature soever, ever did or could allow it.

The Hanoverian Oxonian was made to reply not only with a systematic defence of the sufficiency of Scripture without (as the Nonjuror insisted) the traditions of the Church, but with a defence of the conduct of Oxford

6 Boswell, *Journal*, p. 375 (5 November 1773).

7 See above, pp. 17–18.

8 Recent monographs on Johnson's spiritual life do not attend to the Nonjuror tradition except in passing: Maurice J. Quinlan, *Samuel Johnson: A Layman's Religion* (Madison, Wisc., 1964); Chester F. Chapin, *The Religious Thought of Samuel Johnson* (Ann Arbor, 1968); Charles E. Pierce, Jr., *The Religious Life of Samuel Johnson* (London, 1983). Nor does Owen Chadwick, 'The Religion of Samuel Johnson', *Yale University Library Gazette* 60 (1986), 119–36.

9 *An Address to the University of Oxford, Occasioned by a Sermon, intitled, The divine Institution of the Ministry, and the absolute necessity of Church-Government; preached before that University by the Reverend Mr. Joseph Betty, on the 21st of September 1729. By I.W.L.* (2nd edn, London, 1730).

10 [Charles Leslie], *The Best Answer Ever was Made ... Address'd in a Letter to the said Mr. Hoadly Himself* (London, [1709]).

Whigs in 1688, and a lament for the Nonjuror Dr George Hickes; 'And the same, I judge of you, Sir, and all others who are of his unfortunate party; and continue in your wishes, prayers and endeavours to unsettle and overturn our present blessed security under a *protestant royal family*.'[11]

Those who rejected the validity of the new regime fell into three classes. The first openly refused the oaths, whether on their initiative or when challenged to take them; separated from the Church, and worshipped in congregations served by clergy who had also lost their benefices and continued the ordination of priests and consecration of bishops in a separate and apostolical succession. The second, like Bishop Francis Atterbury or (presumably) Dr William King, took the oaths of allegiance and abjuration with mental reservations, and remained disaffected or even conspired against the new dynasty from within the Establishment. The third group avoided the oaths but continued to worship with the juring Church of England. Of these, the second was probably larger than the first, and the third was probably far larger again than the second;[12] it was to this third group that Johnson evidently belonged. Of the Nonjuring bishop Archibald Campbell, Johnson wrote in 1784 that at the Revolution he 'adhered not only to the Nonjurors, but to those who refused to communicate with the Church of England, or to be present at any worship where the usurper was mentioned as king':[13] such a group Johnson clearly regarded as a hard core minority within the larger body of those who would not take the oaths.

By the time Johnson embarked on his career in London, the Nonjurors dissenting from and worshipping separately from the Church of England were much reduced in numbers.[14] The bishops deprived at the Revolution were long dead: Robert Frampton (1622–1708), Thomas Ken (1637–1711), John Lake (1624–89), William Lloyd (1637–1710), William Sancroft (1617–93), William Thomas (1613–89), Francis Turner (1636–1700), Thomas White (1628–98). So were famous clergy like John Kettlewell (1653–95) and Charles Leslie (1650–1722). So were the earliest bishops consecrated in Nonjuror communions, George Hickes (1642–1715) and Thomas Wagstaffe (1645–1712). So were the next batch of consecrations: Nathaniel Spinckes (1653–1727), Jeremy Collier (1650–1726), and Samuel

[11] *Causa Dei et Reipublicae contra Novatores. An Epistolary Conference Between a Reverend Nonjuror and a Loyal Oxonian, On The Standard of Christianity. The Standard of Civil Power & Obedience* (London, [1748]), pp. 10, 29. The pamphlet evidently continued a former controversy, as in [Hopton Haynes], *Causa Dei contra Novatores: or, The Religion of the Bible And The Religion of the Pulpit compared. In a Letter to the Reverend Mr. [Samuel] Wilson* (London, 1747).

[12] J. Wickham Legg, *English Church Life from the Restoration to the Tractarian Movement* (London, 1914), pp. 16–20.

[13] Boswell, *Life*, vol. 5 (*Tour*), p. 357.

[14] Henry Broxap, *The Later Non-jurors* (Cambridge, 1924), passim.

Hawes (? –1722). The next consecrations, in 1716, of Henry Gandy (1649–1734) and Thomas Brett (1667–1743), just reached to Johnson's public life. Only a few other famous Nonjurors did so, like Matthias Earbery (1690–1740). Although London in particular still supported separate Nonjuring congregations, theirs was a visibly declining cause.[15] Nonjuring laymen generally worshipped with the juring Church of England, served where possible, it may be presumed, by clergy of High Church sympathies. Most of those who rejected the authority of the regime had no opportunity to worship with a separate Nonjuring congregation, even if they wished to do so. This was the problem which confronted Thomas Hearne in Oxford in January 1730. He chose one solution: 'As for my own part, there being no nonjuring place for worship in Oxford, I continue in my own Room and pray by myself, using the Common Prayer, and that with greater consistence than go to the publick Churches and joyn with them but partly'[16] – that is, to join only in parts of the service, silently omitting the state prayers for the usurping dynasty. Clearly, however, Hearne recognised that others did just that. Even William Law, ordained deacon in 1711, deprived in 1714, ordained priest in the Nonjuring communion in 1727, regularly worshipped in his parish church at King's Cliffe.[17] Johnson, profoundly influenced by William Law's theology, evidently did the same.

Johnson seems to have entertained a low moral view of the minority of Nonjurors who worshipped separately. In March 1775, he recorded that he had once told an Irish Whig clergyman, Dr Samuel Madden,

> '... that perhaps a Nonjuror would have been less criminal in taking the oaths imposed by the ruling power, than refusing them; because refusing them, necessarily laid him under an irresistable temptation to be more criminal; for, a man *must* live, and if he precludes himself from the support furnished by the establishment, will probably be reduced to very wicked shifts to maintain himself'. BOSWELL. 'I should think, Sir, that a man who took the oaths contrary to his principles, was a determined wicked man, because he was sure he was committing perjury; whereas a Nonjuror might be insensibly led to do what was wrong, without being so directly conscious of it.' JOHNSON. 'Why, Sir, a man who goes to bed to his patron's wife is pretty sure that he is committing wickedness.' BOSWELL. 'Did the nonjuring clergymen do so, Sir?' JOHNSON. 'I am afraid many of them did.'

Boswell thought this unconvincing, and that 'had not his own father complied with the requisition of government ... he would probably have thought more unfavourably of a Jacobite who took the oaths'.[18] But Johnson's categorical assertion seems to stem from personal knowledge.

Hawkins was aware of his subject's early associations, but relegated to a

[15] J. H. Overton, *The Nonjurors* (London, 1902), pp. 282–4, 323–4, 340–5.
[16] John Buchanan-Brown (ed.), *The Remains of Thomas Hearne* (London, 1966), p. 369.
[17] Overton, *The Nonjurors*, pp. 331–2. [18] Boswell, *Life*, vol. 2, pp. 321–2.

footnote his most telling observation on them: 'Johnson in his early years associated with this sect of nonjurors, and from them, probably, imbibed many of his religious and political principles.'[19] This sympathy he showed on his journey to the Western Islands, in which, as Hawkins observed, 'he has noted his joining in public worship at the English non-juring episcopal chapel at Aberdeen'.[20] This was not strictly correct. In Scotland, the episcopalians had divided after 1688 into Nonjurors and congregations served by licensed ministers, as Johnson knowledgeably explained, 'by tacit connivance quietly permitted in separate congregations supplied with ministers by the successors of the bishops who were deprived at the Revolution': at Aberdeen and Inverness, Johnson worshipped with the latter.[21] His remark to Boswell that he had never been in a 'nonjuring meeting-house' is not contradicted by any evidence. Boswell too appreciated the difference by 1779, when he wrote to Johnson from Edinburgh with a story which was sure to interest him:

On Saturday last, being the 30th of January, I drank coffee and old port, and had solemn conversation with the Reverend Mr. [William] Falconer, a nonjuring bishop, a very learned and worthy man. He gave two toasts, which you will believe I drank with cordiality, Dr Samuel Johnson, and Flora Macdonald. I sat about four hours with him, and it was really as if I had been living in the last century.[22] The Episcopal Church of Scotland, though faithful to the royal house of Stuart, has never accepted of any *congé d'élire*, since the Revolution; it is the only true Episcopal Church in Scotland, as it has its own succession of bishops. For as to the episcopal clergy who take the oaths to the present government, they indeed follow the rites of the Church of England, but, as Bishop Falconer observed, 'they are not *Epsicopals*; for they are under no bishop, as a bishop cannot have authority beyond his diocese'. This venerable gentleman did me the honour to dine with me yesterday, and he laid his hands upon the heads of my little ones. We had a good deal of curious literary conversation, particularly about Mr. Thomas Ruddiman, with whom he lived in great friendship.[23]

Johnson and Ruddiman shared a vital allegiance.

II. THE THEOLOGY OF THE NONJURORS

Hawkins knew something of Johnson's theological views: 'He would no more have put his name to an Arian or Socinian tract than to a defence of

[19] Hawkins, *Life*, pp. 448–51. [20] Ibid., p. 485.

[21] Samuel Johnson, *A Journey to the Western Islands of Scotland*, ed. J.D. Fleeman (Oxford, 1985), pp. 12–13, 21; John Parker Lawson, *History of the Scottish Episcopal Church from the Revolution to the Present Time* (Edinburgh, 1843), p. 300.

[22] Few remarks more clearly emphasise the generation gap between Johnson (b. 1709) and Boswell (b. 1740).

[23] Boswell to Johnson, 2 February 1779: Boswell, *Life*, vol. 3, pp. 371–2.

Atheism.'[24] Yet debates on the Trinity by no means exhausted the subjects of disagreement within the Church of England, and Johnson had a particular interest in one group of Anglicans who came to be distinguished by their theology as well as by their political affirmations: the Nonjurors. Sir John Hawkins deeply disapproved of his subject's views in one respect in particular:

> The truth is, that Johnson's political prejudices were a mist that the eye of his judgement could not penetrate: in all the measures of government he could see nothing right; nor could he be convinced, in his invectives against a standing army, as the Jacobites affected to call it, that the peasantry of a country was not an adequate defence against an invasion of it by an armed force.[25] He almost asserted in terms, that the succession to the crown had been illegally interrupted, and that from whig-politics none of the benefits of government could be expected. He could but just endure the opposition to the minister[26] because conducted on whig principles; and I have heard him say, that during the whole course of it, the two parties were bidding for the people. At other times, and in the heat of his resentment, I have heard him assert, that, since the death of Queen Anne, it had been the policy of the administration to promote to ecclesiastical dignities none but the most worthless and undeserving men: nor would he then exclude from this bigotted censure those illustrious divines, Wake, Gibson, Sherlock, Butler, Herring, Pearce, and least of all Hoadly;[27] in competition with whom he would set Hickes, Brett, Leslie,[28] and others of the nonjurors, whose names are scarcely now remembered.[29]

Such names might be scarcely remembered by Whigs like Hawkins, but for Johnson they constituted a formidable battery of talent. In the much-revised fourth edition of his *Dictionary*, published in 1773, Johnson included as authorities extensive quotations from four Nonjurors in particular: John Kettlewell (1653–95), Robert Nelson (1656–1715), Charles Leslie (1650–1722) and William Law (1686–1761).[30] The choice of Leslie in particular

[24] Hawkins, *Life*, p. 85.

[25] Johnson nevertheless refused to serve in the Trained Bands of the City of London: see above, p. 121.

[26] Hawkins refers to Sir Robert Walpole.

[27] William Wake (1657–1737), Archbishop of Canterbury (1716–d.); Edmund Gibson (1669–1748), Bishop of London (1720–d.); William Sherlock (1641?–1707), Dean of St Paul's (1691–d.); Joseph Butler (1692–1752), Bishop of Durham (1750–d.); Thomas Herring (1693–1757), Archbishop of Canterbury (1747–d.); Zachary Pearce (1690–1774), Bishop of Rochester (1755–d.); Benjamin Hoadly (1676–1761), Bishop of Winchester (1734–d.).

[28] George Hickes (1642–1715), Dean of Worcester (1683–90), deprived at the Revolution; Thomas Brett (1667–1744), Rector of Ruckinge, Kent (1705–14), resigned at the accession of George I, consecrated Nonjuring bishop 1716; Charles Leslie (1650–1722), Chancellor of Connor (1687–90), deprived at the Revolution, Nonjuring theologian.

[29] Hawkins, *Life*, pp. 80–1.

[30] Allen Reddick, *The Making of Johnson's Dictionary 1746–1773* (Cambridge, 1990), pp. 141–69, at 142, 155–6.

was significant, for among a school which inclined to pietistic otherworldliness Leslie stood out not only as a theological writer but as an author profoundly committed to political controversy. In the 1773 edition of the *Dictionary* Johnson quoted from Leslie's treatise of 1700, *The Case of the Regale And of the Pontificat, stated. In a Conference Concerning the Independency of the Church, Upon any Power on Earth, in the Exercise of her Purely Spiritual Power and Authority.* Like Johnson in 1773, Leslie in 1700 had sought to defend the independence of the Church in the realm of ecclesiastical polity as a necessary precondition of the defence of doctrinal orthodoxy against Deists, Arians and Socinians. For similar purposes, Johnson quoted John Kettlewell's *Of Christian Communion, to be Kept on in the Unity of Christ's Church, and Among the Professors of Truth and Holiness. And of the Obligations, both of Faithful People, to Communicate in the Same. Fitted for Persecuted, or Divided, or Corrupt States of Churches; when They are Either Born Down by Secular Persecutions, or Broken with Schisms, or Defiled with Sinful Offices and Ministrations* (London, 1693), a plain reference to the state of the Church of England after the Revolution of 1688.

As significant as Johnson's use of the Nonjurors was that he joined to them, without remarking on any inconsistency, other Anglican theologians who had distinguished themselves as opponents of heterodoxy. One such was Daniel Waterland, author of *A Vindication of Christ's Divinity* (Cambridge, 1719) and *A Second Vindication of Christ's Divinity: Or, a Second Defense of Some Queries Relating to Dr Clarke's Scheme of the Holy Trinity* (London, 1723), an author widely regarded as having played a major part in checking the advance of anti-Trinitarian ideas in those decades. With Waterland went a group of seventeenth-century Anglican divines who had suffered during the Great Rebellion and often been deprived Nonjurors or even exiles during the 1650s, including Henry Hammond (1605–60), Barten Holyday (1593–1661), Peter Heylyn (1600–62), Richard Allestree (1619–81), John Pearson (1613–86) and John Fell (1625–86), together with Charles I's Bishop of Ely Francis White (?1564–1638),[31] authors whom Johnson quoted in order to establish the defensibility of Anglican liturgy and Articles, the dependence of order in Church and State on the divinely sanctioned institution of kingship, and the dangers of Dissenting zealotry.

Johnson's most provocative move was, of course, his public commendation of the Nonjurors. His first biographer sought to excuse this and to derive at least one advantage from it. At least, argued Hawkins, it proved that Johnson was not a Catholic: his use of prayers for the souls of the departed was attributed by his biographer to the influence not of 'the

[31] Reddick, *Making of Johnson's Dictionary*, pp. 158–60.

Romish tenet of Purgatory' but of 'certain divines of a Protestant communion ... These were, the non-juring clergy of the time; of whom, and also of their writings, Johnson was ever used to speak with great respect.' This referred to a controversy triggered by Jeremy Collier's call for restoring (inter alia) prayers for the dead,[32] replied to by Nathaniel Spinckes' denial;[33] Hawkins explained:

> the controversy was carried on to a great length; the result of it was, a schism among the nonjurors: those, for restoring the prayers, compiled a new communion-office; others, who were against widening the breach with the national church, chose to abide by the present form; and this diversity of sentiments and practice was, as Johnson once told me, the ruin of the nonjuring cause.

It would have taken a sympathiser to believe that this alone frustrated that cause, which was in terminal decline for many other reasons; but Johnson's interest was not merely theoretical. He was, indeed, learned in that subject: 'In the study of this controversy, which I have reason to think interested Johnson very deeply,' wrote Hawkins, 'he seems to have taken part with Dr Brett[34] and the separatists his followers.'[35] The schism among the Nonjurors to which Hawkins referred had been triggered by the 'usages controversy'.[36] This centred on the proposal of amending the worship of the Church of England by the introduction of four 'usages', which certain English Nonjurors argued were both primitive, and acknowledged in the first liturgy of Edward VI in 1549. As Thomas Deacon listed them:

1 The mixture of the Wine and Water in the sacrificial cup.
2 The oblation of the Eucharistic elements as the representative sacrifice of Christ's Body and Blood.
3 The blessing of them or the Invocation of the Holy Ghost upon them.
4 The recommending of the faithful departed to God's mercy at the Celebration of the Christian Sacrifice.[37]

32 [Jeremy Collier], *Reasons For Restoring some Prayers and Directions, As they stand in the Communion-Service Of the First English Reform'd Liturgy, Compiled by the Bishops in the 2d and 3d Years of the Reign of King Edward VI* (London, 1717), p. 10.

33 [Nathaniel Spinckes], *No Sufficient Reason For Restoring the Prayers and Directions of King Edward the Sixth's First Liturgy* (London, 1718), replied to by Thomas Brett, *Tradition Necessary to explain and interpret the Holy Scriptures* (London, 1718).

34 Thomas Brett, *A Collection Of the Principal Liturgies, Used by the Christian Church in the Celebration of the Holy Eucharist* (London, 1720).

35 Hawkins, *Life*, pp. 448–51.

36 Overton, *Nonjurors*, pp. 290–308; Broxap, *Later Non-jurors*, pp. 35–65 (pp. 63–5 provides a bibliography of the controversy).

37 Lawson, *History of the Scottish Episcopal Church*, p. 229; Henry Broxap, *A Biography of Thomas Deacon* (Manchester, 1911), pp. 25–49, at 29.

Collier and Brett supported these innovations; Spinckes defended the Book of Common Prayer as settled in 1662. This schism within the ranks of the Nonjurors was only reconciled in 1732.[38]

Johnson's knowledge of the issue came from one source in particular. He explained to the Duchess of Argyll in 1773 that the doctrine of Purgatory or 'a middle state' could be defended by a book of her kinsman, the Nonjuring bishop Archibald Campbell; Johnson's own copy later appeared in the sale catalogue of his library, and at Oxford in June 1784 he revised the account he had given Boswell of Archibald Campbell's life in such detail as to suggest that Johnson's acquaintance with Campbell went far beyond a cursory inspection of the Nonjuror's library.[39] It was on that occasion, in Johnson's 75th year, that he gave Boswell his most detailed view of Nonjuror theology.

Johnson made a remark this evening which struck me a good deal. 'I never (said he) knew a non-juror who could reason.' Surely he did not mean to deny that faculty to many of their writers; to Hickes, Brett, and other eminent divines of that persuasion; and did not recollect that the seven Bishops, so justly celebrated for their magnanimous resistance of arbitrary power, were yet Nonjurors to the new Government. The non-juring clergy of Scotland, indeed, who, excepting a few, have lately [in 1788], by a sudden stroke, cut off all ties of allegiance to the house of Stuart, and resolved to pray for our present lawful Sovereign by name, may be thought to have confirmed this remark; as it may be said, that the divine indefeasible hereditary right which they professed to believe, if ever true, must be equally true still. Many of my readers will be surprized when I mention, that Johnson assured me he had never in his life been in a nonjuring meeting house.

Evidently, Johnson's reputation among his readers was that of a Nonjuror. Boswell, who did not fully understand English ecclesiastical politics, failed to explain or record Johnson's explanation of his puzzling remark that he never knew a Nonjuror who could reason. Instead, Boswell tried to throw light on Johnson's position by printing an exchange with the scholar John Henderson (1757–88) of Pembroke College, Oxford:

HENDERSON. 'What do you think, Sir, of William Law?' JOHNSON. 'William Law, Sir, wrote the best piece of Parenetick[40] Divinity; but William Law was no reasoner.' HENDERSON. 'Jeremy Collier, Sir?' JOHNSON. 'Jeremy Collier fought without a rival, and therefore could not claim the victory.' Mr. Henderson

[38] Broxap, *Deacon*, pp. 89–97, argues that this was more of a compromise than a triumph of the 'usagers'.

[39] Archibald Campbell, *The Doctrines of a Middle State between Death and the Resurrection: Of Prayers for the Dead ... Together with Judgement of the Reverend Dr Hickes concerning this Book, so far as relates to a Middle State, Particular Judgement, and Prayers for the Dead ... Also a Preservative against several of the Errors of the Roman Church ...* (London, 1721); Boswell, *Journal*, p. 354 (25 October 1773); Boswell, *Life*, vol. 5 (*Tour*), p. 356; vol. 4, p. 286.

[40] I.e., exhortatory.

mentioned Kenn and Kettlewell; but some objections were made; at last he said, 'But, Sir, what do you think of Lesley?' JOHNSON. 'Charles Lesley I had forgotten. Lesley *was* a reasoner, and *a reasoner who was not to be reasoned against*.'[41]

But this was evidently Johnson in argumentative mood, drawing fine distinctions of merit among writers with whom he was sympathetic and familiar, not dismissing a group of authors of whom he disapproved.

Although Johnson's reading in philosophy and theology was wide, he took care not to include the works of the heterodox in his *Dictionary* as sources. As Hester Thrale explained, 'I have heard Mr. Johnson say myself that he never would give Shaftesbury [Thomas] Chubb or any wicked Writer's Authority for a Word, lest it should send People to look in a Book that might injure them forever.' It meant a complete ban on Thomas Hobbes. This ban extended to one of Johnson's favourite theologians, Samuel Clarke, ignored in the *Dictionary* because of his Arianism.[42] This renunciation only applied in public pronouncements; in private, his wide sympathies could be expressed. Dr Richard Brocklesby recorded of Johnson: 'He pressed me to study Dr [Samuel] Clarke and to read his Sermons. I asked him why he pressed Dr Clarke, an Arian. "Because, (said he,) he is fullest on the *propitiatory sacrifice*."'[43] Johnson was 'ever an admirer' of Dr Samuel Clarke, recorded Hawkins, and agreed with him in 'most . . . of his opinions, excepting in that of the Trinity, in which he said, as Dr Bentley, though no very sound believer, had done before, that Dr Waterland had foiled him'.[44]

Daniel Waterland, Johnson's contemporary, pointed to Johnson's interest in the Caroline divines. In Johnson's last years, Hawkins recommended to him Bishop Jeremy Taylor's *Holy Living* and *Holy Dying*, and, secondly, Taylor's *Ductor Dubitantium*:

Of the former, though he placed the author at the head of all the divines that have succeeded the fathers, he said, that in the reading thereof, he had found little more than he brought himself; and, at the mention of the latter, he seemed to shrink. His Greek testament was generally within his reach, and he re[a]d much in it. He was competently skilled in the writings of the fathers, yet was he more conversant with those of the great English church-men, namely, Hooker, Usher, Mede, Hammond, Sanderson, Hall, and others of that class.[45]

It was this group that, in 1688, found their apotheosis (or their nemesis) in the Nonjurors.

41 Boswell, *Life*, vol. 4, pp. 286–8.

42 Reddick, *Making of Johnson's Dictionary*, p. 34, citing Katharine Balderston (ed.), *Thraliana* (2nd edn, Oxford, 1951), p. 34.

43 Boswell, *Life*, vol. 4, p. 416; Waingrow, *Correspondence*, p. 32.

44 Hawkins, *Life*, pp. 253–4.

45 Hawkins, *Life*, p. 543.

Johnson was profoundly influenced in his religious life by reading, while at Oxford, the Nonjuror William Law's *A Serious Call to a Devout and Holy Life*, published in December, 1728;[46] the sale catalogue of his library shows that he also owned a copy of the two folio volumes of *The Theological Works of the Reverend Mr. Charles Leslie* (London, 1721), as well as Archibald Campbell's *The Doctrines of a Middle State*, 'Waterland on the Trinity', presumably *A Second Vindication of Christ's Divinity* (1728) and the four volumes of the 1684 collected edition of the works of Henry Hammond.[47] Johnson bought the seventh (1732) edition of Jeremy Collier's *Essays upon several Moral Subjects* for the Thrales' library at Streatham.[48] Hawkins too wrote that Johnson 'was extremely fond of Dr Hammond's Works, and sometimes gave them as a present to young men going into orders: he also bought them for the library at Streatham'.[49] *The Whole Duty of Man*, Nelson's *Festivals and Fasts* and Fleetwood on the Sacrament[50] were the books which Johnson, on his deathbed, urged on his friend John Hoole to confirm his religious beliefs.[51] Two of these three were Nonjuring tracts. Johnson was well aware that Fleetwood was a Whig:[52] his reading and his commitment was not limited to the Nonjuring tradition, though it centred there. If his library as sold at auction on 16 February 1785 did not contain other obviously Tory or Nonjuror texts, this is, of course, not conclusive evidence of Johnson's reading or library more than forty years earlier.[53]

46 Boswell, *Life*, vol. 1, p. 68; Katharine C. Balderston, 'Doctor Johnson and William Law', *Proceedings of the Modern Language Association* 75 (1960), 382–94, and 'Dr Johnson's Use of William Law in the Dictionary', *Philological Quarterly* 39 (1960), 379–88, corrected by Reddick, *Making of Johnson's Dictionary*, p. 230, n. 60.

47 *A Catalogue of the Valuable Library of Books, Of the late learned Samuel Johnson, Esq; LL. D.* [London, 1785], p. 26; for an annotated version see Donald Greene (ed.), *Samuel Johnson's Library: An Annotated Guide* (Victoria, British Columbia, 1975).

48 J. D. Fleeman (ed.), *A Preliminary Handlist of Copies of Books associated with Dr Samuel Johnson* (Oxford, 1984), p. 11.

49 *Johnsonian Miscellanies*, vol. 2, p. 19, quoted in Reddick, *Making of Johnson's Dictionary*, p. 231, n. 66.

50 [? Richard Allestree], *The Whole Duty of Man* (London, 1659; many subsequent editions, including one by the Edinburgh publishers T. and W. Ruddiman, 1741); Robert Nelson, *A Companion for the Festivals and Fasts of the Church of England* (London, 1704; it had reached at least its 25th edition by 1781); Bishop William Fleetwood, *The Reasonable Communicant: or, an Explanation of the Doctrine of the Sacrament of the Lord's-Supper* (London, 1704; 22nd edition by 1784).

51 O M Brack, Jr., *Journal Narrative relative to Doctor Johnson's last Illness three Weeks before his Death kept by John Hoole* (Iowa City, 1972), 20, 21 November 1784.

52 Johnson, *Lives of the Poets*, vol. 2, p. 361.

53 J. D. Fleeman (ed.), *The Sale Catalogue of Samuel Johnson's Library: A Facsimile Edition* (Victoria, British Columbia, 1975), estimates that the sale included only some 2922 volumes, many described at the time as 'in most woful condition', and that the catalogue was hastily and carelessly compiled: p. 7.

III. POLITICS AND RELIGIOUS COMMITMENT

It is demonstrable that Johnson's politics took their rise from his religious commitments. This was, of course, the normal source of principled political attitudes throughout the eighteenth century for men of all religious denominations,[54] and Johnson was unusual only in the depth of his knowledge of the Anglican tradition. Yet in the highly politicised conflict of religious groups that scarred English public life in Johnson's lifetime, one group in particular – the Nonjurors – preserved an unusually heightened sense of the rationale for their agonizing predicament of internal exile and disinheritance. Although pietist, otherworldly disengagement from public affairs ultimately predominated in the outlook of the remaining English Nonjurors of the 1730s and 40s, a counter current threatened to draw some of them towards resistance, even rebellion, and did so in the political setting with which Johnson was involved at the outset of his career.[55]

By the 1760s this alignment had dissolved, and a newcomer to England might not have been fully aware of a world that had now been lost. In the early years of their acquaintance, Boswell, still ill-informed about English ecclesiastical affairs, did not appreciate their force or significance. In August 1763 he touched off Johnson's wrath by relaying to him as one of the 'absurd stories' people told that 'David Hume told me, that you would stand before a battery of cannon, to restore the Convocation to its full powers'. Johnson's 'eyes flashed with indignation', for he had actually said this to Hume; 'And would I not, Sir? Shall the Presbyterian *Kirk* of Scotland have its General Assembly, and the Church of England be denied its Convocation?'[56] This, too, was consistent with Johnson's being a Nonjuror. The Convocation controversy had indeed owed more to the defence of that institution by deprived Nonjurors in the immediate aftermath of the Revolution than to the conformist Francis Atterbury's more famous pamphlet *A Letter to a Convocation Man* (1696).[57] Ten years later, Boswell understood these matters better. In November 1773, Boswell took Johnson

54 This is a leading theme of J. C. D. Clark, *The Language of Liberty 1660–1832: Political Discourse and Social Dynamics in the Anglo-American World* (Cambridge, 1993).

55 The letters of the Nonjuror Thomas Brett for 1737–40, Bodleian MS Eng Th c. 34, are full of cryptic references to negotiations about renewing 'leases' with an unnamed 'landlord'. They presumably refer to attempts among the Nonjuring community to agree on terms (or possibly a reconciliation) for some anticipated event, presumably a restoration. They include letters from Thomas Wagstaffe (1692–1770), Anglican chaplain to James III and Prince Charles, then in Paris (e.g. Wagstaffe to Brett, 14 August 1738, 7 January 1739: ibid., ff. 251, 397).

56 Boswell, *Life*, vol. 1, p. 464.

57 Mark Goldie, 'The Nonjurors, Episcopacy, and the Origins of the Convocation Controversy', in Eveline Cruickshanks (ed.), *Ideology and Conspiracy: Aspects of Jacobitism, 1689–1759* (Edinburgh, 1982), pp. 15–35.

to stay with his father, the judge Lord Auchinleck, who, on the basis of Johnson's 'supposed political tenets which were so discordant to his own that, instead of speaking of him with that respect to which he was entitled, used to call him "a Jacobite fellow"'.[58] Boswell expected trouble: his father 'was as sanguine a Whig and Presbyterian as Dr Johnson was a Tory and Church of England man'. Johnson agreed to steer off subjects which would offend his host, and the visit began well:

> Our first day went off very smoothly. It rained, and we could not get out; but my father showed Dr Johnson his library, which, in curious editions of the Greek and Roman classics is, I suppose, not excelled by any private collection in Great Britain. My father had studied at Leyden and been very intimate with the Gronovii and other learned men there. He was a sound scholar, and, in particular, had collated manuscripts and different editions of Anacreon, and others of the Greek lyric poets, with great care; so that my friend and he had much matter for conversation, without touching on the fatal topics of difference.

This truce lasted until

> my father was showing him his collection of medals; and Oliver Cromwell's coin unfortunately introduced Charles the First, and Toryism. They became exceedingly warm and violent, and I was very much distressed by being present at such an altercation between two men, both of whom I reverenced; yet I durst not interfere ... In the course of their altercation, Whiggism and Presbyterianism, Toryism and Episcopacy, were terribly buffeted.[59]

The dependence of Johnson's politics on his theology is most evident in the central question of allegiance. His *Dictionary* remarkably contained no definition of 'Jacobite', but defined 'Nonjuror' as 'One who conceiving James II. unjustly deposed, refuses to swear allegiance to those who have succeeded him', and 'nonjuring' as 'Belonging to those who will not swear allegiance to the Hanoverian family'. In support of which, Johnson quoted Swift: 'This objection was offered me by a very pious, learned, and worthy gentleman of the *nonjuring* party.'[60] Johnson did not confine the term 'nonjuror' to the clergy, or to those who had been ejected from some office or church preferment;[61] he interpreted it widely as covering all those who would not take the oath of allegiance. Nor did Johnson's definition entail that a Nonjuror must refuse to participate in the services of the juring church, though he was aware that some Nonjurors did feel obliged to form

58 Boswell, *Journal*, p. 370 (2 November 1773); Boswell, *Life*, vol. 5 (*Tour*), p. 376.
59 Boswell, *Journal*, pp. 370, 375–6 (2, 6 November 1773).
60 Samuel Johnson, *A Dictionary of the English Language* (London, 1755).
61 Greene (*Politics*, p. xxx) argues that 'As Johnson was well aware, the term was normally applied to those clergy of the Church of England who in 1689 refused to take the oaths of allegiance to William and Mary and consequently were deprived of their church appointments.' It is clear from Johnson himself that 'Nonjuror' had a more extensive meaning.

Plate 5

Johnson's London milieu. St Clement Danes church in the Strand was a centre for High Churchmen and Nonjurors. The Crown and Anchor tavern, home of the Oak Society, is shown opposite; a row of sympathetic booksellers and publishers faced the west end of the church. In the distance is Temple Bar with its row of Jacobite heads.

separate congregations. Johnson's claim that 'he had never in his life been in a nonjuring meeting-house'[62] has been interpreted as a condemnation of the Nonjuring cause; but this was not Johnson's view.

What is known of Johnson's own religious life bears out in practical form these abstract commitments. In mid 1765, Johnson moved from chambers in the Temple to a house in Johnson's Court, Fleet Street. Hawkins recorded that, at that time, 'The church he frequented was that of St Clement Danes,[63] which, though not his parish-church, he preferred to that of the Temple, which I recommended to him, as being free from noise, and, in other respects, more commodious. His only reason was, that in the former he was best known.'[64] Boswell too recorded in 1773 that Johnson 'had his seat' at St Clement Danes.[65] St Clement Danes would, of course, have been within easy walking distance of Johnson's other residences, including Gough Square and Bolt Court. Hawkins was not fully informed about Johnson's religion, 'having never been present with him at church but once', and evidently failed to appreciate his friend's preference for St Clement Danes.[66] If Johnson was indeed better known there, it was among the High Church, Nonjuror, Tory and quasi-Jacobite circles who found St Clement Danes congenial.[67]

Johnson's obiter dicta on Jacobitism indeed centred on religion rather than hereditary right:

A Jacobite, Sir, believes in the divine right of Kings. He that believes in the divine right of Kings believes in a Divinity. A Jacobite believes in the divine right of Bishops. He that believes in the divine right of Bishops believes in the divine

62 Boswell, *Life*, vol. 4, p. 288.

63 According to Hume, Charles Edward Stuart was received into the Church of England during his clandestine visit in 'the new church in the Strand'. Greene, *Politics*, p. xxxv, argues that this was St Martin-in-the-Fields. It might more probably be St Mary-le-Strand, built 1714–23; but St Clement Danes (whose tower and steeple were completed in 1719) was still sometimes known as the 'new church', and its proximity to Lady Primrose's house in Essex Street, where the Prince stayed, points to the latter. Cf. Woolf, *Medallic Record*, p. 119, for the medal distributed on James III's instructions on that occasion.

64 Hawkins, *Life*, p. 452.

65 Boswell, *Life*, vol. 2, p. 214. For other visits in 1775, 1776, 1778, 1779, 1781, 1783 and 1784 see ibid., pp. 356–7; vol. 3, pp. 17, 24, 26, 302, 313, 379; vol. 4, pp. 90, 203, 209, 270n.

66 Hawkins, *Life*, p. 453.

67 The Jacobite John Byrom regularly attended St Clement Danes while in London in 1735–6 (Byrom, *Journal*, vol. 1, pp. 569, 572, 576, 579, 595, 695; vol. 2, pp. 7, 20, 26). William Bowyer (1663–1737), the eminent London printer, a Nonjuror, had his second son Thomas baptised there in 1730 (John Nichols, *Literary Anecdotes of the Eighteenth Century* (9 vols, London, 1812–15), vol. 1, p. 457). In 1721 St Clement's was complimented for its new painting of Charles I, and in 1725 caused a sensation by its new altarpiece, in which an angel was widely recognised as a portrait of James III's queen Clementina Sobieska (J. Wickham Legg, *English Church Life from the Restoration to the Tractarian Movement* (London, 1914), pp. 130–1). The church was even reputed to use the reservation of the Sacrament, an exceptional practice at that time (Archibald Campbell (who lived in the parish) to

authority of the Christian religion. Therefore, Sir, a Jacobite is neither an Atheist nor a Deist. That cannot be said of a Whig; for *Whiggism is a negation of all principle.*[68]

Such remarks seem like jests only if their ideological underpinning is forgotten. Perhaps it was because David Hume lacked this grounding in English political theology that Johnson said of him, 'Sir, he was a Tory by chance.'[69] By contrast, Johnson's friend Richard Savage, though scarcely a man of personal piety, had turned his poem *The Convocation* (1717) into an eloquent defence of the Church and denunciation of its main Whig enemy, Benjamin Hoadly, Bishop of Bangor.[70] Yet Johnson's fame from the 1760s onwards must not be read back into the 1730s or 40s: his long obscurity is marked even among that group with whose outlook he had most sympathy. In the correspondence of the Nonjurors of this period 'Mr. Johnson' signifies not the Grub Street hack, a person of no standing, but John Johnson (1662–1725), vicar of Cranbrook, author of *The Unbloody Sacrifice ... in which the nature of the Eucharist is explain'd according to the sentiments of the Christian Church in the first four centuries* (London, 1714) and other serious theological monographs, a man with whom even the great Daniel Waterland had to contend.

Thomas Brett, 3 February 1729/30: Bodl MS Eng. Th. c 30 f 495). I owe the information in this note, and other material on St Clement Danes, to Mr. Richard Sharp.

68 Boswell, *Life*, vol. 1, pp. 430–1.

69 Boswell, *Life*, vol. 4, p. 194; 'Hume is a Tory by chance, as being a Scotsman, but not upon principle of duty; for he has no principle. If he is anything, he is a Hobbist': Boswell, *Journal*, pp. 238–9 (1 October 1773); Boswell, *Life*, vol. 5 (*Tour*), p. 272.

70 In Clarence Tracy (ed.), *The Poetical Works of Richard Savage* (Cambridge, 1962), pp. 26–40. Tracy observes that Johnson had not read it, but his friend's views were unlikely to have been kept from Johnson.

6

JOHNSON'S POLITICAL CONDUCT, 1737–1760

I. POLITICAL CONTACTS, 1737–1744, AND JOHNSON'S *LONDON*

Some fragmentary evidence exists for the partisanship of Johnson's early acquaintances and for the circles in which he moved after his arrival in London in 1737.[1] Edward Cave, proprietor of the *Gentleman's Magazine*, commended himself to Johnson in two ways. When Johnson came to write Cave's obituary in 1754, he described early years of poverty and rejection reminiscent of the themes of Johnson's *Life of Savage*. But more important were Cave's politics:

> When his apprenticeship was over he worked as a Journeyman at the printing house of Mr. *Barber*, a man much distinguished and employed by the tories, whose principles had at that time so much prevalence with *Cave*, that he was for some years a writer in *Mist's* Journal, which though he afterwards obtained, by his wife's interest, a small place in the post office, he for some time continued. But as interest is powerful, and conversation, however mean, in time persuasive, he by degrees inclined to another party; in which, however, he was always moderate, though steady and determined.[2]

As soon as Johnson found his way to the *Gentleman's Magazine* he would have met there his near contemporary William Guthrie (1708–70), already employed on the journal and perhaps congenial to its proprietor for similar reasons. Guthrie was the son of a Scots episcopalian clergyman, born at Brechin in Forfarshire, educated like Ruddiman at Aberdeen University while it was still a potent centre of episcopalian humanism, who had come to London in 1730.[3] According to Boswell, who would have recognised the politics of his countryman, Guthrie was a Nonjuror.

1 For this phase of his life, and a different interpretation, see especially Thomas Kaminski, *The Early Career of Samuel Johnson* (New York, 1987). For the political context, see especially Eveline Cruickshanks, *Political Untouchables: The Tories and the '45* (London, 1979).

2 [Samuel Johnson], 'An Account of the Life of the late Mr. Edward Cave', *Gentleman's Magazine* 24 (February 1754), 55–8, at 56. For the Jacobite Alderman Barber and *Mist's Journal*, see below, pp. 147, 149, 155n, 158.

3 *Dictionary of National Biography*.

He was descended of an ancient family in Scotland; but having a small patrimony, and being an adherent of the unfortunate house of Stuart, he could not accept of any office in the state; he therefore came to London, and employed his talents and learning as an 'Authour by profession' ... such was the power of his political pen, that, at an early period, Government thought it worth their while to keep it quiet by a pension, which he enjoyed till his death.[4]

Boswell referred to the pension of £200 p.a. which Guthrie obtained from the Pelham ministry in 1745/6 and which Bute renewed in 1762.[5] Despite Guthrie's meanness and vanity, Johnson respected him as, he said, 'a man of parts' and, as Boswell recorded, 'Johnson esteemed him enough to wish that his life should be written':[6] perhaps prudently, it never was. But it seems that Johnson, certainly before Guthrie's pension, was drawn to his fellow author; and if Johnson has been correctly identified as a Nonjuror, it would have been natural that Guthrie should introduce Johnson to such circles in London.

One contact which Johnson certainly made in or before 1744 was with a Scots Nonjuring bishop and author. In April 1773, 'Johnson observed, that there were very few books printed in Scotland before the Union. He had seen a complete collection of them in the possession of the Hon. Archibald Campbell, a non-juring Bishop', a man of whom, in 1773, Johnson gave Boswell 'a full history'. Boswell added: 'I wish this collection had been kept entire. Many of them are in the library of the Faculty of Advocates at Edinburgh.'[7] Archibald Campbell (c. 1669–1744) was consecrated Bishop of Dundee in 1711 and of Aberdeen in 1721, but generally resided in London, where, resigning his offices in 1725 after the usages controversy, he headed a separate Nonjuror congregation.[8] It was a minority taste that Johnson displayed, and this sort of acquaintance was to lead him also to the fugitive rebel William Drummond in 1746.[9] But it did not take knowledge of these conspiracies to interpret Johnson's first published works.

Among Johnson's early friends in London was Richard Savage, brilliant, charming and, in Johnson's account, strangely doomed. It was a friendship which was to give rise to Johnson's first mature biography, published anonymously in 1744 as *An Account of the Life of Mr. Richard Savage*, a bitter

[4] Boswell, *Life*, vol. 1, pp. 116–7.

[5] Guthrie to unnamed [? Bute], 3 June 1762, in Boswell, *Life*, vol. 1, p. 117.

[6] Boswell, *Life*, vol. 2, p. 52; vol. 1, p. 117. For James Edward Oglethorpe's similar refusal to allow Johnson to write his life, see below, p. 200.

[7] Boswell, *Journal*, p. 354 (25 October 1773); Boswell, *Life*, vol. 2, p. 216. Since this was before Johnson's Scottish tour, he could only have seen the books in Campbell's possession in London.

[8] *Dictionary of National Biography*; John Parker Lawson, *History of the Scottish Episcopal Church from the Revolution to the Present Time* (Edinburgh, 1843), pp. 211–2, 225, 228, 232, 234–7, 524.

[9] For whom, see below, pp. 173–4.

and powerful work whose tragic sense reveals the strength of Johnson's identification with his subject. For those unaware of Savage's political views, Johnson's loyalty to him was almost inexplicable: Hawkins described it as 'an intimacy, the motives to which, at first view, may probably seem harder to be accounted for than any one particular in his life'. Hawkins saw that they shared a 'resentment against the possessors of wealth'; shared too

> those principles of patriotism, that both, for some years after, avowed; they both with the same eye saw, or believed they saw, that the then minister meditated the ruin of this country; that excise laws, standing armies, and penal statutes, were the means by which he meant to effect it; and, at the risque of their liberty, they were bent to oppose his measures.[10]

This was true as far as it went; but the two men had a deeper affinity. Hawkins could not have known that Savage's earliest poetry was Jacobite propaganda verse produced at the moment of the rebellion of 1715:[11] *An ironical panagerick on his pretended Majesty G[eorge] by the Curse of G[od] Userper of Great-Brittan ffrance and Ireland, Non-defender of the faith &c.*, a second entitled *The Pretender*, a third, *Britannia's Miseries* and other works. Already the authorities had taken an interest in him: in November 1715 he had been arrested and tried for 'having a treasonable Pamphlet in his possession' and only escaped conviction when he 'impeach'd one of Mr. Berington the Printer's Men'.[12]

Johnson saw in Savage one of those who were 'always zealous in their Assertions of the Justice of the late Opposition, jealous of the Rights of the People, and alarmed by the long continued Triumph of the Court'; although Johnson professed Savage's 'avowed Neutrality with regard to Party', he recorded also that his friend 'was very far from approving the Conduct of Sir *Robert Walpole*, and in Conversation mentioned him sometimes with Acrimony, and generally with Contempt', which cast some doubt on his alleged neutrality. Savage did indeed publish 'a Panegyric on Sir *Robert Walpole*, for which he was rewarded by him with twenty Guineas'; Johnson recorded the excuse:

> He alleged, that he was then dependent upon the Lord *Tyrconnel*, who was an implicite Follower of the Ministry, and that being enjoined by him, not without Menaces, to write in Praise of his Leader, he had not Resolution sufficient to sacrifice the Pleasure of Affluence to that of Integrity.[13]

10 Hawkins, *Life*, pp. 51–4.

11 It survives in the reports of a spy submitted in 1717, PRO SPD 35/7/78: Clarence Tracy, *The Artificial Bastard: A Biography of Richard Savage* (Cambridge, Mass., 1953), pp. 28–37. The general amnesty on 6 July 1717 freed him from the threat of prosecution.

12 Tracy, *Artificial Bastard*, p. 30.

13 [Samuel Johnson], *An Account of the Life of Mr. Richard Savage, Son of the Earl Rivers* (London, 1744), pp. 63–4.

It was a strange anticipation of Johnson's own moral dilemma in accepting a pension from George III in 1762. It seems, too, that Johnson, even in his anonymous biography of 1744, was not entirely candid about his friend's political commitments. These evidently extended beyond the complaints of the Whig opposition, although he shared with them one characteristic which qualified Johnson's attachment to him: 'He was an indefatigable Opposer of all the Claims of Ecclesiastical Power, though he did not know on what they were founded.'[14]

Savage obtained a promise of a place from Walpole; it was never forthcoming. This was not surprising:

> He did not indeed deny that he had given the Minister some Reason to believe that he should not strengthen his own Interest by advancing him, for he had taken Care to distinguish himself in Coffee-Houses as an Advocate for the Ministry of the last Years of Queen *Anne*,[15] and was always ready to justify the Conduct, and exalt the Character of Lord Bolingbroke, whom he mentions with great Regard in an Epistle upon Authors, which he wrote about that Time, but was too wise to publish.[16]

The ministry of the last four years of Queen Anne was the Tory high water mark, made possible by the wave of legitimist sentiment unleashed by the trial of Dr Sacheverel.

Johnson's first published work, the poem *London*, which appeared anonymously in May 1738, may have anticipated a scheme by Savage's friends to rescue their alcoholic and feckless fellow-author. Sir John Hawkins recorded this as fact, and although it has been denied that any direct evidence links Savage with 'Thales' in Johnson's poem or with Johnson himself before the publication of *London*,[17] the circumstantial evidence deserves to be weighed. Johnson recorded the plan for his friend to renounce the corruptions and expense of the metropolis for an Arcadian

[14] [Johnson], *Life of Savage*, p. 108.

[15] Jonathan Swift's *Four Last Years of the Queen* had been written in 1712–13 but, following the Hanoverian accession, not published. In July 1737 Swift arranged for John Boyle, 5th Earl of Orrery, to deliver the manuscript to William King (Swift to Orrery, 2 July 1737, in Harold Williams (ed.), *The Correspondence of Jonathan Swift* (5 vols., Oxford, 1963–5), vol. 4, p. 542) to organise its publication. King still delayed on the grounds that 'the publication of this work, as excellent as it is, would involve the printer, author, and every one concerned, in the greatest difficulties, if not in certain ruin' (King to Deane Swift, 25 April 1738: ibid., p. 107): it did not finally appear in print until 1758 (Harold Williams, 'Jonathan Swift and the Four Last Years of the Queen', *The Library*, 4th series 16 (1935), 61–90; Greenwood, *William King*, pp. 80–5). Johnson knew that this work was, after Swift's death, 'in the hands of Lord Orrery and Dr King'; Johnson had heard of its contents 'from a conversation which I once heard between the Earl of Orrery and old Mr. Lewis': Johnson, *Lives of the Poets*, vol. 3, p. 140.

[16] [Johnson], *Life of Savage*, p. 116.

[17] Waingrow (ed.), *Correspondence*, p. 233; Thomas Kaminski, 'Was Savage "Thales"?: Johnson's *London* and Biographical Speculation', *Bulletin of Research in the Humanities* 85 (1982), 322–35.

retreat in a place which would combine rural innocence with mythic patriotism:

> The Scheme proposed for this happy and independent Subsistence, was, that he should retire into *Wales*, and receive an Allowance of fifty Pounds a Year, to be raised by a Subscription, on which he was to live privately in a cheap Place, without aspiring any more to Affluence, or having any farther Care of Reputation.
>
> This Offer Mr. *Savage* gladly accepted, tho' with Intentions very different from those of his Friends; for they proposed, that he should continue an Exile from *London* for ever, and spend all the remaining Part of his Life at *Swansea*; but he designed only to take the Opportunity, which their Scheme offered him, of retreating for a short Time, that he might prepare his Play for the Stage, and his other Works for the Press, and then return to *London* to exhibit his Tragedy, and live upon the Profits of his own Labour.

Savage left London in July 1739, having 'parted from the Author of this Narrative with Tears in his Eyes'.[18] He died in gaol, in Bristol, in 1743.

Similarly, *London* was ostensibly a poem about the rejection of the corruptions of the town for the virtues of the country; but the characterisation of that corruption was profoundly political, and evoked by certain images which would have been understood as such. Thales's departure for Wales, which would 'Give to St DAVID one *true Briton* more' was a clear allusion to the Jacobite periodical *The True Briton*.[19] Thales, invoking the memory of Elizabeth I, turns his back on London, and, about to embark at Greenwich, says:

> Here let those reign, whom Pensions can incite
> To vote a Patriot black, a Courtier white;
> Explain their Country's dear-bought Rights away,
> And plead for Pirates in the Face of Day;
> With slavish Tenets taint our poison'd Youth,
> And lend a Lye the Confidence of Truth.[20]

England displayed a dispiriting prospect:

> Behold rebellious virtue quite o'erthrown.

The word 'rebellious' had no obvious meaning in that context apart from political allusion. Thales drives home the point by linking parliamentary corruption to George II's regular visits to his favourite electorate:

18 [Johnson], *Life of Savage*, pp. 145, 151.

19 Edited by Philip, Duke of Wharton; published from 3 June 1723 to 17 February 1724, when it was suppressed by legal persecution.

20 [Samuel Johnson], *London: A Poem, In Imitation of the Third Satire of Juvenal* (London, 1738), pp. 3, 6–7.

Scarce can our Fields, such Crowds at *Tyburn* die,
With Hemp the Gallows and the Fleet supply.
Propose your Schemes, ye Senatorian Band,
Whose *Ways and Means* support the sinking Land;
Lest Ropes be wanting in the tempting Spring,
To rig another Convoy for the K[in]g.[21]

Clearly, the fleet should sail: Thales looked forward to the king's departure. So, presumably, did Alexander Pope. His imitation of Horace's sixth Epistle of Book I[22] was addressed to the young lawyer William Murray, who only a decade before had given clear evidence of his Stuart commitment.[23] With its invocation of 'Tully' and 'Hyde', Pope's version alluded certainly to Cicero, probably to Clarendon, but possibly to a later Hyde, Lord Cornbury, who in 1731 had undertaken a mission to the Jacobite court at Rome.[24]

Johnson's *London* was an immediate success: Robert Dodsley printed a second and a third edition in 1738, a fourth in 1739, and a fifth in 1750. But another edition of 1738, though carrying Dodsley's name on the title page, has been ascribed on internal evidence to the Edinburgh publishing firm of T. and W. Ruddiman.[25] The episcopalian and Jacobite Thomas Ruddiman[26] would naturally have recognised the implications of Johnson's poem. Whether the two men ever met is not known, though it may be relevant that Ruddiman paid, his only recorded visit to the capital in 1737 on business connected with the investigation by the House of Lords into the Porteous riots.[27]

When in the 1760s the *North Briton* mounted a violent attack on the pensions granted by George III, it included an assault on Johnson's *London* for its '*distant hints* and *dark allusions*'. These were soon to be made explicit in Johnson's anonymous pamphlets of 1739, and made intelligible the *North Briton*'s heavy irony:

Mr. Johnson's many writings in the cause of liberty, his steady attachment to the present Royal Family, his gentleman-like compliments to his Majesty's Grand-

21 [Johnson], *London*, p. 18.
22 Alexander Pope, *The Sixth Epistle of the First Book of Horace Imitated* was published in London on 23 January 1738.
23 See above, pp. 92, 117.
24 Howard Erskine-Hill, *The Augustan Idea in English Literature* (London, 1983), pp. 334–9.
25 D. F. Foxon, *English Verse 1701–1750* (2 vols., Cambridge, 1975), vol. 1, p. 389; vol. 2, p. 193. Also on the evidence of publisher's ornaments, the Ruddimans have been credited with Edinburgh editions of Alexander Pope's *One Thousand Seven Hundred and Thirty Eight. A Dialogue something like Horace* and *One Thousand Seven Hundred and Thirty Eight. Dialogue II*: Foxon, English Verse, vol. 1, pp. 630–1.
26 For whom, see above, pp. 21, 34–6.
27 Duncan, *Thomas Ruddiman*, p. 4. It is possible that William Guthrie or Archibald Campbell told Ruddiman of Johnson, or introduced them; but no evidence survives.

father, and his decent treatment of the Parliament, intitle him to a share of the royal bounty ... No man, who has read only one poem of his, *London*, but must congratulate the good sense and discernment of the minister, who bestows such a part of the public treasure on this distinguished friend of the Public, of his Master's family, and of the Constitution of the country.[28]

Where Johnson in his anonymous *Taxation no Tyranny* (1775) condemned the pro-Americans as those who had 'blindly hated their country', the charge was thrown back at him. One pamphleteer quoted four lines from *London*[29] as proof of the proposition:

There have been men, and he himself must know it, even in this nation, who have ever declaimed loudly in behalf of high prerogative; have supported all the measures, and even all the pretensions, of the *Stuart* family; have inveighed with rancor against the *House of Hanover*; traduced the glorious Revolution; and employed all their art in writing to abet despotism in all its shapes ... Who can *hate their country* more than these?[30]

Why did Johnson now mock those who had fled to America to escape oppression at home? In *London* he had envisaged just such a refuge from tyranny in England, as the pamphleteer of 1775 now quoted:

> Has Heav'n reserv'd, in pity to the poor,
> No pathless waste, or undiscover'd shore?
> No secret island in the boundless main?
> No peaceful desert yet unclaim'd by Spain?
> Quick let us rise, the happy seats explore,
> And bear oppression's insolence no more.[31]

'Oppression's insolence' had a different meaning for the young Johnson. The threat of prosecution, fine, the pillory, imprisonment and even execution gave critics of the Whig regime a powerful inducement to disguise their attacks behind allegory, irony or a parallel case. Even then they were not safe, since until Fox's Libel Act of 1792 the law gave the jury the task of interpreting innuendos, and judicial guidance allowed a pro-Hanoverian jury a wide scope. In *Rex v. Clarke* (1729), the trial of the publisher of *Mist's Weekly Journal* who had attacked the royal family under fictional names, Lord Chief Justice Raymond agreed with the Attorney General's argument

[28] *The North Briton*, no. 12 (21 August 1762).

[29] Explain their Country's dear-bought-Rights away / ... And lend a Lye the Confidence of Truth.

[30] *Tyranny Unmasked. An Answer to a late Pamphlet, entitled Taxation no Tyranny* (London, 1775), pp. 21–2.

[31] *Tyranny Unmasked*, pp. 23–4.

that a passage's meaning was 'such as the generality of readers must take it in, according to the obvious and natural sense of it'.[32]

The state of the law gave ministries considerable scope to suppress criticism, and from 1714 into the 1740s they often sought to exploit those grey areas. Government lawyers continually harassed hostile publications:[33] as Philip, Duke of Wharton, complained, such a '*Political* Lawyer' would use the idea of an 'Inuendo' to place the most unfavourable construction on the satirist's words: the innuendo 'makes past Times present, and can bring all the different Periods and Revolutions of History into fresh Action before us. It can change Countries, and make *Ancient Greece* and *Old Rome*, *Spain*, *Poland*, &c. appear to be only different Names for one and the same Nation; and shew that they all signify the same as the Word ENGLAND, in their Turns. It can make *Evil Ministers*, that liv'd never so many Ages ago, revive again, and prove them to be actually opening the New Year with their Sinister Operations.' The innuendo was a '*new-invented* Piece of *Law-Artifice*, that will not allow Writers to have their own Meanings, but will be ever devising new Meanings for them'; it 'can make as many Transformations out of a *plain* and *literal* Narrative, as are to be found in the *Metamorphosis* of Ovid'.[34] One ministerial apologist

> complains heavily, that the whole Artillery of Pamphleteers, Ballad-mongers, and Libellers was drawn out to asperse the Government; and charges the Writers of the *Craftsman* with shewing by what Steps Revolutions may be form'd, and resolving, since they could not prevail on the King to change his Ministry, to try if they could not persuade the People to change their King.

Had this been true, replied the opposition's defender, 'there had been no need of putting forced Constructions upon every Paper, and torturing and

32 Thomas Barnardiston, *Reports of Cases Determined in the Court of King's Bench* (2 vols., In the Savoy, 1744), vol. 1, pp. 304–5; Francis Ludlow Holt, *The Law of Libel* (2nd edn, London, 1816), p. 96n; Lawrence Hanson, *Government and the Press 1695–1763* (London, 1936), pp. 24–6.

33 For an anthology of arrest warrants signed by Secretaries of State and directed against authors, journalists, printers and publishers, see [Philip Carteret Webb, ed.], *Copies taken from the Records of the Court of King's Bench at Westminster; The original Office-Books of the Secretaries of State, remaining in the Paper, and Secretaries of State's Offices, or from the Originals under Seal. Of Warrants issued by Secretaries of State, for seizing persons suspected of being guilty of various Crimes, particularly, of being the Authors, Printers and Publishers of Libels, from the Restoration to the present Time* (London, 1763). For the originals, PRO SPD 44/82, 44/83 and 44/84.

34 *The True Briton*, 13 January 1724. The paper generally appeared under a Latin tag taken from Virgil, Horace, Ovid, Sallust, Cornelius Nepos, Pliny, Juvenal, Ausonius, Tacitus, Cicero, Lucan, Martial, Claudian, or Propertius.

wresting the Author's Meaning to support unreasonable Prosecutions', since the law of treason would have covered it.[35]

With the law as it then stood, however, there were few legal restraints on a ministerial campaign of repression. Nathaniel Mist, publisher of *Mist's Weekly Journal*, was broken in health and financially ruined by a long detention in prison awaiting trial in 1721, an action finally dismissed in December that year in the King's Bench for lack of evidence. The ministry tried again in 1723, and in 1728 the entire staff of *Mist's*, writers, printers and distributors, was taken into custody, a total of twenty two persons. In the 1720s this policy of repeated harassment suppressed two leading Jacobite newspapers, the *True Briton* and the *Freeholder's Journal*; in 1727, 1729, 1730, 1731, 1737 and 1739 the ministry did its best similarly to silence *The Craftsman*.[36] In 1726 Lord Orrery explained to James III that 'tho there is no formal law to restrain the Liberty of the press, yet several Printers have been so severely prosecuted, that 'tis allmost impossible to gett any thing published, that does but look like a reflection upon the Gouvernment'.[37]

Henry Haines, printer of *The Craftsman*, was arrested for its issue of 2 July 1737, which according to Nicholas Paxton, the Treasury Solicitor, 'contains several Quotations from Shakespear's Play of King John which are, by the Observations made thereupon, endeavoured to be applied to his present Majesty'.[38] Before his trial, Haines was again arrested for the issue of 10 December, with its author, Nicholas Amhurst; in May 1738 Haines received sentence of a year's imprisonment, a £200 fine, and had to find sureties of £2000 for seven years for his good behaviour.[39] These were the stakes in the desperate game of opposition journalism, and, by those criteria, William Guthrie's career developed more successfully than Johnson's. By 1740 he was writing steadily for the two main opposition papers, *Common Sense* and *Old England*, and to such effect that on 17 March a warrant was issued for his arrest; but a more effective gag was found to be a pension of £200 in return for not writing against the ministry, a reward which he received from 1746 to his death.[40]

35 *The Doctrine of Innuendo's Discuss'd; or the Liberty of the Press Maintain'd: Being some Thoughts upon the present Treatment of the Printer and Publishers of the Craftsman* (London, 1731), pp. 15–16.

36 [Webb], *Copies taken from the Records of the Court of King's Bench*, pp. 28–35; Hanson, *Government and the Press*, pp. 45, 47, 65.

37 Orrery to James III, 6 August 1726, Stuart Papers, Royal Archives 96/17, quoted in Paul Chapman, 'Jacobite Political Argument in England, 1714–1766' (Cambridge Ph.D. thesis, 1982), p. 103.

38 'State of Prosecutions now depending ...', BL Add MSS 33052 f. 150.

39 Hanson, *Government and the Press*, pp. 69–70.

40 PRO SPD 44/83/391, 395; Guthrie to Newcastle, 21 March 1754: BL Add MSS 32734 f. 299; Sir Lewis Namier, *The Structure of Politics at the Accession of George III* (2nd edn., London, 1963), p. 229.

Johnson's poem soon achieved classic status. But Hawkins rightly noted that *London* did not do for Johnson's career what he had hoped: 'it procured him fame but no patronage'.[41] It may not have added to Johnson's safety, for the threat of arrest hung over the known critics of the government and may at this point have deterred even a famous and well-connected author. In May 1738 appeared Alexander Pope's *One Thousand Seven Hundred and Thirty Eight. A Dialogue something like Horace*, and in July the same year *One Thousand Seven Hundred and Thirty Eight. Dialogue II.*[42] One observer wrote a year later: 'Mr Pope has published nothing new this winter, some people say he had a piece or two ready, but was deterred by the Lords ordering one Paul Whitehead into custody for publishing an impudent poem called Manners, in which there were many scandalous & barefaced reflections upon several of the Peers.'[43]

II. THE POLITICAL PAMPHLETS OF 1739

If Johnson has been correctly identified as a Nonjuror with Tory views and a proclivity towards Jacobitism, this makes both intelligible and important his early political writings, especially the pamphlet *Marmor Norfolciense*, published anonymously in May 1739.[44] This work, though concealed behind the stylistic devices of allegory and irony, spoke clearly to the political options of its age.

How the interest of James III could best be promoted had been open to interpretation. An undercurrent of conspiracy and violence had never been far beneath the surface.[45] In 1733 *Fog's Weekly Journal* seemed to hint at the assassination of Sir Robert Walpole, a meaning which had to be quickly denied.[46] In parliamentary terms, some saw the best hope in creating an anti-Walpole coalition from any components that could be combined together. It was a commonplace of the ministry in the 1730s that the opposition was an unnatural alliance of republicans and Jacobites, a group of 'Malecontents' who 'want a THOROUGH CHANGE; ANOTHER REVOLUTION'.[47] This was, essentially, a correct perception. In 1736 the Oxford

41 Hawkins, *Life*, p. 61. 42 Erskine-Hill, *The Augustan Idea*, pp. 344–9.
43 Thomas Edwards to Lewis Crusius, 8 June 1739: Bodleian MS Bodl 1009, f. 36.
44 It has been conventional to dismiss *Marmor Norfolciense* and *A Compleat Vindication of the Licensers of the Stage*, published some two weeks later: for this, and an alternative explanation, see Kaminski, *Early Career of Samuel Johnson*, pp. 91–2.
45 Eveline Cruickshanks, 'Lord Cornbury, Bolingbroke and a Plan to Restore the Stuarts, 1731–35', *Royal Stuart Papers* 27 (Huntingdon, 1986).
46 *Fog's Weekly Journal*, 31 March, 7 April 1733; *Remarks on Fog's Journal, of February 10. 1732/3. Exciting the People to an Assassination* (London, 1733).
47 *A Coalition of Patriots Delineated. Or, A Just Dsplay of the Union of Jacobites, Malecontents, Republicans, and False Friends, with an Attainted Old Traitor, to revile the Ministry; impose upon the People; set aside the Succession; and bring in the Pretender* (London, 1735), p. 21.

Jacobite William King wrote while in Paris to James Edgar, confidential clerk to James III, to report on King's recent visits to Ireland and Scotland and to urge:

I could heartily wish some proper steps were taken to unite Garth [the king's friends] and Mercer [the opposition Whigs] in ye same interest, which I conceive would not be at all difficult to be effected at this juncture. I mean the same Mercer, who is such a professed enemy to all the measures of 500 [the Elector of Hanover] and 503 [Walpole]. I cannot help intimating this, because I am fully persuaded 473 [the king's restoration] in a great measure depends on that union.[48]

Walpole's response was to attempt to conciliate the Tories and divide them from their opposition Whig allies, in part by overtures to James III himself, in part by winning the confidence of the Jacobite emissary Colonel William Cecil. James wrote: ''tis fit my friends should know that I have not the least reason to think that Walpole or any other of the present Ministers are anyways favourably disposed towards me'. But according to William King, Cecil was duped by Walpole into the belief that Sir Robert 'had formed a design to restore the House of STUART':

For this reason he communicated to Sir ROBERT all his despatches, and there was not a scheme which the CHEVALIER's court or the jacobites in *England* had projected during Sir ROBERT's long administration, of which that minister was not early informed, and was therefore able to defeat it without any noise or expense.[49]

Tories were never united about the best strategy to adopt. William King clearly hinted at his own party when he wrote in the early 1760s:

Some very worthy gentlemen and true lovers of their country were inclined to pray for the continuance of Sir ROBERT's ministry, as the old woman prayed for the life of *Dionysius* the tyrant. They judged that his successors would be worse ministers, and worse men; that they would pursue his measures without his abilities: and the event has verified their prediction.[50]

The late 1730s were, however, a period of expectation and excitement in Jacobite circles. During the summer of 1736, with George II absent in Hanover from 22 May, Lord Hervey noticed that 'a licentious, riotous, seditious, and almost ungovernable spirit in the people showed itself in many tumults and disorders, in different shapes, and in several parts of the kingdom'.[51] On 14 July 1736 Robert Nixon, a Nonjuring clergyman,

48 William King to James Edgar, 24 November 1736: Stuart Papers, Windsor, 191/168, in Greenwood, *William King*, pp. 74–5.

49 James III to Col. William Cecil, n.d., Stuart Papers, Windsor, 140/195; William King, *Anecdotes*, p. 37, quoted in Greenwood, *William King*, pp. 75–6.

50 William King, *Anecdotes*, pp. 41–2.

51 John, Lord Hervey, *Some Materials towards Memoirs of the Reign of King George II*, ed. Romney Sedgwick (3 vols., London, 1931), vol. 2, p. 565.

caused an explosion in Westminster Hall while the law courts were in session in order to publicise his opposition to recent Acts of Parliament (including the Gin Act) and to George II, whom he styled 'a Foreign Prince';[52] on and after 26 July serious rioting disturbed Shoreditch and Spitalfields, disturbances in which Walpole's spies discovered a Jacobite undercurrent, and which Sir Robert described as a Jacobite attempt 'to influence the people, and to raise great tumults upon Michaelmas-day, when the Gin-act takes place'.[53] It did not take secret agents to discover this: Lord Hervey too noted that the Spitalfields weavers 'began with railing against Irishmen, but came in twenty-four hours to cursing of Germans, reviling the King and the Queen, and huzzaing for James III'.[54]

Disorder continued across England, fuelling the ministry's sense of anxiety. On 7 September an armed mob seized Edinburgh and lynched Captain John Porteous, an army captain under sentence of death for murder when his troops had fired on an Edinburgh crowd, killing eight of them. This outrage, and the shielding of those reponsible by a conspiracy of silence in Edinburgh, could only be interpreted in one way. Walpole believed that despite the crushing of the Spitalfields riots by military force, 'the fire kindled anew'.[55] Disturbances rumbled on, a threatening backdrop to the actions of Whig politicians and a cause of expectation among their opponents. Lord Orrery's friends called him to town: 'They tell me of strange Things that must inevitably happen in a short Time. Knights to be conquer'd in Battle – mighty Champions to be slain – new Lords – new Commons – I had almost said new K . . .'[56]

Bolingbroke's doctrine that the identities of Whig and Tory 'either had, or long before now ought to have, sunk into those of Court and Country' was only partly persuasive:

[52] *The Tryal of Robert Nixon, a Nonjuring Clergy-Man, for a High Crime and Misdemeanour* (London, 1737). For this pamphlet two printers, Samuel Slow of St Clement Danes and Dormer, and the bookseller John Torbuck, also of St Clement Danes, were 'taken up for Republishing ye Libel for which Nixon was convicted': Nicholas Paxton, 'State of Prosecutions now depending agt. Persons taken up by Virtue of his Grace the Duke of Newcastle's Warrants. 13 February 1737', BL Add MSS 33052 f. 150; PRO SPD 44/82/146, 151. An arrest warrant was also issued for, among others, Ann Dodd: PRO SPD 44/82/136. In January 1736/7 Nixon was again arrested for republishing James II's proclamation ordering a day of thanksgiving for the birth of an heir on 10 June 1688: PRO SPD 44/82/143.

[53] Sir Robert Walpole to Horatio Walpole, 29 July 1736: W. Cobbett (ed.), *The Parliamentary History of England, from the Earliest Period to the year 1803* (36 vols, London, 1806–20), vol. 9, col. 1283; Vincent J. Liesenfeld, *The Licensing Act of 1737* (Madison, Wisconsin, 1984), p. 62. For this episode in general see ibid., pp. 60–6.

[54] Hervey, *Memoirs*, vol. 2, p. 566.

[55] Sir Robert Walpole to Horatio Walpole, 30 September 1736: Cobbett (ed.), *Parliamentary History*, vol. 9, col. 1287; Liesenfeld, *Licensing Act*, p. 63.

[56] Orrery to William Cecil, 2 February 1738/9: *Orrery Papers*, vol. 1, p. 252.

Though this Doctrine has prevailed with a good many to look upon the Court and Country as two Interests incompatible with one another, yet I am surpriz'd that there should be so great Force in meer Names and Words as to impose upon his Party. These Distinctions, Sir, of Whig and Tory, &c. while they prevail'd, were used by each Party to signify, in their Sense of the Word, the Country, and the Denomination under which the other Party went, the Court. Had you ask'd a Tory why he stood up for the Prerogative, he would have answer'd you, because I think it is for the Good of my Country. Ask a Whig why he struggled so hard for what he call'd Liberty, and to pull down *France*, and to keep out the *Pretender*, &c. he would have answered, because unless such and such things are done *my Country is endanger'd*. Ask the same Men over again separately what their Opinion is of their Antagonists, each will tell you that they want to betray their Country to those in Power, that is, in other words, *The Court*.[57]

Bolingbroke, visiting England in late 1738 and still attached to his ideal of a united Country party as the only way of ousting Walpole, was 'disgusted' to see it polarising into its Whig and Tory components as 'the spirit ... of Jacobitism rises anew among the Torys'.[58] By the summer of 1739 this threatened to split the opposition; as Walpole told Dudley Ryder in October, there existed a

great difference between the Jacobites and the patriot Whigs, particularly those of the Prince's [Frederick, Hanoverian Prince of Wales] court; that they had a meeting in the vacation when one of the Prince's friends proposed a revolution in favour of the Prince, saying that the King's [George II's] interest was entirely lost and he could not support it, but the Jacobites said if there was to be an alteration, it should be a restoration. These broke off that Treaty.[59]

The prospect of war with Spain, urged on by a Tory-dominated City of London despite Walpole's reluctance and declared on 19 October 1739, seemed to provide an opportunity for political destabilisation. This opportunity was recognised, and some people attempted to seize it. Seven Scottish peers formed an association like that of 1688 and invited James III to invade; James sent an emissary, Colonel Arthur Brett, to tour England and gauge support, who reported back in March 1740 that despite the caution of peers and MPs to be involved in practical conspiracy, 'The City of London is full of spirit and gives effectual proofs of it.'[60] Even Sir Robert Walpole, perhaps as an insurance policy, perhaps in an attempt to subvert

57 *An Historical View of the Principles, Characters, Persons &c. of the Political Writers in Great Britain* (London, 1740), pp. 43–4.

58 [Bolingbroke] to Lord Denbigh, 20 November 1738: HMC *Denbigh* 5 (1911), p. 231; H.T. Dickinson, *Bolingbroke* (London, 1970), pp. 255–68.

59 Sir Dudley Ryder's diary, 6 October 1739, Harrowby MSS, quoted in Romney Sedgwick (ed.), *The History of Parliament: The House of Commons 1715–1754* (2 vols., London, 1970), p. 70.

60 Cruickshanks, *Political Untouchables*, pp. 16–21.

his opponents' organisation, was in negotiation with James via the historian and Nonjuring clergyman Thomas Carte, Atterbury's former secretary.[61] On 1 August 1739 two Nonjurors, John Byrom and William Law, exchanged confidences, which Byrom recorded in his shorthand journal. Law

said that they talked of the Pretender's coming, was I not afraid of it? I said, No, not at all; and he talked in his favour, and that the m. was satisfactorily concluded between the psw and ldstm, and, as we came away, gave him (the father [i.e. James III]) a most excellent character for experience, wisdom, piety; I said that I saw him once; he said, Where? I said, At A[vignon]; he said, Did you kiss hands? I said, Yes, and parted; he said that Mr. Morden and Clutton had been with him, that there should not be so much talk about such matters, that the time was not now, that he loved a man of taciturnity.[62]

Shortly before, in May 1739, Johnson published his first political pamphlet. *Marmor Norfolciense* was, as its title page recorded, 'Printed for J. Brett at the *Golden-Ball*, opposite St *Clement's* Church in the *Strand*'. Already, Johnson was no stranger to the locality of that centre of High Church and Nonjuring Anglicanism that was to be his preferred place of worship into the 1780s.[63] St Clement Danes continued to attract Anglicans of a certain stamp.[64] Daniel Waterland followed his tract *A Review of the Doctrine of the Eucharist, As laid down in Scripture and Antiquity* (2nd edn, London, 1737) with his charge to his clergy, delivered as Archdeacon of Middlesex: *The Christian Sacrifice explained, In a Charge Delivered in part to the Middlesex Clergy At St Clement-Danes, April the 20th, 1738* (London, 1738). Opposite St Clement Danes, on the corner of the Strand and Arundel Street, stood the Crown and Anchor tavern. Although Whigs also used it, it was the meeting place both for the Academy of Ancient Music, which had a distinct political orientation, and also from c. 1740 for the Oak Society, whose politics were unmistakable; Prince Charles Edward may have attended one of its meetings on his clandestine visit of 1750, an event evidently anticipated by the society with a commemorative medal ordered in 1749,[65] reportedly by John Baptist Caryll, later the patron of the journal *The True Briton* (1751–3).

61 James III to Carte, 10 July 1739, printed in Lord Mahon, *History of England from the Peace of Utrecht to the Peace of Versailles 1713–1783* (5th edn, 7 vols, London, 1858), vol. 3, appendix, p. l.

62 Richard Parkinson (ed.), *The Private Journal and Literary Remains of John Byrom* (4 parts in 2 vols., Manchester, 1854–7), vol. 2, p. 259. The meaning of the abbreviations is not known.

63 See above, pp. 139–40.

64 The Nonjuror Mathias Earbery was resident in the parish of St Clement Danes when arrested in September 1732 for publishing 'several Scandalous, Seditious and Treasonable Libels, intituled The Universal Spy, or the Royal Oak Journal': PRO SPD 44/82/93, 96.

65 Noel Woolf, *The Medallic Record of the Jacobite Movement* (London, 1988), pp. 116–8.

It was a centre for sympathetic publishers and booksellers, too.[66] In 1738 the Nonjuror Bishop Archibald Campbell shared with his fellow Nonjuror Bishop Thomas Brett his delight at

a 12 penny Pamphlet called A Letter to a Member of Parlt containing a Proposal for bringing in A Bill to Revise, Amend, or Repeal certain Obsolete Statutes commonly called the X Commandments. Printed by Minors in Clements Chu: Yard in the Strand. The 3d Edit: is more than half sold off, & it is like to have a 4th. I was much diverted with its having bitt the Infidels among whom it had a great run for the 1st 2 or 3 days after it was published & sett them a Cursing the Author & Bookseller, but their Outcry agt. it made the Christians buy it so fast that the 2nd Edition went off in about a 4[t] night.[67]

Another bookseller announced himself on the title pages of his works as 'Printed for A. MILLAR, at *Buchanan's-Head*, over-against St *Clement's* Church, in the *Strand*'. In 1738 Andrew Millar had published *The Life of James Fitz-James, Duke of Berwick*, the natural son of James II by Arabella Churchill, a work translated from the French which openly accepted James Francis Edward Stuart as James II's legitimate son and heir and described the Revolution of 1688 as the result of James being 'forced to abandon' his kingdoms by a 'fickle and inconstant' nation.[68] In 1739 he followed this with David Mallett's anonymous *Mustapha. A Tragedy. Acted at the Theatre-Royal in Drury-Lane*, and James Thomson's banned *Edward and Eleonora. A Tragedy. As it was to have been Acted at the Theatre-Royal in Covent-Garden.*

Millar's customers, Johnson no doubt among them, could also buy the two volumes of a work published in the same year, Thomas Carte's *A Collection of Original Letters and Papers, Concerning the Affairs of England, From the Year 1641 to 1660. Found among the Duke of Ormonde's Papers*, and a work by Archibald Campbell (Regius Professor of Divinity and Ecclesiastical History at St Andrews), printed by William Bowyer (a Nonjuror) entitled *The Necessity of Revelation: or an Enquiry into the Extent of Human Powers With Respect to Matters of Religion*. In 1740 Millar's was one of the shops selling the third edition of the works of a loyal courtier of Charles II and James II, a Tory after the Revolution and a man deprived of all his offices at the Hanoverian accession, *The Works of John Sheffield, Earl of Mulgrave, Marquis of Normanby and Duke of Buckingham*.[69] If such works did not please, Johnson

66 For the examination of Ruth Charlton, of St Clement Danes parish, on 28 June 1737, for selling a suspected paper entitled *The Alchymist or Weekly Laboratory*, see BL Add MSS 32690 f. 333.

67 Archibald Campbell to Thomas Brett, 2 December 1738: Bodleian MS Eng Th c. 34, f. 377.

68 *The Life of James Fitz-James, Duke of Berwick* (London, 1738), pp. 20, 29.

69 Millar evidently took over the work after the opulently-produced second edition of 1723, 'Printed by John Barber, Alderman of London', a known Jacobite. For Lord Carteret's warrant dated 26 January 1722/3 to search for and seize the second volume of this work as

might have also found next to St Clement's churchyard the shop of Ralph Minors, who in 1739 published *The Contempt of the Clergy Considered. In a Letter to a Friend*, a defence of the Anglican priesthood,[70] though not refusing to issue a Freethinking counterblast, *The Tryal of William Whiston, Clerk. For Defaming and Denying the Holy Trinity, before the Lord Chief Justice Reason.* In 1739 Minors published *An Essay for The Better Regulation and Improvement of Free-Thinking. In a Letter to a Friend*, an inflated parody of that position.

Had Johnson continued to browse in these bookshops in 1740, he would have found Millar affirming the Anglo-Latin tradition by printing and publishing a two-volume English translation from the French of Abbé Banier's *The Mythology and Fables of the Ancients, Explain'd from History*, and appealing to a Jacobite hero by selling the three volumes of *The Military History of Charles XII. King of Sweden, Written by the express Order of his Majesty, by M. Gustavus Adlerfeld, Chamberlain to the King*. Millar then followed this with William Patterson's anonymous *Arminius. A Tragedy. As it was to have been Acted at the Theatre-Royal in Drury-Lane* and Mallett and Thomson's *Alfred: A Masque. Represented before Their Royal Highnesses The Prince and Princess of Wales, At Cliffden, On the First of August, 1740*. Andrew Millar in due course became the 'principal proprietor' of the consortium of booksellers that financed Johnson's *Dictionary*,[71] and in 1749 published Lord Bolingbroke's *Letters, on the Spirit of Patriotism: on the Idea of a Patriot King: and On the State of Parties, At the Accession of King George the First.*[72]

John Brett was no less significant as Johnson's chosen publisher.[73] Brett was a useful figure for those intent on destabilising the Hanoverian regime. His publications in 1738 and 1739 included a series of tracts intent on stirring up war with Spain.[74] But his interests were wider than that: in 1739

'a seditious and scandalous Libel', see [Webb], *Copies taken from the Records of the Court of King's Bench*, p. 26.

70 Its author maintained that 'as our Laws now stand, the Church is wholly independent of the State as to her spiritual Powers and Authorities', and called for the revival of Convocation (pp. 130, 136, 151).

71 Hawkins, *Life*, p. 342.

72 Johnson was known in this area: in 1749 was published *A Criticism on Mahomet and Irene. In a Letter to the Author*, 'Printed and sold by *W. Reeve*, in *Fleet-Street*; and *A. Dodd*, opposite St *Clement's* Church, in the *Strand*'. Mahomet referred to the character in Johnson's play.

73 Johnson had sided with the Nonjuring bishop Thomas Brett (1667–1743) in the 'usages' controversy that had divided that communion; it may be that the printer John Brett was a kinsman, perhaps one of the bishop's twelve children.

74 E.g. *Two Letters wherein the sovereignty of the British seas, and that the sole right of fishing in them, appertaineth to the King of Great-Britain, &c. is demonstratively maintain'd* (1738); *The Conduct of His Catholick Majesty compared with that of the British King ...* (1739); *A Congratulatory poem: humbly inscribed to the Right Honourable Sir Robert Walpole, on the conclusion of the convention between their Majesties of Great-Britain and Spain* (1739); *French Counsels Destructive to Great-Britain; or Seasonable Advice to Sir R[obert] W[alpole], in the present Critical Conjuncture* (1739); *The True Interest of the Princes of Europe, at this Present Juncture* (1739); *Spanish treachery, baseness*

he published *The Fear of Death. An Ode*, attributed to the Jacobite Philip, Duke of Wharton (1698–1731); in 1740 he published Benjamin Loveling's *The First Satire of Persius Imitated*;[75] in 1745 he was to issue, without the author's name, Sir Thomas Burnet's *Some new proofs by which it appears that the Pretender is truly James the Third; with observations on the depositions filed in the court of Chancery ... in order to convince the world that the then pretended Prince of Wales was not spurious*,[76] and extracts from Sir Richard Steele's *The Crisis* under the title *The Wisdom of our Fore-fathers, recommended.*

John Brett also published the Tory-Jacobite *Common Sense: or, the Englishman's Journal*;[77] although he escaped prosecution for *Marmor Norfolciense*, he was soon hauled before the Court of King's Bench for publishing a seditious libel in *Common Sense* for 23 June 1739, perhaps a less embarrassing charge for the ministry to pursue, and in 1740 was again prosecuted for selling the *London Evening Post* of 1 April.[78] *Common Sense* ran from 5 February 1737 to the end of 1743, quickly overtaking in popularity its flagging rival *The Craftsman* and its more openly Jacobite forerunner. *Fog's Weekly Journal* had declined in the mid 1730s, avoiding politics; in June 1737 it was revamped and begun 'by a new hand', John Kelly, but with the seventh issue the printer and publisher were arrested for an allegory 'upon the History of the Emperor Augustus and his Empress', denounced by the ministry as a seditious libel. With that, the paper finally collapsed,[79] and the field was left open for *Common Sense*. It drew on the support and copy of a younger generation of the opposition Whigs, especially Chesterfield, Lyttelton and Pitt. Yet its political purposes were more complex. Despite

and cruelty displayed; from fifteen hundred eighty-eight to seventeen hundred thirty-nine (1739); *A Letter To the Right Honourable Sir R— W—, &c. Upon the present Posture of Affairs, Wherein, amongst other Things, the Convention Will be set in a clear Light* (1739).

75 For which, see above, pp. 20–1, 55.

76 Thomas Burnet (1694–1753), third son of Gilbert Burnet, Bishop of Salisbury, debauchee, wit and religious sceptic, had published *Some New Proofs, By which it Appears that the Pretender is truly James the Third* anonymously in 1713. It argued that the 'Old Pretender' was not only a supposititious child, but the second impostor: Queen Mary had first miscarried; the child smuggled into the bedchamber in a warming pan had also died soon after; a third baby (James the third) had been found to take its place. Why was this republished by John Brett in 1745? Brett evidently needed to establish his loyalty in the eyes of the government; this pamphlet would have been well chosen to do so, as well as congenial to its author, a judge in the court of common pleas from October 1741 and knighted in November 1745. At the same time, the crudity and simplicity of the pamphlet's arguments could only have discredited the anti-Stuart case in the eyes of those who were not rabid Whigs: James III, now adult, bore an unmistakable resemblance to his royal father.

77 H.R. Plomer, G.H. Bushnell and E.R.McC. Dix, *A Dictionary of the Printers and Booksellers who were at work in England Scotland and Ireland from 1726 to 1775* (Oxford, 1932), p. 33.

78 PRO SPD 36/48/34–39, 36/50/270, 44/82/174, 182. In January 1743/4 Katherine Brett, bookseller of St Clement Danes, was arrested for selling William Shropshire's *Old England's Te Deum*: PRO SPD 44/82/194–6. John Brett was again in court in June 1745: ibid., f. 223.

79 PRO SPD 36/41/200, 36/41/240, cited in Chapman, 'Jacobite Political Argument in England', pp. 74–5.

opposition Whig support, *Common Sense* 'was actually run and mainly written by an Irish playwright named Charles Molloy', formerly a contributor to the Jacobite *Mist's Weekly Journal* and then editor of its successor, *Fog's Weekly*.[80] As this pedigree would suggest, Molloy too was a Jacobite, who had obtained funds from James III to launch his new paper and had, in those negotiations, indicated that the similarly-inclined Alexander Pope would be a contributor. Although it is not known whether Pope did supply copy, one who did was the Oxford Jacobite Dr William King.[81]

Charles Molloy was described by one fellow journalist as 'an *Irish* Roman Catholic, and ... a Nonjuring Counsellor at Law'. His journal *Common Sense* 'soon gain'd a good many Readers. But a Schism soon following betwixt the Author and Printer it was divided into two *Common Senses*, which were publish'd by different Printers, and wrote by different Authors ... but the Printer who opposed *M[ollo]y* dying, his Paper after languishing for some time died too, and *M[ollo]y* remain'd Master of the Field.'

> I was told that the first thing that brought it into request was the *Vision of the Golden Rump*, a most impudent Satire upon the K[ing] and the late Q[ueen], not to mention the Ministry and the Court; and as I have been inform'd it was wrote by Dr *K[in]g* of *O[xfor]d*, a noted Jacobite.[82]

Common Sense would have been congenial to the young Johnson. If he knew of the journal before his arrival in London in March 1737, he might have bought it in time to read William King's satirical article in the issue of 28 May that year, recommending a remodelled monarchical government for 'Corsica', a thin disguise for Britain. King ironically suggested replacing the monarch of that island with a king carved from oak, who would not be a tyrant and who would be immune from a variety of human failings (by implication, those of George II) like pride, avarice, lust and (a devastating understatement) 'Unevenness of Temper'. The article concluded: 'Reason, which is the distinguishing Excellence of Human Nature, can only prove a Blessing to those, whether Princes or private Persons, who are Men of Honour and Virtue.'[83] Its issue for 13 August 1737, though purportedly about 'a neighbouring Kingdom', by implication cast doubt on the title of the Hanoverians if they found it prudent to surrender the beneficent 'Prerogative (if that Name may be bestowed on an Act supposed to work by

80 Alvin Sullivan (ed.), *British Literary Magazines: The Augustan Age and the Age of Johnson 1698–1788* (Westport, Conn., 1983), pp. 43–6.

81 George Hilton Jones, 'The Jacobites, Charles Molloy, and *Common Sense*', *Review of English Studies* 4 (1953), 144–7.

82 *An Historical View of the Principles, Characters, Persons &c. of the Political Writers in Great Britain*, pp. 19–22.

83 Greenwood, *William King*, pp. 78–80.

a Divine Power from Heaven) called *Touching for the King's* Evil'. The issue of 22 April 1738 was unfashionably complimentary to that Tory achievement, the treaty of Utrecht, and began a campaign for a declaration of war on Spain; that of 27 January 1739 was an ironic attack on the avarice and military aggression of George II as Elector of Hanover.

It was in this setting that *Marmor Norfolciense* appeared in May 1739, without the author's name but purporting to be by 'Probus Britannicus', a 'True Briton'. Johnson presented a copy to an unknown recipient,[84] so that his anonymity had its limits: clearly, it was intended to be used among certain groups of sympathisers but to be unacknowledged among the public at large. In the light of the explosive contents of the tract, this was not surprising. It pretended to be a commentary on an ancient Latin inscription, recently discovered near the town of Lynn in Norfolk (for which borough Sir Robert Walpole was the sitting MP). Johnson's pamphlet printed the inscription (in fact a Latin poem of some distinction by Johnson himself) and added an English version, supposedly translated by a protégé of 'the *Maecenas* of *Norfolk*'. This translation purported to include a prediction of the state of the nation on its discovery:

TO POSTERITY

Whene'er this Stone, now hid beneath the Lake,
The Horse shall trample, or the Plough shall break,
Then, O my Country! shalt thou groan distrest,
Grief swell thine Eyes, and Terror chill thy Breast.
Thy Streets with Violence of Woe shall sound.
Loud as the Billows bursting on the Ground.
Then thro' thy Fields shall scarlet Reptiles stray,
And Rapine and Pollution mark their Way.
Their hungry Swarms the peaceful Vale shall fright
Still fierce to threaten, still afraid to fight;
The teeming Year's whole Product shall devour,
Insatiate pluck the Fruit, and crop the Flow'r:
Shall glutton on the industrious Peasants spoil,
Rob without Fear, and fatten without Toil.
Then o'er the World shall Discord stretch her Wings,
Kings change their Laws, and Kingdoms change their Kings.
The Bear enrag'd th' affrighted Moon shall dread;
The Lilies o'er the Vales triumphan[t] spread;
Nor shall the Lyon, wont of old to reign
Despotic o'er the desolated Plain,
Henceforth th' inviolable Bloom invade,

[84] J. D. Fleeman, *A Preliminary Handlist of Copies of Books associated with Dr Samuel Johnson* (Oxford, 1984), p. 26; D. Nichol Smith and E. L. McAdam (eds.), *The Poems of Samuel Johnson* (2nd edn, Oxford, 1974), pp. 85ff.

Or dare to murmur in the flow'ry Glade;
His tortur'd Sons shall die before his Face,
While he lies melting in a lewd Embrace;
And, yet more strange! his Veins a Horse shall drain,
Nor shall the passive Coward once complain.[85]

Was the monkish author a Briton or a Saxon? It was inconclusive that he had used the word 'Patria', argued Johnson, adopting the persona of a naive Whig antiquarian commenting on this archaeological discovery, 'since we find that in all Ages, Foreigners have affected to call *England* their Country, even when like the *Saxons* of old they came only to plunder it'.[86] But he was probably 'BORN A BRITON' since 'it has been rarely, very rarely known that Foreigners however well treated, carressd, enriched, flatter'd or exalted, have regarded this Country with the least Gratitude or Affection, till the Race has by long Continuance, after many Generations, been naturaliz'd and assimilated'. 'Patria' might mean '*the Land of my Father*'; but this did not prove his ancestors' residence in England, since Johnson observed 'how common it is for Intruders of Yesterday, to pretend the same Title with the ancient Proprietors, and having just received an Estate by voluntary Grant, to erect a claim of *hereditary Right*'.[87] George I and George II claimed just such an hereditary title to their new kingdom.[88]

With thinly veiled irony, Johnson insisted that the prophecy was not fulfilled: 'Is not all at Home Satisfaction and Tranquillity? all Abroad Submission and Compliance? ... To me the present State of the Nation seems so far from any Resemblance to the Noise and Agitation of a tempestuous Sea, that it may be much more properly compared to the dead Stilness of the Waves before a Storm.' It was an open threat.[89] Of the 'scarlet Reptiles' (soldiers) he added: 'the Mischief done by them, their Ravages, Devastations and Robberies, must be only the Consequences of Cowardice in the Sufferers, who are harrassed and oppressed only because they suffer it without Resistance'.[90] Resistance, indeed rebellion, was the moral of Johnson's satire.

Continuing his pose as a Whiggish antiquarian labouring to explain the inscription, Johnson joined the growing wave of demands for war. The passive lion was a similarly inappropriate image, argued the antiquary, if it suggested the extension of French power. And

85 [Samuel Johnson], *Marmor Norfolciense: or an Essay on an Ancient Prophetical Inscription, In Monkish Rhyme, Lately Discover'd near Lynn in Norfolk. By Probus Britannicus* (London, 1739), pp. 10–12.

86 Ibid., pp. 15–16.

87 Ibid., pp. 16–18.

88 J. C. D. Clark, *English Society 1688–1832: Ideology, social structure and political practice during the ancien regime* (Cambridge, 1985), pp. 124–37.

89 [Johnson], *Marmor Norfolciense*, pp. 29–30.

90 Ibid., pp. 34, 37.

can the *English* be said to be trampled or tortur'd? Where are they treated with Injustice or Contempt? What Nation is there from Pole to Pole that does not reverence the Nod of the *British* King? Is not our Commerce unrestrained? Are not the Riches of the World our own? Do not our Ships sail unmolested, and our Merchants traffick in perfect Security? Is not the very Name of *England* treated by Foreigners in a Manner never known before? Or if some slight Injuries have been offered, if some of our petty Traders have been stopped, our Possessions threaten'd, our Effects confiscated, our Flag insulted, or our Ears crop'd, have we lain sluggish and unactive? have not our Fleets been seen in Triumph at Spithead? did not *Hosier* visit the *Bastimentos*, and is not *Haddock* now stationed at *Port Mahon*?[91]

How was the image of the horse sucking the lion's blood to be construed? Metaphorically, Johnson's antiquary blundered on, 'I might observe that a Horse is born in the Arms of H[anover]. But how then does the Horse suck the Lyon's Blood? Money is the Blood of the Body politic. – But my zeal for the present happy Establishment will not suffer me to pursue a Train of Thought that leads to such shocking Conclusions. The Idea is detestable, and such as, it ought to be hoped, can enter into the Mind of none but a virulent Republican, or bloody Jacobite.'[92] It would have occurred most readily to the latter, for the image of the white horse of Hanover trampling the British lion had been appropriated by Stuart propaganda. Perhaps the most vivid image of all those devised by Stuart engravers was precisely such a scene which appeared on a Jacobite medal struck at Rome by the elder Hamerani in 1721, played out against a background of London's skyline and before a grieving Britannia, and beneath the caption 'QVID GRAVIVS CAPTA' (what more grievous than being in captivity). It was the last such medal to bear the portrait of James III, with the legend VNICA SALVS (the only security) conveying a particularly poignant double meaning in the year of the South Sea Bubble. Johnson's poem was, in effect, the same image versified.[93]

Marmor Norfolciense was a plain and open incitement to war against Spain, and perhaps France: a conflict which Walpole had long sought to avert and which Jacobites had eagerly anticipated as a means of destabilising the Hanoverian regime. So, in 1744 and 1745, it proved to be. Johnson had, at this time, no principled objection to war as such, and *Marmor*

91 Ibid., pp. 38–9. Bastimentos was an island off Panama, visited by Admiral Francis Hosier's unsuccessful punitive expedition in 1726. Port Mahon was the British naval base in the island of Minorca, to which a fleet commanded by Admiral Nicholas Haddock was sent in May 1738.

92 Ibid., pp. 40–1.

93 Woolf, *Medallic Record of the Jacobite Movement*, p. 83. Such medals were a prevalent, easily-circulated form of publicity. For William King showing a similar medal to the equally loyal antiquary Thomas Hearne in November 1722 see Greenwood, *William King*, p. 21.

(a) 'Unica Salus': medal by Ermenegildo Hamerani, 1721

(b) 'Redeat': medal attributed to Thomas Pingo, 1752

Plate 6 The image and the text. Jacobite medals were a significant propoganda medium and exchanged imagery with literature and oratory

incited war fever on flimsy grounds of offended xenophobia. By the 1760s, the dynastic setting had changed. Johnson wrote against war with Spain over the Falkland Islands dispute; in *The Patriot* he urged:

As war is one of the heaviest of national evils, a calamity, in which every species of misery is involved; as it sets the general safety to hazard, suspends commerce, and desolates the country; as it exposes great numbers to hardships, dangers, captivity and death; no man, who desires the public prosperity, will inflame national resentment by aggravating minute injuries, or enforcing disputable rights of little importance.[94]

The significance of Johnson's first political work was easy to discern, and long remembered. In 1775, *Marmor Norfolciense* was republished with notes by a savage critic of Johnson, indignant at his anti-American pamphlets, ironically pretending to absolve him of authority for the earlier piece, which had been published anonymously and which Johnson had never acknowledged as his:

I urged in your Vindication, learned Sir! that it was impossible so pointed an Attack on the glorious Revolution; such bitter Reflections, keen Sarcasms, and personal Invectives against the illustrious HOUSE OF HANOVER, *which are to be found in the following Essay; could proceed from the Pen of the* now *renowned Champion for the Honour and Glory of One of the House of* Brunswick; *whose Exaltation to the Throne of these Realms has ever been Matter of the* greatest *Distress, Trouble, and Disappointment to* Tories *and* Jacobites; *neither of whom can ever discover Zeal or Attachment to* any *reigning Monarch, unless the Maxims of his Government should be the same with those, which, in their warmest Wishes, they would desire to see the cursed and expelled Race of the* STUARTS *adopt and pursue. This indeed may gain a temporary Allegiance, and procure an outward Shew of Obedience, as it would not only gratify their high-flown extravagant Notions of* hereditary Right *and* unlimited Authority, *but afford some distant Prospect and Hope, that a Deviation from all Principles and Maxims that first, in the Opinion of the* Whigs, *vindicated the Deposition of the* STUARTS, *and Elevation of the House of* Hanover, *might, by a happy Train of political Consequences, restore the imperial Diadem to that Head, round which every Jacobite would wish to see it cast its* hereditary *Splendor. No Man can be hardy enough to impute to Dr* JOHNSON *Wishes or Expectations of such a Nature*

which would be more unacceptable to him than '*The Doctrine of Ghosts and Phantoms*', or '*the Pretensions to Second Sight in the Highlands of* Scotland'.[95] There was no doubt about the meaning of *Marmor Norfolciense*; '*it is manifest, that the Essayist was a high-flown* Jacobite, *and* really *wrote upon* Principle'.

94 [Samuel Johnson], *The Patriot. Addressed to the Electors of Great Britain* (London, 1774), pp. 19–20.

95 [Francis Webb, ed.], *Marmor Norfolciense: or, an Essay on an Ancient Prophetical Inscription, in Monkish Rhyme, Lately discovered near Lynn in Norfolk. By Probus Britannicus. Printed and Published in the Year M.DCC.XXXIX. A New Edition, With Notes, and a Dedication to Samuel Johnson, LL.D. By Tribunus* (London, 1775), pp iii–v. See below, pp. 230–1.

Such an author could never have accepted a pension from a Hanoverian. The critic quoted six lines from *London*, in which Johnson had put his view of pensions on record: he could hardly therefore be the author of this seditious work.[96]

The anonymous editor then reprinted the text of *Marmor Norfolciense* with barbed footnotes. Where the author had observed 'how common it is for Intruders of Yesterday, to pretend the same Title with the ancient Proprietors, and having just received an Estate by voluntary Grant, to erect a Claim of *hereditary Right*', the editor noted: 'Could the Defenders of the illustrious House of *Hanover* ever have pensioned such a Jacobitical Libeller of the first illustrious Heroes of the *Brunswick* Line?' The author had affirmed his 'natural Affection to Monarchy, and a prevailing Inclination to believe that *every* Excellence is inherently in a King'; the editor glossed: 'Without yielding in the least to the Suspicion that Dr *Johnson* is the Author of this Essay, we may venture to suggest, that perhaps the Doctor's Loyalty may be owing to such a Predilection in favour of Monarchy.'[97]

When Boswell drew this republication to his attention, Johnson 'looked at it and laughed, and seemed to be much diverted with the feeble efforts of his unknown adversary',[98] but evidently said nothing more quotable about his youthful sedition. By 1775 it did him no harm, according to Thomas Tyers, writing in the *Gentleman's Magazine*. Johnson's 'high tory principles in church and state were well known. But neither his Prophecy of the Hanover House, lately maliciously reprinted, nor his political principles or conversations, got him into any personal difficulties, nor prevented the offer of a pension, nor his acceptance ... The present royal family are winning the hearts of all the friends of the house of Stuart.' Johnson, excused Tyers, had a weakness in his belief in ghosts; but 'Posterity must be permitted to smile at the credulity of that period. Johnson had otherwise a vulnerable side; for he was one of the few non-jurors that were left, and it was supposed that he would never bow the knee to the Baal of Whiggism.'[99]

96 Ibid., pp. ix, xi.

97 Ibid., pp. 12, 15. This pamphlet should be set against Greene's suggestion (*Politics*, p. xxii) that in all of Johnson's publications 'there is not a single statement indicating sympathy with Jacobitism'.

98 Boswell, *Life*, vol. 1, p. 142.

99 Tyers, 'A Biographical Sketch of Dr Samuel Johnson', *Gentleman's Magazine* 54 (December 1784), 899–911, reprinted in Brack and Kelley (eds.), *Early Biographies*, pp. 61–90, at 68, 74. When Johnson was introduced to Thomas Tyers, he misheard Tyers's name and assumed him to be Robert Thyer (1709–81), Chetham's librarian at Manchester 'and a non-juror. This mistake was rather beneficial than otherwise to the person introduced', recorded Tyers: ibid., p. 78. It is noteworthy that Johnson was aware that Thyer was a Nonjuror, a fact likely to be best known within Nonjuring circles.

When *Marmor Norfolciense* was republished, it was denounced by one of the two leading literary reviews:

This is a bloody Jacobitical pamphlet, on the most avowed anti-revolutional principles, prophesying the evils impending on this nation in consequence of the accession of the present R[oyal] F[amily] and said (*nem. con.*) to have been written by the *now notorious* Gentleman, to whom this new edition is addressed. It is, indeed, a little unfortunate for him, if he *is* the Author, that it should be dragged out of its lurking-hole at the present time; that is, if he may be supposed to feel it; for, as *he* would say, *the man who has arrived to such a degree of moral turpitude, as to militate against the best interests of mankind, must be indurated to conviction, and obtunded to remorse.* The substance of the pamphlet has been retailed in almost every newspaper.[100]

None of the early biographers of Johnson denied or protested against this identification.

Johnson's second pamphlet of 1739 is less well known, but no less political in its significance; indeed it engaged with a more specific conflict in the public arena. The most recent student of the subject is in no doubt that 'Enemies of the state, particularly Jacobites, manipulated the London stage during 1736 and 1737 as part of their larger plan to create disaffection in Britain and overthrow the government and ultimately the Crown itself.'[101]

The ministry had been badly stung by the satirical plays of the 1730s, especially the opposition Whig Henry Fielding's *The Historical Register*, *Pasquin* and *Eurydice Hissed*, but in order to take legislative action it needed the excuse of a more virulent example with fewer claims to protection as a work of art. This was duly provided in the spring of 1737 when a farce entitled *The Golden Rump*[102] was offered to Henry Giffard, manager of the theatre at Lincoln's Inn Fields. Though no copies are extant, it took its cue from an allegory, probably by William King, published in *Common Sense* for 19 and 26 March 1737.[103] Thomas Davies, then an actor in Henry Fielding's theatrical company, described it as 'no less than a most outrageous satire against the king, the royal family, and many of the highest and most respected persons in the kingdom ... the author of The Golden Calf [sc. Rump] had wantonly exceeded every limit of decency, and even loyalty, and put to defiance the laws of the land. The piece was replete with

100 *The Monthly Review* 53 (1775), 360.

101 Liesenfeld, *The Licensing Act of 1737*, p. xi.

102 George II, an authoritarian with a violent temper, was known sometimes to kick his Whig ministers. This demonstration of crudity on one side and servility on the other was, understandably, relished by Tory satirists.

103 For which, see Liesenfeld, *Licensing Act*, pp. 92–101. The journal soon warranted a collected edition, proudly reprinting 'The Vision of the Golden Rump': *Common Sense: or, the Englishman's Journal. Being A Collection of Letters, Political, Humourous, and Moral; Publish'd Weekly under that Title, For the First Year* (London, 1738). It threw in, for good measure, three issues of *Fog's Weekly Journal*.

Jacobite principles, at a time when they were much more offensive to the people than the persons of Jacobites.'[104] It is alleged that Giffard prudently showed it to Sir Robert Walpole; Walpole shrewdly chose his moment on 24 or 25 May to have passages from the play read to a shocked House of Commons and produced a conveniently-prepared Bill for pre-performance censorship of the stage; it received its third reading on 3 June. *The Golden Rump* may have been written at his instigation for just such a purpose.[105]

The Act remained uninvoked until February 1739, when Henry Brooke's play *Gustavus Vasa, the Deliverer of his Country*, already in rehearsal at the Drury Lane theatre, was refused a license. It could still be printed, however, and Brooke recouped his loss with a handsome edition published on 5 May and patronised by nearly nine hundred subscribers. Samuel Johnson, who was among them, then read a sensational play about Christiern, a Danish usurper on the Swedish throne, challenged by Gustavus, with a better hereditary title, who secures the expulsion of the usurper and the downfall of his corrupt prime minister. The allegory was not difficult to decode. Sir John Hawkins was indignant that Henry Brooke, author of *Gustavus Vasa*, 'having with his eyes open, and the statute of the tenth of George the second staring him in the face, [had] written a tragedy, in which ... under pretence of a laudable zeal for the cause of liberty, he inculcates principles, not only anti-monarchical, but scarcely consistent with any system of civil subordination'. When it was banned, 'This interposition of legal authority was looked upon by the author's friends, in which number were included all the Jacobites in the kingdom, as an infraction of a natural right, and as affecting the cause of liberty.'[106]

Samuel Johnson, though anonymously, now took part as one of 'the author's friends', and against the examiner of plays, Walter Chetwynd, a member of an active political family from Staffordshire which had deserted the Tories to support Walpole.[107] On 25 May was advertised for sale Johnson's second pamphlet,[108] hard on the heels of *Marmor Norfolciense* (advertised on 11 May). Once more Johnson adopted the device of extended irony, this time to condemn by overstatement the position he

104 Thomas Davies, *Memoirs of the Life of David Garrick, Esq.* (2 vols., London, 1780), vol. 2, pp. 203–6.

105 No evidence supports such contemporary accounts of its authorship, or the means by which Walpole obtained a copy. For this episode, see Liesenfeld, *The Licensing Act of 1737*, passim; Martin C. Battestin and Ruthe R. Battestin, *Henry Fielding: A Life* (Routledge, 1989), pp. 217–28.

106 Hawkins, *Life*, p. 76.

107 For Johnson's possible resentment at the Chetwynds' apostacy see D.J. Greene in Johnson, *Works*, vol. 10, p. 53.

108 [Samuel Johnson], *A Compleat Vindication of the Licensers of the Stage, From the Malicious and Scandalous Aspersions of Mr. Brooke, Author of Gustavus Vasa. With A Proposal for making the Office of Licenser more Extensive and Effectual* (London, 1739).

wished to destroy. Ironically, he condemned in the opposition their altruism: 'This Fondness for Posterity is a kind of Madness which at *Rome* was once almost epidemical.' Ironically, he pretended to condemn their doctrine:

This Temper which I have been describing is almost always complicated with Ideas of the high Prerogatives of human Nature, of a sacred unalienable Birthright, which no Man has conferr'd upon us, and which neither Kings can take, nor Senates give away, which we may justly assert whenever and by whomsoever it is attacked, and which, if ever it should happen to be lost, we may take the first Opportunity to recover.

Ironically, Johnson defended the authorities: 'Unhappy would it be for Men in Power, were they always obliged to publish the Motives of their Conduct. What is Power but the Liberty of acting without being accountable?' The opposition absurdly and inconveniently demanded *reasons* for the ministry's conduct:

They have made it their Practice to demand once a Year the Reasons for which we maintain a Standing Army.

One Year we told them that it was necessary, because all the Nations round us were involved in War; this had no Effect upon them, and therefore resolving to do our utmost for their Satisfaction, we told them the next Year that it was necessary, because all the Nations round us were at Peace.

This Reason finding no better Reception than the other, we had Recourse to our Apprehensions of an Invasion from the Pretender, of an Insurrection in Favour of *Gin*, and of a general disaffection among the People.

And Johnson clearly identified himself with Brooke's design:

His Prologue is filled with such Insinuations as no Friend of our excellent Government can read without Indignation and Abhorrence, and cannot but be owned to be a proper Introduction to such Scenes as seem designed to kindle in the Audience a Flame of Opposition, Patriotism, publick Spirit, and Independency, that Spirit which we have so long endeavoured to suppress, and which cannot be revived without the entire Subversion of all our Schemes.[109]

No one could then have foreseen that the Licensing Act was to stand alone. The *Daily Gazetter*, a government newspaper, had aired the further possibility of press censorship in December 1737, and *Common Sense* and *The Craftsman* kept this threat before the public into the spring of 1738.[110] Johnson's pamphlet was a heightened denunciation not of a single piece of legislation but of a corrupt and illegitimate regime which was shielding itself from honest scrutiny first by a campaign of harassment against

109 [Johnson], *Compleat Vindication*, pp. 9, 11, 16–19.

110 Hanson, *Government and the Press*, pp. 13–14.

printers, booksellers and authors, and finally by legally-enacted pre-performance censorship. Johnson's political message was plain, and was understood (evidently at or soon after publication) by his Whig friend. Sir John Hawkins refused to undertake 'a minute examination' of the two pamphlets of 1739 as literature, and contented himself with condemning Johnson's politics. The strategic danger, thought Hawkins, as all Whigs thought, excused the conduct of the ministry, and condemned its critics:

Did it become a man of his discernment, endowed with such powers of reasoning and eloquence as he possesssed, to adopt vulgar prejudices, or, in the cant of the opposition, to clamor against place-men, and pensioners and standing armies? to ridicule the apprehension of that invasion in favour of the pretender, which himself, but a few years after became a witness to, or to compare the improbability of such an event with that of a general insurrection of all who were prohibited the use of gin?[111]

Nor was Johnson alone in his stand against the Act. It may be that William King's Latin poem *Sermo Pedestris*, published in 1739, is also an attack on stage censorship; it has been suggested that it falls into the genre of Latin dialogue satires brilliantly exploited by John Randolph, Fellow of All Souls, in his attack on the South Sea Bubble *Commercium ad Mare Australe* (1720).[112] The most vocal opponents of censorship were those who had most to lose from its imposition.

III. REBELLION AND SURVIVAL, 1739–1746

Hawkins, who probably knew Johnson at that period, wrote candidly of *Marmor Norfolciense*:

A publication so inflammatory as this, could hardly escape the notice of any government, under which the legal idea of a libel might be supposed to exist. The principles it contained were such as the Jacobites of the time openly avowed; and warrants were issued and messengers employed to apprehend the author, who, though he had forborne to subscribe his name to the pamphlet, the vigilance of those in pursuit of him had discovered. To elude the search after him, he, together with his wife, took an obscure lodging in a house in Lambeth-marsh, and lay there concealed till the scent after him was grown cold.[113]

Hawkins's story was long discredited by Boswell's claim that one of the Secretaries of the Treasury, Thomas Steele, had at Boswell's request searched for but found no such warrant.[114] But even if no warrant had been

111 Hawkins, *Life*, p. 78.

112 Greenwood, *William King*, pp. 98–105. The disguised allusions to individuals are harder to decipher than in King's *Miltonis Epistola ad Pollionem*.

113 Hawkins, *Life*, p. 72.

114 Boswell, *Life*, vol. 1, pp. 141–2, confirmed by Thomas Steele to Boswell, 13 January 1790, in Waingrow (ed.), *Correspondence*, p. 302. Thomas Steele (1753–1823) was joint secretary to the Treasury in 1783–91. No warrant is recorded in PRO SPD 44/82, 44/83 or 44/84.

issued, Johnson's fears may have been well founded: in June 1739 the publisher of *Common Sense* was imprisoned for an attack on the Walpole ministry; the same month Edward Cave, editor of the *Gentleman's Magazine*, reprinted Johnson's English translation of his fictional Latin inscription, but omitted Johnson's really inflammatory commentary on it. Johnson may have removed to an obscure lodging as a precaution.[115]

Johnson was caught between every author's need of fame and fear of retribution. If *London* and the pamphlets of 1739 won him recognition, it was, presumably, within one social milieu in particular. William King became Principal of St Mary Hall in 1720: at what time he first met Johnson is not known, but King was in London, at the Temple and visiting Tom's Coffee House, in May 1739, when Johnson's first two political pamphlets appeared, and spent part of the same month with Alexander Pope as the guest of Lord Orrery at his seat of Marston, Somerset.[116] King, too, continued his propaganda campaign in his chosen genre. In March 1740 appeared *Scamnum, Ecloga*, King's third Latin political satire, this time in the form of a Virgilian eclogue, dedicated to George Keith (?1693–1778), Marshall of Scotland,[117] who had commanded troops in the Fifteen, was attainted, commanded the expedition of 1719 and was still living in exile in Spain. In 1744 he was intended to command a small French invasion force aimed at Scotland, while the main landing threatened London. As poetry, *Scamnum, Ecloga* was 'one of the most impressive examples in European literature of the grand eclogue: in its way grander than any of Vergil's own'. But its real point was political: in *Scamnum, Ecloga* one of King's highly formalised shepherds, Tityrus, expresses 'barely disguised hopes' for a 'golden age in the future under the restored House of Stuart'.[118]

When the first book of William King's Latin epic *Templum Libertatis* was published in 1742, the anonymous reviewer in the *London Magazine* praised the enterprise: 'it must be agreeable to every *True Briton*, to see this difficult Task attempted with Success by a *British* Bard, and in as pure *Latin* as was wrote by any of the Authors of the *Augustan* Age'. If readers were in any doubt about the application of this eulogy of liberty, the second book of the poem, published in 1743, spoke openly of '*Ita quidem regnantur Europae gentes*

115 Bertram H. Davis, *Johnson before Boswell: A Study of Sir John Hawkins's Life of Samuel Johnson* (New Haven, Conn., 1960), pp. 100–2.

116 Greenwood, *William King*, pp. 106–7. Probably this was the Tom's Coffee House in Devereux Court, which ran between the Strand and Essex Street, near St Clement's church.

117 Greenwood, *William King*, pp. 110–18. English translations were published in 1741 and 1744. For King's admission that 'G. K. S. M.' should be read '*Georgio Keith Scotiae Marescallo*' see King to Orrery, 25 March 1740: Bodleian MS Eng hist d. 103, f. 11.

118 Greenwood, *William King*, p. 118.

fere omnes trans fretum Britannicum. Britanniae vero Regum legitimo & sacrato jure continetur: & Rex ipse ita est, ut Phoenix, avis magna, admiranda, unica.'[119]

Johnson cannot have been unaware that his venture into political pamphleteering, like *London*, had failed to win him influential patronage. This was scarcely his fault. James III's patronage of the Jacobite press in England was fitful, unsystematic, and on a hopelessly inadequate scale; by contrast, Walpole spent some £50,000 on press propaganda between 1731 and 1741. Nor, when Jacobite journalists and publishers were harassed by the Whig authorities, were they consistently supported and protected by their own side.[120] It is no surprise that a sympathetic and potentially immensely useful writer like Samuel Johnson was not enlisted in a systematic campaign: none such existed. Most Jacobite propaganda was uncoordinated, the result of the personal commitment of individuals.[121] Johnson was one such individual. His pamphlets of 1739 might have rendered some service to the Stuart cause, but they evidently yielded Johnson none of the patronage which he desperately needed, and, perhaps intimidated by the fear of arrest, he wrote no others.

He did not, however, abandon his beliefs. Johnson's commitment to the cause of monarchical legitimacy was further evidenced in 1741 when he edited as a pamphlet, and abridged for publication in the *Gentleman's Magazine* of February, a tract of 1660 which called for just that restoration which occurred later the same year. Johnson closely followed the title of 1660: *Monarchy Asserted to Be the Best, Most Antient, and Legall Form of Government. In a Conference Held at Whitehall, with Oliver, Lord Protector.* The original work reprinted verbatim the speeches of the members of the Parliamentary committee who, on 9 April 1657 and following days, had laboured in vain to persuade Cromwell to adopt the title of king, rehearsing a range of arguments from law, history and expediency to prove that only monarchy, grounded in the ancient constitution and in the affection of the people, offered the prospect of peace and a stable order.[122] It had been 'much in the thoughts of the Parliament', Sir Charles Woolesley had declared, 'that the reason why things of late have been so unsettled

119 Greenwood, *William King*, pp. 119–56, at 145–6, 155: 'The diabolical loftiness of the second book is not greatly inferior to that of the comparable sections of *Paradise Lost*. The indictments against contemporary venality are written with a Swiftian force and with a conscious grandeur absent from those of the Dean.'

120 Hanson, *Government and the Press*, pp. 108–18; G.A. Cranfield, *The Press and Society* (London, 1978), pp. 44–6; Chapman, 'Jacobite Political Argument', pp. 96–144.

121 Chapman, 'Jacobite Political Argument', p. 162.

122 Greene, *Politics*, p. 264 reverses the significance of this piece: 'Is it possible that he was attracted by the idea of an elective, rather than a hereditary, monarchy, with men like Cromwell, whose abilities Johnson admired so highly, at its head?' It might be suggested that the pamphlet showed the usurper Cromwell wisely refusing what the usurper William of Orange unexpectedly seized.

throughout in the nations, hath been because, that to the body of this people, there hath not been a legall head'.[123] Johnson's readers were free to apply the moral to George II.

To the years 1742 and 1746 belong the two momentous episodes of disillusionment which marked off the cultural politics of Johnson's later years from his youthful commitments. James III finally overcame his aversion for the opposition Whigs so far as to instruct the Tories to co-operate with them in bringing down Walpole; his majority now paper-thin and still eroding, Sir Robert finally resigned on 2 February 1742. It should have been the apotheosis of the young Johnson's political aspirations. The reality proved otherwise, as Hawkins best explained. To 'party-opposition', recorded Hawkins, Johnson

> ever expressed great aversion; and, of the pretences of patriots, always spoke with indignation and contempt. He partook of the short-lived joy that infatuated the public, when Sir Robert Walpole ceased to have the direction of the national councils, and trusted to the professions of Mr. Pulteney and his adherents, who called themselves the country-party, that all elections should thenceforward be free and uninfluenced, and that bribery and corruption, which were never practiced but by courtiers and their agents, should be no more. A few weeks, nay, a few days, convinced Johnson, and indeed all England, that what had assumed the appearance of patriotism, was personal hatred and inveterate malice in some, and in others, an ambition for that power, which, when they had got it, they knew not how to exercise. A change of men, and in some respect, of measures, took place: Mr. Pulteney's ambition was gratified by a peerage; the wants of his associates were relieved by places, and seats at the public boards; and, in a short time, the stream of government resumed its former channel, and ran with a current as even as it had ever done.[124]

Apart from Lord Gower, who was given the post of Lord Privy Seal and abandoned his party, no Tories received office. The object of the Walpolian machine was to ensure its survival by buying off enough of the opposition Whigs, and in this it was successful. Pulteney became Earl of Bath in 1742; Carteret was squeezed out of office by a Pelhamite coup in 1744 and marginalised by a removal to the House of Lords as Earl Granville. Johnson long remembered the Whig opposition of the 1730s, declaring in 1773: 'Pulteney was as paltry a fellow who could be. He was a Whig who pretended to be honest; and you know it is ridiculous for a Whig to pretend to be honest. He cannot hold it out.'[125] But his remark was one of bitter disillusion, not throwaway parody.

The political options facing Johnson's generation were about to be

[123] [Nathaniel Fiennes], *Monarchy Asserted to Be the Best, most Antient, and Legall Form of Government*... (London, 1742), p. 6.
[124] Hawkins, *Life*, p. 506.
[125] Boswell, *Journal*, p. 340 (20 October 1773).

transformed a second time by armed rebellion. If Johnson had indeed changed his lodgings as a precaution after the publication of *Marmor Norfolciense*, it becomes more plausible that he might also have cast a veil over his whereabouts during part of a much more dangerous period for men of his political principles in 1744–6. Sensationally, English Jacobites now faced the challenge that their long-repeated promises might have to be translated into action. In November 1743, Louis XV was finally persuaded that domestic English support for a rising would be sufficient, and began preparations for a French invasion as the necessary catalyst. A force of 10,000 troops was organised in secret, a larger number than the English troops around London, intended to embark from Dunkirk in January 1744 under cover of a naval diversion from Brest: it was the scheme which English Jacobites since 1715 had pleaded for as the necessary precondition of success. Preparations were pressed forward with efficiency and secrecy on the French side; but, postponed for a month at the insistence of Tory MPs, the scheme was betrayed in February by one of Newcastle's secret agents, François de Bussy, a senior official in the French Foreign Office. With extreme urgency military preparations and displays of Hanoverian loyalty were now urged forward in England too, and suspected persons taken into custody.[126] Lord Orrery was afraid of arrest, writing to warn his wife:

> poor Col: Cecil is sent to the Tower; many more are suspected: (would to God my real Sentiments were known as fully to the Privy Council as they are to you!) and from Suspicions all dangers are to be apprehended ... Ld Barrimore is apprehended, and old Dr Beaufort, the Physician who attends Col: Cecil; Tom Carte, and some others as little worth naming. In short, these are gloomy times ... As to my own Part, I am so entirely innocent that I have no Fears (as you and you only can tell, yet Appearances may perhaps be against me).[127]

The immense advantage of surprise had been lost, the papers of suspected English Tories were systematically searched, and the English side of the enterprise effectively inhibited. Worse was to follow: on 7 March an impending clash off Dungeness between the Portsmouth and the Brest fleets was prevented by a devastating storm that drove both back into port in disorder, and smashed many of the smaller vessels in Dunkirk harbour awaiting the embarkation of French forces.[128] It had been the high point of Jacobite hopes, the most plausible and best-equipped expedition ever mounted in their favour; again, the Stuarts' supporters were cheated by

[126] Cruickshanks, *Political Untouchables*, pp. 50–9.

[127] Lord Orrery to Lady Orrery, 28 February 1743/4: *Orrery Papers*, vol. 2, p. 186. Orrery clearly expected his letters to be intercepted and read by the regime's security service, as they certainly were in 1746: Lady Orrery to Lord Orrery, 1 May 1746: ibid., vol. 2, p. 208.

[128] Cruickshanks, *Political Untouchables*, pp. 60–5.

vain hope. It is not known that Johnson ventured any written comment on this episode.

What happened next was, by comparison, a hopeless gamble. On 3/14 July Prince Charles Edward Stuart, acting on his own initiative, embarked from St Nazaire with only two small ships, and landed in Eriskay on 3 August (n.s.): the Forty-five had begun. There is an hiatus in Johnson's correspondence between January 1744 and June 1746,[129] and very little other evidence survives for Johnson's activities between early 1745 and early 1746.[130] Little of what evidence exists ties Johnson to any date or place.[131] Boswell merely guessed that

> In 1746 it is probable that he was still employed upon his Shakespeare ... It is somewhat curious, that his literary career appears to have been almost totally suspended in the years 1745 and 1746, those years which were marked by a civil war in Great-Britain, when a rash attempt was made to restore the House of Stuart to the throne. That he had a tenderness for that unfortunate House, is well known; and some may fancifully imagine, that a sympathetick anxiety impeded the exertion of his intellectual powers; but I am inclined to think, that he was, during this time, sketching the outlines of his great philological work.[132]

Once again, Boswell sought to frame excuses for his subject. But where a direct question to Johnson might have produced hard evidence to resolve this momentous issue, Boswell could offer no specific information. In another context, however, he noted a relevant circumstance. One of Johnson's friends was 'Mr. William Drummond, bookseller in Edinburgh, a gentleman of good family, but small estate, who took arms for the house of Stuart in 1745; and during his concealment in London till the act of general pardon came out, obtained the acquaintance of Dr Johnson, who justly esteemed him as a very worthy man'.[133] How they met, Boswell failed to record, but that they did so strongly suggests that Johnson moved at that time in fugitive Jacobite circles. Nor was this a passing acquaintance:

[129] Johnson, *Letters*, vol. 1, pp. 38–40. Since Johnson's surviving letters from the 1740s number only 15, this is not in itself decisive evidence.

[130] 'This is the period of his life about which least is known': James L. Clifford, *Young Samuel Johnson* (London, 1955), p. 273. For a similar lacuna in the evidence for the life of the Jacobite Dr William King between July 1745 and April 1746 see Greenwood, *William King*, pp. 176–7.

[131] Johnson composed a sermon for the Rev. Henry Hervey Aston, preached at St Paul's on 2 May 1745; but when he wrote it is unknown, and there is no evidence that he was present at the service. Similarly, Johnson revised for Samuel Madden the latter's poem, *Boulter's Monument*, published in October 1745; but when and where the work was done is not recorded: Clifford, *Young Samuel Johnson*, pp. 274–8. Greene (*Politics*, p. xxxii) can add nothing between a dinner engagement in February 1745 and April 1746.

[132] Boswell, *Life*, vol. 1, p. 176.

[133] Boswell, *Life*, vol. 2, pp. 26–7. This was William Drummond (c. 1708–74) of Callendar, Perthshire. A William Drummond was imprisoned in Newgate in May 1746: PRO SPD 44/82/306. It is not known whether he was the same man.

Johnson continued to correspond with Drummond through the 1750s and 1760s,[134] and visited him during Johnson's Scottish tour of 1773.[135] It may not be unrelated to Johnson's brief but disastrous patronage of William Lauder that it occurred during a period in which Johnson was actively helping other Scots in difficult circumstances. At different times, Johnson employed six amanuenses to help him with the compilation of his *Dictionary*: five of them were Scots. What their political views were, how they came to be in London, and why Johnson chose this unusual balance of nationalities is not known.[136]

It may be that another, and unexplained, friendship had a similar origin. Mystery has surrounded the figure of 'Dr' Robert Levett (1705–82), once a waiter in Paris who had acquired some medical knowledge (though no degree), whom Johnson maintained in his household for 'many years' before Boswell knew Johnson and, indeed, until Levett's death. According to Thomas Percy, Johnson had known Levett 'from about [17]46.'[137] Boswell also noted: 'It appears from Johnson's diary, that their acquaintance commenced about the year 1746'.[138] Evidently this was the diary Johnson destroyed. It may be only a coincidence of names[139] that an early friend of the Johnson family in Lichfield was Theophilus Levett (1693–1746) who in 1718 and 1721 narrowly escaped prosecution for sedition after his alleged open declarations of Jacobite allegiance;[140] Samuel Johnson would have known Theophilus before going to Oxford in 1728.[141] In 1743 Johnson intervened to pay interest on a debt owed by his mother to Theophilus Levett, pleading for more time to pay, and assuring him: 'I think myself very much obliged by Your Forbearance, and shall esteem it a great happiness to be able to serve You. I have great opportunities of dispersing any thing that You may think it proper to make publick.'[142]

134 Johnson, *Letters*, vol. 1, pp. 168, 268, 280, 289.

135 Boswell, *Life*, vol. 5 (*Tour*), pp. 385, 394, 400.

136 Allen Reddick, *The Making of Johnson's Dictionary 1746–1773* (Cambridge, 1990), pp. 37, 62–5; James L. Clifford, *Dictionary Johnson: Samuel Johnson's Middle Years* (New York, 1979), pp. 52–4.

137 Bodleian MS Percy d. 11, f. 15v.

138 Boswell, *Life*, vol. 1, pp. 243.

139 After his death in 1782, Johnson wrote: 'I have by advertising found poor Mr. Levet's brothers in Yorkshire': Johnson to Lucy Porter, 19 March 1782: Johnson, *Letters*, vol. 4, p. 21. But Johnson was not unaware of Levett's background: he knew the year and place of his birth, his education, 'his early course of life', 'what relations had he, and how many are now living': Johnson to Charles Patrick, 14 February 1782: Johnson, *Letters*, vol. 4, p. 10. This suggests that Johnson knew much more.

140 Paul Kléber Monod, *Jacobitism and the English People 1688–1788* (Cambridge, 1989), p. 237.

141 The Levetts were an extensive family (Reade, *Johnsonian Gleanings*, vol. 4, pp. 182–92; vol. 11, pp. 295–6); it is possible, though not established, that Robert Levett may have been a distant kinsman of Theophilus.

142 Boswell, *Life*, vol. 1, pp. 81, 160–1; Johnson to Levett, 1 December 1743: Johnson, *Letters*, vol. 1, p. 37. Johnson and his mother mortgaged their Lichfield house to Theophilus Levett for £80 on 31 January 1739; Johnson finally cleared this debt, including outstand-

This last sentence, overlooked by biographers, hints at one of the advantages of a career in journalism for a man of Johnson's views.

It may not be appropriate to be too confident about the otherworldliness of men of letters in the light of the evidence that Daniel Defoe was an armed participant in Monmouth's rising of 1685, and narrowly escaped capture.[143] It must be emphasised that there is no evidence that Johnson himself participated in the rising of 1745. But given what is now known of the extent of Jacobite commitment, as well as the unexplained circumstances of Johnson's life, it is a realistic possibility rather than a romantic speculation that for a time in 1745–6 he held himself in readiness for dramatic events in circumstances which may have arisen but, as only hindsight makes self-evident, did not. A stronger and not inconsistent possibility is supported by another literary parallel. Those suspected of disaffection could be summoned to take the oaths before a magistrate, and, if they refused, their refusal would be formally recorded. It has been suggested that the understandably cautious Alexander Pope evaded such a challenge to declare himself in the fraught years of 1715–17 by 'adroit footwork' and by escaping the official attention which naturally focused on men of property.[144] It may be that in 1745–6 Johnson, living in relative poverty and obscurity, found a larger degree of anonymity a distinct advantage. He was, in any case, not a widely-known figure either in political or literary circles: the fame he sought in his early career largely eluded him until the publication of the *Dictionary*. *The Vanity of Human Wishes* (1749) was the first of his works openly to acknowledge his authorship. In 1746, Johnson escaped the notice of his contemporaries. Their attention was fixed elsewhere.

Johnson submitted his 'Short Scheme for compiling a new Dictionary' to the booksellers at the end of April 1746,[145] and probably would have been working on it on 16 April, the date of the Battle of Culloden. By that stage the rebel cause was clearly lost. But from the landing of Prince Charles (3 August 1745 n.s.) through the battle of Preston Pans (21 September) to the arrival of the rebel army in Derby (4 December), the prospects for a military destabilisation of the Hanoverian regime seemed considerably greater. Even in London, Jacobite supporters were almost certainly a

ing interest, on 27 June 1757: Reade, *Johnsonian Gleanings*, vol. 4, pp. 8–10. By 1761–2, it may have been Theophilus's son John Levett of whom Johnson lamented 'My only remaining friend [at Lichfield] has changed his principles, and was become the tool of the predominant faction': Johnson to Giuseppe Baretti, 20 July 1762: Johnson, *Letters*, vol. 1, p. 205.

143 Paula R. Backscheider, *Daniel Defoe: His Life* (Baltimore, 1989), pp. 35–40.

144 Howard Erskine-Hill, 'Alexander Pope: The Political Poet in His Time', *Eighteenth Century Studies* 15 (1981–82), 123–48, at 133.

145 Clifford, *Young Samuel Johnson*, p. 280.

minority, though a dangerous minority, and known sympathisers with the Stuart cause ran significant risks. Openly Jacobite propaganda was potentially fatal to its authors and publishers, and was distributed by various clandestine means. In December 1745 the Whig magistrate Sir Thomas De Veil reported that he had 'Receiv'd from different Persons some of the Pretender's printed Declarations which are every night thrust under Doors & putt into key holes'.[146] In 1717 a pamphleteer had complained that a rival Jacobite publication, *To Robert Walpole Esq.*, had been 'thrown about the Streets at Midnight, and privately dropt in the Shops'.[147] Such evidence suggests the informal, local networks of distribution appropriate to a genuinely populist movement; but it suggests also how ineffective and unsystematic was their impact. Government surveillance fragmented the Jacobite movement, prevented it from mounting an effective propaganda campaign, and intimidated its adherents. During the Forty-five at least six aldermen fled London to escape arrest.[148] Even after Culloden, recorded the Whig Alexander Hume Campbell to his brother, 'The printer of the National Journal is cast into Newgate for the paper of 10 June [the birthday of James III] which is so silly a Jacobite paper that it is wonderfull how it come out.'[149] At popular level, xenophobia, libertarianism and anti-Catholicism reinforced each other and could at times take pro-Hanoverian or anti-Jacobite forms: a swathe of labourers, artisans, tradesmen and craftsmen were apprehended, often by their social equals, prosecuted and sometimes jailed for indiscreet declarations of their allegiance to the House of Stuart.[150] Johnson was a political realist: his caution was appropriate.

IV. THE AFTERMATH, 1747–1760

The Anglo-Latin movement, combining moral satire and political subversion, had failed. William King's poetical invocations to Alexander, second Earl of Marchmont[151] did not succeed in cementing the loyalty of

146 PRO SPD 36/71/219, 36/76/195, quoted in Chapman, 'Jacobite Political Argument', p. 83.

147 *A Vindication Of the Honour and Justice of His Majesty's Government* (London, 1717), p. 4, quoted ibid., pp. 212–3.

148 Monod, *Jacobitism and the English People*, pp. 281–2.

149 Alexander Hume Campbell to Hugh, 3rd Earl of Marchmont, 17 June 1746: HMC *Polwarth*, vol. 5, p. 180.

150 Nicholas Rogers, 'Popular Disaffection in London During the Forty-Five', *The London Journal* 1 (1975), 5–27; Dr Rogers argues (p. 25) that judicial records 'suggest that mid-century Jacobitism was an ethno-religious phenomenon', confined to ethnic minorities. It seems more likely that High Church and Nonjuring English Tories were more discreet than the Irish and Scots communities.

151 See above, pp. 37–8.

that family. After the second Earl's death in 1740, Walpole's fall allowed their reconciliation to the Whig cause. In 1747 Alexander Hume Campbell wrote to his brother the third Earl: 'I have seen Dr King. He is well and seems to expect us not to continue with his (Jacobite) friends. I joking confirm'd our aversion to that cause and caution'd him against the folly.'[152] Yet, folly or not, Johnson's sympathies did not quickly subside. They were, naturally, carefully discriminating between individuals. Johnson took a low view of the character of Simon, Lord Lovat, executed for his part in the Forty-five, but in 1773 could still repeat the verses from the *Gentleman's Magazine* of April 1747 on the 'several personages who suffered' with Lovat on Tower Hill. Lovat, a graduate of Aberdeen, among whose final words on the scaffold were quotations from Horace and Ovid, would have appreciated the long Latin poem in his honour by 'Poneromastiae', dated from Berwick 31 January, but less pleased by an English verse:

> Pity'd by *gentle minds* KILMARNOCK dy'd;
> The *brave*, BALMERINO, were on thy side;
> RADCLIFFE, unhappy in his crimes of youth,
> Steady in what he still mistook for truth,
> Beheld his death so decently unmov'd,
> The *soft* lamented, and the *brave* approv'd.
> But LOVAT's end indiff'rently we view,
> True to no *King*, to no *religion* true:
> No *fair* forgets the *ruin* he has done;
> No *child* laments the *tyrant* of his *son*;
> No *tory* pities, thinking what he *was*;
> No *whig* compassions, for he *left the cause*;
> The *brave* regret not, for he was not brave;
> The *honest* mourn not, knowing him a *knave*.[153]

In 1749 Johnson 'formed a club that met weekly at the King's head, a famous beef-steak house, in Ivy Lane near St Paul's, every Tuesday evening'. There Johnson was 'transformed into a new creature'. This frankness had its problems, as Hawkins, one of the members, recorded:

> It required, however, on the part of us, who considered ourselves as his disciples, some degree of compliance with his political prejudices: the greater number of our company were whigs, and I was not a tory, and we all saw the prudence of avoiding to call the then late adventurer in Scotland, or his adherents, by those names which

[152] Alexander Hume Campbell to Hugh, 3rd Earl of Marchmont, 24 March 1746/7, in HMC *Polwarth* 5 (1961), p. 226.

[153] Boswell, *Journal*, p. 197 (21 September 1773); Boswell, *Life*, vol. 1, pp. 180–1; *Gentleman's Magazine* 17 (1747), 162–3, 194. Johnson had reason to remember this issue, since it contained (p. 189) William Lauder's 'Further Charges against Milton' (see above, pp. 59–66).

others hesitated not to give them, or to bring to remembrance what had passed, a few years before, on Tower-hill.[154]

The same year, Johnson's poem *The Vanity of Human Wishes* prominently included a plain allusion to the Forty-five:

> Let Hist'ry tell where rival Kings command,
> And dubious Title shakes the madded Land,
> When Statutes glean the Refuse of the Sword,
> How much more safe the Vassal than the Lord,
> Low sculks the Hind beneath the Rage of Pow'r,
> And leaves the *bonny Traytor* in the *Tow'r*.[155]

Four Scots peers had been imprisoned in the Tower of London for their role in the rebellion – Cromarty, Balmerino, Kilmarnock and Lovat. The first was pardoned, the last three executed. It was in this context that Johnson was still reproaching his countrymen for their lack of patriotism:

> Our supple Tribes repress their Patriot Throats,
> And ask no Questions but the Price of Votes;
> With Weekly Libels and Septennial Ale,
> Their Wish is full to riot and to rail.[156]

But Johnson's position was far sharper than any amorphous deploring of declining virtue. His servant Francis Barber gave Boswell an account of 'the friends who visited' Johnson in Gough Square in 1752; they included John Boyle, 5th Earl of Orrery and Baron Boyle (1707–62).[157] Johnson's intimacy with Orrery was not based on much respect for the peer's literary abilities. Johnson called him 'a feeble-minded man ... his conversation was like his writing, neat and elegant, but without strength ... he grasped at more than his abilities could reach. Tried to pass for a better talker, and a better writer, and a better thinker than he was.'[158] What drew the two men together was more political affinity than literary esteem. Orrery was a prominent Jacobite conspirator from the visit to England of the Jacobite agent Colonel Arthur Brett in 1739–40, a close friend of William King[159] and one of the group of peers and MPs who had addressed the French court in early 1743 with a request for military support for a restoration. That summer, Orrery had been proposed as one of Charles Edward's council of

154 Hawkins, *Life*, pp. 219, 250.
155 In the 1755 edition, 'bonny' was changed to 'wealthy'.
156 Samuel Johnson, *The Vanity of Human Wishes. The Tenth Satire of Juvenal, imitated* (London, 1749), pp. 5, 10.
157 Boswell, *Life*, vol. 1, p. 243; he may have known Johnson earlier: cf. Orrery to Dr Birch, 30 December 1747, ibid., vol. 1, p. 185. Waingrow (ed.), *Correspondence*, p. 169.
158 Boswell, *Journal*, p. 202 (22 September 1773).
159 See the letters of King to Orrery, Bodleian MS Eng hist d. 103, and of Orrery to King, in *Orrery Papers*.

regency (together with the 7th Earl of Westmoreland, elected Chancellor of Oxford University in 1759).[160] Johnson was even presented by Orrery with a copy of that author's *Remarks on the Life and Writings of Dr Jonathan Swift* (London, '1752' [sc. November 1751]).[161] That Orrery should have favoured with his friendship a person in Johnson's humble station in life was, at least, unusual.[162] Johnson's relations with the Tory and Jacobite MP Sir John Philipps, 6th Bt. (1700–64)[163] are unknown, but Johnson was evidently familiar with the domestic arrangements in Philipps's family,[164] in 1758 he franked a letter for Johnson's use,[165] and in 1760 Johnson asked anxiously after his health when the newspapers reported him dangerously ill.[166]

Yet Jacobite conspiracy and propaganda did not cease even after 1746. In that year William King wrote his bitter Latin satire *Hydra*, which he wisely left unpublished for obvious reasons.[167] Bitter resentment at the frustration of long-nurtured hopes in 1744 and 1745–6 paradoxically fuelled even more bitter, if more impractical, manifestations of allegiance in the few years which followed. One plan envisaged a rebellion timed to begin at the Lichfield races in September 1747, and although it was successively postponed Dr William King visited the same event in September 1749 and drew up a list of 275 loyal gentlemen who had attended.[168] From 1749 a series of projects for a coup in London, to be backed by French troops, were explored by Charles Edward's sympathisers and even induced him to make a clandestine visit of five days to the capital in 1750. These schemes, collectively known as the Elibank plot,[169] were foiled by the arrest

160 Cruickshanks, *Political Untouchables*, pp. 18, 20–1, 38, 46, 54, 77, 104, 108.

161 J. D. Fleeman, *A Preliminary Handlist of Copies of books associated with Dr Samuel Johnson* (Oxford, 1984), p. 51. This work, critical of Swift's choice of friends, caused a breach between Orrery and William King: Greenwood, *William King*, pp. 248–9.

162 For the warmth of their relationship see their exchange of letters, 15 February, 9, 12 July 1752: *Orrery Papers*, vol. 2, pp. 99, 111–14.

163 For whom, see Sedgwick (ed.), *The House of Commons 1715–1754*, vol. 2, p. 334. Philipps was a graduate and benefactor of Pembroke College, Oxford; was granted an Oxford DCL at the festivities surrounding the opening of the Radcliffe Camera in 1749; and had not stood for re-election to Parliament in 1747, as Horace Walpole put it, 'on the desperate situation of the Jacobite cause'.

164 Boswell, *Journal*, p. 241 (2 October 1773).

165 Johnson to Robert Chambers, 8 April 1758: Johnson, *Letters*, vol. 1, p. 160. MPs and peers had the privilege of free postage on letters which they franked with their signature: this minor perquisite could be used to help their clients and protégés.

166 Johnson to Robert Chambers, 31 December 1760: Johnson, *Letters*, vol. 1, p. 195.

167 Greenwood, *William King*, pp. 177ff.

168 Greenwood, *William King*, pp. 234–5; Cruickshanks, *Political Untouchables*, pp. 106–8. How far Johnson's local contacts in Lichfield would have given him intimations of these plans is unknown.

169 For which, see Sir Charles Petrie, *The Jacobite Movement: The Last Phase 1716–1807* (London, 1950), pp. 140–59; Frank McLynn, *Charles Edward Stuart* (London, 1988), pp. 395–414.

of their leading organiser, Dr Archibald Cameron, and his execution on 7 June 1753: it was after this individual had been hung, drawn and quartered that, addressing the Hanoverian supporter William Hogarth, Johnson 'burst out into an invective against George the Second, as one, who, upon all occasions, was unrelenting and barbarous'.[170]

Archibald Cameron was not alone, as the execution of Lieutenant Thomas Anderson in 1753 reminded his sympathisers.[171] The government's campaign against the press also continued with scarcely-relaxed vigilance. In 1753 James Ralph's paper *The Protester* was almost prosecuted, Newcastle complaining: 'the Paper is serious Jacobitism; a Comparison in favour of the Tory Ministry in Queen Ann's Time, against the Whig Ministers, at all Times – a most severe Reflection upon the King, & his Family; and a most strong Attack, & Censure of Sir Robert Walpole, & His Administration'.[172] In 1754 Richard Nutt was sentenced to a fine of £500, the pillory and two years' imprisonment for ascribing the country's ills to the Revolution settlement;[173] in 1757 *A Sixth Letter to the People of England* contained an openly Jacobite allusion, and was seized by government messengers.

Yet the Stuart cause had long survived such repression, and one of its chief adherents gave a different reason for its dramatic weakening in that decade. Charles Edward's visit to his capital in 1750[174] was doubly unwise, thought William King, for it gave evidence to his supporters not only of his and his advisers' poor political judgement of the practical prospects for military action, but also, and now increasingly, of his personal unsuitability, especially when measured against the exalted image of him that had been manufactured in his absence. Even William King, who met him on this visit, wrote in retrospect that 'in a polite company he would not pass for a genteel man ... very little care seems to have been taken of his education. He had not made the belles lettres or any of the finer arts his study, which surprised me much, considering his preceptors, and the noble opportunities he must have always had in that nursery of all the elegant and liberal arts and science', Rome: evidently King expected a Virgilian hero, the embodiment of the Anglo-Latin culture of which the Principal of St Mary Hall was the last great creative exponent but not the last adherent.

But I was still more astonished, when I found him unacquainted with the history and constitution of *England*, in which he ought to have been very early instructed. I

170 Boswell, *Life*, vol. 1, p. 147.

171 Monod, *Jacobitism and the English People*, p. 104.

172 Newcastle to Henry Pelham, 17 July 1753: BL Add MSS 32732 f. 295. *The Protester* was however patronised by the Duke of Bedford, and escaped prosecution.

173 Hanson, *Government and the Press*, p. 72.

174 He evidently stayed with Lady Primrose at her home in Essex Street, which ran south from the Strand just east of St Clements church.

never heard him espress any noble or benevolent sentiments, the certain indications of a great soul and a good heart; or discover any sorrow or compassion for the misfortunes of so many worthy men who had suffered in his cause. But the most odious part of his character is his love of money, a vice which I do not remember to have been imputed by our historians to any of his ancestors, and is the certain index of a base and little mind ... To this spirit of avarice may be added his insolent manner of treating his immediate dependants, very unbecoming a great prince, and a sure prognostic of what might be expected from him if ever he acquired sovereign power.[175]

A worse circumstance 'occasioned the defection of the most powerful of his friends and adherents in England, and by some concurring accidents totally blasted all his hopes and pretensions'. In Scotland during the Forty-five he had acquired a mistress, Clementina Walkinshaw, whose sister was housekeeper at Leicester House. This mistress 'soon acquired such a dominion over him, that she was acquainted with all his schemes, and trusted with the most secret correspondence'. Charles's adherents in England, fearing that Walkinshaw had been planted as a spy by the English ministry, sent an emissary named M'Namara to the Prince in Paris to demand her removal; he refused. 'She had no elegance of manners: and as they had both contracted an odious habit of drinking, so they exposed themselves very frequently, not only to their own family, but to all their neighbours. They often quarreled and sometimes fought: they were some of these drunken scenes which, probably, occasioned the report of his madness.' Those 'persons of distinction' in England who had despatched M'Namara then 'determined no longer to serve a man who could not be persuaded to serve himself, and chose rather to endanger the lives of his best and most faithful friends, than part with an harlot, whom, as he often declared, he neither loved nor esteemed'. William King concluded: 'from this era may truly be dated the ruin of his cause; which, for the future, can only subsist in the N[o]n[jur]ing congregations, which are generally formed of the meanest people, from whom no danger to the present government need ever be apprehended'.[176] King, the Oxford humanist, worshipping with the juring Church of England, had no hesitation in dismissing as plebeian those Nonjurors who worshipped separately; Johnson's disapproval of those congregations was not essentially different. So the active Jacobites were disillusioned with the Prince whose propaganda had elevated him to the dangerous and fragile position of a cultural icon.

Disillusion was the keynote of Jacobite sympathisers in England in the 1750s, and it is difficult to imagine that such feelings were not expressed when William King brought Samuel Johnson the diploma of his Oxford

175 William King, *Anecdotes*, pp. 198–203. 176 Ibid., pp. 204–11.

degree in 1755. In his Latin letter of thanks to the Vice Chancellor, acknowledging his honorary MA, Johnson concluded:

I would appear ungrateful indeed unless I were to acknowledge and praise the graciousness with which the distinguished gentleman [William King] personally delivered the testimony of your regard. If anything can add satisfaction to something already so satisfying, the honour pleases me all the more in that I have been selected to re-enter academic ranks in the very season when crafty (albeit unintelligent) men attempt by all available means to lessen your authority and to injure the reputation of the University – men whom I (insofar as someone on the sidelines can) have always opposed and will always oppose. I hold that any man who shall have betrayed you or the Academy would be the betrayer of virtue and literature and of himself and future generations.[177]

It was a strange letter, incongruously combining elegant thanks with a denunciation of 'crafty men' who had 'betrayed' the University. But Johnson thereby aligned himself squarely with William King and against those embattled Whigs who thought they had a duty to tell the world of Oxford's concealed Jacobitism.

Since the riot on 23 February 1747/8, King had been involved in a running controversy with Oxford Whigs who sought to pin the blame on him: Richard Blacow of Brasenose (who exploited the issue to demonstrate his loyalty to the regime and after much toad-eating obtained a canonry of Windsor) pressed first the vice chancellor, then the ministry, to prosecute the rioters; Edward Bentham of Oriel, another Whig placehunter, published in 1748 *A Letter to a Young Gentleman of Oxford* with a denunciation of Oxford Jacobitism, making sure that the bishop of Oxford and the Lord Chancellor received copies. King hit back in 1748 with his satirical *A Proposal for Publishing a Poetical Translation, Both in Latin and English, of the Reverend Mr. Tutor Bentham's Letter to a Young Gentleman of Oxford*, and in 1749 followed it with *A Poetical Abridgement, Both in Latin and English, of the Reverend Mr. Tutor Bentham's Letter to a Young Gentleman of Oxford*: both brilliantly denigrated Bentham's scholarship, intelligence and literary ability. His oration at the opening of the Radcliffe Camera in 1749 also contained an attack on Oxford's Whig informers,[178] which they returned on King's head in sustained denunciations. It was a theme which the 1754 general election kept at fever pitch when Oxfordshire was the scene of a bitterly-fought contest.[179] King, as a leading campaigner on the side of the 'Old Interest', published in February 1755 *Doctor King's Apology*, printed with the vice chancellor's approval at the university printing house in the

177 Johnson to George Huddesford, 26 February 1755: Johnson, *Letters*, vol. 5, p. 49 (translation).
178 Greenwood, *William King*, pp. 182–278, at 198.
179 R. J. Robson, *The Oxfordshire Election of 1754* (London, 1949).

Sheldonian; its object was to vindicate King's conduct during the election from the aspersions of a 'Society of Informers' (the Whig dons of Exeter College) and 'the Grand Informer', Richard Blacow of Brasenose. This continuing campaign of mutual denigration prompted Richard Blacow, seven years after the riot, to publish the most revealing account of all: *A Letter to William King LL.D., Principal of St Mary Hall in Oxford; containing a Particular Account of the Treasonable Riot in Oxford, in February 1747* (London, 1755).[180]

It was with the defence of men like Blacow in mind that one pamphleteer condemned the practice in principle only:

> where Informations are made, only for the sake of repairing broken Fortunes, or satisfying personal Revenge, or where the Accusation of Innocence may be contrived to gratify the Cruelty of a Tyrant, or the Violence of despotic Power; there Informations, which in the first Case would be public Virtue, in these last Instances, would become the Pest of Society, and highly deserve that Character that *Tacitus* gives of the Informers in *Tiberius* his Reign; *Delatores, hominum genus publico exitio, repertum.*

But this could not apply to those bound by the oath of allegiance to the king to 'a Discovery of all such Practices as tend to propagate Discontent, and alienate the Affections of his People from him, by false Suggestions, and spiriting up Disobedience to his Laws, and legal Authority, and abetting the Cause of a Competitor to his Crown'. Informers, in that sense, were 'the *laudable and necessary Means* of defending and supporting good Governments against the open or concealed Enemies of it'.[181] To 'loyal' Oxonians, such men were anathema, and denounced as spies and informers.

Such frank affirmations should be set against other evidence that Johnson's position might be evolving. In some ways, changes can be securely documented. Disillusion was the keynote of his observations on the celebrations of the peace of Aix-la-Chapelle, signed in 1748: 'The powers of this part of the world, after long preparations, deep intrigues, and subtile schemes, have set Europe in a flame, and, after having gazed awhile at their fireworks, have laid themselves down where they rose, to enquire for what they have been contending.'[182] It was a sentiment far removed from the passion with which Johnson had urged his country into war in 1739.

In other respects, it is not clear that Johnson ever modified the theoretical structure of his ideology in the 1750s. In 1753 the *Gentleman's Magazine* issued a consolidated index to its first twenty volumes. It carried a

[180] For Blacow's activities as an informer see especially Greenwood, *William King*, pp. 270–3.

[181] *A Discourse upon Informations and Informers* (London, [1755]), pp. 11–12, 23, 26.

[182] 'O.N.' in the *Gentleman's Magazine*, 19 (January 1749), p. 8; Johnson, *Works*, vol. 10, p. 114.

two-page Preface, of which John Nichols, writing a preface to a later index, recalled: 'the greater part of that Preface was written, and the whole of it corrected, by my illustrious Predecessor, Dr SAMUEL JOHNSON'.[183] Johnson's prose and interests can be detected in some passages, especially his pride in the *Magazine* as an 'Historical Chronicle' of 'Publick Events': 'nor is there any Period in which Publick Events have been more numerous or more important. For since the Commencement of our Volumes Two Wars by which almost all the known World was in some degree affected, have been begun and concluded', with consequences for 'every State in *Europe*'. This was neutral enough. Johnson then turned to England.

> With respect to our own Country, the deep and extensive designs of a Statesman, as able perhaps as any that ever existed, and the Opposition that was inflexibly maintained against him, have produced such a Series of Argumentation as has comprized all Political Science, and ascertained the Right of the Crown and the Privileges of the People, so as for ever to prevent their being confounded in the Cause either of Tyranny or of Faction.

This was, at least, a cool appraisal of Walpole, author of 'deep ... designs'. By 1753 Johnson disapproved equally of the minister and his opponents. Nothing is credited to either: the elucidation of the issues is ascribed to the controversy, and the right of the Crown and privileges of the People are only held to have been publicly aired, not constitutionally secured. Johnson now turned to a still more sensitive point.

> This Period will be render'd still more remarkable in *English* History by a Rebellion, which was not less contemptible in its beginning than threatening in its progress and consequences; but which, through the Favour of Providence, was crushed at once, when our Enemies abroad had the highest expectations from it, and has contributed to our greater security.[184]

Did this passage signify Johnson's repudiation of the Stuart cause? The evidence is inconclusive. His *Dictionary* in 1755 defined 'contemptible' as 'deserving scorn' but also, neutrally, as 'scorned', and in this paragraph it might carry the meaning 'small'. To attribute its defeat to Providence was a cool comment on the extent of Hanoverian loyalty or the prowess of Hanoverian arms. Finally, the clause 'and has contributed to our greater security' is ungrammatical, referring to no antecedent noun, and suggests that part of the paragraph, possibly everything after the semicolon, was added by another hand.

Whatever Johnson's pragmatic statements about events of the moment,

183 *General Index to the Gentleman's Magazine, from the year 1787 to 1818 ... with a Prefaratory Introduction ... by John Nichols*, vol. 3 (London, 1821), pp. iii, xlviii.

184 *A General Index to the First Twenty Volumes of the Gentleman's Magazine, in five parts* (London, 1753), pp. i–ii.

one work in particular contained clear statements of a traditional ideology. *A Dictionary of the English Language*, finally published in 1755 but composed in the years since 1746, only partly echoed Johnson's political dilemmas of the 1750s. Its definitions of tyranny ('Absolute monarchy imperiously administered') and tyrant ('An absolute monarch governing imperiously') argued no great admiration for the memory of James II, a characteristic which Johnson shared with most English Tories. Other key terms were, however, defined in ways which James II's conduct had made problematic. 'Abdication' was defined as 'The act of abdicating; resignation; quitting an office by one's own proper act before the usual or stated expiration', and exemplified from Swift's *Sentiments of a Church of England-man*: 'Neither doth it appear how a prince's *abdication* can make any other sort of vacancy in the throne, than would be caused by his death; since he cannot *abdicate* for his children, otherwise than by his own consent in form to a bill from the two houses.'

The primary meaning of 'loyal' was given as 'Obedient; true to the prince', as in Dryden's satiric lines:

> *Loyal* subjects often seize their prince
> Yet mean his sacred person not the least offence.

'Loyalty', 'Firm and faithful adherence to a prince', was illustrated from Shakespeare:

> Though *loyalty*, well held, to fools does make
> Our faith meer folly; yet he that can endure
> To follow with allegiance a fall'n lord,
> Does conquer him that did his master conquer.

To exemplify 'prince', Johnson made an ironic use of a passage from John Locke: 'The succession of crowns, in several countries, places it on different heads, and he comes, by succession, to be a *prince* in one place, who would be a subject in another.' But he made the irony clear by following it with Pope's lines

> Our tottering state still distracted stands
> While that *prince* threatens, and while this commands.

'Defeasible' was defined as 'That which may be annulled or abrogated', as in Sir John Davies's tract on Ireland: 'He came to the crown by a *defeasible* title, so was never well settled.'

Johnson's *Dictionary* defined 'Rightful' as '1. Having the right; having the just claim. 2. Honest; just', and supported it with lines from Shakespeare's *Richard II*:

> Some will mourn in ashes, some coal black,
> For the deposing of a *rightful* king.

If the moral was unclear, Johnson followed it by defining 'Rightfully' as 'According to right; according to justice', as in Dryden's *Preface to Fables*: 'Henry, who claimed by succession, was sensible that his title was not sound, but was *rightfully* in Mortimer, who had married the heir of York.' One of the meanings of 'succession' was 'The power or right of coming to the inheritance of ancestors', as in Dryden's lines

> What people is so void of common sense,
> To vote *succession* from a native prince?

Dryden also provided one of a long list of instances of the verb 'usurp', 'To possess by force or intrusion; to seize, or possess without right':

> Who next *usurps*, will a just prince appear,
> So much your ruin will his reign endear.

With crushing emphasis, Johnson added 'usurper', 'One who seizes or possesses that to which he has no right. It is generally used of one who excludes the right heir from the throne', as in Milton's lines

> But this *usurper*, his encroachment proud,
> Stays not on man; to God his tow'r intends
> Siege and defiance.

Or in Dryden's:

> Few *usurpers* to the shades descend
> by a dry death, or with a quiet end.[185]

One Whig reader complained that Johnson had cited authors 'who are often of no authority', like the Restoration royalist Sir Roger L'Estrange, and perceptively complained: 'Beside which he seems to have contrived to make his Dictionary a vehicle for Jacobite and High-flying tenets by giving many examples from the party pamphlets of Swift, from South's Sermons and other authors in that way of thinking, a remarkable instance of which is in the verb *abdicate*.'[186] John Wilkes too correctly realised that Johnson's *Dictionary* was 'a complete system of English politics and history'. His

[185] These terms should supplement those chosen for study in Robert DeMaria, Jr., *Johnson's Dictionary and the Language of Learning* (Chapel Hill, 1986), listed on pp. 287–95.

[186] Thomas Edwards (1699–1757) to Daniel Wray (1701–83), 23 May 1755, in Bodleian MS Bodl. 1012, f. 208. Edwards's Whiggism was clear: he referred to the Old Interest in the Oxfordshire election of 1754 as 'the enemy': ibid., f. 90. For a different interpretation of the *Dictionary*, see Robert DeMaria, *The Life of Samuel Johnson: A Critical Biography* (Oxford, 1993), p. 123, and idem, 'The Politics of Johnson's *Dictionary*', *Publications of the Modern Language Association* 104 (1989), 64–74.

purpose was naturally satirical: quoting Johnson's definition of 'revolution' as 'the change produced by the admission of King William and Queen Mary', Wilkes was appalled at this minimalist account of the Whig deliverance: 'What noble words! what a bold, glowing expression.'[187] Johnson's full definition had actually been 'Change in the state of a government or country. It is used among us κατ' ἐξοχήν [especially], for the change produced by the admission of king William and queen Mary'. But although Johnson had conceded (as was indeed true) that the term 'revolution' was *especially* used of the events of 1688–9, his brief characterisation of that episode as the 'admission' of new monarchs was neutral to the point of frigidity.

The publication of the *Dictionary* was, most famously, the occasion for Johnson's reproof of the fourth Earl of Chesterfield, whose patronage he had solicited in 1746 and who had evidently done nothing to lighten the burdens which Johnson had carried in the intervening years. Yet although Chesterfield may not have supported Johnson financially when he was compiling the *Dictionary*, his two essays[188] in *The World* drawing attention to that work before its publication were full of seemingly genuine praise almost to the point of adulation: Johnson could hardly have expected better publicity, and behind his hostile reaction to Chesterfield may be a political motive. It is possible that Johnson had turned to Chesterfield as a man in sympathy with his own cause, for in August 1741 Chesterfield, on behalf of the opposition Whigs, had undertaken a mission to Paris and Avignon to offer his party's support for a restoration in return for Tory aid in bringing down Walpole. The mission succeeded, producing James III's circular letter to his supporters of 16/27 September 1741 asking them to join with the Whig opposition in just such a campaign, and it was to this alliance (temporary though it proved) that Walpole's fall was due.[189] The two most senior men to whom Johnson had turned for patronage, Gower and Chesterfield, had not only failed as patrons; they had deserted the cause. Johnson's personal frustration was possibly heightened by political disillusion.

Johnson's *Dictionary* was a scholarly exercise, composed in the busy isolation of a garret. That labour completed, Johnson's attention surveyed a wider scene. The launch of his new periodical *The Literary Magazine, or Universal Review* in April 1756, coinciding with the outbreak of a new

187 *The North Briton*, no. 12 (21 August 1762).

188 *The World* 100 (28 November 1754), 101 (5 December 1754).

189 Cruickshanks, *Political Untouchables*, pp. 27–8. Chesterfield protested, after receiving Johnson's crushing letter in 1755, that he had never turned Johnson away; 'that Dr Johnson would have been always more than welcome – that he had sent frequently to invite him but that he had changed his Lodgings or could not be found etc': W. Adams to Boswell, 17 February 1785: Waingrow (ed.), *Correspondence*, pp. 56–63, at 62.

Anglo-French war in America and India which was already even greater in geographical extent than the last, confirmed Johnson's close attention to the momentous public events of his age.[190] His magazine gave them full coverage, not only reporting diplomatic and military news but printing the texts of treaties and dispatches in an attempt to provide a serious history of the war. For the first issue of the *Literary Magazine*, Johnson wrote a survey of the relations between England and her continental European neighbours since the reign of Elizabeth. Although only a summary, it was markedly different from anything Johnson had produced before: in the breadth of the chronological and geographical sweep, it signalled the supersession of the narrow preoccupations of the English political nation in the first four decades of Johnson's life.

These old issues were not erased by being set in a wider context. The Englishmen of 1756, contemplating their nation being dragged into a world war, were still treated by Johnson to an account of James II: 'He was not ignorant of the real interest of his country; he desired its power and its happiness, and thought rightly, that there is no happiness without religion; but he thought very erroneously and absurdly, that there is no religion without popery.' This was, it seems, always Johnson's position. So was his rejection of the Whig myth that 1688 had represented James II's abdication: it was 'the necessity of self-preservation' which had 'impelled the subjects of James to drive him from the throne',[191] a form of words with which Johnson markedly failed to disclaim a belief in James's or his son's title to the throne. Johnson had not abandoned his position; it had merely receded further and further from practical relevance. Even one of his most patriotic essays only narrowly replaced a piece of 1730s invective. According to Thomas Percy, Johnson originally wrote a paper 'in ridicule of the Army', but 'wch. he afterwds. suppressd. substituting in its place one entirely opposite "On the bravery of the Eng. Com. Soldiers".'[192]

The last French-backed invasion attempt associated with plans for some form of Stuart restoration was quickly famous only for leading to a succession of resplendent British naval victories in 1759.[193] Johnson was well aware of the absence of domestic conspiracy at that date (a confidence

190 His occasional writings on the Seven Years' War were greater in bulk than either his published political works of 1739–49 in the dynastic idiom identified above, or his political pamphlets of the 1770s: Johnson, *Works*, vol. 10, pp. 116–289.

191 [Samuel Johnson], 'An Introduction to the Political State of Great-Britain', *The Literary Magazine, or Universal Review* no. 1 (15 April – 15 May 1756), 1–9, in Johnson, *Works*, vol. 10, pp. 126–50, at 142.

192 Bodleian MS Percy d. 11, f. 7v.

193 Claude Nordmann, 'Choiseul and the Last Jacobite Attempt of 1759' in Eveline Cruickshanks (ed.), *Ideology and Conspiracy: Aspects of Jacobitism, 1689–1759* (Edinburgh, 1982), pp. 201–17.

which may suggest that he had had some knowledge of earlier schemes). On Skye in 1773,

> Sandie MacLeod had assured us that the Prince was in London in 1759 when there was a plan in agitation for him. We could hardly believe it, and Mr. Johnson said there could be no probable plan then. Dr MacLeod said with warmth that there was. The present Royal Family were all to have been seized and put aboard a ship; he was to have been in London; a number of persons of great consequence, among which was the Lord Mayor of London, were in the plot, and James III of Britain would have been proclaimed at Charing Cross; the Prince Regent would have issued writs and called a Parliament, and all would have gone well. 'But,' said the Doctor [MacLeod], 'it failed from the pusillanimity of some of those who were to have acted.' Mr. Johnson said it could not have done, unless the King of Prussia had stopped the Army in Germany; for that the Army would have fought without orders, and the fleet would have fought without orders, for the king under whom they served.[194]

Johnson was a political realist.

[194] Boswell, *Journal*, p. 162 (13 September 1773). Sandie MacLeod 'was aide-de-camp to the Prince in 1745, and remained eighteen years in exile on that account': ibid., p. 132 (8 September 1773).

7

JOHNSON'S POLITICAL OPINIONS, 1760–1784

I. THE CONVERSION OF THE INTELLIGENTSIA AND JOHNSON'S PENSION

What remained of popular Jacobitism largely evaporated in the 1750s. By the end of that decade even those who had been most committed to the Stuart cause were wavering or equivocal in their allegiance. By 1760 William King himself, in his Latin poem *Aviti Epistola ad Perillam, Virginem Scotam*, joined in the prevalent triumphalism generated by the success of the Seven Years' War and began to speak in glowing terms of the liberties enjoyed by Britons.[1] In this new scene the Stuarts had nothing new to say. Appropriately, James III's death in 1766 was marked by a Latin oration evidently directed at an Anglo-Latin audience;[2] but England's cultural politics had moved on. By the 1770s, Johnson like King looked back with pride on the Seven Years' War, 'when France was disgraced and overpowered in every quarter of the globe, when Spain coming to her assistance only shared her calamities, and the name of an Englishman was reverenced through Europe'.[3] This astonishing military triumph changed fundamentally the political options which confronted Englishmen, including those of Johnson's persuasion. These wider metamorphoses, combined with the rending factional conflicts of the 1750s, weakened the party to which he had typically looked. In September 1759 King also confided to a visitor his opinion that 'the Tories have not one man amongst them at present capable to be put at their head',[4] and the death of George II on 25 October 1760 provided an opportunity for King like others to draw new conclusions from their old premises. On 4 August 1761 the Oxford lawyer Sir William Blackstone met King, and reported to Shelburne: 'The Doctor desired me

[1] Greenwood, *William King*, pp. 289–99.

[2] A. Fabroni, *In Funere Jacobi III. Magnae Britanniae Regis Oratio* (Rome, 1766).

[3] Johnson, *Lives of the Poets*, vol. 3, p. 11.

[4] General Robert Clark to Lord Fitzmaurice, 15 September 1759, Shelburne MSS, Bowood, quoted in Greenwood, *William King*, p. 300.

to assure You, upon his Word and Honour, that he had no Attachments whatever, either public or secret, to that Cause in which the Sentiment of the World has usually ranked him as a Principal.'

Shelburne duly wrote to Bute to warn him that King intended to go to court to kiss the hand of George III as one of the delegation to be sent by Oxford University with a loyal address:

I take the liberty to mention it to Your Lordship, that if the King does not think a man who has indulged himself in Republican Sentiments worse than a Jacobite, he may oblige an old, and I have reason to think, a good man, consequently a vain one, who has nothing left to ask but an exception from absolute insignificance at the end of his days.[5]

Oxford's loyal address was presented at court on 16 September 1761, with William King as one of its bearers, and King was presented to the new monarch by the young Lord Shelburne.

William King evidently took no oath; there was no formal need for him to do so. But the position of this eminent Latinist, who presumably had taken the oaths in order to hold his fellowship, now drew closer to that of Johnson, who had held out as a Nonjuror. King, too, like Johnson, now paid a price for his gesture: in November 1761 he was the victim of a newspaper attack by Robert Gordon, a surviving Nonjuring bishop, 'with whom', King recorded, 'I had once lived in some degree of friendship'. King now openly condemned the bishop:

I don't know whether he would be a martyr, but no man is a greater enthusiast in religion than he is in the Jacobite cause. *Hereditary right* and *passive obedience* are the chief articles of his creed. Talk to him of *public spirit* and the *amor patriae*, 'tis a language which he does not understand; for he would be content to see the nation involved in a general ruin, and the extirpation of three or four millions of our people, if by that means the House of *Stuart* might be restored. And this is the doctrine which he teaches in the little congregation over which he presides as pastor; where, while he boasts of the purity of his religion, and a steady adherence to his political system, he departs from every principle of humanity, and devotes his country to ruin.

Robert Gordon was motivated by personal resentment, argued King, and despair at the failure of his cause:

Our zealot is enraged to see the extinction of faction, and such an harmony established amongst all orders and degrees as must necessarily prove our principal security. The nonjurors are now become a very insignificant and contemptible party. And although the Roman Catholics would certainly be very glad to see their religion re-established in this country, yet there are few amongst them who would

[5] Blackstone to Shelburne, 4 August 1761; Shelburne to Bute, 18 August 1761; Shelburne MSS, Bowood, quoted in Greenwood, *William King*, pp. 300–1.

engage in any desperate measure for this purpose; and desperate they must be, when the odds are perhaps more than a thousand to one that an attempt of this kind does not succeed: which, as long as the present union of our people and their attachment to the sovereign subsist, may fairly be asserted.

This assertion prompted King in 1761 to a reflection on the profound changes which had recast English attitudes in the 1750s:

The means by which this union hath been effected must needs be a matter of inquiry amongst all foreign politicians, since our own observe it with a kind of wonder. A continual success in the conduct of our public affairs, and a series of victories, may justly be alleged as one of the principal causes of uniting many of those (however they have been distinguished by party) who are real lovers of their country. But this would not have reduced the Jacobite interest to the low condition in which we see it at present, unless some more powerful motives had influenced the leaders of that party to change their principles and desert a cause, to which they had so stedfastly adhered for so many years. As I can in some measure account for this defection, I shall probably render an acceptable service to many of my countrymen and satisfy the inquiries of posterity by publishing an anecdote, which I am now under no obligations to conceal, and which as the affairs of Britain are at present circumstanced, it would, in my opinion, be criminal in me to suppress.

William King proceeded to record the facts of Prince Charles Edward's visit to London in 1750 and the progressive disillusion which demoralised his English supporters once they met their all-too-human idol.[6]

Scotland was changing too. When Thomas Ruddiman, aged 78, finally resigned the post of Keeper of the Advocates' Library in Edinburgh, a post he had held since 1730, he was replaced by David Hume. The death of Ruddiman in 1757 symbolised 'the decline of Latinity, and of the old humanist disciplines associated with it, as a dominant force in Scottish culture'.[7] Its decline some time before had indeed been disguised by the survival of its most distinguished practitioner.[8] The death of his English counterpart William King in 1763 was equally symbolic for the republic of letters south of the border.[9] With those men went much of the cultural medium within which a certain sort of antiquarian scholarship, and assertions or denials of hereditary right, had been nurtured and communicated. The times changed, but Johnson only partly obeyed the classical precept to change with them. How far this entailed a betrayal of principle becomes a central question for his biographers. Johnson's professed account of his new disposition was disarmingly simple:

6 William King, *Anecdotes*, pp. 190–6; Greenwood, *William King*, pp. 302–4.
7 Duncan, *Thomas Ruddiman*, p. vii.
8 Duncan, *Thomas Ruddiman*, pp. 147ff, discerns a decline in Scotland from the 1720s.
9 Greenwood, *William King*, pp. 327–61.

We were so weary of our old King, that we are much pleased with his successor; of whom we are so much inclined to hope great things, that most of us begin already to believe them. The young man is hitherto blameless; but it would be unreasonable to expect much from the immaturity of juvenile years, and the ignorance of princely education. He has been long in the hands of the Scots, and has already favoured them more than the English will contentedly endure. But perhaps he scarcely knows whom he has distinguished, or whom he has disgusted.[10]

More fundamental issues were, however, at stake. The argument that Johnson was not ruled by principle in matters of allegiance, and that his expressions of Jacobitism were, at most, romantic gestures, is sometimes defended by the circumstances of his acceptance of a pension of £300 p.a. from the new First Lord of the Treasury, Lord Bute, in 1762.[11] Yet the evidence for the circumstances of that grant does not easily bear that conclusion. The anonymous letter to Bute recommending a royal pension openly hinted that Johnson was a Nonjuror and that to accept a place would involve him in perjury:

If it be objected that his political principles render him an unfit object of His Majesty's favor, I would only say that he is to be the more pitied on this account, and that it may sometimes happen that our opinions, however erroneous, are not always in our power. Add to this that a disregard to this would be a further prosecution of his Majesty's noble plan, the total abolition of all party distinctions . . . I am told that his political principles make him incapable of being in any place of trust, by incapacitating him from qualifying himself for any such office. But a pension my Lord requires no such performances – and my Lord it would seem but a just condescension to human infirmity that the man who has endeavored in such a forcible manner to correct all our failings and errors should be excused one himself.[12]

The 'political principles' which would make Johnson an 'unfit object' of George III's favour cannot have been Toryism alone, since many former Tories had already been honoured by the new monarch with places or titles. But the author of the letter made those principles clear: Johnson was incapable of 'qualifying himself'. The only qualification required of all placeholders was subscription of the oaths of allegiance and abjuration. These were the 'performances' which a pension would not require.

Johnson was not the most obvious candidate for a pension from the ministry's point of view, and his inclusion may have been chiefly the result of the new policy of even-handedness towards Whig and Tory, English and

10 Johnson to Giuseppe Baretti, 10 June 1761: Johnson, *Letters*, vol. 1, p. 196.

11 Greene (*Politics*, p. xxii) argues (without evidence) that the pension was a reward for Johnson's writings in the 1750s against the Seven Years' War, which Bute and George III were attempting to end. This would not be inconsistent with the arguments advanced here.

12 Unknown to Bute, Cambridge, 15 November 1761: Waingrow (ed.), *Correspondence*, p. 512.

Scots Scourge N° 27.

Alex.r Mackenzie Inv.t et Sculp 1762 L.d Bute hired a number of writers, as Smollett &c &c See Almons Anecdotes L.d Bute. Vol. II. p. 5.

The HUNGRY MOB of SCRIBLERS and Etchers

If thine Enemy be hungry give him Bread to eat;
and if he be thirsty. give him water to drink Proverbs. 25. 21.

Let each Scribler that will ply his Needle or Quill
In Despite. of the Beadle or Gallow's
And their Venom throw out all the Kingdom about
No Regard should be paid to such Fellows

Was a God to alight from Olimpus height
Or Pallas to Guide in this Nation
The hungry Tribe 'gainst her Rules would Subscribe.
And endeavour to blacken her Station.

Then in Pit-y behold; how they Scratch and they Scold
And Spew from their Airy Dominions.
Not any of Sense can sure take Offence?
Or be Bi-Ass'd by such weak Opinions?

If their snarling you'd stop give the Hellhounds a Sop
Like Cerberus, that Infernal Growler.
They'l Riggle and bow; and Praises bestow,
Tho' now they breathe nothing but Foul Air. 1762.

Plate 7

Johnson's pension. Bute's patronage of the arts was consistently denounced as politically biassed

Scots. Thomas Percy, writing notes on Boswell's *Life of Johnson*, observed: 'About the Pension. B[oswell] does not tell that J[ohnson] was pension'd to keep Home's Pension in Countenance.'[13] If these were the problems on the Hanoverian side, Sir John Hawkins recognised the same principled dilemma in the mind of his subject: 'Upon receiving the news, Johnson was in doubt what answer to return, being, perhaps, disturbed with the reflection, that whatever he might deserve from the public, he had very little claim to the favour of any of the descendants of the house of Hanover.' And he drew an historical analogy:

Johnson, it is true, had laid himself open to reproach, by his interpretation of the word Pension in his Dictionary, written, it is evident, at a time when his political prejudices were strongest, and he found himself in a predicament similar to that of Dr [William] Sherlock, who, at the Revolution, was a non-juror to king William, but, after deliberating on his refusal as a case of conscience, took the side that made for his interest, but against his reputation.[14] But who, except the Great Searcher of Hearts, can know, that in the case of Sherlock or Johnson, either made a sacrifice of his conscience? Or, seeing that the grant of Johnson's pension was confessedly unconditional, and bound him neither to the renunciation of any of his political principles, nor the exercise of his pen in the defence of any set of men or series of measures, who will have the face to say, that his acceptance of it was criminal; or that it was in the power of any one to pervert the integrity of a man, who, in the time of his necessity, had, from scruples of his own raising, declined the offer of a valuable ecclesiastical preferment, and thereby renounced an independent provision for the whole of his life?[15]

Hawkins referred to the offer of a rectory made to Johnson about 1758 by Mr. Langton of Langton, Lincolnshire.

The Whig historian Thomas Birch (1705–66) knew Johnson from 1741, perhaps even from 1739; Boswell called him Johnson's 'friend'.[16] On 24 July 1762, Birch wrote to Philip Yorke, son of the 1st Earl of Hardwicke, with news about royal pensions in the new reign: 'Sam. Johnson likewise,

[13] Thomas Percy's notes, Bodleian MS Percy d. 11, f. 7r. For John Home (1722–1808) see Kenneth Simpson, *The Protean Scot: The Crisis of Identity in Eighteenth Century Scottish Literature* (Aberdeen, 1988), pp. 97–116: 'Above all else, Scotland had to produce a tragedian for her claims for literary recognition to be taken seriously; or so the *literati* believed.' Home was acclaimed, like James Macpherson, because he addressed an opportunity in the cultural politics of his age. His tragedy *Douglas*, partly based on a Scots ballad, was first performed in 1756; in 1757 Home became private secretary to Lord Bute; encouraged James Macpherson; and received a pension of £300, at Bute's instigation, at the accession of George III in 1760.

[14] On Sherlock's change of allegiance see William Sherlock, *The Case of Allegiance due to the Sovereign Powers* (London, 1691); Jeremy Collier, *Dr Sherlock's Case of Allegiance Consider'd* (London, 1691); John Kettlewell, *The Duty of Allegiance Settled upon its True Grounds* (London, 1691); Erskine-Hill, 'Literature and the Jacobite Cause', p. 16; J. P. Kenyon, *Revolution Principles: The Politics of Party 1689–1720* (Cambridge, 1977), pp. 24–9.

[15] Hawkins, *Life*, pp. 393–4.

[16] Boswell, *Life*, vol. 1, pp. 139, 151, 153, 160, 226, 285.

who would lately scarce have own'd the King's title, is now a Royal Pensioner with 300 £ a year. Monsr. Colbert was more delicate in his recommendations to Louis XIV. of Men of Genius & Learning than the great Courtier of more modern Times.' Two weeks later he added:

Sam. Johnson's becoming a pensioner has occasioned his Dictionary to be turn'd to in the Word *Pension* thus defined by him; 'an allowance made to any one without an Equivalent. In England it is generally understood to mean Pay given to a State-hireling for Treason to his Country.' I do not know, whether the Acceptance of his pension obliges him to an Oath to the Government. If he now takes that Oath, I know what to determine about the Conscience of this *third Cato*.[17]

Johnson never took such an oath. Charles Churchill, in Book II and Book III of his poem *The Ghost* (March and October 1762), bitterly attacked Johnson as

> POMPOSO (insolent and loud,
> Vain idol of a *scribbling* crowd . . .
> Who, proudly seiz'd of *Learning's* throne,
> Now damns all Learning but his own . . .
> He damns the *Pension* which he takes,
> And loves the STUART he forsakes.

Johnson replied by excluding Churchill from the *Lives of the Poets*.

The Scots clergyman William Shaw, a collaborator of Johnson's, gave an account of his friend's pension:

when proposed to his Majesty, a certain Lord, whom he [Johnson] would not name, was abundantly sarcastic on his character, and mentioned his political principles as inimical to the House of Hanover. Lord Bute's answer was, that if these were the Doctor's principles, there was merit in his suppressing them; that if he had not made an improper use of them without any acknowledgement from court, it was not very likely he would, when that should take place, and that it was intended to

17 Thomas Birch to Philip Yorke, Lord Royston, 24 July, 7 August 1762: British Library Add MSS 35399 ff. 305, 316; on 14 August Birch reported that the *North Briton* of that date not only attacked Arthur Murphy 'but likewise Sam. Johnson, the new pensioner, who has been latterly seen at Lord Bute's Levee': ibid., f. 320. On 4 September he added: 'Hawkesworth, in the last Gentleman's Magazine, is angry, your Ldp sees, with the *North Briton* for animadverting upon the giving a pension to Sam. Johnson, which the candid & modest Superintendant of the Magazine stiles *encouraging literary merit without regard to party principles*; a gentle Expression for furious Jacobitism. A Friend of Johnson's told me, that when he mention'd to him the Design of giving him a pension, he answer'd with a supercilious Air, "If they offer me a small Matter, I will not accept of it"': ibid., f. 341. Lord Royston replied on 7 September: 'I took notice of Hawkesworth's most indecent Remark on the Pension given to his Fellow Labourer in Declamatory Impertinence Johnson; & I presume from several Symptoms in his *Collection*, that he flatters himself with the honor of standing next Oars in yt literary List. Both he & Smollet have changed their *Livery* lately, & Let them Wear Whose they will, I shall have a most sovereign Contempt for such Hackney Sycophants & Scriblers': ibid., f. 345.

reward his writings which were before the public, without any regard to such principles as he kept to himself.[18]

Boswell placed in 1763 Johnson's self-justification:

I have accepted of a pension as a reward which has been thought due to my literary merit; and now that I have this pension, I am the same man in every respect that I have ever been; I retain the same principles. It is true, that I cannot now curse (smiling) the House of Hanover; nor would it be decent for me to drink King James's health in the wine that King George gives me money to pay for. But, Sir, I think that the pleasure of cursing the House of Hanover, and drinking King James's health, are amply overbalanced by three hundred pounds a year.[19]

Johnson implied that he had formerly taken 'pleasure' in doing both. Boswell, horrified, argued in extenuation of this passage: that it was rhetorical exaggeration to show Johnson's dexterity in argument; that Boswell had 'heard him declare, that if holding up his right hand would have secured victory at Culloden to Prince Charles's army, he was not sure he would have held it up'; that he had said to Bennett Langton: 'Nothing has ever offered, that has made it worth my while to consider the question fully.' But these arguments hardly strengthened Boswell's case. Johnson was evidently moderating his earlier position, not rhetorically heightening it; his remark on Culloden verged on open treason; and his disclaimer to Bennett Langton was evasive and implausible in the light of Johnson's intellectual milieu. However much his position had changed by the 1760s, Boswell was obliged to concede: 'there is no doubt that at earlier periods he was wont often to exercise both his pleasantry and ingenuity in talking Jacobitism'.[20]

II. CONSTANCY OR COMPROMISE, 1760–1784

Although Johnson's political sympathies before 1760 are well evidenced, there is doubt about the extent to which he retained them, modified or unmodified, into the reign of George III. Some evidence, impossible to verify, points to a larger degree of continuity. The *London Evening Post* of 6 June 1775 regaled its readers with a Johnsonian anecdote:

POMPOSO some time ago being in company with a select number of friends, where they spoke without the least reserve, was asked by one of the company, how he came to *change his political sentiments*? 'Sir', says the other, in his usual *base* voice, 'I have not changed my political sentiments, though political sentiments have changed to mine; for I would have you to know, I am as much a *Jacobite* now as ever.'

[18] [William Shaw], *Memoirs of the Life and Writings of the late Dr Samuel Johnson* (London, 1785), pp. 136–7.

[19] Boswell, *Life*, vol. 1, p. 429.

[20] Boswell, *Life*, vol. 1, p. 430.

This may refer to the episode recorded by William Burke, who in 1779 argued for the irrelevance of the Pretender in the current invasion threat:

> what uses the French can make of him I don't see, unless Dr Johnson's, is the Sentiment of all the quondam Jacobites, that they have only lent, not sold, their principles; or, that they make his Majesty Tenant at Will of their Loyalty; but I remember about two Years agoe that Leviathan Jacobite, saying in Company 'No Madam, we have not relinquished our principles, we think the right to be, where we always thought it; various circumstances induce us to an acquiescence in what *is*, without abandoning our opinions of what *ought to be*.'

William Burke was naturally sceptical: 'this sort of occasional conformity, must be accredited by the success of some Battles in support of indefeasible hereditary Right' before he would see 'many avowed partizans of Johnson's Doctrine'.[21] As a man of self-consciously inflexible principle, Johnson may plausibly have argued (as Boswell elsewhere recorded) that his political sentiments were not compromised, especially when (as now) doubt could be cast on that claim.

But Johnson's feelings about the monarch had evolved. In 1779 he had the early impressions of his *Lives of the Poets* bound, and sent to George III: 'If the King is a Whig, he will not like them; but is any King a Whig?'[22] He would not have posed such a rhetorical question in the reign of George II. In 1770 Johnson condemned the Wilkesites as 'low-born railers' who had

> attacked not only the authority, but the character of their Sovereign, and have endeavoured, surely without effect, to alienate the affections of the people from the only king, who, for almost a century, has much appeared to desire, or much endeavoured to deserve them. They have insulted him with rudeness and with menaces, which were never excited by the gloomy sullenness of William, even when half the nation denied him their allegiance; nor by the dangerous bigotry of James, unless when he was finally driven from his palace, and with which scarcely the open hostilities of rebellion ventured to vilify the unhappy Charles, even in the remarks on the cabinet of Naseby.[23]

There was a timelessness in Johnson's account of the polarities in public life, as, at the end of the 1770s, in his account of Milton's politics:

> Milton's republicanism was, I am afraid, founded in an envious hatred of greatness, and a sullen desire of independence; in petulance impatient of controul, and pride disdainful of superiority. He hated monarchs in the state, and prelates in the church; for he hated all whom he was required to obey. It is to be suspected, that his

21 William Burke to Duke of Portland, 26 July 1779: Portland Papers (Nottingham University Library), Pw F 2149; Kaminski, *Early Career of Samuel Johnson*, p. 229.

22 Johnson to Hester Thrale, 10 March 1779: Johnson, *Letters*, vol. 3, p. 155.

23 [Samuel Johnson], *The False Alarm* (London, 1770), p. 50. Charles I's 'cabinet' of papers was captured at the battle of Naseby in 1645 and a selection later published in an attempt to denigrate him.

predominant desire was to destroy rather than establish, and that he felt not so much the love of liberty as repugnance to authority.[24]

But if Johnson's views suggested their long antecedents, so did the views of his opponents. The Dissenter Joseph Towers seized on Johnson's remark in *The False Alarm* that the party struggle in the reign of Anne 'was to exclude or restore an exiled king'. Towers observed:

All your newly acquired loyalty to George III cannot make you forget your much-favoured House of Stuart, nor wholly remove your attachment to it. It was too deeply rooted, and become too natural to you, to be totally eradicated: *Naturam expelles furca, tamen usque recurret.*[25]

Johnson continued to move in sympathetic circles. His close friendship from the mid 1760s with the brewer Henry Thrale may have owed something to the views of the latter's father Ralph Thrale (c. 1698–1758), MP for Southwark in 1741–7 and listed among the 'gentilhommes incorruptibles' in the list of persons expected to favour a restoration given to the Jacobite emissary James Butler in 1743.[26] Oliver Goldsmith was another of Johnson's close companions. In April 1773, Johnson quoted Dryden's lines:

For colleges on bounteous kings depend
And never rebel was to arts a friend.

For Johnson, as for Dryden (and as for the whole tradition which embraced William King, Thomas Ruddiman, and all who opposed Bentley in the controversy over the *Epistles of Phalaris*) polite literature, the state of the Church and the fortunes of the Universities were bound up with the cause of dynastic legitimacy. Boswell recorded the revealing exchange which followed:

General Paoli observed, that successful rebels might. MARTINELLI. 'Happy rebellions'. GOLDSMITH. 'We have no such phrase.' GENERAL PAOLI. 'But have you not the *thing*?' GOLDSMITH. 'Yes; all our *happy* revolutions. They have hurt our constitution, and will hurt it, till we mend it by another HAPPY REVOLUTION.' – I never before discovered that my friend Goldsmith had so much of the old prejudice in him.[27]

24 Johnson, *Lives of the Poets*, vol. 1, p. 217.

25 [Joseph Towers], *A Letter to Dr Samuel Johnson: occasioned by his late Periodical Publications. With an Appendix, containing some Observations on a Pamphlet lately published by Dr Shebbeare* (London, 1775), p. 43.

26 Eveline Cruickshanks, *Political Untouchables: The Tories and the '45* (London, 1979), pp. 44, 115–38, at 121, 135. For the son, see J. D. Fleeman, 'Dr Johnson and Henry Thrale, MP' in Mary Lascelles et al. (eds.), *Johnson, Boswell and their Circle* (Oxford, 1965), pp. 170–89.

27 Boswell, *Life*, vol. 2, pp. 223–4.

Boswell was in no doubt about the nature of this 'old prejudice'. The same month, Johnson confirmed that these were indeed Goldsmith's views by telling Boswell Johnson's anecdote of being with Goldsmith in Poets' Corner of Westminster Abbey and quoting Ovid's line *Forsitan et nostrum nomen miscebitur istis* (it may be that our names too will mingle with these); walking home, Goldsmith pointed to the heads of the executed rebels of the Forty-five impaled above Temple Bar and 'slyly whispered' the same line.[28]

In March 1783 Boswell recorded a similar exchange with Johnson's old and close friend General James Edward Oglethorpe (1696–1785),[29] who had introduced Boswell to Dr John Shebbeare and had been 'one of the warmest patrons' of Johnson's poem *London* in 1738:

> OGLETHORPE. 'The House of Commons has usurped the power of the nation's money, and used it tyrannically. Government is now carried on by corrupt influence, instead of the inherent right in the King.' JOHNSON. 'Sir, the want of inherent right in the King occasions all this disturbance. What we did at the Revolution was necessary: but it broke our constitution.' OGLETHORPE. 'My father did not think it necessary.'

In what circles Johnson and Oglethorpe had first met is not recorded; but for Oglethorpe to have approved of *London*, and for them to have met within a short time of its publication, suggests a shared social milieu in the metropolis. The nature of that milieu is, in Oglethorpe's case, easy to discover. His father, Sir Theophilus Oglethorpe (1650–1702), had been Brigadier-General of James II's army.[30] His daughters had been raised as Catholics. James Edward Oglethorpe had been an early hero of the covertly-Jacobite Richard Savage, and the general helped the indigent poet financially on several occasions:[31] possibly Savage's company led Oglethorpe to Johnson's. General Oglethorpe, embarrassingly bearing the Christian names of James III, had been unhappily drawn into the Forty-five as a subordinate of the inert Field Marshal George Wade. Even more than his superior, the energetic Oglethorpe had proved strangely lacking in zeal or military ability, even missing a major opportunity to cut off the retreating rebel army at Penrith, and was the subject of a court martial

28 Boswell, *Life*, vol. 2, p. 238; the incident is undated.

29 Johnson had offered to write Oglethorpe's life; the general prudently refused: Boswell, *Life*, vol. 2, p. 351. For Oglethorpe's Jacobitism see Paul Kléber Monod, *Jacobitism and the English People 1688–1788* (Cambridge, 1989), pp. 34, 231, 272.

30 Boswell, *Life*, vol. 4, pp. 112, 170–1; vol. 1, p. 127. For Sir Theophilus's involvement in active conspiracies in the 1690s, and his son's Jacobite upbringing, see Amos Aschbach Ettinger, *James Edward Oglethorpe: Imperial Idealist* (Oxford, 1936), pp. 31–80.

31 Clarence Tracy, *The Artificial Bastard: A Biography of Richard Savage* (Cambridge, Mass., 1953), p. 127.

after the campaign was over.[32] His sister Eleanor, marquise de Mézières, had been a channel of communication from Charles Edward Stuart to the English Jacobites during the Elibank plot;[33] General Oglethorpe himself provided funds for John Baptist Caryll's Jacobite paper *The True Briton*, published in 1751–3. In the general election of 1754 he stood as a candidate for Westminster, his ignominious failure revealing the disintegration of that potent Jacobite electoral organisation of the 1740s, the Independent Electors of Westminster.[34] But his sympathies were clear.

Another of Johnson's friends in later life continued an earlier tradition. The ex-Jacobite William King delivered his last oration before the University of Oxford at the Encaenia of 8 July 1763. How far the oration was King's own work is, however, open to doubt. *Jackson's Oxford Journal* described it as 'a most spirited and elegant Oration, delivered with a Grace and Dignity, which notwithstanding his acknowledged Powers, could scarce be expected from a Gentleman in his 79th Year'. Perhaps indeed Johnson had helped, for Dr Richard Powney, writing from Oxford, had earlier approached Dr John Douglas: 'If you should see Mr. Sam: Johnson I wish you would ask him if he would prepare a handsome English Oration to close the Encaenia. It will give him a desirable opportunity of returning his Obligations to the King, and his Ministry. I speak this from the Vice Chancellor who would be glad of so able a hand, to do honour to the intended celebrity', for it was still expected that George III might attend the Encaenia as part of the celebrations of the end of the Seven Years' War.[35] The text of King's oration does not survive, but according to one hearer 'The purport of his speech was this: "that we had gained great honour by acting with steadiness and integrity in a time of general corruption: and that now, without any alteration in our conduct, we had the happiness of being in some degree of favour with a Prince, who is one of the best that ever lived".'[36] He died, at Bath, on 30 December 1763 and was succeeded as Principal of St Mary Hall by Nowell, preacher of a famous

32 Frank McLynn, *Charles Edward Stuart* (London, 1988), pp. 195, 197–8; Ettinger, *James Edward Oglethorpe*, pp. 255–69.

33 McLynn, *Charles Edward Stuart*, p. 404.

34 Monod, *Jacobitism and the English People*, pp. 34, 230–1. In 1738, as well as encouraging Johnson's *London*, Oglethorpe had subscribed ten guineas to the Jacobite Thomas Carte's *History of England*: John Nichols, *Illustrations of the Literary History of the Eighteenth Century* (8 vols, London, 1817–58), vol. 5, p. 166.

35 Richard Powney to John Douglas, 15 March 1763: BL Egerton MSS 2183 f. 60; a few days later he added 'I have found out a way of applying to Johnson', ibid. f. 62 [n.d.]; I. G. P[hilp], 'Doctor Johnson and the Encaenia Oration', *Bodleian Library Record*, new series 8 (February 1969), 122–3. I owe this reference to Mr. J. S. G. Simmons.

36 Charles Godwyn to John Hutchins, 1 August 1763, in John Nichols (ed.), *Literary Anecdotes of the Eighteenth Century* (9 vols., London, 1812–15), vol. 8, p. 236, quoted Greenwood, *William King*, pp. 318–9.

fast sermon before the House of Commons on 30 January 1772, the House's thanks for which were deleted from the Journal when absent Whig MPs discovered its monarchical sentiments. Nowell duly became Johnson's friend, and in June 1784 Johnson, Boswell and Dr Adams of Pembroke were guests at Nowell's house in Oxford, 'where was a very agreeable company, and we drank "Church and King" after dinner, with true Tory cordiality'. 'Dr Johnson said to me, "Sir, the Court will be very much to blame, if he is not promoted."'[37] But Thomas Nowell rose no higher: Hanoverian generosity had its limits.

If these were Johnson's closest friends, he retained a clear sense also of those with whom he was not in instinctive harmony. In 1777 Johnson regretted the increase in numbers of the second and more distinguished club of which he was a member, 'as we have several in it whom I do not much like to consort with'; Boswell added a note: 'On account of their differing from him as to religion and politics'.[38] The thesis of a profound transition in the political options facing the English public in the late 1750s and early 1760s makes sense of Johnson's decision to accept a pension and shows the degree of truth in his claim that his principles were unchanged. It throws light, too, on the survival of the term 'Tory'[39] even after it had become inappropriate as the description of any parliamentary grouping.[40] Mrs. Piozzi (formerly Mrs. Henry Thrale) was using the term in this anachronistic way in writing that 'Of Mr. Johnson's toryism the world has long been witness, and the political pamphlets written by him in defence of his party, are vigorous and elegant.' Nevertheless, his commitments were vehement: 'No man however was more zealously attached to his party; he not only loved a tory himself, but he loved a man the better if he heard he hated a Whig. "Dear Bathhurst[41] (said he to me one day) was a man to my heart's content: he hated a fool, and he hated a rogue, and he hated a *Whig*; he was a very good *hater.*"'[42] Johnson did his best to adhere to what he understood as the older conception of party, and even in 1773 maintained that his friend Burke

> was wrong in his maxim of sticking to a certain set of *men* on all occasions. 'I can see that a man may do right to stick to a *party*', said he; 'that is to say, he is a *Whig*, or he

37 Boswell, *Life*, vol. 4, p. 296.

38 Johnson to Boswell, 11 March 1777: Johnson, *Letters*, vol. 3, p. 11. Bruce Redford suggests (ibid.) that those to whom Johnson objected included Charles James Fox, Edward Gibbon and Adam Smith.

39 For which, see especially James J. Sack, *From Jacobite to Conservative: Reaction and orthodoxy in Britain, c. 1760–1832* (Cambridge, 1993).

40 Ian R. Christie, 'Party in Politics in the Age of Lord North's Administration', *Parliamentary History* 6 (1987), 47–68.

41 Dr Richard Bathurst, physician (d. 1762).

42 Hester Lynch Piozzi, *Anecdotes of the Late Samuel Johnson*, pp. 40, 83.

is a *Tory*, and he thinks one of those parties upon the whole the best, and that to make it prevail, it must be generally supported, though in particulars it may be wrong. He takes its faggot of principles, in which there are fewer rotten sticks than in the other, though some rotten sticks, to be sure; and they cannot well be separated. But to bind one's self to one man, or one set of men (who may be right today and wrong to-morrow), without any general preference of system, I must disapprove.'[43]

This was not a fair summary of Burke's position, but Johnson was right to discern a profound contrast between the party system of his youth and early adult life, expressed as a clear ideological antithesis of Whig and Tory, and the new rationale for party cohesion which Burke attempted to devise for the Rockingham group in the 1760s after that early-Hanoverian antithesis was no more.

This degeneration Johnson dated to the administration of Sir Robert Walpole. Johnson still adhered to a vision of the constitution which also allowed a greater scope for the personal role of the monarch. This was evident also in the account of the Rev. Dr William Maxwell, who knew Johnson from 1754:

In politicks he was deemed a Tory, but certainly was not so in the obnoxious or party sense of the term; for while he asserted the legal and salutary prerogatives of the crown, he no less respected the constitutional liberties of the people. Whiggism, at the time of the Revolution [of 1688], he said, was accompanied with certain principles; but latterly, as a mere party distinction under Walpole and the Pelhams, was no better than the politicks of stock-jobbers, and the religion of infidels.

He detested the idea of governing by parliamentary corruption, and asserted most strenuously, that a prince steadily and conspicuously pursuing the interests of his people, could not fail of parliamentary concurrence. A prince of ability, he contended, might and should be the directing soul and spirit of his own administration; in short, his own minister, and not the mere head of a party: and then, and not till then, would the royal dignity be sincerely respected.[44]

Hawkins's daughter recalled her father's view of Johnson's dilemma:

in his political pamphlets he [Hawkins] admired him, and unwillingly was he driven to confess, even to us his children, that Johnson could ever have written on principles opposite to those which he afterwards adopted. It appears now, indeed, little less than virtue to have been what was called a Jacobite; and certainly there was no small degree of virtue, and of many virtues, in the adherence to a royal cause, more perhaps than *could* be practised on the other side; but still it would be a

43 Boswell, *Journal*, p. 21; Boswell, *Life*, vol. 5 (*Tour*), p. 36.
44 Printed in Boswell, *Life*, vol. 2, pp. 116–33, at 117.

hardy champion who would venture to defend the two parts of Johnson's conduct, and a subtle sophist who could reconcile his opinions.[45]

She confessed that she had wished to see *Marmor Norfolciense* reprinted in her father's edition of Johnson's *Works*, published in 1787: 'The time was passed, I thought, when any thing written against the Protestant succession could be offensive, and we were at a point of time when such an obstinate adherence was rising in estimation ... but he had much more wisdom than his daughter', and omitted it.[46]

Hawkins, as a Whig, provided a summary of Johnson's 'political principles' which, like Boswell, tried to place his subject's embarrassing views in the best light:

That he was a tory, he not only never hesitated to confess, but, by his frequent invectives against the whigs, was forward to proclaim: yet, was he not so besotted in his notions, as to abett what is called the patriarchal scheme, as delineated by Sir Robert Filmer and other writers on government; nor, with others of a more sober cast, to acquiesce in the opinion that, because submission to governors is, in general terms, inculcated in the Holy Scriptures, the resistance of tyranny and oppression is, in all cases, unlawful: he seemed rather to adopt the sentiments of Hooker on the subject, as explained by Hoadly, and, by consequence, to look on submission to lawful authority as a moral obligation: he, therefore, condemned the conduct of James the second during his short reign; and, had he been a subject of that weak and infatuated monarch, would, I am persuaded, have resisted any invasion of his right or unwarrantable exertion of power, with the same spirit, as did the president and fellows of Magdalen college, or those conscientious divines the seven bishops. This disposition, as it leads to whiggism, one would have thought, might have reconciled him to the memory of his successor, whose exercise of the regal authority among us merited better returns than were made him; but, it had no such effect: he never spoke of king William but in terms of reproach, and, in his opinion of him, seemed to adopt all the prejudices of jacobite bigotry and rancour.[47]

But his disillusion with the leaders of the opposition which toppled Walpole was bitter, recorded Hawkins, and discredited patriotism in his eyes. Latterly, his 'frequent reflections on the politics of this country, and the willingness of the people to be deceived, had begot in Johnson such an apathy, as rendered him deaf to the calls of those who were watching over our dearest rights'.[48] The Whig attorney understood much about the politics of his nonjuring subject, but not all; he never finally sympathised, or felt free from the obligation to censure Johnson's views. Nor was Johnson immune to the attractions of patriarchal theory, declaring of Raasay in

45 Laetitia-Matilda Hawkins, *Memoirs, Anecdotes, Facts and Opinions* (2 vols., London, 1824), vol. 1, pp. 89–90.
46 Ibid., pp. 161–2. 47 Hawkins, *Life*, pp. 504–5. 48 Ibid., pp. 506–8.

1773: 'This is truly the patriarchal life. This is what we came to find.'[49] Four years later, he reflected: 'The admission of money into the Highlands will soon put an end to the feudal modes of life, by making those men landlords who were not chiefs. I do not know that the people will suffer by the change, but there was in the patriarchal authority something venerable and pleasing.'[50]

There is substantial evidence that Johnson's early dynastic commitments were carried over and influential on his thinking in the years after 1760, and little evidence which points the other way. One such possible indication to the contrary occurred late in Johnson's life; perhaps on 7 May 1781, when Boswell 'told him that I was a zealous Tory, but not enough "according to knowledge", and should be obliged to him for "a reason"'. Johnson replied with what looked on the surface like an eirenic statement:

> A wise Tory and a wise Whig, I believe, will agree. Their principles are the same, though their modes of thinking are different. A high Tory makes government unintelligible: it is lost in the clouds. A violent Whig makes it impracticable: he is for allowing so much liberty to every man, that there is not power enough to govern any man. The prejudice of the Tory is for establishment; the prejudice of the Whig is for innovation. A Tory does not wish to give more real power to Government; but that Government should have more reverence. Then they differ as to the Church. The Tory is not for giving more legal power to the Clergy, but wishes they should have a considerable influence, founded on the opinion of mankind; the Whig is for limiting and watching them with a narrow jealousy.[51]

Examined more closely, however, it is clear that Johnson's attempt to frame a formula of tranquil reconciliation quickly broke down. The 'modes of thinking' of Whigs and Tories prove to be so different, indeed antithetical, in Johnson's account that it is not clear how 'their principles are the same'. Nor was his account of the two sides equal: his Whig was a 'violent Whig' with a prejudice for 'innovation' who would make government 'impracticable', and was a plain enemy of the Church.

Even this quickly-unsuccessful search for common ground was a rare pronouncement by Johnson, and not necessarily inconsistent with what he continued to say into the 1780s on the dynastic issue. On 13 September 1773, during their Highland tour, Boswell tried to summarise his and his mentor's positions:

> I must here explain a little Mr. Johnson's political notions as well as my own. We are both *Tories*; both convinced of the utility of monarchichal power, and both lovers of that reverence and affection for a sovereign which constitute loyalty, a

49 Boswell, *Journal*, p. 135 (9 September 1773).
50 Johnson to Boswell, 22 July 1777: Johnson, *Letters*, vol. 3, p. 39.
51 Boswell, *Life*, vol. 4, p. 118.

principle which I take to be absolutely extinguished in Britain, which is one of the worst consequences of the Revolution. Mr. Johnson is not properly a *Jacobite.* He does not hold the *jus divinum* of kings. He founds their right on long possession, which ought not to be disturbed upon slight grounds. He said to me once that he did not know but it was become necessary to remove the King at the time of the Revolution; and after the present family have had so long a possession, it appears to him that their right becomes the same that the Stuarts had. His difficulty is as to the right still in some measure belonging to that unfortunate family. In short, he is dubious; and he would not involve the nation in a civil war to restore the Stuarts. Nay, I have heard him say he was so dubious that if holding up his right hand would have gained the victory to the Highland army in 1745, he does not know if he would have done it. Beauclerk told me he heard him say so before he had his pension. I, again, have all that Mr. Johnson has, and something more, for my high notions of male succession make me mount up to distant times; and when I find how the Stuart family's right has been formed, it appears to me as but very casual and artificial. I find not the firm feudal hold for which I wish and which my imagination figures. I might fix my eye at the point of James IV, from whom my ancestor Thomas Boswell got the estate of Auchinleck, and look no further, had I a line of males from that Prince. But Queen Mary comes in the way; and I see the sons of Lennox on the throne. Besides, I consider that even supposing Prince Charles to have the right, it may be very generous for one to support another's right at every risk, but it is not wise, and I would not do it. Mr. Johnson's argument of right being formed by possession and acknowledgement of the people, settles my mind, and I have now no uneasiness. With all this, he and I have a kind of *liking* for Jacobitism, something that it is not easy to define. I should guard against it; for from what I have now put down, it is certain that my calm reasoning stops short at action, so that doing anything violent in support of the cause would only be following a sort of passion or warm whim. And talking much in favour of it may even in this secure and more liberal reign hurt a man in his rising in life.[52]

Boswell's desire to think as Johnson did is almost pathetically obvious; but in that attempt he evidently made Johnson approach closer to Boswell's own position. Boswell's claim that Johnson did not hold 'the *jus divinum* of kings' is difficult to reconcile with Johnson's youthful loyalty or with his current acknowledgement of a 'right still in some measure belonging' to the Stuarts, for if right were merely pragmatic then only one dynasty could hold it. Nor is it clear how a merely pragmatic conception of right would cause Johnson to be a Nonjuror, for there is no evidence that he ever took an oath of allegiance in person to James III. It is more likely that Johnson had clear intellectual grounds for his position that his companion only partly grasped, but which would have been clearer to his friends in the years before Johnson met Boswell in 1763. It seems likely that the charge against Boswell is not that he made an apolitical, sceptical man of letters

52 Boswell, *Journal*, pp. 162–3.

into a prototype of a figure from the novels of Sir Walter Scott, but rather that Boswell failed to appreciate the full extent of Johnson's earlier principled commitment to the Stuart cause. Johnson was more of a Jacobite than Boswell portrayed him, not less.

Hawkins's claim that Johnson did not endorse Filmer (an author on whom he did not rely in the *Dictionary*) and Boswell's possibly misconceived version of this, that his mentor 'does not hold the *jus divinum* of kings', can however be reinforced from another source, though the testimony comes by a tenuous route. Thomas Cooper (1759–1840), friend of Priestley, from 1792 an émigré to America, defended Johnson from the charge that he had been 'a bigot in politics and religion': 'In a political conversation which I had with Dr Johnson he said, "I believe in no such thing as the *jure divino* of kings. I have no such belief; but I believe that monarchy is the most conducive to the happiness and safety of the people of every nation, and therefore I am a monarchist, but as to its divine right, that is all stuff. I think every people have the right to establish such government as they may think most conducive to their interest and happiness."'[53]

Cooper's anecdote is the only surviving evidence that the two ever met.[54] If Johnson made such a remark, which is open to some doubt, he presumably did so between the summer of 1780, when Cooper was attending anatomical lectures in London, and Johnson's death in 1784; but by the time Cooper's report was recorded in the 1820s he had had an active career as a Jacobin agitator and author in Manchester, London and Paris in the 1790s and continued his turbulent political involvement as a Jeffersonian politician in the United States. This undoubtedly coloured his recollection of Johnson's position.[55] In particular, Cooper endorsed the utilitarianism and materialism of his friend Joseph Priestley, and by the end of his life declared himself a Benthamite.[56] It is clear that Johnson was in no doubt in grounding political obligation on law and long possession: that alone was sufficient to identify the Revolution of 1688 as an illegal act, despite disapproval of the conduct of James II. It is not securely established, however, on what grounds Johnson still conceded a right remaining in the

[53] Cooper's table talk, in or after the 1820s, noted by his political ally Colonel D.J. M'Cord, in Evert A. and George L. Duyckinck, *Cyclopaedia of American Literature* (2 vols., New York, 1855), vol. 2, p. 333. Cooper matriculated at University College, Oxford in 1779 and was called to the bar at the Inner Temple in 1787.

[54] He did, however, record other anecdotes of Johnson, e.g. in *Memoirs of Dr Joseph Priestley: to the Year 1795, written by Himself ... and Observations on his Writings, by Thomas Cooper* (2 vols., London, 1807), vol. 1, p. 411.

[55] Cooper once at least declared Johnson 'very ignorant and very bigoted': Maurice Kelly, *Additional Chapters on Thomas Cooper*, University of Maine Studies, Second Series no. 15 (Orono, Maine, 1930), pp. 62–3.

[56] Dumas Malone, *The Public Life of Thomas Cooper 1783–1839* (New Haven, 1926), pp. 14–15, 370 and passim.

House of Stuart once long possession was on the side of the Hanoverians. Boswell in 1773 rightly recorded that he was 'dubious', and this may have recognised a move by Johnson towards a utilitarian position that Thomas Cooper either recorded or exaggerated. Johnson's politics remained, however, firmly based on his Anglicanism.

Johnson's perception of the balance of opinion against the Hanoverian dynasty was closely bound up with his view of the Church and of the moral decline of English society. It was this which led him to what would, out of that context, seem a wild exaggeration. In 1773, Boswell

> asked if it was not strange that Government should permit so many infidel writings to pass without censure. Mr. Johnson said, 'Sir, it is mighty foolish. It is for want of knowing their own power. The present family on the throne came to the crown against the will of nine-tenths of the people. Whether these nine-tenths were right or wrong is not our business now to inquire.[57] But such being the situation of the Royal Family, they were glad to encourage all who would be their friends. Now you know every bad man is a Whig; every man who has loose notions. The Church was against this family. They were, as I said, glad to encourage any friends; and therefore, since the accession of this family, there is no instance of any man being kept back on account of his bad principles – and hence this inundation of impiety.'[58]

In April 1775, Boswell recorded Johnson's 'extraordinary partiality' for Charles II, perhaps not least because 'The Church was at no time better filled than in his reign.'[59] Charles II he thought 'the best King we have had from his time till the reign of his present Majesty, except James the Second, who was a very good King, but unhappily believed that it was necessary for the salvation of his subjects that they should be Roman Catholicks'. George I 'knew nothing, and desired to know nothing; did nothing, and desired to do nothing: and the only good thing that is told of him is, that he wished to restore the crown to its hereditary successor'. He 'roared with prodigious violence against George the Second'.[60]

Johnson declared in 1775 that 'the nation in general has ever been loyal, has been at all times attached to the monarch, though a few daring rebels have been wonderfully powerful for a time'.[61] On 17 September 1777, Boswell recorded:

57 This formula implies an answer. Had the opponents of the Hanoverian succession been wrong, Johnson could easily have said so.

58 Boswell, *Journal*, p. 236 (30 September 1773).

59 Johnson looked back on the reign of Charles II as an age of principle; 'Politicks (said he) are now [April 1775] nothing more than means of rising in the world': Boswell, *Life*, vol. 2, p. 369.

60 Boswell, *Life*, vol. 2, pp. 341–2.

61 Boswell, *Life*, vol. 2, p. 370.

He had this evening, partly, I suppose, from the spirit of contradiction to his Whig friend, a violent argument with Dr Taylor, as to the inclinations of the people of England at this time towards the Royal Family of Stuart. He grew so outrageous as to say, 'that, if England were fairly polled, the present King would be sent away to-night, and his adherents hanged tomorrow'. Taylor, who was as violent a Whig as Johnson was a Tory, was roused by this to a pitch of bellowing. He denied, loudly, what Johnson said; and maintained, that there was an abhorrence against the Stuart family, though he admitted that the people were not much attached to the present King. JOHNSON. 'Sir, the state of the country is this: the people knowing it to be agreed on all hands that this King has not the hereditary right to the crown, and there being no hope that he who has it can be restored, have grown cold and indifferent upon the subject of loyalty, and to have no warm attachment to any King. They would not, therefore, risk any thing to restore the exiled family. They would not give twenty shillings a piece to bring it about. But, if a mere vote could do it, there would be twenty to one; at least, there would be a very great majority of voices for it. For, Sir, you are to consider, that all those who think a King has a right to his crown, as a man has to his estate, which is the just opinion, would be for restoring the King who certainly has the hereditary right,[62] could he be trusted with it; in which there would be no danger now, when laws and everything else are so much advanced: and every King will govern by the laws.[63] And you must also consider, Sir, that there is nothing on the other side to oppose to this; for it is not alledged by any one that the present family has any inherent right: so that the Whigs could not have a contest between two rights.'

Dr Taylor admitted, that if the question as to hereditary right were to be tried by a poll of the people of England, to be sure the abstract doctrine would be given in favour of the family of Stuart; but he said, the conduct of that family, which occasioned their expulsion, was so fresh in the minds of the people, that they would not vote for a restoration. Dr Johnson, I think, was contented with the admission as to the hereditary right, leaving the original point in dispute, *viz.* what the people upon the whole would do, taking in right and affection; for he said, people were afraid of a change, even though they think it right. Dr Taylor said something of the slight foundation of the hereditary right of the house of Stuart. 'Sir, (said Johnson,) the house of Stuart succeeded to the full right of both the houses of York and Lancaster, whose common source had the undisputed right. A right to a throne is like a right to any thing else. Possession is sufficient, where no better right can be shown.[64] This was the case with the Royal Family of England, as it is now with the King of France: for as to the first beginning of the right, we are in the dark.'[65]

[62] Johnson here affirms his belief in a legal title, but accepts that a legally-grounded hereditary title remains with the Stuarts.

[63] Cf. Greene (*Politics*, p. xxxiv): 'There is never a hint in Johnson's writings . . . of support for . . . a restoration'.

[64] Johnson thereby distanced himself from the belief of Sir Robert Filmer and others that hereditary titles could be traced back with sufficient exactness.

[65] Boswell, *Life*, vol. 3, pp. 155–7.

This matter of principle coloured Johnson's view of party manoeuvre. In 1781, Boswell drew a contrast between the fortunes of parties which he implied were constant: 'when I mentioned that Mr. Burke had boasted how quiet the nation was in George the Second's reign, when Whigs were in power, compared with the present reign, when Tories governed; – 'Why, Sir, (said he,) you are to consider that Tories having more reverence for government, will not oppose with the same violence as Whigs, who being unrestrained by that principle, will oppose by any means.'[66] In March 1783, Johnson

> talked with regret and indignation of the factious opposition to Government at this time, and imputed it, in a great measure, to the Revolution. 'Sir, (said he, in a low voice, having come nearer to me, while his old prejudices seemed to be fermenting in his mind,) this Hanoverian family is *isolée* here. They have no friends. Now the Stuarts had friends who stuck by them so late as 1745. When the right of the King is not reverenced, there will not be reverence for those appointed by the King.'

Boswell commented: 'His observation that the present royal family has no friends, has been too much justified by the very ungrateful behaviour of many who were under great obligations to his Majesty.'[67] He wrote of Lord North and his adherents, who in March 1783 joined with their inveterate enemies, the associates of Charles James Fox, to compel the King to accept this improbable and unwelcome coalition as his ministers.[68]

66 Boswell, *Life*, vol. 4, p. 100. 67 Boswell, *Life*, vol. 4, pp. 164–5.
68 John Cannon, *The Fox-North Coalition: Crisis of the Constitution, 1782–4* (Cambridge, 1969).

8

JOHNSON'S WRITINGS, 1760–1781

I. THE *DICTIONARY* AND THE POLITICAL PAMPHLETS OF 1770–1774

Johnson's pamphlets of 1770–4 lacked detailed annotation, and their sources and idiom are not self-evident from their texts; but another work on which Johnson was engaged at that time inevitably made his references plain. In the summer of 1771, Johnson embarked on an extensive revision of his *Dictionary*, eventually published as the fourth edition in March 1773. For the great deal of additional material now included, Johnson 'relied heavily upon his current reading ... The many illustrative quotations that he added, particularly to the second volume, seem to reflect a concerted attempt to alter the reading and interpretation of many entries according to ideological and religious aims.' In particular, Johnson added a wealth of new examples from religious writers, so often drawing attention to the theological meanings of words. It was a deliberate attempt 'to infuse many of the entries with a more conscious religious and/or political presence and purpose'.[1] Especially prominent as sources of new quotations were Anglican and Nonjuror authors: in order of frequency, William Law (1686–1761), Bishop John Fell (1625–86), Bishop John Wilkins (1614–72), John Kettlewell (1653–95), Bishop Francis White (?1564–1638), Archdeacon Daniel Waterland (1683–1740), Henry Hammond (1605–60), Archdeacon Barten Holyday (1593–1661), Peter Heylyn (1600–62), Robert Nelson (1656–1715), Richard Allestree (1619–81), Charles Leslie (1650–1722) and Bishop John Pearson (1613–86). John Milton headed the list, which included also the Puritan William Perkins (1558–1602), but *Paradise Lost* was set in a context created by a phalanx of Caroline divines.[2]

Johnson's revision of his *Dictionary* coincided in time with his re-entry into political controversy in the early 1770s, with his pamphlets *The False*

[1] Allen Reddick, *The Making of Johnson's Dictionary 1746–1773* (Cambridge, 1990), pp. 89–91, 94. This paragraph is indebted to the research of Professor Reddick, on which it largely draws.

[2] Reddick, *Johnson's Dictionary*, pp. 121–2.

Alarm (1770), *Thoughts on the Late Transactions Respecting Falkland's Islands* (1771), *The Patriot* (1774) and *Taxation no Tyranny* (1775). Johnson was, in some sense, clearly aligning himself behind the civil power in the face of what he perceived as major threats to the social order. But his politics had always stemmed from his prior commitment to the Church, a commitment which often led him partly to condone the events of 1688 by placing the defence of Anglicanism before the claims of dynastic allegiance. It was natural that Johnson's defence of the civil order in the early 1770s should have been matched by a renewed emphasis on the religious premises of civil society, and natural too that Johnson should have turned for support to the group of authors, often Nonjurors, who had in their own time most vigorously rebutted similar challenges to the Church.[3] In this, Johnson was not merely responding to the secular political challenges of John Wilkes, the Falkland Islands crisis or the American problem; he was responding, like others of his generation, to successive attacks on the doctrine, liturgy and establishment of the Church in the late 1760s and early 1770s.[4]

He was also echoing a much older commitment. Hawkins observed of the opposition to Walpole that 'some of the writers on the side of it were such avowed enemies to religion, as might beget, in those acquainted with their characters, a suspicion that, as in the language of politics, there is an alliance between church and state, a similar relation subsists between infidelity and patriotism, proofs whereof have not been wanting in these our late times'.[5] Johnson's political message in the first edition of the *Dictionary* had been conveyed chiefly in his definitions of terms like 'abdication', 'loyal', 'prince', 'defeasible', 'rightful', 'succession' and 'usurper';[6] by contrast, the 'religious presence' in the first edition has been described as 'for the most part politically neutral'.[7] For the fourth edition of 1773, Johnson responded to the political problems of the previous decade with a reassertion not of dynastic legitimism but of Anglican orthodoxy. These principles illuminate some aspects of Johnson's later works, especially his political pamphlets;[8] his record of his highland tour, *A Journey to the Western Islands of Scotland* (1775); and *The Lives of the Poets* (1779–81).

By 1770, Johnson's position had changed. In that year he defended the ministry against the threat posed by John Wilkes, and wrote a pamphlet sceptical of popular cries in which he envisaged a sensible observer trying

3 For the rehabilitation of Nonjuring writings at the end of the eighteenth century for exactly this reason, see J. C. D. Clark, *English Society 1688–1832: Ideology, social structure and political practice during the ancien regime*, pp. 220–2, 224, 226–7, 249.

4 Reddick, *Johnson's Dictionary*, pp. 143–50; Clark, *English Society 1688–1832*, pp. 335–9.

5 Hawkins, *Life*, p. 332.

6 For which, see above, pp. 185–6.

7 Reddick, *Making of Johnson's Dictionary*, p. 144.

8 Published in a collected edition as *Political Tracts* (London, 1776), still without acknowledgement of Johnson's authorship.

vainly to correct the illusions of an ignorant tailor, draper and blacksmith discussing politics at 'an honest alehouse': not half of what he had to say 'will be heard; his opponents will stun him and themselves with a confused sound of places, venality and corruption, oppression and invasion, slavery and ruin'.[9] The opposition idiom of the 1720s and 30s had sunk deep into the popular consciousness, and survived for decades after its inital dynastic setting was no more.

The False Alarm termed Wilkes a 'retailer of sedition and obscenity'; it sought to demonstrate that the House of Commons was constitutionally entitled to nullify his return as a member for Middlesex and declare his rival, Colonel Luttrell, elected in his place. Johnson argued for such a power in the Commons on the grounds of 'political necessity': the indivisibility of legislative sovereignty entailed that where there was no redress, there was no wrong. The legislative powers of Parliament were 'unaccountable, for to whom must that power account, which has no superiour?' As for the House of Commons, 'its own resolutions must be its laws, at least, if there is no antecedent decision of the whole legislature'. This was a privilege 'not confirmed by any written law or positive compact, but by the resistless power of political necessity', or, as Johnson later put it, discussing whether a vote of the Commons could render a man incapable of subsequent election,

> Here we must again recur, not to positive institutions, but to the unwritten law of social nature, to the great and pregnant principle of political necessity. All government supposes subjects, all authority implies obedience. To suppose in one the right to command what another has the right to refuse is absurd and contradictory. A state so constituted must rest for ever in motionless equipoise ...[10]

Johnson considered that the Wilkesite issue ought to align men more clearly than it did.

> None can indeed wonder that it has been supported by the sectaries, the constant fomenters of sedition, and never-failing confederates of the rabble, of whose religion little now remains but hatred of establishments, and who are angry to find separation now only tolerated, which was once rewarded;[11] but every honest man must lament, that it has been regarded with frigid neutrality by the Tories,[12] who, being long accustomed to signalize their principles by opposition to the court, do

[9] [Samuel Johnson], *The False Alarm* (London, 1770), pp. 38, 40.

[10] *Ibid.*, pp. 9–10, 18, 35.

[11] I.e. during the reigns of the first two Georges.

[12] The disintegration of the early-eighteenth-century Tory party meant that its members were found on both sides of a question: in the division over General Warrants of 18 February 1764, former Tories divided 41 to 45: Sir Lewis Namier, 'Country Gentlemen in Parliament', in *Crossroads of Power* (London, 1962), pp. 42–3.

not yet consider that they have at last a king who knows not the name of party, and who wishes to be the common father of all his people.[13]

Yet the subject of the pamphlet did not interpret it in merely functional terms. John Wilkes addressed Johnson: 'You have ambitiously declared yourself the spitter forth of that effusion of servility and bombast. You *could not* have been concealed.' Wilkes was outraged that Johnson should have defended the right of the House of Commons to expel a Member on the grounds of 'political necessity'. Wilkes's position was:

The RIGHTS OF THE PEOPLE are not what the Commons have ceded to them, but what they have reserved to themselves; the *privileges of the Commons* are not what they have an indefeasible pretension ot [to] by arbitrary and discretionary claim, but what THE PEOPLE, for their own benefit, have allowed them.

Johnson had been bought off by Bute for £300 a year:

Yet, surely, if it be upon such terms that you are become a PENSIONER, it were far better to return back to that poor but honest state, when you and the miserable *Savage*, on default of the pittance that should have secured your quarters at the club, were contented – *in the open air* – to growl at the *moon*, and Whigs, and Walpole, and the house of Brunswick.[14]

Wilkes's final shot was the most telling:

In the midst of these contradictions, there is one point in which you are consistent. You discover in every line a rooted attachment to '*the unhappy family*' whom 'the gloomy, sullen William' drove out: – and, in the blindness of your zeal, or in the candor of Jacobitism, when you even mean to pay a compliment to the best of princes, you are betrayed into the detestable and traiterous insinuation, that he is the only king since the Revolution, whose character, or whose measures, have borne any resemblance to those of the abdicated line.

But it was part of a trend:

It is but too notorious, that you are not the only person who has been suffered to approach St James's, with all the principles and prejudices of *St Germains*. What better, then, was to be expected, than unheard-of exertions of unconstitutional powers, on the part of administration: and the prostitution of some HIRELING PEN, in the cause of passive obedience and non-resistance, but thinly veiled in their new-fangled disguise of A GREAT AND PREGNANT PRINCIPLE OF POLITICAL NECESSITY?[15]

13 [Samuel Johnson], *The False Alarm* (London, 1770), pp. 52–3.
14 [John Wilkes], *A Letter to Samuel Johnson, LL.D.* (London, 1770), pp. 5, 14, 23–4, 33.
15 [Wilkes], *Letter to Samuel Johnson*, pp. 52–4; [Philip Rosenhagen], *The Crisis. In Answer to the False Alarm* (London, 1770), p. 21.

John Scott denied Johnson's claim that the advance of political knowledge had not kept pace with the advance of natural knowledge, and proved it by one key claim: 'The doctrines of divine hereditary right, and passive obedience to the will of kings, were doctrines readily adopted by those who believed the comet and the eclipse, prognosticks of publick calamity: but to the honour of this nation, the gloom both of philosophical and political prejudice, has been long since dissipated.' Johnson's argument from precedent that the House of Commons had a power to regulate its membership, to fine, to imprison, and to disable men from election, Scott condemned as just such a precedent drawn from 'the age of witchcraft and astrology, of terrifying meteors and prognosticating eclipses'. The threat to the state now came, argued Scott, from bribery and the general loss of 'virtue'. Johnson was part of that trend: 'To the troublesome opponent of administration, the tempting bait of a place or pension is presented' and accepted by 'the base deserter of his country'.[16] How had Johnson's position changed, argued Scott, since *London*, 'a most bitter Satyr against the Great' which would have aligned Johnson on the side of what he now termed 'plebeian grossness', or *The Vanity of Human Wishes*, with its open approval of 'Not only Petitions ... but even Remonstrances':

> Thro' Freedom's sons no more *Remonstrance* rings,
> Degrading Nobles and controuling Kings;
> Our supple tribes repress their Patriot throats,
> And ask no questions but the price of votes.

Not satisfied with that, Scott quoted *The Rambler* no. 68: 'However vanity or insolence may look down with contempt on the suffrage of men, undignified by wealth, and unenlightened by education, it very seldom happens, that they commend or blame without justice. Vice and Virtue are easily distinguished ...'[17]

In 1770–1 renewed conflict with Spain was narrowly averted when the governor of Buenos Aires sanctioned an invasion of Falkland's Islands, to which both nations laid claim. Johnson's intervention gave expression both to a profound aversion to war, and a scepticism even of that most successful conflict of 1756–63: 'Not many years have passed since the cruelties of war were filling the world with terror and with sorrow' was not a triumphalist verdict on the conquest of Canada. Johnson then gave a cool, balanced account of the claims of the two sides, of the diplomatic exchanges, and of the practical worthlessness of a group of barren and storm-lashed islands: 'This is the country of which we have now possession, and of which a

[16] [John Scott], *The Constitution defended, and Pensioner exposed; in Remarks on the False Alarm* (London, 1770), pp. 1–3, 11. The author was the Quaker poet John Scott (1730–83).

[17] [Scott], *The Constitution defended*, pp. 26–7.

numerous party pretends to wish that we had murdered thousands for the titular sovereignty'. War promoted only 'the sudden glories of paymasters and agents, contractors and commissaries'.[18]

Again the reaction of the pamphleteers was hostile, denouncing Johnson (this time by an ironical vindication of him) as 'remarkable for his attachment to despotism and tyranny'. How could the author be Johnson? 'From your infancy you have invariably opposed the encroachments of the Tories on our laws and liberties, and the treasonable attacks of the Jacobites on the Protestant succession. Your pen has never defended an usurping king or a corrupt minister.' This anonymous pamphleteer now turned on Johnson precisely the cultural critique of William King, Thomas Ruddiman and scores of their contemporaries: 'The decay of public spirit, and the corruption of genuine taste, go always hand in hand.'[19] And he linked it with an historical scheme: 'Charles the Second's Tories sold Dunkirk to the enemy: Queen Anne's Tories gave up innumerable conquests by the treaty of Utrecht; and George the Third's Tories resigned still more by the peace of Versailles.' He went further: 'You and your party have been so long accustomed to consider France and Spain as the friends of your friend over the water, that you may well mistake them sometimes for friends to England, and therefore be disposed, out of pure gratitude, to treat them with moderation and generosity.' For reasons like this, the ministry was to be wholly condemned; 'No man but a Tory or a Jacobite will have the effrontery to stand up in their defence.'[20] Johnson's anonymous call for war in 1739 was forgotten when he counselled peace in the Falkland Islands dispute of 1770. It was alleged that 'Dr J — n writ a pamphlet in defence of the Spaniard's claim ... a Jacobite was pensioned *by England*, for pleading the cause of *Spain!*'; 'Where was Doctor J — n's regard for English Honour, when he suffered his pen to attempt restraining the English lyon's rage, while roaring for vengeance against the Spaniards?'[21]

Johnson's *The Patriot* echoed in the 1770s the preoccupations of the 1730s and 40s. It was in that earlier decade that 'patriotism', a new term seemingly coined only in the 1720s, was dissected and discussed, and the claims of politicians to the title of patriot weighed.[22] This was the structure

18 [Samuel Johnson], *Thoughts on the Late Transactions respecting Falkland's Islands* (London, 1771), pp. 1, 41, 44.

19 *A Refutation Of a Pamphlet, called Thoughts on the Late Transactions respecting Falkland's Islands; in a Letter Addressed to the Author, and dedicated to Dr Samuel Johnson* (London, 1771), pp. i, 2.

20 *A Refutation of a Pamphlet*, pp. 20, 28–9, 39.

21 *The Pamphlet entitled 'Taxation no Tyranny', candidly considered, and it's Arguments and Pernicious Doctrines, Exposed and Refuted* (London, [1775]), pp. 6–7, 12.

22 E.g. *Patriotism Delineated: with Advice How to distinguish the True Patriot From the False One* (London, 1731); *Modern Patriotism, a poem* (London, 1734); *The Patriot at Full Length* (London, 1735); *A Vindication of the Conduct of a Certain Eminent Patriot* (London, 1742); *The Patriot and the Minister review'd ...* (London, 1743).

of Johnson's pamphlet of 1774: 'Some claim a place in the list of Patriots by an acrimonious and unremitting opposition to the Court. This mark is by no means infallible. Patriotism is not necessarily included in rebellion. A man may hate his King, yet not love his Country.' It was a far remove from Johnson's sentiments in the 1730s. Now, Johnson resorted to *ad hominem* arguments to disparage the opposition:

> He that has been refused a reasonable or unreasonable request, who thinks his merit underrated, and sees his influence declining, begins soon to talk of natural equality, the absurdity of *many made for one*, the original compact, the foundation of authority, and the majesty of the people. As his political melancholy increases, he tells, and perhaps dreams of the advances of the prerogative, and the dangers of arbitrary power; yet his design in all his declamation is not to benefit his country, but to gratify his malice.

There was worse: this group Johnson characterised as 'the most honest of the opponents of government' since they did at least 'feel some part of what they express'; 'But the greater, far the greater number of those who rave and rail, and enquire and accuse, neither suspect, nor fear, nor care for the public; but hope to force their way to riches by virulence and invective, and are vehement and clamorous, only that they may be sooner hired to be silent.'[23] A 'true Patriot', according to Johnson, was 'no lavish promiser: he undertakes not to shortern parliaments; to repeal laws; or to change the mode of representation, transmitted by our ancestors':[24] yet all these things had been promised by the Patriot opposition of the 1730s. As for the use of military force to check the actions of the American colonists, 'This infliction of promiscuous evil may therefore be lamented, but cannot be blamed. The power of lawful government must be maintained; and the miseries which rebellion produces, can be charged only on the rebels.'[25] This was not the Johnson of 1745.

The Patriot was a timeless and generalised attack on the members of the opposition, published just before the general election of 1774. Yet, again, the reactions to *The Patriot* showed opposition figures resisting a functional interpretation of the issues and asserting an ideological one which had many resonances with the ideological conflicts of earlier decades. Johnson's definition of a patriot was disputed as insufficently specific. To say that it was 'love of his country' was not enough: 'A man must know what is the true interest of his country, and use his best endeavours to promote it, before he can have a just title to the honourable distinction of a Patriot.' It looked implausible that Johnson 'begins with striking off the list of Patriots,

[23] [Samuel Johnson], *The Patriot. Addressed to the Electors of Great Britain* (London, 1774), pp. 4–6.
[24] Ibid., pp. 16–17. [25] Ibid., p. 26.

all opponents of the present Government'. Johnson's disparagement of 'natural equality, the absurdity of *many made for one*, the original compact, the foundation of authority, and the majesty of the people' was inappropriate. Scott quoted Bolingbroke's *Patriot King* against him: '*Majesty* (says a celebrated writer) *is not an inherent, but a reflected light.*'[26] The alternative was an outdated superstition, with which, by implication, Scott credited Johnson:

> In former ages, the vulgar entertained an idea of some super-human anomalous quality inherent in the wearer of a crown. They deified their Kings, and obeyed them with implicit veneration; there are those who wish this idea still to exist, but knowledge is increased, if virtue is not; men cannot be awed, and therefore they must be bribed into submission.

As to Johnson's claim that patriots were merely 'disseminating discontent ... He is no lover of his country that unnecessarily disturbs its peace', Scott innocently advanced the truth of these claims of menaces to 'the safety of [the nation's] liberties'.

Johnson had scorned the opposition cry 'that because the French, in the new conquests, enjoy their own laws, there is a design at court of abolishing in England the trial by juries ... that the Protestant religion is in danger, because *Popery is established in the extensive province of Quebec*'. Scott insinuated that such things were not impossible: 'the power which establishes Popery in one place, may establish it in another be they ten or ten thousand miles distant'.[27] Anti-Catholicism had never been as convincing to Tories and Nonjurors as it was to Whigs and Dissenters; now, the increasingly tolerant policies of the Westminster government were confronted by the recrudescence of a much older force.

Johnson had charged that patriots' appeals to 'the people' were stirring up not 'the wise and steady, but the violent and the rash ... the idle and the dissolute'. But should not the patriot accept any assistance? The man was no patriot, argued Johnson, who wished to rob his country of its rights over its American colonies; but, replied Scott, Britain's rights over them were as disputable as its claims to Falkland's Islands, for which Johnson thought war unjustifiable. Scott was already reaching towards a Jacobin religion of humanity:

> Patriotism has been generally understood to be a virtue; but that Patriotism seems to have little claim to the appellation, which is nothing more than a local attachment; a passion, which, for the advantage of one favourite nation, will not scruple to

[26] [Johnson], *The Patriot*, p. 5; [Lord Bolingbroke], *Letters, on the Spirit of Patriotism: on the Idea of a Patriot King; and On the State of Parties, At the Accession of King George the First* (London, 1749), p. 88.

[27] [John Scott], *Remarks on the Patriot. Including some Hints respecting the Americans: with an Address to the Electors of Great Britain* (London, 1775), pp. 5, 7–8, 11–16.

ravage and enslave all others ... Patriotism seems better defined, a rational and liberal sentiment, which, on conviction of what is the greatest good of a part, will wish to extend it to the whole of society. The lover of freedom would gladly establish it not only in one, but in every political system in the universe.[28]

Johnson's patriotism, like Burke's in reply to Richard Price's *A Discourse on the Love of Our Country* (1789), was still defined by the intellectual matrix of monarchical allegiance.[29] Now as earlier, the main threat to that nexus of ideas would have to be a dynastic challenge.

II. EXPIATION: THE SCOTTISH TOUR

Just such dynastic problems were raised, and avoided, in *A Journey to the Western Islands of Scotland*. This has traditionally been the hardest of Johnson's major works to explain. It demonstrates no romantic sensibility which might anticipate, and respond to, the beauties of a bleak and mountainous terrain. Johnson largely overlooked the flora and fauna of the country through which he travelled. He did not, like Thomas Pennant, the most industrious tourist of his age, display an urge to list and catalogue antiquities. His interest in Scottish society was more than offset by his reactions to primitive material circumstances, and to Scots' religion. His book has normally been thought to lack the social purpose which is present as a thinly-concealed sub-text in the English tours of Daniel Defoe and William Cobbett.

Johnson could hardly have looked forward to his Scottish journey with the tourist's usual expectations. At Newcastle, on the road north, he wrote a letter which he posted in Edinburgh:

You have often heard me complain of finding myself disappointed by books of travels, I am afraid travel itself will end likewise in disappointment. One town, one country is very like another. Civilized nations have the same customs, and barbarous nations have the same nature. There are indeed minute discriminations both of places and of manners, which perhaps are not unworthy of curiosity, but which a traveller seldom stays long enough to investigate and compare.[30]

Johnson was well aware of the illusions which his age entertained about nature. From Skye he wrote:

You are perhaps imagining that I am withdrawn from the gay and the busy world into regions of peace and pastoral felicity, and am enjoying the reliques of the golden age; that I am surveying Nature's magnificence from a mountain, or

[28] [Scott], *Remarks*, pp. 18–19, 25–7, 34.
[29] For which, see J. C. D. Clark, *The Language of Liberty 1660–1832: Political Discourse and Social Dynamics in the Anglo-American World* (Cambridge, 1993), pp. 46–62.
[30] Johnson to Hester Thrale, 12 August 1773: Johnson, *Letters*, vol. 2, p. 50.

remarking her minuter beauties on the flowery bank of a winding rivulet, that I am invigorating myself in the sunshine, or delighting my imagination with being hidden from the invasion of human evils and human passions, in the darkness of a Thicket, that I am busy in gathering shells and pebbles on the Shore, or contemplative on a rock, from which I look upon the water and consider how many waves are rolling between me and Streatham.

These illusions he only rehearsed in order to puncture them:

The use of travelling is to regulate imagination by reality, and instead of thinking how things may be, to see them as they are. Here are mountains which I should once have climbed, but to climb steeps is now very laborious, and to descend them dangerous, and I am now content with knowing that by a Scrambling up a rock, I shall only see other rocks, and a wider circuit of barren desolation. Of streams we have here a sufficient number, but they murmer not upon pebbles but upon rocks; of flowers, if Chloris herself were here, I could present her only with the bloom of Heath. Of Lawns and Thickets, he must read, that would know them, for here is so little sun and no shade. On the sea I look from my window, but am not much tempted to the shore for since I came to this Island, almost every Breath of air has been a storm, and what is worse, a storm with all its severity, but without its magnificence, for the sea is here so broken into channels, that there is not a sufficient volume of water either for lofty surges, or loud roar.[31]

The feature of Highland society which most won Johnson's appreciation, and which recurred again and again in his accounts, was that society's 'feudal hospitality ... We have found ourselves treated at every house as if we came to confer a benefit'. But this did not disguise the basic fact about the people he was among: 'They are a Nation just rising from barbarity.'[32]

Even Sir John Hawkins was at a loss to explain the stormy autumn journey to the Western Islands: 'The motives that induced him to undertake a labour so formidable to a man of his age, as his tour must be thought, I will not enquire into: doubtless, curiosity was one of them; but, it was curiosity directed to no peculiar object.'[33] Evidently, Johnson had not explained himself to his friend. Yet his tour of the Highlands was soon the subject of comment: as one journalist recorded, it was a journey which Johnson 'undertook, it is said, with a view of collecting authentic materials for presenting the world with a genuine history of the escape of the Young Chevalier after the battle of Culloden'.[34]

Johnson's *A Journey to the Western Islands of Scotland* was published in

31 Johnson to Hester Thrale, 21 September 1773: Johnson, *Letters*, vol. 2, pp. 78–9.
32 Johnson to Hester Thrale, 30 September 1773: Johnson, *Letters*, vol. 2, pp. 91–2, 96; Johnson to Boswell, 27 May 1775: ibid., p. 214.
33 Hawkins, *Life*, pp. 480–1.
34 [? Isaac Reed], in *Westminster Magazine* 2 (September 1774), 443–6, printed in Brack and Kelley (eds.), *Early Biographies*, pp. 13–18, at 15–16.

January 1775 and incurred similar criticism to his political pamphlet *The Patriot* (October 1774). A critic of James Macpherson emphasised how the government's 'very being depends upon the Revolution's being acknowledged as a salutary measure' and stigmatised those who, he claimed, were aligned against it, including 'Dr Johnson, a writer whose partiality to the exiled family of Stuart shines in every page of his works'. Why had men like Johnson and Shebbeare been pensioned? The writer reproached himself:

> if it be quite agreeable to his Majesty, King George, that his subjects should be taught, that James II was the best of Men and of Kings, and that William III was the worst of both; that the Revolution was a state trick, contrived by a parcel of scoundrels, only to save their necks; a measure so detested by every man, without exception, in these realms, that even they who had brought it about, wished it undone again, and entered into measures to overturn it: If, I say, this is the system which his present Majesty wishes to be inculcated into the minds of the inhabitants of these kingdoms, that Great Personage must be presumed to know best the interest of his august family.

The anonymous pamphleteer sought to associate Macpherson with these royal pensioners on the grounds that he had given too much credence to 'the agents of James the Second', in the Stuart papers which he had used for his *History*.[35]

It seems that Johnson was reluctant to be aligned in this way, however, for on the most sensitive of political questions his reticence was marked, and on one subject he published less than he knew. In Glenmoriston, Johnson was pleasantly surprised that the landlord of his inn 'had learnt his [Latin] Grammar, and ... justly observed that a man is the better for that as long as he lives'. But perhaps this was not unrelated to another fact: the landlord, Macqueen, 'had joined Prince Charles at Fort Augustus, and continued in the Highland army till after the battle of Culloden'.[36] This did not feature in Johnson's book. He did not record that Charles Boyd, one of his hosts at Slanes Castle, had been in arms in the Forty-five and spent twenty years in exile. Boswell did.[37] He did not record visiting the site of the battle of Glenshiel, when on 10 June 1719 a Highland rising in favour of the Stuarts, backed by Spanish troops, was defeated by British regular forces. Boswell did.[38] On the short sea passage to Skye, they were 'shown

35 *A Letter to James Macpherson, Esq. with an Address to the Public, on his History of Great Britain, and his Original Papers* (London, 1775), pp. iii–iv, 2.

36 Boswell, *Journal*, pp. 102–3, 106 (31 August, 1 September 1773).

37 Johnson, *Journey* (ed. Fleeman), pp. 13–15; Boswell, *Journal*, p. 70 (24 August 1773); Boswell, *Life*, vol. 5 (*Tour*), p. 99.

38 Johnson, *Journey* (ed. Fleeman), pp. 32–3; Boswell, *Journal*, p. 107 (1 September 1773); Boswell, *Life*, vol. 5 (*Tour*), p. 140. The military expedition had been organised by Cardinal Alberoni and James Butler, 2nd Duke of Ormonde, in exile from his attainder in

the land of Moidart where Prince Charles first landed' in 1745: Boswell again recorded it, Johnson did not.[39] The pattern was repeated six days later when Boswell recorded, but Johnson omitted, their meeting with 'Malcolm MacLeod, one of the Raasay family, celebrated in the year 1745 for conducting the Prince with fidelity from Raasay to the Laird of Mackinnon's'.[40] The same happened on 3 October, when they again passed Loch Moidart en route for Coll. Boswell reflected: 'The hills around, or rather mountains, are black and wild in an uncommon degree. I gazed upon them with much feeling. There was a rude grandeur that seemed like a consciousness of the royal enterprise, and a solemn dreariness as if a melancholy remembrance of its events had remained.'[41] Johnson recorded no comment.

At Coirechatachan on Skye, Johnson was well pleased with his welcome: 'There were several good books here: Hector Boethius in Latin, Cave's *Lives of the Fathers*, Baker's *Chronicle*, Jeremy Collier's *Church History*' – perhaps because the house also possessed 'a head of Prince Charles in Paris plaster. Also a print of Ranald Macdonald of Clanranald, with a Latin inscription about the Culloden cruelties'. Johnson soon found a kindred spirit in his host's wife:

> While we were at dinner, Mr. Johnson kept a close whispering conference with Mrs. Mackinnon about the particulars that she knew of the Prince's escape. The company were entertained and pleased to observe it. Upon that subject there was a warm union between the soul of Mr. Samuel Johnson and that of an Isle of Skye farmer's wife. It is curious to see people, though ever so much removed from each other in the general system of their lives, come close together on a particular point which is common to each ... Upon her saying something, which I did not hear or cannot recollect, he seized her hand keenly and kissed it. Here was loyalty strongly exemplified.[42]

Discussing the population of Raasay, Johnson noted: 'Not many years ago, the late Laird led out one hundred men upon a military expedition'; only in a private letter did he reveal (what Boswell openly printed) that the military expedition had been the Forty-five.[43] It was Boswell who recorded at Kingsburgh on the Isle of Skye that Johnson slept in the same bed as Charles Edward Stuart, listened 'with placid attention' to Flora Macdonald's stories of that Prince's escape, and said 'All this should be written down'; but Johnson did not do so. Again, it was Boswell who compiled a

1715 to his death in 1745, and brother of the Chancellor of Oxford University. For Ormonde's role see W. K. Dickson, *The Jacobite Attempt of 1719* (Edinburgh, 1895).

39 Boswell, *Journal*, p. 113 (2 September 1773).

40 Ibid., p. 126 (8 September 1773).

41 Ibid., p. 247 (3 October 1773).

42 Ibid., pp. 121, 229 (7, 28 September 1773).

43 Johnson, *Journey* (ed. Fleeman), pp. 51; Johnson, *Letters*, vol. 2, p. 87; Boswell, *Journal*, p. 134 (8 September 1773); Boswell, *Life*, vol. 5 (*Tour*), pp. 171, 174.

careful account, from Scots witnesses, of the Prince's escape.[44] Boswell noted, of their listening to Flora Macdonald's account: 'Mr. Johnson and I were both visibly of the *old interest* (to use the Oxford expression), kindly affectioned at least, and perhaps too openly so.'[45] Privately, to Hester Thrale, Johnson confessed that he could not help being impressed at Kingsburgh, where 'I had the honour of saluting the farfamed Miss Flora Macdonald, who conducted the Prince dressed as her maid through the English forces from the Island of Lewes' and 'slept in the bed, on which the Prince reposed in his distress'. Johnson found himself in congenial company. 'These are not Whigs', he wrote with laconic understatement.[46] Yet, remarkably, Charles Edward Stuart was never mentioned in the published text of Johnson's *Journey to the Western Islands*: Johnson's book is *Hamlet* without the Prince.

Johnson's strange reticence was quickly remarked on. In *Taxation no Tyranny*, Johnson was held in places to have punished the Whigs 'by an indignant silence'; but of this

> severity, the reader who hath perused a Journey to the Western Isles of Scotland, may call to mind as singular an instance. May I presume to ask you, Sir, whether, if victory had declared against the Whigs, you would so cautiously have concealed from us that the field of Culloden was lately honoured with your presence?

For once speculation was wrong: Johnson and Boswell had not visited the site of the battle. But it was a good guess. Before, like Johnson, dismissing the military abilities of the American colonists, continued the critic,

> it would be politic to wait the issue of a battle, before we undervalued them. It was acknowledged by some impartial Generals that a disturbance in the North,[47] (of which you, probably, have heard) might more easily have been quelled, if such a multitude of their fellow-soldiers had not reported that the insurgents were at once timid, and undisciplined.[48]

Johnson deliberately skirted around the events of 1745–6, but sometimes his feelings could not be restrained. He lamented the decline of the clan chiefs: 'Their pride has been crushed by the heavy hand of a vindictive conqueror', whom Johnson did not name.[49] But his book avoided the central issue with an implausible disclaimer:

44 Boswell, *Journal*, p. 160 (13 September); Boswell, *Life*, vol. 5 (*Tour*), pp. 185–205.
45 Boswell, *Journal*, p. 162 (13 September 1773).
46 Johnson to Hester Thrale, 30 Sept. 1773: Johnson, *Letters*, vol. 2, p. 87.
47 The Forty-five.
48 *Taxation, Tyranny. Addressed to Samuel Johnson, LL.D.* (London, 1775), pp. 6–7, 78.
49 Johnson, *Journey* (ed. Fleeman), p. 74.

The political tenets of the Islanders I was not curious to investigate, and they were not eager to obtrude. Their conversation is decent and inoffensive. They disdain to drink for their principles, and there is no disaffection at their tables. I never heard a health offered by a Highlander that might not have circulated with propriety within the precincts of the King's palace.[50]

Somewhat different was his private account: recording the participation of the men of Raasay in the Forty-five, he added: 'You may guess at the opinions that prevail in this country, they are however content with fighting for their king, they do not drink for him, we had no foolish healths.'[51]

Human society was at the centre of Johnson's attention; human society, dignified by scholarship and uplifted by religion, rather than nature or architecture. Even in Paris he complained: 'upon the whole I cannot make much acquaintance here, and though the churches, palaces, and some private houses are very magnificent, there is no very great pleasure after having seen many, in seeing more'.[52] Yet Johnson was inhibited from a scholarly engagement with those aspects of Scottish society which most interested him. The last recorded set-piece conversation on his Scottish tour, at his return to Edinburgh on 11 November 1773, was a discussion of the Forty-five with the historian William Robertson, Lord Elibank and Sir William Forbes; Johnson urged the compilation of a history of that event, and argued that 'being in rebellion from a notion of another's right, was not connected with depravity'; but, again, Boswell recorded the episode, and Johnson's account passed over it in silence.[53] His profound interest in this historical episode was unassuaged. Four years later, driving with Johnson in Derbyshire in September 1777, Boswell 'observed, that we were this day to stop just where the Highland army did in 1745. JOHNSON. "It was a noble attempt."' How they came to be at that spot is unexplained; it seems most unlikely to have been mere coincidence and equally probably was another stage of Johnson's tour of the scenes of that event. Boswell expressed a wish to write 'an authentic history of the Forty-five', but knew that he 'could not have the advantage of it in my life-time', that is, that it would be treasonable to publish it in England. Johnson suggested that this problem could be avoided by printing it in Holland.[54] In his sense of the risks of political candour, Johnson was still living in the 1740s.

Even the title of Johnson's book is puzzling: his journey took him around

50 Ibid., p. 88.
51 Johnson to Hester Thrale, 24 Sept. 1773: Johnson, *Letters*, vol. 2, p. 81.
52 Johnson to Robert Levett, 22 October 1775: Johnson, *Letters*, vol. 2, pp. 272–3. Levett's Parisian experience, whatever it was, had evidently not escaped Johnson.
53 Boswell, *Journal*, pp. 384–5 (11 November 1773); Boswell, *Life*, vol. 5 (*Tour*), pp. 392–4.
54 Boswell, *Life*, vol. 3, p. 162.

the coast of much of Scotland, from Edinburgh to St Andrews, Montrose and Aberdeen in the east, from Inverness and along Loch Ness, then south from Inverary and Dumbarton to Glasgow; but the work is entitled *A Journey to the Western Islands of Scotland.* There, evidently, was the focus of Johnson's interest, and in that part of his narrative occur his most profound reflections on the decline of a patriarchal and military social structure after the failure of the rebellion. It may not be fanciful to see in the journey a deeper cause than curiosity. Guilt, remorse and atonement were major elements in Johnson's psyche. His refusal to stand in for his aged father in running the family stall at Uttoxeter market so troubled him that fifty years later he travelled to the place and stood on the same spot 'for a considerable time bareheaded in the rain ... In contrition I stood, and I hope my pennance was expiatory.'[55] Given Johnson's political views, his failure more actively to support the Stuart cause, and his moral dilemma in accepting a pension from a Hanoverian, it may not be fanciful to see his physically arduous journey to the Highlands both as a pilgrimage and an expiation.

Yet Johnson was lastingly inhibited about public discussion of Jacobitism, as was natural for a man born in an era when such things were treason, not romance. The contrast between the two men was perfectly captured by the very title pages of their books. Johnson's, in 1775, lacked the author's name and was austerely titled *A Journey to the Western Islands of Scotland.* In 1785, Boswell's read: *The Journal of A Tour to the Hebrides, with Samuel Johnson, LL.D. Containing Some Poetical Pieces by Dr Johnson, relative to the Tour, and never before published; A Series of his Conversation, Literary Anecdotes, and Opinions of Men and Books: With an Authentick Account of The Distresses and Escape of the Grandson of King James II. in the Year 1746.* For Johnson in 1775, the rebellion was politics; for Boswell in 1785, it was history.

III. THE AMERICAN REVOLUTION

The Stuart cause had receded into irrelevance in the 1750s. James III's death in 1766 had caused no ripples in domestic English politics. By the mid 1770s a quite different, though no less momentous problem preoccupied the English elite: the impending rebellion in America. It was this which called forth Johnson's longest political reflection. *Taxation no Tyranny* was written at the request of the ministry, which insisted on alterations to the text in the interest of moderation. Johnson agreed to these, and even defended Lord North's motion of 27 February for conciliating the colonies: 'if Lives can be saved, some deviation from rigid policy may be excused'. But this did not raise his estimate of the ministers' abilities: 'are such men fit

[55] Boswell, *Life*, vol. 4, p. 373.

to be the governours of kingdoms?'[56] His intervention in the American crisis was not the act of a government hireling, but the statement of a position in which he profoundly believed.

Johnson's tract, a pamphlet of 91 pages, was published in March 1775. Although anonymous, the marks of Johnson's prose style and doctrines were unmistakable. All activities, he insisted, including politics, had 'fundamental principles'; yet first principles were difficult to prove except by more fundamental principles, and it was difficult to demonstrate theoretically those principles which had arisen from practice. One such was that '*the supreme power of every community has the right of requiring from all its subjects such contributions as are necessary to the public safety or public prosperity*'.[57]

Johnson's references to George III were now unambiguous. Colonists were disputing 'the authority of their lawful sovereign'. Society had so progressed that 'Every man is taught to consider his own happiness as combined with the publick prosperity, and to think himself great and powerful, in proportion to the greatness and power of his Governors'. 'All Government is ultimately and essentially absolute ... In sovereignty there are no gradations. There may be limited royalty, there may be limited consulships but there can be no limited government.' Liberties were 'emanations' from this absolute authority, from whose decisions there was no appeal. In the current conflict, 'To be quiet is disaffection, to be loyal is treason'.[58]

The weightiest critic of Johnson's anti-revolutionary politics was pre-committed in the same way as many of the others. Joseph Towers (1737–99), autodidact, Socinian, ordained as a Dissenting minister in 1774, was at the centre of a group of heterodox Dissenters in London. He had already gone into print to urge his theological doctrines;[59] to reprove John Wesley for his praise of George III and censure of Wilkesite disorder;[60] to attack Dr Nowell for his 30 January sermon before the House of Commons;[61] and to support the petition to Parliament against subscription to the Thirty-nine Articles.[62]

56 Johnson to William Strahan, 3 March 1775: Johnson, *Letters*, vol. 2, p. 185–6.

57 [Samuel Johnson], *Taxation no Tyranny; an Answer to the Resolutions and Address of the American Congress* (London, 1775), pp. 1–2.

58 [Johnson], *Taxation no Tyranny*, pp. 2–3, 19, 23–5, 55.

59 Joseph Towers, *A Review of the Genuine Doctrines of Christianity. Comprehending Remarks on Several Principal Calvinistical Doctrines* (London, 1763).

60 [Joseph Towers], *A Letter to the Rev. Mr. John Wesley; In Answer to His late Pamphlet, entitled, 'Free Thoughts on the Present State of Public Affairs'* (London, 1771).

61 [Joseph Towers], *A Letter to the Rev. Dr Nowell, Principal of St Mary Hall ... occasioned by his very extraordinary Sermon, preached before the House of Commons on the thirtieth of January, 1772* (London, 1772).

62 [Joseph Towers], *A Dialogue between two Gentlemen, concerning The late Application to Parliament for Relief in the Matter of Subscription to the Thirty-nine Articles and Liturgy of the Church of England* (London, 1772).

Towers took Johnson's authorship of the four pamphlets of the 1770s as securely established. His complaint was that Johnson had intruded into a province not his own:

> When a man, who has rendered himself eminent by his productions in morals, and in polite literature, engages in political contentions, and in those which are apprehended to be of great national importance, it may reasonably be expected of such a writer, that he should distinguish himself not by party violence and rancour, but by moderation and by wisdom: and that at least he should not wholly lose sight of that liberality of sentiment, which should characterise the scholar; nor of that decency and politeness, which should adorn the gentleman.

Instead, Johnson's political pamphlets had been marked by 'bitterness of invective, unjust and uncandid representations, the most bigotted prejudices against them whom you oppose, and the highest strains of contemptuous insolence'.[63]

Towers was clear that Johnson's pension was of a piece with his politics. It might have first seemed the reward of merit; but

> the use that has since been made of you, renders it sufficiently apparent, that a pension was conferred on you with other views. It now seems probable, that your known Jacobitical principles, which, however strange it may be thought, appear now to be in high estimation at court, were among your chief recommendations; and that it was these, added to the hope of employing you in the service of your new masters, which really occasioned your being placed in the list of royal pensioners.[64]

This was plausible since Towers could remind his readers that 'During the last reign' Johnson was 'generally considered as one of the most bigotted Jacobites in the kingdom'. Somewhat inconsistently, Towers recalled Johnson's libertarian commitments, quoting *London* as evidence: 'It was then a subject of your most pathetic complaints, that England was *oppressed with excise*, that it was a *cheated* and a *groaning nation*, and a *beggar'd land*. We were then cursed with a *pensioned band*, and with *hireling senators*; and it was a *thoughtless age lull'd* to SERVITUDE.'

By what 'revolution' had the public evils which oppressed England in the reign of George II been dissipated in that of George III? It was thanks to Johnson's pension, argued Towers, quoting *The False Alarm*, that we now possess 'a government approaching nearer to perfection, than any that experience has known, or history related', and because, under George III, 'principles were now adopted at court, similar to those of that family, whose attempts to enslave the nation had been the cause of their expulsion

63 [Joseph Towers], *A Letter to Dr Samuel Johnson: Occasioned by his Late Political Publications. With an Appendix, containing some Observations on a Pamphlet lately Published by Dr Shebbeare* (London, 1775), pp. 1–2.

64 [Towers], *Letter to Dr Samuel Johnson*, pp. 2–3.

from the throne'.[65] Only after the reader had been introduced to Johnson's alleged Jacobite principles did Towers let slip his most bitter resentment. In *The False Alarm*, Johnson had written: 'None can indeed wonder that it [the opposition] has been supported by the sectaries, the constant fomentors of sedition, and never-failing confederates of the rabble, of whose religion little now remains but hatred of establishments.'[66] It had gone to the heart of Towers's position, and it compelled him to denounce Johnson for bigotry and invective.

Others of Johnson's opponents dwelt first on the terms of the dispute with the American colonists. Pro-Americans claimed that the argument had already been decided in favour of the exemption of the colonies from taxation when Johnson changed the terms of the argument, 'thus shaking off at once all the shackles of local circumstances, specific rights, and constitutional liberties; cutting asunder the several knots, which all former combatants, finding themselves bound by them, had patiently tried to untie'.[67] Yet Johnson was not alone in subscribing to the doctrine of the absoluteness of government that his critics regarded as novel. Johnson's arguments were fully in line with those of other anti-revolutionary pamphleteers.[68] John Gray had laid down the same axiom in terms which echoed Blackstone:

> A fundamental principle that has ever been regarded as such by all writers of government is, that in every civilized state, there must be, some where, a Supreme all-controling Power. In the British state this supreme power is by the constitution fixed in the united wills of the king, lords, and representatives of the people in parliament assembled.

From this he proceeded similarly to deduce, denying Locke, that 'the right of taxation is not in the people, but in the Supreme Superintending Power'. 'It is the general superintendance that gives a right to taxation, by implying the necessity of being supported; and where the constitution of the state has placed that superintendance, it of necessity places the right of demanding supplies, and regulating the mode of raising them.'[69]

Johnson's commitment was engaged not least by the arguments used in favour of the colonists. The English were told 'that the continent of North America contains three millions, not of men merely, but of Whigs, of Whigs

65 [Towers], *Letter to Dr Samuel Johnson*, pp. 4–6, 8.

66 [Towers], *Letter to Dr Samuel Johnson*, p. 31.

67 *Tyranny Unmasked. An Answer to a late Pamphlet, entitled Taxation no Tyranny* (London, 1775), p. 3.

68 E.g. *A Short Appeal to the People of Great-Britain; upon the Unavoidable Necessity of the Present War with our Disaffected Colonies* (2nd edn, London, 1775).

69 [John Gray], *The Right of the British Legislature To Tax the American Colonies Vindicated; And the Means of Asserting that Right proposed* (London, 1774), pp. 2, 8.

fierce for liberty, and disdainful of dominion':[70] if such was the alignment, Johnson's preference was not in doubt. Against Whigs in rebellion, Johnson rehearsed arguments more familiar to his father's generation:

How any man can have consented to institutions established in distant ages, it will be difficult to explain. In the most favourite residence of liberty, the consent of individuals is merely passive, a tacit admission in every community of the terms which that community grants and requires. As all are born the subjects of some state or other, we may be said to have been all born consenting to some system of Government. Other consent than this, the condition of civil life does not allow. It is the unmeaning clamour of the pedants of policy, the delirious dream of republican fanaticism.[71]

Johnson had claimed, wrote one critic, that his thesis about the necessarily absolute nature of the state's authority and its right to levy taxation on all its subjects was 'as old as Government'; his critic insisted that 'it is evidently of modern structure'. Government's power was not unlimited; 'in *extreme* cases' it was limited by the people, 'with whom *alone* the supreme power *unlimited* of any community can reside'.[72] Another critic seized at once on Johnson's conception of 'supreme power' as 'too arbitrary in its sound for any Englishman the least conversant in the nature of the Constitution'. The principle of no taxation without representation was clearly embodied in that constitution, claimed the author, and especially in Magna Carta; to argue otherwise was to

explain a country's dear-bought rights away

– a quotation which he identified in a footnote: 'See a Spirited Poem, intitled LONDON, and written in the reign of George the *Second*, by Doctor SAMUEL JOHNSON.'[73]

From the proposition that 'Power is derived from the people', one pamphleteer argued to a conclusion that rhetorically denounced Johnson's position: government was a trust; when that trust was broken, 'subjects are absolved from obedience'; resistance therefore was not treason,

Unless, according to the Tory creed, we could supposed the people made for Kings, and not Kings *for*, as well as *by*, the people ... And although the old doctrine of a divine right, which held bigots of a Monkish age in fetters of brass, be given up for another fraud of a less pious, but more plausible nature, the supremacy of Parliament, it matters not a rush to considerate men, whether the Crown be made absolute by religious prejudices, or the cant and quibble of law; by a church, or

70 [Johnson], *Taxation no Tyranny*, p. 7.
71 [Johnson], *Taxation no Tyranny*, pp. 34–5.
72 *An Answer to a Pamphlet, entitled Taxation no Tyranny. Addressed to the Author, and to Persons in Power* (London, 1775), pp. 6, 11.
73 *Taxation, Tyranny. Addressed to Samuel Johnson, LL.D.* (London, 1775), pp. 2, 27.

Parliamentary JUGGLE; by the papal insolence of a LAUD, or the insidious treachery of a MANSFIELD.[74]

Replies to Johnson played on a scenario more familiar in the pages of nineteenth-century historians but fully developed in the 1770s: 'Until the Tories got into power at the commencement of this reign, Great Britain and America were thought, by each country, to have interests inseparable.' The Stamp Act, 'an arbitrary encroachment', began the troubles.

As Tories have forced us into a situation which threatens shipwreck – it cannot be wondered that Jacobites applaud the helms-man. True to the interests of their staunch friends, they fight their battles – they vindicate the most destructive measures. A professed Jacobite becomes the champion of an administration, chosen by a king of the Brunswick line! – Dr J—n approves of his government – pretends a zeal for the rights of a monarch, whose title to the crown, *he reprobates!*[75]

One pamphleteer similarly observed how it was

exceedingly odd to find, so early as in the third generation from the time that we put an absolute exclusion, as we thought, upon Toryism from the government of these realms, Toryism now again making its way upon us in open publications, countenanced even by an administration ... it insinuates, by a most odious implication, an injury done to those, who lost the crown of England for their Tory principles.

Could it really be by Johnson, a man who had 'all his life-long, written of the *Revolution* and the *House of Hanover*' with 'singular virulence'?[76]

For a hostile critic, all of Johnson's arguments could be related back to this one commitment: 'If we review the tenets he espouses, and *must* espouse, to be a *consistent* Jacobite – we shall easily account for the ridicule with which he wishes to treat the necessity of Representation prior to Taxation.' Jacobites were identified also by their religion: 'it is notorious, that the very men who refuse to attend a Church, where George the Third is prayed for, are, notwithstanding, the most vociferous in the praise of his ministers'. A Tory was presented as 'an advocate for arbitrary power – and yet meanly, and cowardly conceals his opinion, that the Hanoverian Family have *no* right to the Crown'. But 'DR. J—N is too honest to conceal his sentiments. His partiality for the Stuarts, is notorious – he is too much a man of honour to deny his principles.'[77] This chorus of certainty about Johnson's early disaffection was not just recollection: it could draw on the republication in 1775 of Johnson's anonymous pamphlet of 1739, *Marmor*

[74] *A Defence of the Resolutions and Address of the American Congress, in reply to Taxation no Tyranny. By the Author of Regulus* (London, [1775]), pp. 93–6.

[75] *The Pamphlet entitled 'Taxation no Tyranny,' candidly considered, and it's Arguments, and pernicious Doctrines, Exposed and Refuted* (London, [1775]), pp. 4–6.

[76] *Tyranny Unmasked*, pp. 5, 7.

[77] *The Pamphlet entitled 'Taxation no Tyranny'*, pp. 9, 30–1, 68.

Norfolciense, now reissued with a new anonymous introduction which made the message of the original text clear to anyone who failed to see it.[78] Like many of Johnson's assailants, the anonymous editor was a Dissenter, Francis Webb (1735–1815), a pupil of Caleb Ashworth at Northampton, a Baptist minister until 1766 and now prospering as a customs officer at Gravesend, who later became a Unitarian.[79] For Johnson as for English society in general, the loudest advocates of American independence were the theologically heterodox Dissenters.

Americans' 'resistance' to 'the several unjust and impolitic acts of our Parliament', argued one of Johnson's opponents, 'has not proceeded from a spirit of disaffection, or rebellion; but is a constitutional assertion of their undoubted rights, as free subjects'. The anonymous author presented no evidence of the inner dispositions of the American colonists, however: his point was to denounce the 'prejudices' of 'English pensioners', and to claim by inference that 'the *Americans*' had been 'actuated by motives of religion and justice'.[80] Attacks on Johnson indeed said little about those internal dynamics of the American colonies which had led them into rebellion: these polemicists were precommitted to the view that the conflict was solely caused by innovations in British policy. So believing, they sought in their attacks on Johnson to settle scores which related almost wholly to older political and religious conflicts in England.

By 1780, one hostile critic of Johnson looked back to his *Life of Savage* to quote its libertarian, pro-colonial sentiments against its author, then notorious as the author of the anti-colonial *Taxation no Tyranny*. Savage had 'asserted the natural equality of mankind, and endeavoured to suppress that pride which inclines men to imagine that right is the consequence of power': 'The benevolent Dr Price himself could not have advanced a doctrine more unsavoury to the palate of Dr Johnson's friends, nor needs it much sagacity to shew how it appears in contrast with *the change which experience hath made in the Doctor's opinions*.'[81]

One critic used the fiction of a 'perfect manuscript of Virgil's works ... lately discovered at Herculaneum' for an attack on Johnson in which literary allusion overwhelmed the meaning.[82] But this was unusual, an echo of a former literary idiom: by the 1770s, the driving force of antagonism was Dissent, and theological heterodoxy, often in combination. Many of Johnson's detractors wrote in the same heterodox idiom as

78 See above, pp. 163–5. 79 *Dictionary of National Biography*.

80 *Resistance no Rebellion: in Answer to Doctor Johnson's Taxation no Tyranny* (London, 1775), Advertisement, pp. 3, 22.

81 [Francis Blackburne], *Remarks on Johnson's Life of Milton* (London, 1780), pp. 151–3.

82 [John Hall Stevenson], *An Essay upon the King's Friends, with an Account of some Discoveries made in Italy, And found in a Virgil, concerning the Tories. To Dr S-l J-n* (London, 1776), p. 4.

Blackburne. One denounced 'The Tory doctrine' as 'always wrapped in creed and mystery'; 'darkness and obscurity' were necessary to hide 'Superstition and tyranny'; Johnson's doctrine would 'effectually bind both the hands and consciences of mankind, and render them tamely subservient to every pious fraud of kings or priests'; 'Of all tyrants, bigotry is the most despotic; and a jure divino lettered slave, in a Protestant, free, and enlightened country, is a monster of the first magnitude.'[83]

The author of *A Defence of the Resolutions and Address of the American Congress, in reply to Taxation no Tyranny* did not confine his arguments to the texts of colonial resolutions. In a second pamphlet addressed to his heterodox hero Dr Price, he expressed his own sense of the relation of civil and religious liberties. Both depended on dispelling '*delusion*', but one delusion in particular:

> When a Nation could be so far gulled by a Priesthood, as to believe a *Wafer* not only the *true Sign* of the human Body, but the Body itself actually existing in many different places at the same time, they became bankrupt in understanding. Their juggling leaders had drawn upon them for the last mite of reason and common sense; and Transubstantiation remained in all the Catholic States, a badge of Spiritual Tyranny on one hand, and Slavery on the other, which infinitely surpassed all the Fable, Superstition, and Imposture of Pagan Rome.
>
> Luckily, in Britain, we have shaken off this creed, and indeed most other religious creeds and prejudices.

The only illusion that remained, he fulminated, was the equal 'imposture' of '*scraps* of paper', i.e. credit.[84]

Another of Johnson's opponents in the American crisis was a Scots Presbyterian, who prefaced his reply to *Taxation no Tyranny* with a reply to Johnson's fellow pensioner Shebbeare and a history of the unmerited sufferings of his fellow Presbyterians since the reign of James I: 'And as I bore arms against the Pretender in 1715, in defence of the liberties and religion of my country, so I shall end life in wishing there may be always found a sufficient number of British subjects, who will be able to defend that happy constitution which that great prince king *William* put us in possession of.'[85] Rebellion in America was being provoked by the English government;

> This case is just the same with what happened in *Scotland* in the reign of *Charles* II. The country was quite peaceable, but by the contrivances of Archbishop *Sharp*, the Duke of *Lauderdale*, and Sir George *Mackenzie* his majesty's advocate, they were

[83] *A Defence of the Resolutions and Address of the American Congress, in reply to Taxation no Tyranny. By the Author of Regulus* (London, [1775]), pp. 4–5, 16.

[84] *A Letter to the Rev. Dr Price* (London, 1776), pp. 27–8.

[85] [Hugh Baillie], *An Appendix to a Letter to Dr Shebbeare. To which are added, Some Observations on a Pamphlet, Entitled, Taxation no Tyranny: In which the Sophistry of that Author's Reasoning is Detected* (London, 1775), p. 32.

persecuted with fines, tortures, and death, for worshipping God in their own way: which obliged them, when they heard their ministers preach in the fields, to carry weapons of defence with them in case of their being attacked by the kings forces, who hunted them every where to destroy them – and this was called rebellion.

This was not mere analogy: 'The people in *America* are mostly *Presbyterians*, and *Protestant Dissenters*'; by resisting oppression 'they are called rebellious, although the whole continent of *America* has always been remarkable for their affection to the royal family'.[86]

One opposition writer claimed that 'every Whig' was against the English ministry, who in turn 'may depend on finding in Doctor J—n, a powerful advocate – ever ready to exert his utmost abilities in the defence of those, *whose principles have so near an affinity with his own*'. This was, of course, rhetorical exaggeration: the anonymous critic's position was drawn not from ministerial Whig thought, but from that extreme strand which placed the most extensive interpretation on the events of 1688: 'If the people had not constitutionally resumed the reins of government at the Revolution – Charles Stuart – the popish Pretender – would at this moment have been the despotick tyrant of Britain.' The Revolution had entailed the dismissal of the monarch, implied the author, not his abdication.[87] By the 1770s, the Whig opposition was increasingly monopolised by such viewpoints; and this in turn contributed to align Johnson and those from a similar background ever more firmly behind the throne.

IV. *THE LIVES OF THE POETS*

Johnson's pamphlets of the 1770s, especially *Taxation no Tyranny*, together with *A Journey to the Western Islands of Scotland*, had reawakened the public to his political preferences. The appearance of the *Lives of the Poets* in 1779–81 did nothing to placate that section of the reading public which had already been roused to indignation by Johnson's principles. Once again, they scrutinised his text for political statements and, once more, these were not hard to find.[88]

The whole orientation of the work was, to begin with, patrician: the highest achievements of English letters were associated with the regime restored in 1660, with only a few anomalous exceptions in the cases of Milton or Addison. Johnson's commitment to Anglicanism clearly jarred with Milton's position: that poet's 'malignity to the Church' was revealed by 'some lines which are interpreted as threatening its extermination'. The

86 [Baillie], *An Appendix*, pp. 9, 42.
87 *The Pamphlet entitled 'Taxation no Tyranny'*, pp. 7, 88.
88 For this theme see Howard Erskine-Hill, 'The Poet and Affairs of State in Johnson's *Lives of the Poets*', *Man and Nature* 6 (1987), 93–113.

cultural centrality of the Restoration was highlighted by Johnson's dismissive censure of Milton's politics ('an acrimonious and surly republican') and evocation of the horrors of the civil war, 'that age, when subordination was broken, and awe was hissed away'.[89] The Cromwellian regime was described unambiguously as 'the rebels', 'the usurping powers', and those responsible for Charles I's death as 'murderers'. The regime of Oliver and Richard Cromwell was a 'system of extemporary government, which had been held together only by force', and which 'naturally fell into fragments when that force was taken away'.[90] Edmund Waller was dismissed with Johnson's 'contempt and indignation' for writing panegyrics to Charles I, Cromwell and Charles II in turn.[91] Johnson wrote with evident relish of Dryden's *Absalom and Achitophel* (1681), that formidable satire on the opposition under Charles II dedicated to the exclusion from the throne of James, Duke of York. Instead of the Whig heroes of an anti-Popery crusade, the opposition became merely 'the faction which, by lord Shaftesbury's incitement, set the duke of Monmouth at its head'.[92] Yet James II was not depicted as a hero: of John Milton's brother Christopher, a royalist and a judge, Johnson wrote that he retired in James's reign 'before any disreputable compliances became necessary'.[93]

Of the Revolution of 1688 Johnson wrote in terms of studied neutrality implying a refusal of endorsement. The genuineness of the heir allegedly born on 10 June 1688 was never challenged. Instead of a triumphalist account of England's deliverance, Johnson merely recorded that 'king James was frighted away, and a new government was to be settled'.[94] Johnson nowhere condoned James II's rule; but equally, Charles Sackville, Earl of Dorset, won no praise for having 'found it necessary to concur in the Revolution'. In 'what is not the most illustrious action of his life, [he] was employed to conduct the Princess Anne to Nottingham with a guard, such as might alarm the populace, as they passed, with false apprehensions of her danger. Whatever end may be designed, there is always something despicable in a trick.'[95] James II's political mistakes did not extinguish his title to the throne; the Whig fiction that he had abdicated was ignored in

[89] Johnson, *Lives of the Poets*, vol. 1, pp. 135, 216–7.

[90] Ibid., vol. 1, pp. 13, 157, 177, 274.

[91] Ibid., vol. 1, pp. 381, 397–8. [92] Ibid., vol. 2, pp. 59–60.

[93] Ibid., vol. 1, p. 127. Dryden's writings for James II were termed 'flattery', and his dislike of the Anglican priesthood explained: 'Malevolence to the clergy is seldom at a great distance from irreverence of religion, and Dryden affords no exception to this observation': ibid., vol. 2, pp. 74, 98–9.

[94] Ibid., vol. 2, p. 285.

[95] Ibid., vol. 1, pp. 438–9. Dryden also had written a panegyric on Oliver Cromwell in 1658, and reversed his loyalties in 1660, but Johnson was decidedly more charitable to him: ibid., vol. 2, p. 6.

the *Lives*. Readers might have sensed Johnson's own position expressed in his description of that of Elijah Fenton (1683–1730):

> He was born near Newcastle in Staffordshire, of an ancient family, whose estate was very considerable; but he was the youngest of twelve children, and being therefore necessarily destined to some lucrative employment, was sent first to school, and afterwards to Cambridge; but, with many other wise and virtuous men, who at that time of discord and debate consulted conscience, whether well or ill informed, more than interest, he doubted the legality of the government, and, refusing to qualify himself for publick employment by the oaths required, left the university without a degree; but I never heard that the enthusiasm of opposition impelled him to separation from the church.[96]

Alexander Pope was in the same situation: 'his religion hindered him from the occupation of any civil employment'.[97] It was extremely rare that a Whig, Sir Richard Blackmore, was praised for adhering 'invariably to his principles and party throughout his whole life'. Johnson's political perceptions were keen: despite the reticence of Addison and Steele, *The Spectator* 'shewed the political tenets of its authors'.[98]

If Johnson's account of 1688 suggested a reluctant acknowledgement of a necessary evil, his account of 1714 was positively hostile. It was merely what occurred when 'the House of Hanover took possession of the throne'. The 'succession of a new family to the throne filled the nation with anxiety, discord, and confusion'. It meant that the Tory George Granville 'was persecuted with the rest of his party'. Queen Anne's creation of twelve new Tory peers to tilt the party balance in the House of Lords had been 'an act of authority violent enough, yet certainly legal, and by no means to be compared with that contempt of national right, with which some time afterwards, by the instigation of Whiggism, the commons, chosen by the people for three years, chose themselves for seven'.[99] Johnson wrote of the Septennial Act of 1716, a Whig electoral strategem to defend both their own precarious advantage and also the new dynasty from the very real dangers of a counter-revolution.

There was no orthodox triumphalism in Johnson's account of 1714: on the contrary, it was an event which blighted careers and drove England's finest men of letters into internal exile. The death of Queen Anne 'broke down at once the whole system of Tory Politicks; and nothing remained [for Swift] but to withdraw from the implacability of triumphant Whiggism, and shelter himself in unenvied obscurity'. Lord Oxford was not the only one who now lived 'under the frown of a victorious faction'.[100]

96 Ibid., vol. 3, pp. 109–10. 97 Ibid., vol. 4, pp. 34–5.
98 Ibid., vol. 3, p. 79; vol. 2, pp. 360–1.
99 Ibid., vol. 2, pp. 379, 388; vol. 3, p. 381; vol. 4, p. 152.
100 Ibid., vol. 3, pp. 408–9; vol. 4, p. 73.

Walpole was presented in, at best, an ambiguous light. In 1781 Johnson could look back sceptically on the politics of the 1730s: 'At this time a long course of opposition to Sir Robert Walpole had filled the nation with clamours for liberty, of which no man felt the want, and with care for liberty, which was not in danger.'[101] This suggested not admiration for the Walpolian regime, but scepticism for the mock patriotism of the Whig opposition. Johnson's taste did not extend to its verse. James Thomson's '*Liberty*, when it first appeared, I tried to read, and soon desisted. I have never tried again, and therefore will not hazard either praise or censure.'[102] Yet this did not condone the Hanoverian regime in stifling criticism by the Licensing Act of 1737; writing of the banning of Henry Brooke's *Gustavus Vasa* and James Thomson's *Edward and Eleonora* under that Act, Johnson remarked: 'It is hard to discover why either play should have been obstructed.'[103]

In the two satires entitled *Seventeen Hundred and Thirty-eight*, Pope's political views were evident to Johnson.

> Pope was then entangled in the opposition; a follower of the Prince of Wales, who dined at his house, and the friend of many who obstructed and censured the conduct of the Ministers. His political partiality was too plainly shewn; he forgot the prudence with which he passed, in his earlier years, uninjured and unoffending through much more violent conflicts of faction.[104]

At this point 'Paul Whitehead, a small poet, was summoned before the Lords for a poem called *Manners*, together with Dodsley his publisher'; Johnson judged that 'the whole process was probably intended rather to intimidate Pope than to punish Whitehead'. In any case,

> Pope never afterwards attempted to join the patriot with the poet, nor drew his pen upon statesmen. That he desisted from his attempts of reformation is imputed, by his commentator, to his despair of prevailing over the corruption of the time. He was not likely to have been ever of opinion that the dread of his satire would countervail the love of power or of money; he pleased himself with being important and formidable, and gratified sometimes his pride, and sometimes his resentment; till at last he began to think he should be more safe, if he were less busy.[105]

Johnson's view of the relation of religion and politics was made clear in his life of the poet Mark Akenside (1721–70), son of 'a butcher of the Presbyterian sect', educated at Edinburgh initially with the intention of ordination in that denomination.

[101] Ibid., vol. 4. p. 260. [102] Ibid., vol. 4, p. 274. [103] Ibid., vol. 4, p. 263.
[104] Ibid., vol. 4, pp. 120–1.
[105] Ibid., vol. 4, p. 122.

> Whether, when he resolved not to be a dissenting minister, he ceased to be a Dissenter, I know not. He certainly retained an unnecessary and outrageous zeal for what he called and thought liberty; a zeal which sometimes disguises from the world, and not rarely from the mind which it possesses, an envious desire of plundering wealth or degrading greatness; and of which the immediate tendency is innovation and anarchy, an impetuous eagerness to subvert and confound, with very little care what shall be established.[106]

Like the *Dictionary*, Johnson's *Lives of the Poets* contained a political agenda.

106 Ibid., vol. 4, pp. 449–50.

9

'SOPHISTRY', 'INDISCRETION', 'FALSEHOOD': THE DENIGRATION OF SAMUEL JOHNSON, 1775–1832

Johnson's reputation varied with that political stance of the observer, and the recasting of his towering reputation, for reasons which were demonstrably political, began during the American war. His memories of feudal hospitality were soon soured by Scots complaints that he had systematically understated the originality and achievements of that nation. The minister of Lismore, Argyllshire, persuaded himself that 'The Doctor hated Scotland; that was his *master-passion*, and it scorned all restraints. He seems to have set out with a design to give a distorted representation of every thing he saw on the north side of the Tweed', a belief which inspired the offended Presbyterian to a 371-page dispute with every paragraph of the erring document: that Johnson had described a Scots library as smaller, a Scots landscape as more treeless, or a Scots literature as more fraudulent, than it was. Anyone who trusted Johnson's account, claimed M'Nichol, would be 'miserably deceived'. Johnson had displayed a 'want of candour'; he had produced a 'deluge of falsehood and abuse'. He was 'disingenuous'; of a 'cynical disposition' and 'blinded by prejudice'. He had been guilty of 'rancour', 'malevolence', 'insincerity', 'literary assassination', 'indiscretion', 'malice', 'calumny', 'wilful misrepresentation' and 'inconsistencies'. His 'stubborn malignity', 'vanity', 'amazing ignorance', 'falsehood', 'bare-faced contradictions' and 'sophistry' were all part of 'the Doctor's injustice to my country'. Happily, the tolerant Caledonian could boast of 'that *good temper* with which the Scots have, of late years, borne the *invectives* of their southern neighbours'.[1] This piece of Scots scholarship may not have been immediately persuasive, but it helped to create a

[1] Donald M'Nichol, *Remarks on Dr Samuel Johnson's Journey to the Hebrides; in which are contained, Observations on the Antiquities, Language, Genius and Manners of the Highlanders of Scotland* (London, 1779), pp. 5–6, 8, 11–12, 24, 38, 46–7, 50, 70, 87, 107, 116, 123, 143, 160–1, 213–4, 218, 258, 371.

climate in which Johnson's reputation could be blackened by Englishmen who had more serious reasons for wishing to do so.

Other comment from north of the Border contributed. Observers quickly saw that Johnson's *Journey* contained 'remarks sufficient to move passions less *irritable* than those which commonly warm a Scotchman's breast'; but these were sufficient to persuade one loudly Presbyterian Scot that Johnson had held his country 'for forty years in contempt' and was moved by 'the malice of his heart'. Johnson's scepticism of the poems of Ossian was merely one proof of this: he must have been swayed by 'pride' and 'arrogance' to question what had been 'proved by a cloud of witnesses'. Dr Blackwell had shown how Homer's poems could have been written in an age 'not the most polished': 'every one who has tasted of the beauties of Homer, or of Ossian, will readily agree, upon comparing them with the productions of our more polished moderns, that in giving up nature and strength, for regularity and delicacy, we have made a wretched exchange'. The anonymous critic boasted of the support of Gray and Warton.[2]

Johnson, like Ruddiman, was predisposed to see Scots society in decay: Johnson's account was therefore very different from Pennant's, and this laid him open to unfavourable comment in the press.

> Mr. Pennant made two Tours into Scotland, in order to get acquainted with the Inhabitants, their Manners and Customs; to see the Face of the Country, and learn the State of Agriculture, Arts, Manufactures, Fisheries and Commerce; to discover its various Productions, Antiquities and Curiosities of Nature and Art; and to observe how far the remotest Creeks and Islands are, or might be made, subservient to the general Good and Prosperity of the British Empire.
>
> Dr Samuel Johnson travelled into Scotland, in order to discover sequestered Glens, and remote Sea-girt Rocks hardly inhabited, where Needles and Ink are scarce, and Halters with Wooden Bitts are used to lead Horses.

The anonymous critic compared the two authors' accounts under a succession of headings, religion being prominently contrasted:

> Mr. Pennant praises the Scotch Clergy for their Learning, Piety, Decency and Dignity of Behaviour; Diligence in their Function; and for their Chearfulness and Hospitality, notwithstanding ther scanty Incomes.
>
> Dr Johnson is grieved to find (and he does not deny that he found them) such Virtues among Presbyterians . . .

The conclusion was again to Johnson's disadvantage:

> Whence can proceed this wide Difference between these two Travellers, as to their Objects, Pursuits, Reception, and Accounts of the same Country in the same Year? Is it because Mr. Pennant is a Gentleman and a Scholar, and Dr Johnson only a

[2] *Remarks on a Voyage to the Hebrides, in a Letter to Samuel Johnson, LL.D.* (London, 1775), pp. 1–2, 28–9, 31, 34.

Scholar? Or is it because Mr. Pennant is a Welchman, and Dr Johnson an Englishman, and the Subject of Discourse, Scotland? Be it as it will, one Thing I observe with Pleasure is, that the learned Doctor is happily reinstated in the Favour of his Countrymen, and that his last Publication has amply atoned for all his Sins. Even his Apostacy, and his Pension from Lord Bute are wiped out by the Merit of his Spleen and Rancour against the Scotch.[3]

The political principles embodied in Johnson's *Lives of the Poets* (1779–81) were similarly apparent to contemporaries predisposed against him, and that work soon attracted close scrutiny. Robert Potter lamented that

it were to be wished that the spirit of party had not been so warmly diffused through this work; it is often disagreeable, but in the Life of Milton it is disgusting: not that I am inclined to defend the religious or political principles of our great poet; I know too well the intolerant spirit of that liberty, which worked its odious purposes through injustice, oppression, and cruelty; but it is of little consequence to the present and future ages whether the author of Paradise Lost was Papist or Presbyterian, Royalist or Republican; it is the Poet that claims our attention . . .[4]

Samuel Beilby, writing as 'a Yorkshire Freeholder', protested against 'many *virulent* and *malevolent* reflections upon the most illustrious characters that ever existed in this nation'; this was not surprising from one who 'has long been the mercenary Hireling of a late despicable Administration'. Systematically, Beilby worked his way through *The Lives of the Poets* to convict the author of political bias. This was easiest in the case of Milton, and Johnson's remark that Milton 'inherited no veneration for the White Rose', as Beilby termed it 'the favourite emblem of the Stewart family', could be returned in kind: 'those bodies that drank Tory and Jacobitical milk in their infancy, still retain an ardent affection for the paler Rose'. Johnson's work, claimed Beilby, was a sustained denunciation of his chosen poets; Johnson was 'a cruel and merciless Critic'. Quoting Charles Churchill's satiric verse on Johnson, Beilby argued: 'Had Churchill been living he dared not have acted thus.'[5]

Beilby was moved to reply by Johnson's characterisation of Gilbert Walmsley: 'He was a Whig, with all the virulence and malevolence of his party.' Since this was Beilby's own party, he felt authorised to cast odium on the Doctor: 'No man was ever so blinded and misled by political prejudices as he has been.'[6] Johnson's 'civility to Butler', suggested Beilby,

[3] 'Staffa', in *The St James's Chronicle*, 16–18 February 1775.

[4] Robert Potter, *An Inquiry into some Passages in Dr Johnson's Lives of the Poets: particularly his Observations on Lyric Poetry, and the Odes of Gray* (London, 1783), p. 3.

[5] [Samuel Beilby], *Remarks on Doctor Johnson's Lives of the most eminent English Poets* (York, 1782), pp. v, 1–3.

[6] [Beilby], *Remarks*, p. 24.

'is owing to his having been a Loyalist'. Johnson's discussion of Waller called forth a defence of Hampden: 'So far from being the Zealot of Rebellion, he was the Zealot of the Rights and Liberties of mankind.' Waller himself had been credited by Johnson with 'hyperbolical complaints of imaginary grievances' in the Long Parliament of 1640; Beilby retorted: 'In the above passage may easily be traced the sentiments of the author of Taxation no Tyranny.' Similarly, Johnson's 'censure upon Dorset's poetical works, entirely arises from his rooted aversion to the Earl's political principles' and conduct during the Revolution of 1688. His praise of Dryden showed him inclining the other way: 'What more could have been said by the meanest zealot for papacy and despotism?' Such principles as Johnson's excused him in republishing 'the filthy and indelicate poems of Swift ... what is not that man capable of doing, who dares openly to vindicate the sentiments of the writer of the Four last Years of Queen Ann?'[7]

The 'greatest blemish' of the *Lives*, wrote one critic, was 'the frequent recurrence of certain political opinions, which are far from enhancing the value of a work, the sole object of which should have been literary instruction and amusement'. Johnson was guilty of

> Sentiments, which do not discriminate the essential difference between resistance and rebellion, which have a tendency to revive the exploded doctrine of passive obedience, and which are inimical, in course, to the glorious principles of the revolution [of 1688], or in other words, to the dearest privileges of Englishmen; sentiments like these might be read in the pages of a Sacheverell or a Filmer with calm contempt.

In Johnson's shining pages, it was impossible to read those sentiments 'without a regret not absolutely devoid of indignation'.[8]

The heterodox Archdeacon Francis Blackburne, author of the anonymous tract *The Confessional* (London, 1766) which began a campaign within the Church for the abrogation of its defining formulae, was indignant at Johnson's cool approval of Milton. Still hiding behind anonymity, Blackburne contrasted Milton's 'magnanimity' with Johnson's 'see-saw meditations, the shifty wiles of a man between two fires, who neither dares to fight nor run away'. The explanation of Johnson's intervention was simple: 'it was not for the reputation of Dr Johnson's politics that Milton should be abused for his principles of Liberty by a less eminent hand than his own'.

[7] [Beilby], *Remarks*, pp. 10, 13–16, 18–20.

[8] 'Memoirs of the Life and Writings of Dr Samuel Johnson' by 'L', *Universal Magazine* 75 (August 1784), 89–97, reprinted in Brack and Kelley (eds.), *Early Biographies*, pp. 29–42, at 41–2.

Plate 8
Reactions to *The Lives of the Poets*. The critic is depicted being scourged by Apollo and the poets who had suffered in Johnson's work

The source of his disaffection to Milton's principles can be no secret to those who have been conversant in the controversies of the times. Dr Johnson's early and well-known attachments will sufficiently account for it; and posterity will be at no loss to determine whether our biographer's veneration was paid to the *White Rose* or the *Red*.[9]

Johnson had censured Milton's defence of the freedom of the press;

But pensions and preferments are wonderful enlighteners; and the free circulation of sedition during the last reign, when many an honest Jacobite propagated his discontents without the least apprehension for his ears, is now become a pernicious policy, unworthy of the wisdom and dignity of an administration under the protection of the respectable Dr Samuel Johnson.

[9] [Francis Blackburne], *Remarks on Johnson's Life of Milton* (London, 1780), pp. vii, 2–4.

Contrasting Johnson's politics with Milton's drove Blackburne to extremes:

In the Doctor's system of government public liberty is the *free grace* of an *hereditary* monarch, and limited in kind and degree, by his gracious will and pleasure; and consequently to controul his arbitrary acts by the interposition of good and wholesome laws is a *manifest usurpation* upon his prerogative ... Upon Johnson's plan, there can be no such thing as public liberty.[10]

After Johnson's death, the Socinian Joseph Towers returned to the anonymous campaign against the Anglican hero that he had begun during the American war. Towers readily conceded Johnson's literary attainment; his point was, rather, that 'Some of the friends of Dr Johnson have been led, by the warmth of their attachment to him, to estimate too highly his moral and religious character.' His virtue was offset by an 'arrogance' and 'bigotry' which led him to side with Strafford and Laud in *The Vanity of Human Wishes* and denigrate Milton's private life and politics. These prejudices committed him, in the political pamphlets of the 1770s, to 'positions ... which are inconsistent with the principles of the English constitution, and repugnant to the common rights of mankind ... few party pamphlets have appeared in this country, which contain greater malignity of misrepresentation'. The outcome of the American war, argued Towers, sufficiently refuted Johnson's position in *Taxation no Tyranny*. Indeed, Johnson's whole world had now passed away:

one of the great features of Johnson's character, was a degree of bigotry, both in politics and in religion, which is now seldom to be met with in persons of a cultivated understanding. Few other men could have been found, in the present age, whose political bigotry would have led them to style the celebrated JOHN HAMPDEN 'the zealot of rebellion'; and the religous bigotry of the man, who, when at Edinburgh, would not go to hear Dr Robertson preach, because he would not be present at a Presbyterian assembly, is not easily to be paralleled in this age, and in this country.[11]

Johnson's form of High Churchmanship came under increasing attack with the Evangelical movement and the growth of that heterodox Dissent which Johnson had resisted. Stories of his indignation on his Scottish tour against the havoc wrought by the Reformation produced a reaction: 'Surely, said a friend of ours ... this man wanted only the lot of being born in Spain, when the inquisition was established, to have been distinguished as the most black-minded and bloody supporter of that barbarous tribunal.'[12]

10 [Blackburne], *Remarks*, pp. 64–5, 85–6.

11 [Joseph Towers], *An Essay on the Life, Character, and Writings, of Dr Samuel Johnson* (London, 1786), pp. 3, 8, 24, 45–7, 50, 56–7. Towers depicted Milton as a moderate Dissenter and reformer: ibid., pp. 62, 78–9.

12 [William Hayley], *Two Dialogues; containing a Comparative View of the Lives, Characters and Writings of Philip, the late Earl of Chesterfield, and Dr Samuel Johnson* (London, 1787), p. 95.

Closely following hostile verdicts like this from unknown or anonymous detractors, Hawkins's *Life* was published in March 1787 and quickly attacked by the reviewers, mostly Johnson's close friends.[13] All of them rushed to defend the memory of their literary hero from what were taken to be the misrepresentations and disparagements of his first major biographer. Yet despite this vindicatory stance, adopted in all the leading journals, none of the reviewers even attempted to argue that Hawkins had misreported Johnson's political views.[14] Most merely repeated them as fact. The *Monthly Review* commented on Johnson's early Jacobitism: 'It is probable that he continued in those principles till he despaired of the cause.'[15] Although Boswell's *Life of Johnson*, published in 1791, sought in many ways to establish its superiority over its rival, Boswell too refrained from questioning Hawkins's account of his subject's politics.

It was, of course, the prevalent public understanding. Throughout the 1760s and 1770s, the London press retailed emphatic stories that Johnson had been, or was, a Jacobite, or that he adhered to Jacobite principles. These assertions were not confined to the *North Briton*, but have been traced in a remarkably wide range of titles: the *St James's Chronicle*, *Public Advertiser*, *Gazetteer*, *Middlesex Journal*, *Whitehall Evening Post*, *Universal Museum*, *General Evening Post*, *London Evening Post*, *London Packet*, *Morning Chronicle* and *London Magazine*. Similarly, Boswell recalled that 'Johnson and Shebbeare[16] were frequently named together, as having in former reigns had no predilection for the family of Hanover':[17] both obtained pensions in the 1760s. It does not appear that this stream of comment called forth protests from Johnson, his friends or early biographers that it was fundamentally misconceived.[18] One noted: 'Insulted and reviled as he was perpetually, when did he write a vindication of himself, or a satire upon his enemies?'[19]

13 Bertram H. Davis (ed.), *The Life of Samuel Johnson, LL.D. by Sir John Hawkins, Knt.* (London, 1961), p. xiv; idem, *Johnson before Boswell: A Study of Sir John Hawkins's Life of Samuel Johnson* (New Haven, Conn., 1960), pp. 14–36.

14 E.g. *The Critical Review* (May, 1787), pp. 339–45 and (June, 1787), pp. 417–24; [? George Steevens], in *The European Magazine* (April, 1787), pp. 223–7 and (May, 1787), pp. 310–3.

15 [Arthur Murphy] in *The Monthly Review* 76 (April, 1787), 273–92; (May, 1787), pp. 369–84; (July, 1787), pp. 56–70; (August, 1787), pp. 131–40.

16 John Shebbeare (1709–88), author of *Letters on the English Nation: By Battista Angeloni, a Jesuit* (2 vols, London, 1755) and six *Letters to the People of England* (London, 1755–7). For the last of these he was in November 1758 sentenced to stand in the pillory, to three years' imprisonment, and to find security for good behaviour for seven years: Boswell, *Life*, vol. 3, p. 315n.

17 Boswell, *Life*, vol. 4, p. 113.

18 Helen Louise McGuffie, *Samuel Johnson in the British Press, 1749–1784. A Chronological Checklist* (New York, 1976), pp. 27, 55, 58, 60–1, 63, 68–9, 71–3, 80, 82–3, 85, 108, 137, 150, 156, 158–60, 167–8, 171, 176, 186, 212, 215, 240.

19 [Hayley], *Two Dialogues*, p. 23.

Many of Johnson's immediate circle idolised him, but for easily-intelligible political reasons these views were not always shared by the wider educated public. That this was the case was readily apparent to Johnson and to his friends; yet neither he nor they sought to argue that his opinions had been fundamentally or generally misunderstood. The silence of contemporaries in a position to correct any misapprehensions is eloquent. The evidence is sufficient to place Johnson's politics against the shifting options of his lifetime, despite his own reticence and concealment of treasonable commitments. Johnson was a lifelong Nonjuror of early-eighteenth-century Tory principles who in the early part of his life found the arguments in favour of the exiled dynasty deeply appealing; these principles he partly adapted to a new monarch in the 1760s. He did not see himself as abandoning them.

Not only did what was later conceptualised as Romanticism supplant the Anglo-Latin culture of Johnson's youth; in the 1790s the Jacobin agenda obscured the Jacobite one. One reformer in 1791 used Johnson to make a point against hereditary titles and wealth:

> There is no man, even though his mind should have acquired strength by personal exertion, who is not more or less hurt by the constant adulation and servility of those who are about him. We see this in the case of such a man as the late Dr S. Johnson, who rose into public notice by his genius, and by exertions which must at times have been laborious and irksome; and yet the flattery that he met with made him extremely conceited and insolent, so that, had it not been checked by his miserable superstition, and a constant fear of death, he would have been as unapproachable as an eastern monarch. Also, the court that was paid to him on account of such attainments in knowledge as he had made, led him to neglect and despise others of infinitely more value; so that though he might be called a giant in the Belles Lettres, he was hardly a child in philosophy, morals, theology, or the theory of government; that is, though he was great in little things, he was contemptibly little in great ones. His great powers were exhausted on the subjects of language and taste; and his acquaintance with human nature, which appears to so much advantage in his Rambler, was not greater than that of many other persons, though his wonderful power of language makes it seem to be so.

If this was true of a man of such 'genius and exertions' as Johnson, 'what can we expect of men who find themselves in the possession of all they can wish as soon as they come of age?'[20] Nor was it only the Jacobin vision which found Johnson's world uncongenial. Sir James Mackintosh (1765–1832), Holland House's preferred historian before the arrival of T. B. Macaulay, naturally recognised Johnson's position: 'He was a Tory, not without some propensities towards Jacobitism, and a high Churchman,

[20] *Political Dialogues. Number I. Of the General Principles of Government* (London, 1791), pp. 14–15.

with more attachment to ecclesiastical authority and a splendid worship than is quite consistent with the spirit of Protestantism. On these subjects he neither permitted himself to doubt nor tolerated difference of opinion in others.' On these topics his understanding was 'bound by his prejudices'; he avoided 'abstruse speculations' partly from a 'secret dread that they might disturb those prejudices in which his mind had found repose from the agitations of doubt'.[21]

The Unitarian William Hazlitt set out systematically to diminish the status of *The Rambler* as a collection of Anglican moral teaching. It fell far short of the *Spectator*, argued Hazlitt; 'the Rambler is a collection of moral Essays, or scholastic theses' marked by 'the dryness of didactic discussion'. They were not original; 'do not disturb the ordinary march of our thoughts'; 'what most distinguishes Dr Johnson from other writers is the pomp and uniformity of his style ... His subjects are familiar, but the author is always upon stilts.'[22] But if Hazlitt damned Johnson's style, his most central objections were aimed at that element in Johnson which was most antithetical to Hazlitt.

> Dr Johnson is also a complete balance-master in the topics of morality. He never encourages hope, but he counteracts it by fear; he never elicits a truth, but he suggests some objection in answer to it. He seizes and alternately quits the clue of reason, lest it should involve him in the labyrinths of endless error: he wants confidence in himself and his fellows ... No advance is made by his writings in any sentiment, or mode of reasoning. Out of the pale of established authority and received dogmas, all is sceptical, loose, and desultory: he seems in imagination to strengthen the dominion of prejudice, as he weakens and dissipates that of reason; and round the rock of faith and power, on the edge of which he slumbers blindfold and uneasy, the waves and billows of uncertain and dangerous opinion roar and heave for evermore. His Rasselas is the most melancholy and debilitating moral speculation that ever was put forth. Doubtful of the faculties of his mind, as of his organs of vision, Johnson trusted only to his feelings and his fears. He cultivated a belief in witches as an out-guard to the evidences of religion; and abused Milton, and patronised Lauder, in spite of his aversion to his countrymen, as a step to secure the existing establishment in church and state.

Hazlitt praised Johnson the man for his blunt talk and practical charity;[23] but he did so in order more effectively to damn Johnson's politics and his religion.

The critical insights of Mackintosh and Hazlitt were now to be combined

21 Sir James Mackintosh, journal for 1811, in R. J. Mackintosh, *Memoirs of the Life of the Right Honourable Sir James Mackintosh* (2 vols., London, 1835), vol. 2, pp. 166–7. The 'ludicrous prejudice which he professed against Scotland' was equally easily traced: 'perhaps because it was a Presbyterian country': ibid., p. 171.

22 William Hazlitt, *Lectures on the English Comic Writers* (London, 1819), pp. 195–8.

23 Hazlitt, *English Comic Writers*, pp. 200–4.

in a devastating polemic by Thomas Babington Macaulay (1800–59). The occasion of Macaulay's campaign was a new edition of Boswell's *Life of Johnson*, published in 1831 and edited by the politician and intellectual John Wilson Croker (1780–1857). Croker, an MP from 1807 to 1832, Secretary to the Admiralty from 1809 to 1830, was closely associated with the support of England's old order against both the French Revolution and domestic challenges including Catholic Emancipation and parliamentary reform. Several times in debates in the House of Commons, Croker's superior knowledge and forensic skill discredited the inexperienced Macaulay's meretricious orations in favour of reform.[24] Now Croker's edition of Boswell's *Johnson* offered Macaulay an opportunity for revenge.

The combination of Johnson with Croker raised Macaulay to a high pitch of indignation. He set out to discredit both, with a string of crude adjectives. Croker had proceeded from 'ignorance' and 'carelessness' to make 'blunders' and 'misstatements' amounting to 'scandalous inaccuracy'. Macaulay obsessively listed some apparent editorial slips over dates (each called a 'monstrous blunder') seemingly to justify his denigrations: the sweeping claim that 'Two of Mr. Croker's three statements must be false' in fact referred to minor questions of dating. Yet the serious object of this invective was to show that Croker was 'entitled to no confidence whatever'.[25] Macaulay then turned to Boswell. His biography was, admittedly, 'a very great work', but its author was

> of the meanest and feeblest intellect . . . Servile and impertinent, – shallow and pedantic, – a bigot and a sot, – bloated with family pride, and eternally blustering about the dignity of a born gentleman, yet stooping to be a talebearer, an eavesdropper, a common butt in the taverns of London, – so curious to know every body who was talked about, that, Tory and High Churchman as he was, he manoeuvred, we have been told, for an introduction to Tom Paine . . .

Boswell was 'a great writer' only because he was 'a great fool'.[26]

This denigration of the editor and the biographer prepared the way for Macaulay's much harder task, the denigration of their subject. It had to be admitted that Johnson was 'really an extraordinary man'. But Macaulay at once undid the effect of that admission by implying that Johnson's extraordinariness lay in his personal oddity: 'his insatiable appetite for fish-sauce and veal-pie with plums, his inextinguishable thirst for tea, his

[24] The editor of Macaulay's letters notes that Croker 'provoked a more virulent hatred' in Macaulay 'than any other public man': Thomas Pinney (ed.), *The Letters of Thomas Babington Macaulay* (6 vols., Cambridge, 1974–81), vol. 1, pp. 286–7n.; cf. ibid., p. 313; vol. 2, pp. 6, 84 ('that impudent leering scoundrel Croker', etc.).

[25] [T. B. Macaulay], review of J. W. Croker (ed.), *The Life of Samuel Johnson, LL.D.* in *The Edinburgh Review* 54 (1831), 1–38, at 1, 3, 6–7.

[26] Ibid., pp. 16–18.

trick of touching the posts as he walked, his mysterious practice of treasuring up scraps of orange-peel ... his contortions, his mutterings, his gruntings, his puffings ...' If his person was absurd, his social standing was also obscure. Macaulay depicted the low social status of authors in the reigns of the first two Georges, and dwelt on the 'faults' of character which so precarious a career imposed on those who followed it: 'abject misery' produced 'dissolute manners'; alternate luxury and beggary made such men 'untameable'. This was the harrowing experience which had deformed Johnson's character before, with his pension, he emerged into polite society in the 1760s.[27]

These premises once established, Macaulay could parody Johnson as 'a complete original' whose virtues were made irrelevant by his compulsive eccentricities: 'He could fast; but when he did not fast, he tore his dinner like a famished wolf, with the veins swelling on his forehead, and the perspiration running down his cheeks.' Macaulay then implicitly applied this model to Johnson's moral and political judgement. 'The characteristic peculiarity of his intellect was the union of great powers with low prejudices': Macaulay had so prepared his readers that they would not allow Johnson's great powers to elevate his beliefs above the level of low prejudices. Johnson was to be seen as (sadly, understandably) irrational, swayed by 'some domineering passion' or 'childish prejudices'.

Johnson's famous scepticism could now be dismissed; he was to be pictured as 'credulous' about 'the invisible world'. 'He rejects the Celtic genealogies and poems without the least hesitaiton; yet he declares himself willing to believe the stories of the second sight.'[28] This tactic allowed Macaulay to subvert Johnson's religion:

> Many of his sentiments on religious subjects are worthy of a liberal and enlarged mind. He could discern clearly enough the folly and meanness of all bigotry except his own ... In Scotland, he thought it his duty to pass several months without joining in public worship, solely because the ministers of the kirk had not been ordained by bishops.[29]

The same tactic had the same effect for Macaulay's account of Johnson's politics:

> Nobody spoke more contemptuously of the cant of patriotism ... His calm and settled opinion seems to have been, that forms of government have little or no influence on the happiness of society. This opinion, erroneous as it is, ought at least to have preserved him from all intemperance on political questions. It did not,

[27] Ibid., pp. 20, 23–5. [28] Ibid., pp. 26–8.
[29] Ibid., p. 29.

however, preserve him from the lowest, fiercest, and most absurd extravagances of party-spirit,

that is, his prejudice 'against all who leaned to Whiggish principles'. So Johnson's views on the Long Parliament and the American Congress became 'torrents of raving abuse'.[30]

It is difficult, in retrospect, to see how Macaulay achieved so great an impact by the use of such extreme language. His arresting adjectives concealed, however, a more subtle rhetorical strategy, and his critique harmonised with the most salient political development of his age. The political changes of the late 1820s and early 1830s produced so substantial a displacement of concepts and ideologies as to make the social order prevailing since the Restoration quickly seem like a previous order which had passed away.[31] With his usual acuteness, Macaulay sensed this paradigm shift, and found an historical parallel. Of Johnson he wrote:

How it chanced that a man who reasoned on his premises so ably, should assume his premises so foolishly, is one of the great mysteries of human nature. The same inconsistency may be observed in the schoolmen of the middle ages. Those writers show so much acuteness and force of mind in arguing on their wretched *data*, that a modern reader is perpetually at a loss to comprehend how such minds came by such *data*.

Johnson never examined his major premises: the excellence of English poetry in the age of Dryden and Pope; the worthlessness of rival poetic idioms; the superiority of Latin to English. So Macaulay depicted himself as the arbiter of the new age, and Johnson as the irrelevant spokesman of a world now lost:

The reputation of those writings, which he probably expected to be immortal, is every day fading; while those peculiarities of manner, and that careless table-talk, the memory of which, he probably thought, would die with him, are likely to be remembered as long as the English language is spoken in any quarter of the globe.[32]

Macaulay privately boasted that 'my article on Croker has ... smashed his book ... Croker looks across the House of Commons at me with a leer of hatred which I repay with a gracious smile of pity.'[33] It was, of course, not

[30] Ibid., p. 30.

[31] For which, see especially J. C. D. Clark, *English Society 1688–1832: Ideology, social structure and political practice during the ancien regime* (Cambridge, 1985), pp. 349–420.

[32] [Macaulay], review, pp. 31–3, 38.

[33] Macaulay had staked his whole career on his performance in the House, and was incensed by Croker's effective replies to him: 'My modesty, – which, as you well know, is my great weakness, will not allow me to repeat all the compliments which I have received': Macaulay to Thomas Flower Ellis, 17 October 1831, in Macaulay, *Letters* (ed. Pinney), vol. 2, p. 104.

Johnson's literary standing that was really at stake but the Reform Bill of 1832, and everything that depended on it. Johnson himself had now become an icon, to be fought over like the alleged epistles of Phalaris, as a key symbol in English cultural politics.

Johnson retained a reputation as an accomplished classicist, but critics ceased to see the point of that facility. Although Johnson was acknowledged as a towering figure in the world of letters, it became steadily harder to see what justified this: not *Irene*; not the political pamphlets of the 1770s; there were no published letters, no novels; the *Dictionary* was an achievement, but was it the achievement of a 'harmless drudge', as its author had defined 'lexicographer'? *The Rambler* and *The Idler* were respected, but were less impressive if regarded as late copies of *The Spectator* or *The Tatler*. Most damaging of all, the tradition of English poetry which Johnson most admired and to which he had briefly contributed was gradually, and finally disastrously, challenged by those new modes of sensibility associated in the 1790s with William Wordsworth and Robert Southey.[34] J. G. Lockhart, writing in *Blackwood's Edinburgh Magazine* in March 1818, claimed that the decisive shift in cultural politics had come in about 1810 when the *Edinburgh Review* decided to become 'a despiser of the poetry of Pope', to talk up the Elizabethan and Jacobean writers, and so implicitly (though often with explicit reservations) to open the door to the Romantics. Francis Jeffrey's reviewing for the *Edinburgh* gives some support to that claim: in the *Edinburgh Review* for August 1811 he had argued that 'In point of real force and originality of genius, neither the age of Pericles, nor the age of Augustus, nor the times of Leo X, nor of Louis XIV, can come at all into comparison' with the age of Shakespeare. There was, however, no clear line to be drawn: even Jeffrey retained much of his regard for the Augustans, though steadily diminishing the scale of their achievement and obscuring its central components. Yet he and his chosen reviewers steadily contributed to that process by which Dryden and Pope were reinterpreted as little more than spokesmen for a polished, refined, gentlemanly but 'artificial' and emotionally limited social order.[35]

Whatever its value in literary criticism 'Romantic' is, of course, too simple and too inclusive a term to locate historically authors as diverse as

34 For a helpful study (which, however, largely ignores politics and the classics) of the eclipse of the cultural project of which Johnson was part, see Upali Amarasinghe, *Dryden and Pope in the Early Nineteenth Century: A Study of Changing Literary Taste 1800–1830* (Cambridge, 1962). This work takes as its motto Leslie Stephen's insight: 'It is a mistake to suppose that the eighteenth century ended with the year 1800. It lasted in the upper currents of opinion till at least 1832.'

35 Amarasinghe, *Dryden and Pope*, pp. 71, 76, 85, 87–8. The *Quarterly Review*, which took a political line opposite to that of the Whig *Edinburgh*, was also much more favourable to the Augustans: ibid., pp. 93–116.

Wordsworth and Coleridge; Southey and Byron; Hazlitt, De Quincey, and Hunt; Keats and Shelley. Each reacted to the classical tradition, and to the English vernacular poetry of c. 1660–1750, in a different way,[36] and was differently interpreted. It is not the object of the present study to offer an account of the cross-currents and complexities of what was later termed Romanticism, a category which would not survive historians' scrutiny, and it is not suggested that Johnson's reputation reached a *terminus ad quem* with any such reification. In the light of the earlier political significance and long cultural persistence of the classical tradition, it may be suggested that 'Romanticism', conventionally depicted as a new mode of sensibility derived from an autonomous vernacular, had as much to do with a reorientation within a surviving classical tradition from a Roman to a Greek axis.

The classics did not disappear from English intellectual life with the defeat of Johnson's Anglo-Latin political enterprise in the 1750s, and their social functions continued to evolve. Yet the next most clearly-defined phase in English classical sensibilities owed little to priorities of William King or Alexander Pope: 'Romantic Hellenism'[37] was built around a reviving interest in Greek. Greek studies had been of secondary importance for much of the eighteenth century. Richard Bentley (1662–1742) gave them a marked orientation towards technical textual criticism and away from their subject matter, and Greek scholarship, Greek translations or imitations, and neo-Greek poetry did not acquire marked political overtones until they began to be fashionable in the circle of Charles James Fox. Again, a political movement found its intellectual credibility in the work of the remarkable Greek scholar Richard Porson (1759–1808), seemingly interpreted by the egregious Whig Samuel Parr (1747–1825), and given their most extreme application with scholar-polemicists like Gilbert Wakefield (1756–1801).[38] It was a school which overwhelmed the interpretation of the 'Tory historian of Greece' William Mitford (1744–1827), a

[36] Amarasinghe, *Dryden and Pope*, pp. 137–76. Southey suggested that the origins of the idiom of the early Romantics could be found in a school 'half-Greek half-Gothick', which, begun by Gilbert West, 'was followed by Mason, Gray, and Warton, and is to be traced in Akenside and Collins': Robert Southey, *Specimens of the Later English Poets* (London, 1807), p. xxxii, quoted in Amarasinghe, *Dryden and Pope*, p. 140.

[37] Bernard Herbert Stern, *The Rise of Romantic Hellenism in English Literature 1732–1786* (Menasha, 1940). Stern accounts for the rise of Hellenism in terms of 'the growth of scientific Greek archaeology ... the growth of sentimental accounts of Greece written by travellers; and ... the rise of a hellenized body of aesthetics produced by artists, painters, and poets (p. 11); he does not discuss the cultural politics of this shift in taste.

[38] M. L. Clarke, *Greek Studies in England 1700–1830* (Cambridge, 1945), pp. 1, 7, 67–101. For a similarly Whig application of his studies by Andrew Dalzel, professor of Greek at Edinburgh 1772–1806, ibid., pp. 44–5.

sceptical critic of Greek democracy who drew parallels between Athens and revolutionary France that incensed the Whig reviewers.[39]

Romantic Hellenism may itself have had its earliest origins in the opposition culture of the 1730s, as in James Thomson's poem *Liberty* (London: A. Millar, 1735) and Richard Glover's *Leonidas* (London, 1737), a commitment that was most successfully carried forward in the Greek antiquarian researches and Pindaric poetry of Thomas Gray. It was left to 'Romanticism ... to transmute the neo-classical worship of the ancients into a bulwark for the "radical" ideas of genius, primitivism, liberty, and equality'.[40] Of the Greek poets only one, Pindar, expressed the full range of ideals which achieved so much prominence in the last decades of the eighteenth and the first decades of the nineteenth century. The themes of military victory, national glory, personal triumph and emancipation linked with the freedom of the community were enforced in Pindar with a 'vehement intensity' which spoke to the new aesthetic; and in England the first poet to respond to these widening opportunities was Gray. 'His Pindaric odes, with their urgency and passion, foreshadow bolder flights that were to come.'[41] But it was exactly this that Johnson, in his account of Gray in the *Lives of the Poets*, had resisted.

In retrospect, Englishmen found a new way of estimating Johnson's stature: he was a moralist. Even Hawkins asked 'whether Johnson possessed all the qualities of a critic', especially 'a truly poetic faculty' and answered in the negative. Instead, 'Moral sentiments, and versification, seem chiefly to have engaged his attention, and on these his criticisms are accurate, but severe, and not always impartial.' His 'spirit of criticism ... by long exercise, may be said to have become mechanical'.[42] William Hayley borrowed from Plutarch the device of parallel lives to draw a moral contrast between Johnson and Chesterfield, a comparison which could be held to show 'the decisive triumph of the once indigent and neglected, but truly great Moralist, over the high-born and fashionable Wit, whose vain talents were, during his life, the idol of his country'. 'An incessant zeal for moral excellence was his ruling passion; and he had an unexampled power of extracting morality from every incident of life, from every appearance in nature.' By contrast, it could be claimed by 1787 that 'much as Johnson had been celebrated for his intimate acquaintance with ancient literature,

39 Clarke, *Greek Studies*, pp. 107–10. For the growing fascination of 'Romantic' poets with Greece, despite an often rudimentary knowledge of the language, ibid., pp. 158–74; for a catalogue of translations of Greek authors into English 1700–1830, pp. 235–45.

40 Stern, *Romantic Hellenism*, pp. 119–27, 151–3, 167.

41 R. M. Ogilvie, *Latin and Greek: A History of the Influence of the Classics on English Life from 1600 to 1918* (London, 1964), pp. 85ff.

42 Hawkins, *Life*, pp. 535–7.

there is not a particle of true atticism, or of Roman urbanity, in all his compositions'.[43] The point of the enterprise had been lost, and the reason for Johnson's inclusion of many minor poets in the *Lives* was forgotten. It has been well observed that the 'most damaging criticism by writers like Wordsworth and Coleridge was aimed not so much at Dryden and Pope as at their imitators'.[44] Potter quoted Johnson on one such: 'Dyer is not a poet of bulk or dignity sufficient to require an elaborate criticism.' Potter replied: 'Does Dr Johnson estimate poetical merit, as Rubens did feminine beauty, *by the stone*?'[45] It was clear enough to Johnson that his host of lesser figures had qualified for their place in the canon as Latinists, as Latin authors, as translators or imitators: in the latter part of his life this steadily weakened as a generally-acknowledged criterion.

If Johnson's politics belonged to a former age, so too did his cultural politics. As the *Lives of the Poets* showed, he had never really abandoned either. The closing scenes of his life also made these priorities clear. In his last year, Johnson wrote: 'When I lay sleepless, I used to drive the night along, by turning Greek epigrams into Latin. I know not if I have not turned a hundred.'[46] This exercise continued into his last illness, recorded Hawkins: Johnson

> succeeded in an attempt to render into Latin metre, from the Greek Anthologia, sundry of the epigrams therein contained, that had been omitted by other translators, alledging as a reason, which he had found in Fabricius, that Henry Stephens, Buchanan, Grotius, and others, had paid a like tribute to literature. The performance of this task was the employment of his sleepless nights, and, as he informed me, it afforded him great relief.[47]

Both Johnson and Boswell turned to the classical tradition for the epitaphs on their cultural achievements, and did so in a revealingly contrasting way. In November 1784, within a month of his death, Johnson made his famous translation of the Seventh Ode of the Fourth Book of Horace:

> Diffugere nives, redeunt iam gramina campis
>   Arboribusque comae;
> Mutat terra vices et decrescentia ripas
>   Flumina praetereunt;
> Gratia cum Nymphis geminisque sororibus audet
>   Ducere nuda choros.

43 [Hayley], *Two Dialogues*, pp. 2, 14–15, 50.
44 Amarasinghe, *Dryden and Pope*, pp. 13, 50.
45 Potter, *An Inquiry into some Passages in Dr Johnson's Lives of the Poets*, p. 5.
46 Johnson to Hester Thrale, 19 April 1784: Johnson, *Letters*, vol. 4, p. 317. Redford identifies Johnson's source as Brodaeus's edition of the *Greek Anthology* (1549).
47 Hawkins, *Life*, pp. 579–80.

Immortalia ne speres, monet annus et almum
  Quae rapit hora diem.
Frigora mitescunt Zephyris, ver proterit aestas
  Interitura, simul
Pomifer Autumnus fruges effuderit, et mox
  Bruma recurrit iners.
Damna tamen celeres reparant caelestia lunae:
  Nos, ubi decidimus,
Quo pater Aeneas, quo Tullus, dives et Ancus,
  Pulvis et umbra sumus . . .

Johnson's version, his last poem in English, summed up his sense of that Roman finality from which his religion offered deliverance:

The snow dissolv'd no more is seen,
The fields, and woods, behold, are green,
The changing year renews the plain,
The rivers know their banks again,
The spritely Nymph and naked Grace
The mazy dance together trace.
The changing year's successive plan
Proclaims mortality to Man.
Rough Winter's blasts to Spring give way,
Spring yield[s] to Summer['s] sovereign ray,
Then Summer sinks in Autumn's reign,
And Winter chils the World again.
Her losses soon the Moon supplies,
But wretched Man, when once he lies
Where Priam and his sons are laid,
Is nought but Ashes and a Shade . . .[48]

Johnson's farewell was a selfless comment on the human condition.

Should these intensely private things be recorded? Had Johnson's most intimate moments and motives now become public property? Boswell anticipated and defended himself against the charge 'that he who has the power of thus exhibiting an exact transcript of conversations is not a desirable member of society'. In the light of Johnson's commitment to the classical tradition, Boswell thought he found the most noble defence of his own literary enterprise in the Ninth Ode of Horace's Fourth Book:

Vixere fortes ante Agamemnona
Multi; sed omnes illacrymabiles
Urgentur, ignotique longa
Nocte, carent quia vate sacro.[49]

[48] David Nichol Smith and Edward L. McAdam (eds.), *The Poems of Samuel Johnson* (2nd edn, Oxford, 1974), p. 265.

[49] Boswell, *Journal*, pp. 401–2.

As Philip Francis, Johnson's favourite translator of Horace, put it:

Before great Agamemnon reign'd,
Reign'd Kings as great as He, and brave,
Whose huge Ambition's now contain'd
In the small Compass of a Grave;
In endless Night they sleep, unwept, unknown,
No Bard had They to make all Time their own.[50]

By comparison with Johnson's apologia, that of his protégé was a vain boast.

[50] Philip Francis, *A Poetical Translation of the Works of Horace* (2 vols., 3rd edn, London: A. Millar, 1749), vol. 1, pp. 384–5.

INDEX

187–8, 195, 199, 203, 206–7, 210, 212, 214, 221, 230, 233–4, 241
riots, Jacobite, 91, 152, 182
Rivers, Richard Savage, 4th Earl (?1654–1712), 58
Robertson, William (1721–93), historian, 224, 243
Rochester, 2nd Earl of (1647–80), poet, 22, 27
Rockingham Whigs, 203
Rogers, Rev. John, 122n
Roman Catholicism, 68, 125, 131–2, 188, 191, 208, 218, 232
'Romanticism', and Greek axis, 2–3, 251–2; and reinterpretation of SJ, 4, 8–9; and changing perspective on English letters, 24, 245, 250–3; and Ossian, 84; and SJ, 219
Roscommon, Wentworth Dillon (c. 1637–85), 4th Earl of, poet, 28
Rowe, Nicholas (1674–1718), poet, 27
Ruddiman, Thomas (1674–1757), Latinist, cultural politics of, 3–4, 8, 21, 47–9, 71; 'patriotic despair', 36, 199, 239; conception of scholarship, 74, 199; respected by SJ, 19, 35; education, 141; as schoolmaster, 60, 118; as publisher, 135n, 146; SJ's ally, 34; and Buchanan, 28; and Lauder, 60–1; and Nonjurors, 129; visits London, 146; death, 192
Rufus, William, 46
Russell, Lord William (1639–83), republican, 100
Ryder, Dudley (1691–1756), MP, 32, 66, 88, 153
Ryswick, peace of (1697), 29

Sacheverell, Rev. Dr Henry (?1674–1724), 29, 111–13, 144, 241
St Andrews, 225
St Aubyn, Sir John (1726–72), 4th Bt, 72
St Clement Danes church, Strand, 52n, 71, 119n, 122n, 139–40, 152n, 154–6, 169n, 180
The St James's Chronicle, 244
St Mary Hall, Oxford, 17, 90–1, 100, 201
Sallust, Gaius Sallustius Crispus (86–34 BC), Roman historian, 15, 19, 32, 148
Salter, Rev. Dr Samuel, 17
Sancroft, William (1617–93), archbishop, Nonjuror, 127
Sanderson, Robert (1587–1663), bishop, 134
Sandford, Rev. John (d. 1739), 45–7
Sandys, George, translator, 30
Sannazaro, Jacopo (1458–1530), Latin poet, 23, 75
Savage, Richard (d. 1743), poet, 9, 40, 43, 57, 140, 142–5, 200, 214, 231
Scaliger, Joseph Justus (1540–1609), and Julius Caesar (1484–1588), 75
Scot, Sir John, of Scotstarvet, 21
Scotland, 3–4, 8, 19, 21, 34–7, 45, 59–66, 74, 77–87, 129, 142, 163, 174, 192, 205, 219–25, 232, 238–40, 246n
Scott, John (1730–83), Quaker, 215, 218
Scott, Sir Walter (1771–1832), novelist, and reinterpretation of SJ, 4, 207
sectaries, *see* Dissenters
Sejanus, Lucius Aelius, favourite of emperor Tiberius, 33
Seneca, Lucius Annaeus Seneca (c. 3 BC–65 AD), philosopher and tragedian, 58, 75n
Senhouse, John, translator, 53
Seven Years' War, 72, 120–1, 188, 190, 201, 215
Seward, Anna (1747–1809), poet, 107
Shaftesbury, Anthony Ashley Cooper (1621–83), 1st Earl of, 111, 234
Shaftesbury, Anthony Ashley Cooper (1671–1713), 3rd Earl of, 134
Shakespeare, William, 24, 72, 76, 110–11, 149, 173, 185, 250
Sharp, James (1613–79), archbishop of St Andrews, 232
Shaw, William (1749–1831), 196
Shebbeare, Dr John (1709–88), pamphleteer, 200, 221, 232, 244
Shelburne, William Petty (1737–1805), 2nd Earl of, 190–1
Shelley, Percy Bysse (1792–1822), poet, 251
Shenstone, William (1714–63), poet, 115
Sheridan, Thomas, translator, 53, 119
Sherlock, William (?1641–1707), Dean, 130, 195
Shropshire, William, 157n
Sidney, Algernon (1622–83), republican, 46
Sidney, Sir Philip (1554–86), poet, 64–5
Skye, isle of, 67, 79, 81, 189, 219, 221–2
Slanes Castle, 221
Sleat, I. of Skye, 16, 79
Slow, Samuel, printer, 152
Smalbroke, Dr Richard (c. 1716–1805), advocate, 119
Smalbroke, Richard, bishop, 119n
Smalridge, George (1663–1719), bishop, 79
Smith, Adam (1723–90), political economist, 202n
Smith, Edmund (1672–1710), poet, 29, 32, 106